The WPA Outcomes Statement—A Decade Later

WRITING PROGRAM ADMINISTRATION
Series Editors: Susan H. McLeod and Margot Soven

The Writing Program Administration series provides a venue for scholarly monographs and projects that are research- or theory-based and that provide insights into important issues in the field. We encourage submissions that examine the work of writing program administration, broadly defined (e.g., not just administration of first-year composition programs). Possible topics include but are not limited to 1) historical studies of writing program administration or administrators (archival work is particularly encouraged); 2) studies evaluating the relevance of theories developed in other fields (e.g., management, sustainability, organizational theory); 3) studies of particular personnel issues (e.g., unionization, use of adjunct faculty); 4) research on developing and articulating curricula; 5) studies of assessment and accountability issues for WPAs; and 6) examinations of the politics of writing program administration work at the community college.

BOOKS IN THE SERIES

Writing Program Administration and the Community College by Heather Ostman (2012)

Writing Program Administration at Small Liberal Arts Colleges by Jill M. Gladstein and Dara Rossman Regaignon (2012)

GenAdmin: Theorizing WPA Identities in the 21st Century by Colin Charlton, Jonikka Charlton, Tarez Samra Graban, Kathleen J. Ryan, and Amy Ferdinandt Stolley (2011).

THE WPA OUTCOMES STATEMENT—A DECADE LATER

Edited by Nicholas N. Behm, Gregory R. Glau, Deborah H. Holdstein, Duane Roen, and Edward M. White

Parlor Press
Anderson, South Carolina
www.parlorpress.com

Parlor Press LLC, Anderson, South Carolina, USA

© 2013 by Parlor Press
All rights reserved.
Printed in the United States of America

SAN: 254-8879

Library of Congress Cataloging-in-Publication Data

The WPA outcomes statement-- a decade later / edited by Nicholas Behm ... [et al.].
  p. cm. -- (Writing program administration)
Includes bibliographical references and index.
  ISBN 978-1-60235-296-4 (pbk. : alk. paper) -- ISBN 978-1-60235-297-1 (alk. paper) -- ISBN 978-1-60235-298-8 (adobe ebook) -- ISBN 978-1-60235-299-5 (epub)
  1. English language--Rhetoric--Study and teaching--United States. 2. Report writing--Study and teaching (Higher)--United States. 3. Writing centers--Administration. I. Behm, Nicholas. II. Council of Writing Program Administrators (U.S.)
  PE1405.U6W723 2012
  808'.042071173--dc22
                                2012005607

1 2 3 4 5

Cover photo, "Eye Candy," courtesy of Greg Glau. See gglau.zenfolio.com for more of Greg's photography.
Cover design by David Blakesley
Printed on acid-free paper.

Parlor Press, LLC is an independent publisher of scholarly and trade titles in print and multimedia formats. This book is available in paper, cloth and eBook formats from Parlor Press on the World Wide Web at http://www.parlorpress.com or through online and brick-and-mortar bookstores. For submission information or to find out about Parlor Press publications, write to Parlor Press, 3015 Brackenberry Drive, Anderson, South Carolina, 29621, or email editor@parlorpress.com.

Contents

Acknowledgments   *vii*
Introduction   *ix*

Part I: Adapting the WPA OS to Develop Curriculum

1 CWPA Outcomes Statement as Heuristic for Inventing Writing-about-Writing Curricula   *3*
   Debra Frank Dew

2 The Politics of Pedagogy: The Outcomes Statement and Basic Writing   *18*
   Wendy Olson

3 Building a Writing Program with the WPA Outcomes: Authority, Ethos, and Professional Identity   *32*
   Kimberly Harrison

4 The Perilous Vision of the Outcomes Statement   *45*
   Teresa Grettano, Rebecca Ingalls, and Tracy Ann Morse

5 The Outcomes Statement as Support for Teacher Creativity: Applying the WPA OS to Develop Assignments   *58*
   Sherry Rankins-Robertson

6 Released from the Ghost of Platonic Idealism: How the Outcomes Statement Affirms Rhetorical Curricula   *71*
   Doug Sweet

7 Beyond Composition: Developing a National Outcomes Statement for Writing Across the Curriculum   *88*
   Paul Anderson, Chris M. Anson, Martha Townsend, and Kathleen Blake Yancey

Part II: Applying the WPA OS to Enact Programmatic, Institutional, and Disciplinary Change

8 The WPA Outcomes Statement and Disciplinary Authority   *107*
   Craig Jacobsen, Susan Miller-Cochran, and Shelley Rodrigo

9 Achieving a Lasting Impact on Faculty Teaching: Using the WPA Outcomes Statement to Develop an Extended WID Seminar   *124*
   Stephen Wilhoit

10 Building Clout in Non-Program Programs by Using the Outcomes Statement   *136*
   Karen Bishop Morris and Lizbeth A. Bryant

11 Reframing the Conversation: Can the
   Outcomes Statement Help?   *154*
   Darsie Bowden

12 The WPA Outcomes Statement: The View from Australia   *165*
   Susan Thomas

13 Ripple Effect: Adopting and Adapting the WPA Outcomes   *179*
   Morgan Gresham

14 Ethos and Topoi: Using The Outcomes Statement Rhetorically To
   Achieve The Centrality and Autonomy of Writing Programs   *191*
   Deirdre Pettipiece and Justin Everett

15 Adoption, Adaptation, Revision: Waves of Collaborative
   Change at a Large University Writing Program   *209*
   J.S. Dunn, Jr. Sarah Fabian, Suzanne Gray, Kimberly
   Coupe Pavlock, Hava Levitt-Phillips, Sarah Soebbing,
   Heidi Estrem, and Linda Adler-Kassner

**Part III: Cultivating the Intellectual Enrichment
of the WPA OS through Critique**

16 Considering the Impact of the WPA Outcomes
   Statement on Second Language Writers   *230*
   Paul Kei Matsuda and Ryan Skinnell

17 Competing Discourses within the WPA
   Outcomes Statement   *242*
   Judy Holiday

18 Is Rhetorical Knowledge the Über-Outcome?   *257*
   Barry M. Maid and Barbara J. D'Angelo

19 The WPA Learning Outcomes: What Role
   Should Technology Play?   *271*
   Micheal Callaway

20 Assessing the Impact of the Outcomes Statement   *285*
   Emily Isaacs and Melinda Knight

Appendix: WPA Outcomes Statement for First-
   Year Composition   *305*
Index   *311*
Contributors   *319*

Acknowledgments

The editors would like to thank David Blakesley for his support of this collection, Susan H. McLeod and Margot Soven for their insightful and gracious feedback on earlier versions, and Jeff Ludwig for his diligent copyediting. The editors are also grateful for having such an intelligent and professional group of contributors and colleagues who populate this collection with their insightful ideas and encouraging experiences. Finally, this collection would not be possible if it were not for the work of colleagues and friends who collaborated to draft the Writing Program Administrators Outcomes Statement for First-Year Composition. The editors thank them for their vision, their investment of time and energy, and their willingness to serve the discipline.

Nicholas Behm expresses appreciation for the invaluable support of the editors, for their grace and wit, and for their investment in and hard work on the collection. Nick is forever indebted to colleagues who have served as mentors, especially Duane Roen, Greg Glau, Keith Miller, Maureen Daly Goggin, Sharon Crowley, and Krista Ratcliffe. They have generously shared their time, knowledge, and love of writing, and Nick is a better teacher, scholar, and person as a result. Finally, Nick wishes to thank his best friend and life-partner, Angie Behm, for her gracious patience, unyielding support, and loving concern.

Greg Glau would like to especially acknowledge the main editor of this project, Nick Behm, who worked tirelessly and managed to keep us moving and on-track. Greg also would like to acknowledge the good and thoughtful work of all contributors to this volume, and—as always—the constant support and help from his wife, Courtney Ann.

Deborah H. Holdstein thanks Duane Roen for inviting her to join everyone on this valuable project—and she thanks the rest of the gang for honoring that invitation and for being fine partners. While this has been an exceptionally collaborative and helpful group to work with, Holdstein particularly wishes to thank Nick Behm for his good humor, good sense, and very hard work. Holdstein also thanks her wonderful husband, Jay Boersma.

Duane Roen thanks Nick Behm and Greg Glau for initiating this project. He also thanks his father, Harley Roen, for his lifelong support. He is grateful to Fred Corey, Director of the School of Letters and Sciences at Arizona State University, for supporting this collection and other scholarly projects. Margaret Munson and Shealyn Campbell have provided invaluable technical assistance for this collection.

Edward M. White would like to thank Duane Roen and the other editors for inviting him to join the editorial team, well after the initial steps had been taken, and Nick Behm in particular for his steady hand and diligence with detail. The WPA OS is unique in its embodiment of collegiality, and this volume continues that tradition.

Introduction

Not even the most prescient among the original "Outcomes Collective" group (the unofficial moniker they gave themselves) could foresee where their discussion was heading, what turns and twists that discussion would take, how many meetings they would attend and emails they would exchange, who would enter into and contribute to their Burkean conversation, and, of course, what any final result might look like. As so often happens as fields develop, the entire enterprise began with a novice inquiry on the WPA listserv (What is the purpose of first-year college composition?), which was followed by a sophisticated question by Edward M. White, who, at the time, was the director of the WPA Consultant-Evaluator service.

White's original 1996 query to the WPA listserv seemed innocuous enough, and reflected what many in the profession had often wondered. White asked,

> Is it an impossible dream to imagine this group coming out with at least a draft set of objectives that might really work and be usable, for instance, distinguishing comp 1 from comp 2 or from 'advanced' comp? We may not have professional consensus on this, though, or even consensus that we *should* have consensus. How would we go about trying? (4)

It is interesting to note that what White requested—a "draft set of objectives that might really work and be usable, for instance, distinguishing comp 1 from comp 2 or from 'advanced' comp"—never really became the focus of the WPA Outcomes Statement for First-Year Composition (WPA OS), because the final document does not help to distinguish why one composition course might be different from another. However, the WPA OS did ultimately center on "objectives" or outcomes, for the Outcomes Collective worked diligently to *not* suggest standards, but rather *outcomes*. Outcomes are goals that can be met on many levels, depending on local conditions (students, teachers, curriculum, etc.); standards are points at which those outcomes can be measured. (For a rich discussion of standards versus outcomes in the history of the WPA OS, see Yancey.)

It is ironic that none of those writing the WPA OS thought of it in terms of assessment. As is clear throughout this book, however, it has had continuing use in program assessment from the beginning. It is now obvious why. An assessment of the value of a writing program—or any program—needs to show how the program has met its designated outcomes. Yet, college writing programs, despite their mission statements, curriculum guidelines, and examinations of all sorts, have rarely attended to student outcomes, and it is those outcomes that provide clear opportunities for assessment and clear data for outsiders looking for accountability. Further, research in composition studies depends on comparative success of different ways of going about the teaching and learning of what matters most in writing, and that, in turn, depends upon clear consensus on outcomes. It should not be surprising that this assessment use of the WPA OS arose from those teaching instead of from outside testing companies usually charged with the task, which is unusual in today's highly charged environment of accountability.

It is interesting to note that White's email does not suggest "let's all chime in with what those objectives might be," which would have initiated an altogether different conversation from the process-oriented approach that he advised: "How might we go about trying?" Immediately, White set the tenor of any subsequent conversation to be all-inclusive ("How might *we* go about trying?"), and started with a focus on figuring out how such a conversation might take place. (For a thorough outline of how the process began and occurred over a period of several years, see Rhodes, Peckham, Bergman, and Condon.)

Nonetheless, one part of White's initial post did become a central question in the first meeting of the Collective, at a workshop planned and chaired by Bill Condon the same year at CCCC: "Would an outcomes statement do more harm than good?" That is, would having a clear statement of outcomes written by those administering first-year college writing courses help our programs communicate with various stakeholders? Two kinds of objections immediately surfaced and remain present in this new volume: Would such a statement serve to depress the creative anarchy that has kept the course alive and well since its introduction into most higher education curricula in America? Or, would it simply be an empty statement ignored by practitioners because it might have little application in real classrooms? Those representing the former statement seemed suspicious of imposed conformity, while those representing the latter suspected that current scholarship and best practice would turn out to be insufficiently persuasive to have much effect. Between these views stood a very slim majority, tentatively in favor of moving forward to draft something that would outspokenly avoid these extremes while embracing opportunities for improving the first-year writing course and perceptions of its purposes that a widely accepted statement could offer.

Unpacking the layers of Edward White's seemingly simple query took more than three years, culminating in the adoption of the WPA OS in April of 2000 by the Council of Writing Program Administrators (and the publication of the WPA OS in the organization's journal in 1999 and again in *College English* in 2001—adding the credibility of publication to the WPA OS).[1] Another layer of credibility appeared in 2005, when the first volume devoted entirely to the WPA OS was published by Utah State University Press. *The Outcomes Book: Debate and Consensus After the WPA Outcomes Statement,* edited by four of the key faculty who developed the document (Harrington, et al.), followed two pages that reprinted the WPA OS with twenty-two chapters examining its uses, challenges, and promise. (We reprint the WPA OS as an Appendix in this volume.)

As intended by the original Outcomes Collective, the conversation has continued: In 2008, a technology plank was added to the original WPA OS after much discussion and deliberation (and hundreds more emails)—a technology plank that had also been part of the original WPA OS conversation, but part of the document that took eight years to codify.

As we reread White's question some sixteen years later, it is interesting to note that such a question would have been extremely difficult to discuss—much less answer—even a few years earlier, because the technology did not exist to facilitate such a discussion. Some 240 faculty eventually participated in the development and revisions of the document. Sure, interested parties would have met at CCCC, WPA or at other conferences; they could have written letters to each other, and memos and proposals; and perhaps at some point, some small group could have come to some consensus. But, before email and the Internet, such a conversation among many people would have been more difficult—or would have taken such a long time that little might have been accomplished. There is some irony in that the lengthy conversation about technology essentially lasted from 1996 through 2008, and was enabled by the technology that was being discussed (and as you will read in this text, that discussion continues).

In this volume, we do not propose to repeat the work of *The Outcomes Book*, the useful 2005 volume that outlines the history of the project, including the process the Outcomes Collective followed in conceiving, drafting, and delivering the WPA OS. During the past decade, we have seen widespread interest in the WPA OS. For example, on October 26, 2011, a Bing Web search on the phrase "WPA Outcomes Statement" yielded 36,800 hits, and a simple Google search yielded 498,000 hits. We suspect that these increased numbers result from an ever-expanding Web and increasing document linkage, but at least to some extent because of an increased interest in the WPA OS. (The first twenty-four pages of a Bing search, for instance, do include references to the WPA OS and nothing tangential.) Further, the WPA OS has been implemented at institutions both in the United States and abroad. In fact, Patricia Freitag Ericsson has generated a table listing more than eighty institutions that report using the WPA OS in some capacity.[2]

In planning for this collection, we thought it would be useful to have some record of how the WPA OS has been adopted, adapted, and modified, and the ways in which the WPA OS is moving outward to affect other parts of the university and university—or college-level writing instruction. Our hope is that this text contributes to the scholarly discussion about the WPA OS by articulating the national and global impact of the WPA OS on various programs and disciplines; serving as a scholarly resource for current and future writing program administrators and scholars within the disciplines of composition studies and writing program administration, as they continue to shape curricula and programs; and forecasting the future impact of the WPA OS.

In working to accomplish this task, we asked scholars in our field to consider some questions: How has the WPA OS affected the discipline as a whole? How has use of the WPA OS affected the political dynamics within institutions? How has the use of the WPA OS affected the teaching of writing in institutions outside the United States?

What does the future hold for the WPA OS, for its use, and what are the implications for students and instructors?

Some of the more local and specific concerns that we asked writers to consider focused on how their own writing programs have used the WPA OS to shape curricula or guide pedagogical practices, evaluate students' writing, assess courses and programs, guide faculty development and perhaps even faculty hiring practices, define "first-year composition" as it applies locally, enable connections to other units on campus that teach writing, and affect the use of digital technologies in writing courses and programs.

Given these considerations, we have grouped the twenty chapters in this new volume into three sections, according to their perspectives on the WPA OS. The seven chapters in the first section, "Adapting the WPA OS to Develop Curriculum," accept the developed version of the WPA OS and use (or adapt) it to improve the writing programs at particular institutions. A common thread that binds this section's essays focuses on the tension inherent when universities and community colleges work to connect a national set of outcomes to their local curriculum. Sometimes, the process of curricular change is facilitated by the WPA OS, although it almost always requires clarification, negotiation, and adaptation. What the WPA OS fosters, we learn in this section of the book, is the value of a bottom-up, generative approach that centers on collaboration requiring the involvement of (and investment by) a large group of stakeholders, ranging from program directors to university librarians, from full-time lecturers and part-time adjunct faculty to graduate teaching assistants. As the original OS Collective determined early on, the WPA OS is designed to be adapted to local conditions: students, faculty, programs, and so on. The WPA OS also serves as the generative grounds for a campus-wide effort focusing on writing as a heuristic for enriching course curricula and writing assignments, and a spur to writing across the curriculum.

Debra Frank Dew opens the first section by describing how the WPA OS affords writing-about-writing (WAW) theorists grounds for dynamic curricula movement. In the second chapter, Wendy Olson focuses on how the WPA OS can be used strategically to interrupt and reshape curricular, programmatic, and institutional structures of basic writing, structures that often constrain pedagogical best practices. Kimberly Harrison then describes one writing program in a large, urban state university as a case study for how the WPA OS can be used to help define programmatic identity; she outlines four specific rhetorical strategies for using the WPA OS to cultivate program ethos. In Chapter 4, Teresa Grettano, Rebecca Ingalls, and Tracy Ann Morse discuss the "perilous vision" of the WPA OS. In addition to establishing a promising vision to set standards for student writing development, the WPA OS is also, they argue, an ideological construct that can guide, challenge, or even obstruct that vision it intends to foster. In Chapter 5, Sherry Rankins-Robertson illustrates methods for applying the WPA OS at the course level to redesign writing assignments to articulate with learning outcomes. Doug Sweet, in Chapter 6, argues for a pluralistic, deliberative, rhetorical curriculum, for which the WPA OS provides a codified and cogent response to the often unacknowledged valorization of binary idealistic epistemologies in composition pedagogy. In Chapter 7, Paul Anderson, Chris M. Anson, Martha Townsend, and Kathleen Blake Yancey describe the theoretical and contextual challenges of developing an outcomes statement for WAC programs.

The eight chapters of the second section, "Applying the WPA OS to Enact Programmatic, Institutional, and Disciplinary Change," take the WPA OS into new territory, exploring methods to use it in ways and sites not really contemplated by the drafters of the original document—even ways in which the WPA OS aided what is described as a "non-program program"; use of the WPA OS enabled the non-program to develop into a real writing program that included a sequenced curriculum and integral portfolio assessment. Other chapters in this section report how the WPA OS aided programs in gaining respect and informed their school's writing curriculum; discuss the international application of the WPA OS; describe how the WPA OS has possibly affected the teaching of writing across an institution; and note the WPA OS's ripple effect on programs and universities.

Craig Jacobsen, Susan Miller, and Shelley Rodrigo open this section by examining the usefulness of the WPA OS in the context of a large-scale, multi-campus, curriculum revision in the Maricopa County Community College District—one of the largest in the country. Next, in Chapter 9, Stephen Wilhoit shows how the WPA OS played a key role in revising a faculty seminar in writing across the curriculum; this chapter offers assessment results documenting the effectiveness of those changes. In Chapter 10, Karen Bishop Morris and Lizbeth A. Bryant demonstrate how the WPA OS can serve as a powerful tool for counteracting institutional inertia by fostering a documentary reality that ultimately strengthened a "non-program program's" identity. Next, in "Reframing the Conversation: Can the Outcomes Statement Help?," Darsie Bowden chronicles the implementation of the WPA OS at a large Catholic university in the Midwest, and recounts how it encourages administrators to take action. In Chapter 12, Susan Thomas presents the view from Australia, showing how the WPA OS facilitated each stage of the development of the Sydney writing program, including a writing center, a virtual exchange program, and the foundations for a WAC program. In Chapter 13, Morgan Gresham speaks to the possibilities and problems adopting and adapting the WPA OS, which she sees as both programmatically stabilizing and oppressive, and she recounts how one program's faculty attempted to counter those oppressive tendencies. Chapter 14 shows a more positive view: Deirdre Pettipiece and Justin Everett argue that the WPA OS, as the core of their strategic plan for writing programs, allowed them to provide reviews of primary research that supported the need for curricula revision and to educate the university community on the disciplinarity of rhetoric and composition. Finally, a collaborative team of co-authors argue, in Chapter 15, that the WPA OS elicits "waves of collaborative change at a large university writing program," allowing literacy professionals in particular institutional settings to collaborate across different ranks and affiliations to document the contributions of their programs for a range of purposes and audiences.

The five chapters of the third section, "Cultivating the Intellectual Enrichment of the WPA OS Through Critique," continue the discourse of the very first workshop in 1996, raising questions about what the writers see as flaws and limitations in the WPA OS that should be addressed in the revisions that surely will occur in the future. The use (and requirement and implementation) of technology has driven one of the competing discourses about the WPA OS from the beginning, and in this section such reflection continues. The apparent centering of the WPA OS on *rhetoric* also generates reflective tension in these chapters, as does the relationship of the WPA OS to the growing body of second-language learners and writers we see in our college classrooms.

Chapter 16 focuses on the impact of the WPA OS on second language writers, a population not much attended to in the document. Paul Kei Matsuda and Ryan Skinnell argue that as a document describing outcomes for all first-year composition students, the WPA OS needs to incorporate language issues more explicitly in recognition of the changing demographics in U.S. higher education, which is increasingly multilingual and multicultural. Next, Judy Holiday presents a reading of the WPA OS that argues that the design of the document weakens its potential for theoretical consistency as well as its efficacy to instantiate the curricular consistency and disciplinary currency it espouses. Barry Maid and Barbara D'Angelo, in Chapter 18, present a rather different critical perspective; their assessment results and student portfolios seem to indicate that rhetorical knowledge emerges as a kind of über-outcome for their students. In Chapter 19, Micheal Callaway registers dissatisfaction with the new technology plank in the WPA OS, which he argues should have less emphasis on technological applications and more emphasis on how writing technologies shape the decisions of writers. The final chapter seeks to assess the impact of the WPA OS, reporting on a survey of 101 four-year colleges and universities selected as type representatives. Emily Isaacs and Melinda Knight inquire into how, and to what extent, the WPA OS, other outcomes, or the values embedded in the document have been adopted or adapted in their research sample.

In essence, the chapters in this concluding section of the book reflect on and push at the WPA OS in ways that will help generate revisions of the document; for now, as in the beginning, the WPA OS is nothing if not a "living" document with significant implications for pedagogy, assessment, curricula—and, consequently, students.

Notes

1. Preliminary drafts of the Outcomes Statement, and notes from conference sessions, can be accessed by visiting the following website: http://www.comppile.org/archives/WPAoutcomes/continue.html. Maintained by Keith Rhodes, this site provides a timeline history of the WPA Outcomes Statement, as well as several resources.

2. This table can be accessed at the following URL: http://www.wsu.edu/~ericsson/OS_table.html. The table lists institutions, as well as how institutions use the WPA OS. For example, some institutions employ the WPA Outcomes Statement to construct and define first-year courses; to prepare teaching assistants and other faculty; or to develop various assessment practices.

Works Cited

Council of Writing Program Administrators. "The WPA Outcomes Statement for First-Year Composition." Council of Writing Program Administrators, July 2008. Web. 27 August 2011.

Ericcson, Patricia Freitag. *Outcomes Use Table: Current Uses of the WPA Outcomes for First-Year Composition*. Washington State University. May 2006. Web. 7 June 2009.

Harrington, Susanmarie, Keith Rhodes, Ruth Overman Fischer, and Rita Malenczyk, eds. *The Outcomes Book: Debate and Consensus after the WPA Outcomes Statement*. Logan, UT: Utah State UP, 2005. Print.

Rhodes, Keith, Irwin Peckham, Linda S. Bergmann, and William Condon. "The Outcomes Project: The Insiders' History." Harrington, et al. 8–17. Print.

Rhodes, Keith. "The Outcomes Statement History." *CompPile*. 14 February 2010. Web. 23 July 2012.

White, Edward M. "The Origins of the Outcomes Statement." Harrington, et al. 3–7. Print.

Yancey, Kathleen Blake. "Standards, Outcomes, and All that Jazz." Harrington, et al. 18–23. Print.

The WPA Outcomes Statement—
A Decade Later

1 CWPA Outcomes Statement as Heuristic for Inventing Writing-about-Writing Curricula

Debra Frank Dew

In "Ideology, Theory and the Genre of Writing Programs," Jeanne Gunner argues that our theoretical efforts to change a writing program or implement new curricula must engage the institution's ideological interest in sustaining its already understood definition of the program's work and its functions, what Gunner calls the "institutional genre" of our programs (9). This "institutional genre" brings with it specific social ends and actions that the institution would have the program accomplish (e.g., testing, sorting, equipping students with specific skills). As an institutional genre of a priori or antecedent status, the institution's ideological hold on the program precedes new theorizing and constrains change, especially when the cultural current of the institution's master discourse enjoys a stronger rhetorical force than that of a WPA's theorizing as a "lesser-status discourse" (15). Unless we reconcile the often competing generic claims upon the program's work, WPAs, in concert with their writing faculty, will struggle to reconstitute the theoretical foundation of the local first-year composition (FYC) curriculum, redesign its forms, and redirect its aims.

In our envisioning of writing-about-writing (WAW) curricula (Russell; Bawarshi; Dew; Sargent and Paraskevas; Downs and Wardle; Wardle), then, we invent in the company of our local institution's already formulated and ideologically invested understanding of FYC and its aims. In pursuit of WAW as a curricular alternative, we might prefer to break radically (Downs and Wardle 558) even heretically (Wardle, "Mutt" 784) from the past, from the constraints of FYC's generic traditions, both the local and the more deftly articulated historical functions of the course. The turn from "'teaching how to write in college' to teaching about writing—from acting as if writing is a basic universal skill to acting as if writing studies is a discipline with content knowledge to which students should be introduced" (Downs and Wardle 553) may be theorized readily in the company of a cohort of progressive curricular theorists. However, FYC is a highly staked curricular space with a deep history that exceeds the local institution, including the earliest frame of Harvard's English A, with its offspring, the current-traditional, five paragraph essay, followed then by process theory and its mantras, and perhaps now the universal academic discourse (UAD) of the general writing skills design. These earlier configurations may likewise be understood as generic antecedents of stronghold status. Not only do earlier configurations persist as FYC genres, but also they recur and habitually expect the "typified rhetorical action" that is their generic due (Miller 157). These curricular constructs often appropriate the FYC space via the expanse of FYC delivering systems (AP, CLEP, dual enrollment) over which we have little, if any, curricular control. The consummate challenge, then, for those of us who would revise FYC is to reconcile the competing definitional claims that pull upon the course—claims of the local institution and its stakeholders, those of the competing delivery systems that enjoy purchase upon FYC's population for multiple ends, and those of peer scholars in the field with those of the newly invented WAW vision. Those of us who would make the curricular turn to a writing-about-writing curriculum face just this conceptual challenge: How do we acknowledge the curricular antecedents that yet over-determine the course and reconcile them anew? The WPA Outcomes Statement for First-Year Composition (WPA OS) as generative heuristic affords us the inventional grounds for just such a move.

Where Is the WPA Outcomes Statement Within the WAW Movement?

The WPA OS as position statement (adopted in 2000) is now likewise antecedent to our most recent WAW theorizing. Even as the WPA OS is "living" in its design, following Kathleen Blake Yancey's reading ("A Comment" 379), the statement looms largely within the WAW movement with its reformist aims either eclipsed, or at least under-articulated, to be sure. The WPA OS is present and formidable in its historical stature as the discipline's FYC curricular statement. Although it is present, we have not yet theorized its relations or found it generatively viable for WAW work. One could claim that the WPA OS enjoys an absent presence within current efforts to reconstitute FYC as a WAW space.

In "Teaching about Writing, Righting Misconceptions," Douglas Downs and Elizabeth Wardle position the WPA OS within their critique of Academic Discourse as Category Mistake. They observe, "These outcomes, which reflect an ideology of access to the academy and a desire to prepare students for academic writing, are increasingly being adopted nationwide" (555). But, they ask, "Can FYC fulfill these expectations?" (555). Their question ends their engagement with the WPA OS, so we might surmise that its conceptual landscape is implicated in the teaching of universal academic discourse as a mistake of category. In this context, do we understand the WPA OS as UAD essence, or perhaps worse, as a DNA composite of the Mutt genre, the pejorative, which Wardle critiques as writing that fails to "respond to rhetorical situations requiring communication . . . to accomplish a purpose that is meaningful to an author" ("Mutt" 77). If, in this association, we fix and flatten the WPA OS as UAD's product-process essence, we can surely implicate the WPA OS in the delivery of the general writing skills curriculum that Downs and Wardle (and others before them, David Russell, in particular) find problematic. To do so, however, to break from the past in their "radical" and "heretical" manner (as cited earlier) via a wholesale dismissal of the WPA OS misses the common rhetorical grounds upon which FYC past may be theorized intelligibly into the WAW present. As Gunner suggests, the agency that WPAs need for curricular change "comes in moments that allow for discursive reshaping" (15) via the "intermingling of discourses of differing cultural value," (15) and in the WAW instance, the WPA OS stands as master discourse relative to those of lesser cultural value, the WAW initiative, which now aspires to and truly needs an alignment with the more powerful cultural discourses of both the field and the local institution.

Part of the WPA OS issue here, as Judy Holiday discusses in Chapter 17, "Competing Discourses within the WPA Outcomes Statement," may be that as an unintended effect of its inclusivity, the WPA OS remains "theoretically problematic" for its ambiguity. While the framers claim that the WPA OS "represents the most current theory and research," it may yet "perpetuate 'service' pedagogies," which are, in kind, the object of the Downs and Wardle critique of universal academic discourse (Holiday). Because the WPA OS can be used generatively to affirm and perpetuate UAD, what we might call a mining of general writing skills, Holiday's "service" function, its theoretical *loosey-gooseyness* risks incoherence. Holiday claims that the WPA OS contains competing discourses that permit both "one-way and multi-directional acculturative approaches to teaching writing." One way to understand Holiday's critique in the company of Downs and Wardle's rejection of universal academic discourse is in light of the WPA OS's epistemological character. Does the WPA OS, by its design, risk more in its inclusivity than it gains in its purported interest in advancing the discipline within a theoretically coherent, research-secured curricular framework? Whether we render the WPA OS's framework as an essence of what we know, or as generative tool for inventing what is visionary by a local context, our terms of epistemological engagement with the WPA OS matter. Whether we reduce the WPA OS to UAD or general writing skills (Downs and Wardle), or critique it for its non-committal nod to the more rhetorically robust "multidirectional acculturative" or "big rhetoric pedagogies" (Holiday), we encounter the WPA OS's living nature, its reformist aims, and most importantly, the heuristic affordances of the genre as generative tool. This is the epistemological challenge that the WPA OS as heuristic posits for our consideration.

To understand the WPA OS as curricular genre used to redesign FYC with a writing-about-writing framework, "we need to look back" mindfully to FYC's history, as Robert Connors advises, and situate the WPA OS within the ebb and flow of reformist and abolitionist impulses across time (4). Upon the WPA OS's adoption in 2000, Kathleen Blake Yancey defined it as our "plural commons" ("A Comment" 380). Providing "a commons," while permitting "a plurality," the WPA OS is a "common curricular text" against which local courses may "be plotted" (380). The WPA OS's "beauty (appeal) is its use of the familiar (audience/conventions) to contextualize the new"—a "new construct of writing is created" with its "use of rhetoric and genre" (Yancey, "Bowling" 218). The WPA OS looks to the past and brings past with it by grounding the knowledge domains in "what composition teachers nationwide have learned from practice, research and theory" (WPA OS). Clearly, it is these claims to a "commons" and to the valuing of a "plurality" that Holiday reframes as a risky ambiguity that is a lesser good than theoretical coherence, if not a research-driven consensus.

In "Bowling Together," her afterward to *The Outcomes Book* of 2005, Yancey's theoretical musing (now extended within her current work on FYC and transfer) gains traction when she asks:

> What is the FYC curriculum? I have to wonder if what is articulated in the Statement is not already our curriculum—genre and language and rhetorical situation: they *are* the curriculum. What would happen if we took this idea seriously and understood that we are a discipline after all, that composition is the content of (any) composition class and program? (220)

The key words "discipline" and "content" both resonate here, as she conceptually bridges the WPA OS with what is now central to the WAW movement. As a discipline, we have a curriculum—genre, language, rhetorical situation—a subject matter with key terms and theories; for content, we have composition itself. Yancey's theorizing grounds the WAW movement with its (1) framing in of FYC as *disciplinary* space within a fully-articulated discourse community, which sanctions (2) the filling of this curricular space with our *subject matter* as content, thus, the writing *about* writing turn. Rather than filling the course anew, I argue that WAW willingly frames what has always already been with us in this space—our disciplinary and theoretical knowledge. Further, this knowledge—as what it is that students "should know" and "understand" (Yancey, "A Brief Introduction" 323)—can be culled from the WPA OS if we use it as a generative tool for staging outcomes along a developmental continuum rather than engaging the outcomes as the landscape of UAD's end product.

In this manner, the WPA OS enabled our local revisioning of FYC into a WAW curriculum in Colorado in 2003, when we reconstituted our general writing skills curriculum as a first-year rhetoric and writing course with a specific content (see Dew). Our starting content was the rhetorical theory we used to engage language matters (language issues in theory and practice) as the subject of course readings, and our practice was rhetorical criticism, where students analyze texts and write in parallel relations to other disciplines in much the same sense as Holiday's "big" rhetoric. With this curricular revision, we aimed to help students gain the meta-rhetorical awareness necessary for transfer by experiencing what Kaufer and Young define as "languaging about a discipline" (83) via writing within a "context-specific, content-rich writing situation" (94). Our first culling of rhetorical theory as content knowledge from the WPA OS helped us further recognize other theoretical domains as likewise embedded within the WPA OS. As we realized the transfer value of explicit instruction in rhetorical knowledge, so have we followed suit with writing process and genre theory. Culling this content knowledge for explicit instruction is linked to expertise in writing and already grounded in the WPA OS's collective knowledge of practice, research, and past theory. The WPA OS, as a heuristic, helps us perennially remember and remix FYC's knowledge domains, and thereby more robustly articulate the WAW content in familiar terms for diverse stakeholders, whose understanding and assent are necessary for any curricular change. This generic remix as a calling up of the WPA OS's ideas and practices of the past can enable historically mindful, theoretically prescient, and locally responsive WAW frames for the course.

How does a generative remix of the WPA OS's knowledge domains help us invent the content that is the signature feature of WAW curricula? What are the content knowledge domains that constitute expertise in writing, and why should we teach them? In "College-Level Writing: What the Research—on Transfer and Elsewhere—Suggests," Yancey posits a short list of transfer-positive knowledge domains to be delivered in FYC as her "Modest Proposal." Her tentative list includes the following: "Composition: Key Terms and Practices; Rhetoric: Key Terms and Practices; Reflection." In her listing here, we see a more deliberate commitment to specific content domains—Key Terms and Practices—that may have been rendered more ambiguous in the WPA OS's original framework, a framework that does not differentiate between content and skills outcomes by design, even as it encompasses both. Anne Beaufort, in *College Writing and Beyond*, offers the most robust account of FYC knowledge domains, which she frames as the "situated domains" of discourse community, subject matter, genre knowledge, rhetorical knowledge, and process knowledge (18). For Beaufort, expertise expects writers to have "mental schema, or heuristics, with which to organize knowledge and aid problem solving and gaining new knowledge in new situations" (17). And further, "[w]e are looking to teach not similarities in the ways writing is done in different contexts, but rather, to teach those broad concepts (discourse community, genre, rhetorical tools, etc.) which will give writers the tools to analyze similarities and differences among the [writing] situations they encounter" (149). When we engage the WPA OS's template generatively with these knowledge domains in view, its outcomes landscape overlays these domains effectively. Rhetorical theory, writing process theory, and genre theory arise as content domains, and I argue that we would do well to commit ourselves to this theoretical scope of work in an ever-expanding reach for a big-rhetoric WAW framework. In doing so with some increasingly strong, research-based grounds for a consensus, we would grant that any program surely begins with local theory-in-hand, drawing from the content knowledge strengths of its faculty. From such a local place, programs might set a robust theoretical course for more expansive work via faculty development. The pedagogical urgency here is the concomitant work in both theory (content) and practice (skills), such that writers have the vocabulary, heuristics, and tools they need to garner intellectual control over their work and account for it (reflection).

Why would a commitment to these three theoretical domains within a WAW framework (1) honor our long-standing desire for inclusivity, (2) admit and respect local constraints, and yet (3) move us more deliberately forward on less ambiguous disciplinary grounds? A cursory review of some of our best research on rhetoric, writing, and genre theory *gets us there*; that is, these research advances that are already imagined and embedded within the WPA OS, but not framed as such, could afford us a more robust expertise that is more powerful cumulatively than any single subset (just process theory and skills, just genre theory and skills) on its own.

Rhetorical Knowledge: Rhetorical Theory + Practice + Meta-Rhetorical Reflection

Using the WPA OS's own terms, what have we learned from practice, research, and theory about the importance of rhetorical knowledge (its nature) to expertise in writing? What happens when we pull our historical "through lines" for rhetorical theory as content? "Through lines" are Yancey's terms for the knowledge students carry forward from context to context, or transfer from here to there ("College-Level"). I extend these terms to encompass the theoretical insights that we as writing professionals carry forward from our research in the teaching of rhetoric and writing.

David Kaufer and Richard Young define expertise as "both an ability to carry out successfully the rhetorical tasks (practice) associated with a subject-matter discipline and an understanding of and ability to articulate the reasons (theory) for the success" (74). Expertise as rhetorical competence within a discipline thus happens when writers both know of (theory) and know how (performance, skill); the one enables the intellectual control over the other. They also define subject matter as "content that has been discussed in recurring and public rhetorical situations" (79). Subject matters have "publically shared histories" that have been analyzed from theoretical perspectives (79). As we learn "history and theory" as the subject matter of a discipline, we gain the "credibility" we need for expertise (79). Through "subject matter encounters," then, we learn the rhetorical practices of a discipline. By practicing, by languaging about the discipline as a subject matter, we learn to write within the discipline (79). In some sense, this account echoes David Bartholomae's notion of novice writers inventing the university in their efforts to take up academic discourse writ large, but Kaufer and Young situate the inventing dynamic more explicitly within the "content-rich" context of a discipline (94). Students aspiring to expertise are "languaging" *with* the discipline's content or subject matter and "languaging" *within* its rich context. In this instance, and in like manner, writing about writing stages rhetoric and writing as the discipline that affords writers both content and skills for such language work.

David Fleming proposes rhetoric as a course of study for our students, understanding rhetoric as a "program of instruction involving both theory and practice and aimed at the moral and intellectual development of student as citizen" (178), with practice as the application or exercise of theory (mindful, critical, purposeful application) (182). Fleming claims that "students need a rhetorical art . . . a theoretical vocabulary providing the language user . . . with a way to isolate, analyze and manage communication situations," and he grounds these claims in rhetoric's earliest of it classical traditions (183). In response to David Russell's call for courses about writing that would replace the FYC general writing skills standard and meet the full criteria for a robust activity system of disciplinary stature (Russell's call for liberal arts courses about writing likewise serves as the generative font for the

Downs and Wardle WAW vision of 2007), Fleming proffers rhetoric in *theory* and *practice* as a course of study.

Thus, as we pull up the WPA OS's theoretical through lines, we discover rhetoric and its key terms as our curriculum (broadening Yancey's earlier musing of *composition* as content) and content for the course. The WPA OS defines rhetorical expertise as outcomes: "focus on a purpose," "respond to needs of different audiences," and "respond . . . to different rhetorical situations" (WPA OS). To realize these outcomes across time developmentally, we need to re-invent the domain of rhetorical knowledge and more robustly envision FYC as encompassing: rhetorical theory—rhetorical practice (criticism, analysis, production) coupled with meta-rhetorical reflection and genre knowledge—and genre theory, coupled with genre practice (criticism, analysis and production) and meta-generic reflection.

Returning again to the WPA OS as what we as a field have learned from "practice, research and theory," we can readily affirm the value of genre knowledge to expertise in writing. In his book-length study, *Genre and the Invention of the Writer*, Anis Bawarshi articulates another vision of writing expertise, as he charges us to: "teach students how to be rhetorically astute and agile, how . . . to use genre analysis . . . to become . . . critical readers of the sites of action within which writing takes place" (165). Teaching "genre analysis as invention technique, [and] heuristic" gives rhetoric a central focus in first-year writing. He continues, "There persists a frustrating assumption that FYW is a contentless course, that it has no inherent subject. FYW does have a subject: it is writing" (168). In such a course, "[s]tudents write arguments, but these arguments are about writing, about the rhetorical choices writers make and how their genred positions of articulation organize and elicit these choices" (163). "Writing is the subject of FYW," he repeats with emphasis, and "not just the process of writing, but writing itself—what writing does, how it works, and why—should be the subject of FYW" (169). He continues, "In other words, FYW should become a course in rhetoric, a course that uses genres to teach students how to recognize and navigate discursive and ideological formations" (169). Bawarshi gives us genre theory and genre criticism in practice, so that writers know of (theory) genre's dynamic nature and know how (practice) to analyze and generate rhetorically effective genres in their own right.

In the earlier *Outcomes Book* of 2005, Barb Little Liu draws explicitly from the WPA OS, and points to three instances where genre outcomes appear: Students should "'understand how genres shape reading and writing processes'"; "'write in many genres'"; and "'develop knowledge of genre conventions'" (qtd. in Liu, 72). Espousing a "genre process" approach, she advises us to "prepare students for the lifelong work of learning to write by exposing them to a number of genres, developing their ability to look critically at communities and genres," and helping them see "both the constraints and the choices within particular writing situations" (79). Expertise here is in gaining "rhetorical consciousness" by "examining particular texts and explicating the ways these texts make use of or break from accepted practices; and second by helping them become ethnographers of discourse communities" (81). She continues: "Instructors should recognize that the ample guidance and detailed feedback often given within writing," (this is *our theorizing* as scaffolding under, articulating over, and determining students' writing practices) "does not follow them," so perhaps our tendency to "initiate and dominate conversations about student writing is misguided" (82). Students should practice "initiating such conversations for themselves, discussing what kinds of questions" would be "useful to ask in new writing situations" (82). Teaching such heuristics would help students develop a "mindset for ethnography" (82) and thereby, I believe, help them secure intellectual control over their work. To teach these heuristics as content is to give students the theoretical tools they need to frame in new writing tasks and negotiate new rhetorical contexts, which is the transfer work that WAW sees as its ends.

Writing Process Knowledge: Writing Process Theory + Writing Practice + Reflection

Once again, using the WPA OS's terms, what have we learned from "practice, research, and theory" about the importance of writing process knowledge to expertise in writing? The WPA OS asks students to understand much about writing process: students should "develop flexible strategies" for managing the process; "understand writing as an open (recursive) process"; "understand the collaborative and social aspects of writing processes"; and "learn to critique their own and other's work" (WPA OS). Our research on writing process defines expertise in now familiar ways: student/expert writer process distinctions (Sommers, "Strategies"); the skillful shifting between writer- and reader-based prose (Flower); gaining meta-cognitive awareness and reflecting critically within the writing portfolio (Yancey, *Reflection*). We deliver much of our best FYC work in scaffolding developing writers through their writing processes as sustained by our own intellectual designs, our writing process knowledge. To what degree, though, does our theoretical oversight and scaffolding enable students' learning of the same, their understanding of the writing process, and the confident securing of intellectual control over their own writing processes? We could more fully cull writing process theory as content knowledge within the WPA OS and position it as an integral domain, a teachable and desirable content outcome.

For example, our lingering concern with peer review in FYC is that students as developing writers do not assess and respond to peers' writing as we do. As Brian Huot notes, "Many [students] are ill-equipped" because a "crucial missing element in most writing pedagogy is any experience or instruction in ascertaining the value of one's work" (169). We support them through amply articulated peer review activities, and trust that the experience we design and the review process over which we maintain intellectual control is sufficient. Huot pushes us further as he defines our work instead as "instructive evaluation" (170), which is the purposeful teaching of writing response, and assessment to our students. They need to set "rhetorical and linguistic targets" for their writing, and then we need to "help them evaluate how well they have met such targets, using this evaluation to help them . . . set new ones" (171.) He uses theory—with a small (t)—as the beliefs and assumptions that inform (give sense to, justify, account for) our practices. Citing James Zebroski, he explains, "'Theory is practice of a specific kind, and practice is always theoretical. The question is whether we are going to become conscious of our theory'" (qtd. in Huot 165). The question, is how can we cull the theoretical content within the WPA OS's writing process outcomes and become "more conscious" (Huot) of our theories and "how they affect the entire act of teaching writing?" (165)? We should teach writers to apply assessment and response theory to their practice.

In her longitudinal study of the writing development of undergraduate students at Harvard, Nancy Sommers helps us to more complexly understand writing expertise as requiring much more than skills work in FYC and the subsequent assessment of the WPA OS's competencies as "end point," either at the close of the first year or beyond (162). She explains, "Without sustained instruction in disciplinary methods, and without expertise in content . . . students learn to write and connect with readers in a more haphazard way, more a process of luck than instruction" (159). Furthermore, "[W]hen students have a chance to build expertise by returning to the same topics, and when they are given instruction and practice in disciplinary methods, they are more likely to engage with writers who have struggled with similar issues and thus find their place in an academic exchange" (159). If "students do not know there is a method in *one* discipline, they are less likely to look for disciplinary conventions elsewhere" (159). To move writers forward developmentally, then, it is vital that we stage fully articulated process experiences that equip writers for the "*reading, questioning, evaluating, interpreting*, and, of course *writing*—that are the sum and the substance—the process—of becoming educated citizens" (162). Sommers does not prescribe a return to the WPA OS, nor call for a remix of its terms as outcomes or as framework; however, a generative culling out of the WPA OS's commitment to disciplinary methods (rhetoric as techne, writing as process) and its content (rhetoric as subject matter, process as subject matter) both complements the WAW curricular turn and refigures its vision along a developmental continuum as Sommers animates it. To the extent that writing about writing equips student writers with methods (skills) and theories (content), accompanied with a mindfulness of their own developing expertise (meta-rhetorical reflection), and the ability to sustain these processes, the WPA OS as heuristic and generative conceptual grounds *can get us there*. The WPA OS offers us the theoretical through lines we need for WAW's robust mapping of process knowledge: writing process (including assessment) theory + process practice + meta-cognitive reflection; and rhetorical knowledge + genre knowledge + process knowledge: all in theory, all in practice, along with critical reflection.

To redesign FYC as WAW, we must reconcile the competing definitions that pull upon its curricular site, including local antecedents as well as the more reductive general writing skills iterations as marketed by the College Board (AP) and ETS (SAT, ACT). The WPA OS as heuristic remains our vital "plural commons" for mediating these competing constructs because it helps us look to the past and reason from what we have learned from practice, research, and theory as we remix FYC's knowledge domains. With such historically mindful work, we may articulate the WAW content in familiar terms for diverse stakeholders, whose understanding and assent are necessary if restless spirits of FYC's past and present are ever to understand our curricular change. In their designing of the WPA OS from the start, the steering committee imagined that the document would "focus on expectations, on what we want students to know, to do, to understand" (Yancey, "A Brief" 323). In our emphasis on general writing skills as the essence of FYC, we have worked deliberately to provide our students with the extensive *practice* they need as developing writers—we excel at teaching what it is that we want them "to do." What the WAW turn in rhetoric and composition asks of us is a continued investment in skills enriched with a similar investment in the theoretical content of our field, rhetoric and composition writ large. In closing, I propose that we deliberately teach students what it is they need "to know" and "to understand" about rhetoric, writing, and genre theory. With a purposeful restructuring and a disentangling of content and skill outcomes, the WPA OS can re-frame FYC as a disciplinary space, and as such, we would move generatively beyond the risky limits of its current design (Holiday), which may yet invite what is "barely doable" rather than advancing what is "visionary" (Yancey, "Standards" 23). We could design and deliver WAW courses that are historically mindful, theoretically prescient, and yet, locally responsive.

Works Cited

Bartholomae, David. "Inventing the University." *Journal of Basic Writing* 5 (1986): 4–23. Print.

Bawarshi, Anis. *Genre and the Invention of the Writer: Reconsidering the Place of Invention in Composition.* Logan: Utah State UP, 2003. Print.

Beaufort, Anne. *College Writing and Beyond: A New Framework for University Writing Instruction.* Logan: Utah State UP, 2007. Print.

Connors, Robert. "The New Abolitionism: Toward a Historical Background." *Reconceiving Writing, Rethinking Writing Instruction.* Ed. Joseph Petraglia. Mahwah, NJ: Lawrence Erlbaum, 1995. 3–26. Print.

Council of Writing Program Administrators. "The WPA Outcomes Statement for First-Year Composition." Council of Writing Program Administrators, July 2008. Web. 12 Mar. 2010.

Dew, Debra Frank. "Language Matters: Rhetoric and Writing I as Content Course." *Writing Program Administration* 26.3 (2003): 87–104. Print.

Downs, Douglass, and Elizabeth Wardle. "Teaching about Writing, Righting Misconceptions: (Re)Envisioning 'First-Year Composition' as Introduction to Writing Studies." *College Composition and Communication* 58.4 (2007): 552–84. Print.

Fleming, David. "Rhetoric as a Course of Study." *College Composition and Communication* 61.2(1998): 169–91. Print.

Flower, Linda. "Writer-Based Prose: A Cognitive Basis for Problems in Writing." *College English* 41.1 (1979): 19–37. Print.

Gunner, Jeanne. "Ideology, Theory and the Genre of Writing Programs." *The WPA as Theorist: Making Knowledge Work.* Ed. Irwin Weiser and Shirley K Rose. Portsmouth, NH: Boynton/Cook, Heinemann P, 2002. 7–18. Print.

Huot, Brian. "Toward a New Discourse of Assessment for the College Writing Classroom." *College English* 65.2 (2002): 163–80. Print.

Kaufer, David, and Richard Young, "Writing in the Content Areas: Some Theoretical Complexities." *Theory and Practice in the Teaching of Writing: Rethinking the Discipline.* Ed. Lee Odell. Carbondale: SIUP, 1993. 71–104. Print.

Liu, Barbara Little. "More than the Latest PC Buzzword for Modes: What Genre Theory Means to Composition." *The Outcomes Book: Debate and Consensus after the WPA Outcomes Statement.* Ed. Susanmarie Harrington, Keith Rhodes, Ruth Overman Fischer, and Rita Malenczyk. Logan: Utah SP, 2005.72–84. Print.

Miller, Carolyn R. "Genre as Social Action." *Quarterly Journal of Speech.* 70 (1984): 154–67.

Russell, David. "Activity Theory and Its Implications for Writing Instruction." *Reconceiving Writing, Rethinking Writing Instruction.* Ed. Joseph Petraglia. Mahwah, NJ: Lawrence Earlbaum, 1995. 51–77. Print.

Sargent, M. Elizabeth, and Cornelia C. Paraskevas. *Conversations about Writing Eavesdropping, Inkshedding, and Joining In.* Toronto: Thomson Nelson, 2005. Print.

Sommers, Nancy. "Strategies of Student Writers and Experienced Adult Writers." *College Composition and Communication* 31.4 (1980): 378–88. Print.

—. "The Call of Research: A Longitudinal View of Writing Development." *College Composition and Communication* 60.1 (2008): 152–64. Print.

Wardle, Elizabeth. "'Mutt Genres' and the Goal of FYC: Can We Help Students Write the Genres of the University." *College Composition and Communication* 60.4 (2009): 765–89. Print.

Yancey, Kathleen Blake. A Brief Introduction. "WPA Outcomes Statement for First-Year Composition." *College English* 63.3 (2001) 321–25. Print.

—. Afterward. "Bowling Together: Developing, Distributing, and Using the WPA Outcomes Statement—and Making Cultural Change." Harrington, et al. 211–21. Print.
—. "College-Level Writing: What the Research—On Transfer and Elsewhere—Suggest." CWPA Conference. Minneapolis, MN. July 2009. Address.
—. "[A Comment on the 'WPA Outcomes Statement for First-Year Composition']: Responds." *College English* 64.3 (2002) 378–80. Print.
—. *Reflection in the Writing Classroom*. Logan, UT: Utah State UP. 1998. Print.
—. "Standards, Outcomes and All That Jazz." Harrington, et al. 18–23. Print.

2 The Politics of Pedagogy: The Outcomes Statement and Basic Writing

Wendy Olson

As evidenced by this collection, along with its 2005 precursor, *The Outcomes Book*, the WPA Outcomes Statement for First-Year Composition (WPA OS) has secured a foothold in our field's conversations about best practices and pedagogies, writing program administration, and writing assessment. At the same time, little dialogue has surfaced to explicitly address how the outcomes might be used to inform basic writing. (See Sternglass for one notable exception.) In this chapter, drawing from my own experience of building a composition program at a regional campus of an RU/VH: Research University (very high research activity), I detail how I use the WPA OS as a guiding curricular frame for both our first-year composition and basic writing classes. In doing so, I speak to the benefits it especially affords our basic writing curriculum. I elaborate how strategic use of the WPA OS allows me to position basic writing classes, which includes one three-credit course and one one-credit tutorial, as part of a holistic curriculum that prepares basic writing students for the expectations of first-year composition. This employment of the WPA OS also functions more broadly to "talk back" to and shape assumptions about what basic writing is and can be in higher education. In particular, I discuss how use of the WPA OS provides a means for foregrounding writing as a complex, meaning-making activity for all students, particularly those enrolled in basic writing classrooms.

As such, this chapter highlights a number of important insights that writing program administrators might consider when adapting the WPA OS for use in their own programs. First, use of the outcomes can provide an important structure for programmatic sequencing and scaffolding between basic writing and first-year composition (FYC). Because the WPA OS focuses on outcomes and not standards, as Mark Wiley and others have suggested, it provides curricular parameters without articulating specific levels of proficiency. In this context, use of the WPA OS can also serve to establish a curricular link for students as they move from one class (basic writing) to the next (first-year composition). This process functions to bring basic writing and first-year composition under the same curricular umbrella. Second, the outcomes in the WPA OS, therefore, act as support for developing, justifying, and sustaining a basic writing classroom with a complex curriculum and an informed pedagogical approach. Third, because this use of the outcomes might simultaneously become the framework by which both institutional and public stakeholders come to know a basic writing program, the WPA OS can also serve as an avenue for the kind of activist framing that Linda Adler-Kassner calls for in *The Activist WPA*—framing that moves to reshape public and institutional assumptions about what constitutes college-level writing and literacy skills. Consequently, while the particulars of my story are context-specific and localized to my campus, this chapter suggests that the WPA OS can provide a potential means for addressing and negotiating the politics of basic writing—from the curriculum up—at other colleges and universities as well. Before moving to a description of our program at Washington State University at Vancouver, I offer a brief overview of what I see as important ideological and political affinities shared between basic writing and the WPA OS.

The Politics Of Basic Writing

As a policy statement drafted and adopted by the Council of Writing Program Administrators, the WPA OS professes current disciplinary values, values informed by disciplinary knowledge. Key among these values is the understanding that "learning to read and write is a complex process" that is both "individual and social" (WPA OS). This focus on the complexity of writing as a social process is, of course, a foundational tenet of the basic writing movement that grew out of CUNY in the 1970s. In fact, it is a fair assessment to note, as many have, that Mina Shaughnessy's work with basic writers has significantly impacted pedagogical approaches across the broader discipline of composition studies. Underlying Shaughnessy's pedagogy is the assertion that basic writing students are not developmentally deficient individuals—a recurring assumption of such students as evidenced in the pejorative language of *remedial* that is still and often used to describe them—but rather writers inexperienced with the context of academic writing.

In particular, Shaughnessy's analytical mapping of error pointed to the complex negotiations writers engage in when producing written texts. A key element to her approach, as highlighted in her satirical essay "Diving In: An Introduction to Basic Writing," required a significant shift in understanding and analyzing error within the context of student writing (236–37). Her understanding of error involved, I would suggest, an acknowledgement of writing as meaning-making and context-specific activity. Similar to the principles outlined in the WPA OS, Shaughnessy's pedagogy required an understanding of the production of writing as a complex act that writers negotiate as both an individual and a social process.

Certainly, much debate and useful critique of Shaughnessy's basic writing pedagogy questioned her pedagogical emphasis on accommodation (see Horner and Lu). Even in its progressiveness, Shaughnessy's pedagogy overemphasized error and correctness. As Nicole Pepinster Greene and Patricia J. McAlexander rightly observe, Shaughnessy's approach was very much ideologically framed and influenced by current-traditional rhetoric (12). At the same time, however, what we see in Shaughnessy's scholarship is a precursory moment. It is a moment that, along with other critiques of cognitivism, like those found in the work of Mike Rose and Patricia Bizzell, anticipated the social turn in composition. One legacy of Shaughnessy's scholarship is a disciplinary understanding of error as contextually situated.

Since Shaughnessy's contributions, the tenets of basic writing pedagogy, at least as expressed in basic writing scholarship, have developed in ways that more or less align with the basic principles highlighted in the original WPA OS: an embracement of the rhetorical nature of writing; an understanding that writing is intricately related to thinking (that form cannot be separate from content); an appreciation of writing processes; and an acknowledgement that writing conventions, including error, are necessarily tied to genre, context, and audience. While error and usage are still often addressed in basic writing pedagogy, the historical obsession with conventions is tempered and circumscribed by an understanding of conventions as both discourse and context specific. In particular, David Bartholomae's contributions to basic writing scholarship furthers our understanding of the complexity surrounding the learning of writing conventions in arguing that entrance into any discourse community is always an act of appropriation and approximation (594). Furthermore, Lu's scholarship uncovers that for some basic writing students, control of particular conventions is not always so much a simple matter of adopting linguistic codes. It is also a process of cultural conflict and struggle ("Redefining").

This emphasis on the social and epistemic nature of writing undergirds the WPA OS. From this observation, we can see how programmatic use of the WPA OS affords the opportunity to make the case for a necessarily complex pedagogy within basic writing classrooms. In doing so, we can also see that, though the primary focus of this chapter is on what strategic use of the WPA OS might do for bolstering basic writing programs, it is equally important to recognize that basic writing pedagogy has significantly influenced the development of the outcomes. As such, the WPA OS can be used as a guiding force that not only professes but also functions, when adapted and adjusted locally, to negotiate the tension between basic writing's theoretical positioning on best practices and pedagogies, and the increasingly political and material forces that often constrain basic writing classrooms, students, and teachers.

Basic Writing at WSU Vancouver

Our composition program at WSU Vancouver is only five years old. Prior to fall 2006, the Vancouver campus was a transfer campus that only offered upper-division coursework, including some graduate courses and programs. In 2005, WSU Vancouver received approval from the Washington State Higher Education Coordinating Board to offer lower-division courses. In anticipation for the fall 2006 admittance of the first first-year class, I was hired in the spring of that same year as part of a cohort of nine tenure track faculty positions across disciplines. As the first director of composition on the Vancouver campus, my initial task was to coordinate and staff the first-year composition curriculum for the incoming first-year class while also contributing to writing-related initiatives across campus.

In retrospect, the first-year composition curriculum at our campus could have taken a very different trajectory. As mentioned above, there was no composition program, *per se*, until my hire. Indeed, I was encouraged to define my position when hired. Before my hire, faculty within the areas of rhetoric and composition included only two full-time faculty members: one faculty member who managed the writing center, and one faculty member who coordinated our secondary education program in addition to serving as associate chair to the department at the time. The English department on our campus offered writing classes, mostly composed of two, upper-division courses, one in argumentation and one in professional and technical writing. These courses primarily served general education requirements, yet there was nothing that held these or other writing courses together programmatically or distinguished them sequentially. In many ways, writing instruction on our campus resembled a collection of classes rather than a program, similar to the kind of curricular and institutional space that Jeffrey Klausman describes as common of composition courses in many community college settings (239).

Before moving to the task of coordinating and staffing the new program, it became clear to me that I would need to re-craft the curriculum that had been recently adopted at Vancouver, a new general education curriculum designed specifically for the Vancouver campus. To do so, I found that I had to mitigate the implicit myths and assumptions that circulate both publicly and institutionally about writing and writing instruction: that writing instruction is remedial education; that literacy is a simple, autonomous skill to be mastered; that students should already know how to write when they enter college, etc. Of note, the proposed curriculum had no provisions for basic writing. Subsequently, to address this oversight in the course of redesigning the curriculum, I made explicit the disciplinary and pedagogical values that informed the direction of the program I was building, using the WPA OS to frame and articulate the philosophy of our burgeoning program.

During my job interview on campus, I gleaned that the newly developed general education program that was underway for the Vancouver campus veered in significant ways from the general education program at the main campus in Pullman. By the time I was hired, the first-year writing requirements within this new model had been reconstructed in at least three significant ways. First, the program had developed and adopted an FYC course that was distinct from the FYC course at the main campus. Envisioned as a large lecture course with weekly break-out lab sessions, the lecture course would be taught by a faculty member, and the lab sections would be facilitated by teaching assistants. Beyond the curricular and pedagogical problems I imagined might likely occur with this model, the immediate implications of this change meant that our Vancouver campus would have to design its own writing placement procedure, whereas the writing placement procedures at the Pullman campus were both well-established and well-respected within our field (Haswell). Second, and attendant, under this general education program, the newly crafted FYC course was optional, though it wasn't entirely clear how students who chose to opt out of the course would otherwise meet their writing requirements, much less their writing needs. Lastly, and arguably most significant, under this model there was no provision for extended or supplemental instruction for students who needed additional writing support.

A few months before the fall semester, I met with administrators and faculty to discuss my concerns about the proposed first-year writing curriculum. I proposed an alternative plan: keep the Pullman model and let me adapt it to the specific needs of our campus and our students. Framing my argument with the WPA OS afforded my proposal a disciplinary ethos. In particular, I argued that given the complexity of learning to write and the varied and numerous writing tasks associated with that complexity, as outlined by national disciplinary experts in the WPA OS, a lecture course with an attendant writing lab was not likely to give students sufficient opportunity to both practice new writing strategies and workshop (not to mention revise) their written work. Furthermore, the first-year course offerings in composition that I wanted to adapt from Pullman included an optional or required (depending upon placement) one-credit supplemental tutorial and a three-credit basic writing course. This three-credit course, required for some students based upon their placement, is the course I primarily focus on below.

The proposal to keep the Pullman model was a conservative move, to be sure, but it was the best move given the circumstances and a confluence of other factors. First, having taught composition in Pullman the four years prior to taking the position at Vancouver, I knew the Pullman model, both its strengths and its weaknesses. I had, in fact, been part of a cohort of instructors who worked with the then-director of composition to redesign the first-year composition program two years prior. Key to this restructuring was a move to portfolio assessment and the construction of a programmatic rubric that aligned with the WPA OS. Thus, I already had both the broader disciplinary knowledge and more specific programmatic understanding needed to re-envision this particular program in a new and different environment. What I needed to carry it out was institutional buy-in and support.

Second, we were short on time. The time I needed to consider and think through, much less implement, a brand new program—whatever its philosophical and pedagogical bent—simply wasn't there. I barely had time to adequately adapt the Pullman model before classes started in fall. Third, and perhaps most important, I was philosophically and pedagogically opposed to the proposed model. I was sympathetic to the logistical contradictions of the model given that the Vancouver faculty and administration had had only just a little over a year to develop, staff, and implement an entirely new general education curriculum—and that they had done so as a group predominately unfamiliar with, or at least greatly distanced from, experiences working with first-year college students. Yet, the question of the role and function of basic writing, particularly given the regional status of the campus and the fact that—at least historically—its transfer population had been primarily non-traditional, had to be addressed. Stressing that the outcomes outlined in the WPA OS were crafted by national writing experts, and based upon disciplinary research and best practices, I was able to draw from its tenets in arguing for a more theoretically and pedagogically informed curricular structure, a structure that included provisions for basic writing.

The exclusion of basic writing from the curriculum until this point was more neglectful than malicious. While I suspect that its absence as even a consideration likely resulted at least in part from a lingering Research I sensibility, I did not necessarily have to fight for its institutional legitimacy in the ways that many of my writing program administrator colleagues have had to do at other institutions. Rather, in making my argument for the need, or at least consideration of basic writing as a potential curricular need on campus, I had to define basic writing and explain its worth. That is, I had to articulate just what it was I meant by the term *basic writing*, and then I had to etch out how its curriculum might serve as some use for our students. Aligning the basic writing courses with a rhetorical framework, in particular, allowed me to demonstrate the need for basic writing as a sequential part of first-year writing instruction on campus. In doing so, I used the WPA OS to frame the overarching curricular and pedagogical philosophies of the emerging program.

Constructed before the technology plank was developed, I used the original outcomes—rhetorical knowledge; critical thinking, reading, and writing; writing processes, and knowledge of conventions—as the curricular link that held together the sequence of writing courses I had adopted from Pullman, a three-credit writing course, a one-credit writing tutorial, and a three-credit FYC course that fulfilled general education requirements. As noted by Barbara D'Angelo and Barry Maid in Chapter 18 of this collection, rhetorical knowledge acts as a kind of über outcome in its relationship to the other outcomes of electronic composing, conventions, writing processes, and critical thinking, reading, and writing. I used this über outcome to guide both the curricular design and the programmatic philosophy of the developing program. In doing so, I was able to complicate and enrich both the content and pedagogical approach of the basic writing course.

Requiring concurrent enrollment in the traditional FYC class, the one-credit class provided supplemental workshop support for FYC writing assignments in the form of weekly group tutorials. What follows includes the course descriptions I drafted and proposed that WSU Vancouver adopt for the traditional FYC class and the three-credit basic writing class, English 101 and English 100/101, in making my case for the inclusion of a basic writing curriculum:

> English 101: This is an introductory course in college-level academic writing, designed to prepare students for writing in the university, emphasizing discipline-specific strategies of academic discourse. Students will read, discuss, and write in a range of academic genres and technological mediums to develop rhetorical skills, critical analytical skills, and research skills. In doing so, students will practice a variety of writing processes and academic conventions. The course theme coincides with the general education campus theme, "global change in a local context" for the 2006–2007 academic year. Final evaluation by portfolio.

> English 100/101: The English 100/101 placement presents the traditional first-year composition curriculum as a two-semester sequence. The linked introductory courses in college-level academic writing are taught by the same instructor and are designed to prepare students for writing in the university, emphasizing discipline-specific strategies of academic discourse. Students will read, discuss, and write in a range of academic genres and technological mediums to develop rhetorical skills, critical analytical skills, and research skills. In doing so, students will practice a variety of writing processes and academic conventions. The two-semester sequence will cover the same curriculum as English 101 but at a less intensive pace in order to provide students with more time to develop their academic writing skills. The course theme coincides with the general education campus theme, "global change in a local context" for the 2006–2007 academic year. Final evaluation by portfolio.

Modeling the curricular design after the Stretch program at Arizona State University (ASU), I developed a sequential set of syllabi and assignments for the three-credit basic writing class and the three-credit first-year composition class, syllabi and assignments that were sequenced and scaffolded through the four outcomes. Though the institutional structure and resources of the programs at ASU and WSU Vancouver differ, I borrowed from the Stretch philosophy in developing my curriculum. Primarily, I culled the emphasis on both reading and writing as inter-dependent skill development and the extended curricular space from one semester to two. Using the outcomes to connect these courses provided basic writing students with a programmatic structure and coherence from one class to the next. Furthermore, it framed the curriculum and shaped the pedagogical approach of the basic writing course at our campus. As part of the first-year curriculum, this basic writing course approached error as context and convention, a part of the whole of an introduction to and practice in academic writing—not as a subset, remedial skill. As such, this framing contributed to local understandings of basic writing curricula and has the generative potential to re-position our institutional assumptions about basic writing courses. In Adler-Kassner's terms, it functions to reframe the dominant narrative about basic writing both on our campus and, potentially, across the surrounding community (169).

In designing the curriculum, I included a rhetorical analysis assignment, cycles of revision and workshop, and portfolio assessment for each course. The major distinctions between the courses as still envisioned include a research paper assignment for the first-year composition course, but fewer pages produced over the course of the semester, and more explicit instruction in knowledge conventions in the basic writing class. These primary distinctions distinguish the courses in levels of achievement more so than in course content (academic writing versus grammar and usage, for example), while the pedagogical approaches to the courses remain strikingly similar.

The Politics of Basic Writing

As we well know, the history of basic writing is fraught with debates concerning its legitimacy. Even if fairly institutionalized across the United States, particularly within open admissions colleges, basic writing remains a contested curriculum at many college and university campuses. Despite decades of literature evidencing the complexity of basic writing as a curriculum and pedagogy, ongoing public and institutional debates concerning remediation and its role in higher education continue to shape and constrain basic writing classrooms. Recent programmatic reforms to the California State University system illustrate one contemporary example (see Fensterwald). In many cases, such as in the California state system, these processes result in attempts to push basic writing programs out of four-year institutions. Another common issue is the framing and crafting of existing programs as generic skills courses. In particular, outside of our writing programs, the assumption that basic writing is—or should be—little more than skills and drills still lingers on, a compelling and often persuasive myth circulated through public and institutional conversations.

The reality, of course, is that developing a keen and useful sense of writing conventions is intricately tied to an awareness of writing as a rhetorical endeavor, an understanding of writing processes, and attention to the relationship between writing and critical reading and critical thinking—elements that the WPA OS focuses upon explicitly. As a field, we generally agree that writing is not just a transactional activity, but also an epistemological one. Given this complexity, as basic writing scholars have noted again and again, basic writing pedagogy must move beyond its historically acontextual, myopic attention to error and singular focus on the conventions of standard, edited English. Yet, doing so in actual practice can sometimes be quite difficult given the varying institutional constraints and limited resources afforded programs, not to mention the broader political pressures and debates, as noted above. Thus, while I, in no way, mean to suggest that a simple solution to these dilemmas is possible or even preferable, I want to suggest that strategic use of the WPA OS can assist writing program administrators in navigating the difficult terrain that makes up the politics of basic writing at their own institutions.

As a teacher greatly influenced by the pedagogical positioning of contemporary basic writing scholarship, one that emphasizes the rhetorical and epistemic nature of writing that is also highlighted in the WPA OS, I have always approached teaching basic writing from a conflicted angst. On the one hand, having worked with a number of non-traditional students in a variety of open admissions institutions, I am well aware of the need to maintain material access for basic writing students, access such as is manifest in the formation of distinct basic writing classes. Without this curricular space, as many have argued—including perhaps most pointedly Mary Soliday in her 2002 monograph—access to higher education is simply limited to some when basic writing classes disappear.

On the other hand, I am ambivalent about the demarcation of basic writing as a distinct curricular space. The content of *what* gets taught in basic writing classrooms, as the work of scholars such as Shaughnessy, Bartholomae, and Lu demonstrates, has always been intricately tied to *how* it gets taught—the underlying pedagogical approach. As noted earlier, one consequence of the influence of basic writing scholarship on the larger field of composition is that the tenets of "good" basic writing pedagogy are also the tenets of "good" composition pedagogy. These pedagogical tenets are authorized through our scholarship and endorsed in such documents as the WPA OS in that it seeks to "[articulate] what composition teachers nationwide have learned from practice, research, and theory" (WPA OS). When we acknowledge this overlap, it calls the curricular and pedagogical uniqueness of basic writing into question. Yet, it is basic writing as a particular pedagogical practice that has so often been called upon by scholars within the field to both afford the subdiscipline its legitimacy and to argue for its material existence as a separate program and/or curriculum. When we acknowledge, however, that good pedagogical practice in basic writing and first-year composition share the same tenets, the historical narrative that constructs basic writing as a unique and distinct pedagogy must be revisited.

Rather than insist on the distinctiveness of basic writing as a curriculum and a pedagogy—a powerful rhetorical trope within basic writing scholarship, I would suggest—we might do better to attend to the "heterogeneity of basic writing," to recognize, that is, basic writing as social material practice. "By recognizing the heterogeneity of basic writing at any given time and place," Horner and Lu write, "teachers can draw on the full range of positions and forces—dominate, alternative, and oppositional as well as residual and emergent—with some of which we might align ourselves and with all of which we must contend" (xiii). And in this political endeavor of negotiating institutional positions and forces, the WPA OS might serve as a useful tool. As I have demonstrated, strategic use of the outcomes, in particular the oppositional affordances made available through the rhetorical knowledge outcome, might allow for a redrawing of the pedagogical and curricular possibilities of basic writing in a way that better aligns basic writing and first-year composition. Such realignment would attend to the complexity of basic writing instruction as well as continue to acknowledge basic writing's function as material access to higher education.

As a document that circulates and codifies the basic tenets that undergird our discipline's pedagogical goals and assumptions about FYC—the valuing of rhetorical knowledge; critical thinking, reading, and writing; writing processes; knowledge of conventions; and composing in electronic environments—the WPA OS provides a means for negotiating the institutional politics of basic writing. By framing the curriculum of both basic writing and first-year composition with the outcomes, pedagogical approaches to teaching basic writing and first-year composition might be programmatically merged.

While such strategizing might not be effective on all campuses and across all institutions, I would suggest that it could prove particularly useful for faculty and administrators at open admissions colleges, especially community colleges, where forty-three percent of U.S. undergraduates are served, and remedial education is among the top institutional agendas (see Ayers; Wilson). At community colleges, basic writing and FYC are often separated not only by curricular goals, but also by different programs and departments. That is, in many two-year institutions, basic writing—or remedial or developmental writing, as it is sometimes referred to as—is structurally housed under basic skills, set aside from the discipline-specific curriculum of English, writing, rhetoric, and/or communication.

Certainly, I do not mean to suggest that the WPA OS is a quick-fix remedy to the politics of basic writing. Furthermore, as many of the contributions in this collection have suggested, negotiating the politics of the WPA OS itself is a complicated and sometimes contradictory landscape. Yet, such an overt move as repositioning basic writing through the WPA OS can make explicit the need for consistency across introductory composition classes. In particular, it can assist in arguing for pedagogical consistency in *how* students are taught while also clarifying and highlighting useful differences among the courses—not so much *what* is taught, the basic content of which also ought to align but sometimes does not—but rather differences in the expectations of proficiency and skill level. It is within this political and pedagogical complexity that I have attempted to situate and shape our basic writing program at WSU Vancouver.

Works Cited

Adler-Kassner, Linda. *The Activist WPA: Changing Stories about Writing and Writers*. Logan: Utah State UP, 2008. Print.

Ayers, David F. "Putting the Community Back into the College." *Academe Online.* American Association of University Professors. 96.3 (2010): n. pag. Web. 19 May 2010.

Bartholomae, David. "Inventing the University." *Cross Talk in Comp Theory: A Reader.* Ed. Victor Villanueva. 1st ed. Urbana, IL: NCTE, 1997. 589–619. Print.

Bizzell, Patricia. "Cognition, Convention, and Certainty: What We Need to Know about Writing." *Pre/Text* 3 (1982): 213–44. Print.

Council of Writing Program Administrators. "The WPA Outcomes Statement for First-Year Composition." Council of Writing Program Administrators, July 2008. Web. 10 July 2010.

Fensterwald, John. "CSU's New Tack to Cut Remediation." *The Educated Guess: Analysis, Opinion, and Ruminations on California Education Policy.* Silicon Valley Education Foundation. 23 March 2010. Web. 29 March 2010.

Greene, Nicole Pepinster, and Patricia J. McAlexander, eds. *Basic Writing in America: The History of Nine College Programs.* Cresskill: Hampton Press, 2008. Print.

Haswell, Richard H., ed. *Beyond Outcomes: Assessment and Instruction Within a University Writing Program*. Westport: Ablex Publishing, 2001. Print.

Horner, Bruce, and Min-Zhan Lu. *Representing the "Other": Basic Writers and the Teaching of Basic Writing*. Urbana, IL: NCTE, 1999. Print.

Klausman, Jeffrey. "Mapping the Terrain: Writing Programs in Two-Year Colleges." *Teaching English in the Two-Year College* 35.3 (2008): 238–251. Print.

Lu, Min-Zhan. "Redefining the Legacy of Mina Shaugnessy: A Critique of the Politics of Linguistic Innocence." *Journal of Basic Writing* 10.1 (1991): 26–40. Print.

Rose, Mike. "The Language of Exclusion: Writing Instruction at the University." *College English* 47.4 (1985): 341–59. Print.

Shaughnessy, Mina P. "Diving In: An Introduction to Basic Writing." *College Composition and Communication* 27.3 (1976): 234–39. Print.

Soliday, Mary. *The Politics of Remediation: Institutional and Student Needs in HigherEducation*. Pittsburgh: U of Pittsburg Press, 2002. Print.

Sternglass, Marilyn S. "Practice: The Road to the Outcomes over Time." *The Outcomes Book: Debate and Consensus after the WPA Outcomes Statement*. Ed. Susanmarie Harrington, Keith Rhodes, Ruth Overman Fischer, and Rita Malenczyk. Logan: Utah State UP, 2005. 201–10. Print.

Wiley, Mark. "Outcomes Are Not Mandates for Standardization." Harrington, et al. 24–31. Print.

Wilson, David McKay. "The Casualties of the Twenty-First-Century Community College. *Academe Online*. American Association of University Professors. 96.3 (2010): n. pag. Web. 19 May 2010.

3 Building a Writing Program with the WPA Outcomes: Authority, Ethos, and Professional Identity

Kimberly Harrison

At Florida International University (FIU), a large, two-campus, urban, Hispanic-serving university, the WPA Outcomes Statement for First-Year Composition (WPA OS) assisted, and initially even enabled, program development. Our program serves as a case study to illustrate the importance of the WPA OS for individual program authority and for ethos-building, and this chapter positions the WPA OS as a foundational document from which programs can define, promote, and further local goals. The ethos of the WPA OS itself lends authority to the discipline of rhetoric and composition as it does to individual WPAs and writing program faculty involved in program and curricular development. This chapter outlines how the WPA OS helped our efforts in cultivating a professional identity for composition and in implementing a first-year curriculum based in writing and rhetoric rather than in literature, a move that has laid the groundwork for further program development, including our recent efforts beyond the English department to prepare teaching assistants from other disciplines to teach college writing.

As Shirley Rose reminds us, writing program administration is "deeply embedded in and dependent upon the cultures of the particular institutions in which individual writing programs are located, the disciplinary cultures of composition studies and English studies more generally, and the broader culture of faculty life and work in higher education" (221). To account for such different contexts, WPA scholarship often takes the form of narratives, which, Rose argues, "help us understand how writing programs evolve—what and how events and circumstances lead to change, how various writing program participants can affect and effect change" (222). As such, I begin by offering a brief narrative to explain how, at our institution, the WPA OS assisted us in initial program development and in establishing program identity beyond identification with literature. I then focus on specific rhetorical uses of the WPA OS that we employed in our efforts, with the goal that perhaps such strategies could help other WPAs who find themselves in, as Karen Bishop Morris and Lizbeth A. Bryant describe in Chapter 10 of this collection, "non-program programs," those in which WPAs often struggle to establish clout.

First-Year Writing: Our Departmental Context

In 2001, when the WPA OS was itself new, the writing program at FIU began efforts to reach consensus about the goals and outcomes of our courses. Patricia Freitag Ericsson, through her survey of the WPA listserv archives and her related email queries of listserv participants, finds that the most common use of the WPA OS has been to shape first-year writing courses (105). In our case, the first-year courses were the obvious starting point as the various goals and outcomes, and subsequently content, of the courses called into question whether there was a writing program at all. Prior to this effort, a glance at the syllabi for our first-year writing courses indicated a wide and disparate set of largely unstated learning goals, ranging from those reflected in the WPA OS to unarticulated goals within courses focused on reading comprehension, modes of discourse, usage rules, and literary or film appreciation. Formal description of the courses was limited to what was found in the undergraduate catalogue:

> ENC 1101 Freshman Composition: Students will be introduced to the principles and process of expository, persuasive, and reflective writing. The first of a two-semester freshman composition sequence.
>
> ENC 1102 Literary Analysis: A continuation of ENC 1101. Develops an analytical, aesthetic, and cultural sensitivity to literature and further explores the techniques of composition and library research.

We could make little collective claim about what students were learning in our courses; instructors of the second-semester composition course could make only a few general assumptions about what their students should have learned in their previous course; and faculty teaching writing-intensive courses in other departments could assume little common ground in the first-year writing curriculum upon which to build. Assessment, which was then just becoming a priority in the university, posed a challenge without some collective agreement on what should be taught, and thus assessed.

As a new WPA, one of two at the time, I saw my job as to begin discussion on reaching consensus about learning outcomes and to define the program as one in rhetoric and composition, as opposed to literature. In doing so within our context, I prioritized developing programmatic internal coherence, which Geoffrey Chase defines as comprising four components:

> (1) [C]ommon goals specific and detailed enough to be meaningful and useful, (2) common assignments, (3) standard methods for evaluation and assessment across multiple sections, and (4) a commitment to examining and discussing these shared features openly. (245)

Such goals were initially met with skepticism: How could faculty in such a large program—one then serving approximately 4,000 students a semester, spread across two campuses—ever agree? What was the value in consensus? Wasn't everyone happy the way things were? Timing was right, though, to respond to such questions with reference to the WPA OS, which had only recently been published in the Fall/Winter 1999 issue of *Writing Program Administration* and the January 2001 issue of *College English*.

As Emily Isaacs and Melinda Knight note in Chapter 20 of this collection, a move toward shared outcomes can be seen as threatening, since composition has "largely originated within a discipline (English) that eschews regulation, standardization, and anything that might compromise what is often characterized as 'academic freedom.'" Kathleen Blake Yancey, in her introduction to the 2001 *College English* publication of the WPA OS, observes the document's efforts to "make visible what we do," a visibility—she suggests—that brings with it vulnerability (323). While Yancey is speaking specifically to the vulnerability of composition programs, she alludes to a larger unease regarding the visibility of the classroom in general. By making visible what goes on in the classroom, and by discussing and attempting to reach consensus on learning outcomes, we might invite interference, regulation, and critique. We might infringe upon instructor individuality and personality. These were local concerns in our early efforts to discuss learning outcomes for first-year writing.

Such questions were not unexpected considering our institutional context. FIU was founded relatively recently (in 1972) and did not serve lower-division students until 1981. The English department, in response to the new student demographics in the 1980s, hired a number of new tenure track literature faculty, who were also charged to teach composition. This arrangement was short-lived, however, with the growth of the university from 16,500 students in 1986 to 39,000 in 2010, and the subsequent shift in literature faculties' teaching responsibilities from lower-division instruction to serving the growing English major and graduate degrees. Yet, the culture of the department in the early 2000s, stemming from its historical context, often equated literary analysis with writing instruction and assumed that a graduate degree in literature automatically carried with it the qualifications for teaching college writing. Some faculty maintained a sense of ownership over the composition program and valued the role that first-year composition played in fostering students' literary appreciation and generating interest in the English (literature) major.

Our strategy to develop a program and an identity based in writing and rhetoric, as opposed to a grouping of loosely related courses identified primarily with literature, was to move gradually.[1] As a then-untenured assistant professor supported by an associate director who was a non-tenure line faculty member, I was eager to avoid as much conflict as possible. Aside from job security issues, a gradual change seemed appropriate, as our goal was not just to change course descriptions and content, but the program culture and the way the program was viewed both in the department and the larger university. As David Blakesley suggests in his account of implementing directed self-placement, "[W]e're better off sacrificing efficiency in the early going, on the promise that our programs in the long run will be much better because of our efforts to involve stakeholders at every stage" (24).

I was hired initially as WPA at the smaller of the university's two campuses (Biscayne Bay). Therefore, we presented curricular reform of the first-semester courses to reflect the WPA OS as a pilot effort on that campus; located twenty miles from the main campus (University Park), which is quite a distance considering Miami traffic, it presented little threat. We had just over twenty-five sections of first-year courses in comparison to the nearly 130 at University Park (recently renamed the Modesto M. Madique campus). The department chair sanctioned our efforts as long as they were labeled as "pilot." Along with a group of interested teaching assistants, adjunct instructors, and some literature faculty serving on the composition committee, the associate composition director and I began to develop a curriculum based on the WPA OS, with attention to internal coherence.

Those of us at Biscayne Bay met frequently as a group, and consensus emerged in support not only of shared outcomes, but also for a shared course structure with a common text and assignment sequence that allowed instructor flexibility but also enough commonality to encourage discussion and collaboration and to shape professional development opportunities. Through regular meetings, roundtables, and workshops, we worked to cultivate both knowledge of and identification with the field of writing studies. By fall 2004, shared learning outcomes defined both first-year courses on our smaller campus, and a shared curriculum based in writing and rhetoric, as opposed to literature, defined our second-term course. The instructors using the shared curriculum met bi-weekly during the first semester of its use, and periodically after the first term, to plan and trouble shoot. We made our pilot effort visible on the program website, where it attracted positive attention from university administrators and some faculty.

We were able to showcase a program with internal coherence. As Chase observes, without such coherence, "it becomes impossible to talk about a program at all and thus impossible to talk about what the relationship should be between what we do in our programs and the larger institution" (246). We were also able to illustrate the benefits that internal coherence had on the faculty who participated in the pilot, who were largely creative writing MFA TAs and adjunct instructors with graduate degrees in literature, with little formal composition training. Discussions about teaching increased; TAs and faculty got to know each other better and shared ideas, participation in frequent workshops and roundtables increased, and assignments were shared, adapted, and discussed. As Chase argues, without such coherence, the chance for collaboration among instructors is limited as "[e]veryone is on their own" (246). The pilot confirmed in our institutional context the benefits of a shared curriculum, not one in which everyone shares the exact syllabus and assignments, but one in which we share basic texts, assignment sequences, and outcomes. As we moved beyond the pilot stages of program development, I encouraged the move to a shared curriculum as we looked to implement the ideas from the pilot campus to the larger program as a whole. I used the WPA OS to make my case.[2]

In 2005, after I was appointed WPA for both campuses, we began laying the groundwork to unify the program across campuses, building on the work of our pilot. On the main campus, with more students and faculty involved, program changes garnered more attention and brought more resistance. Yet, that fall, we met as a department to vote on our proposal for curricular redesign based upon internal coherence and a formal change in the title and description of the courses, from Freshman Composition and Literary Analysis to Writing and Rhetoric I and II. While we received a positive vote, doing so required a compromise in that we agreed to include in our initial redesign one outcome in Writing and Rhetoric II focused on literature: "Students will be able to analyze a literary text focusing on the writer's purpose and textual strategies." Yet, accompanying it were outcomes for rhetorical knowledge, critical thinking, writing, and reading, processes, and knowledge of conventions. That we had shared outcomes at all seemed for us a significant accomplishment. As Jeanne Gunner points out regarding writing program administration, "[W]hat might count as a significant victory in one context is not even the source of a problem in another; what seems a modest programmatic change here is an almost unthinkable act in some programmatic elsewhere" (29).

Aligning our first-year curriculum with the WPA OS was a necessary step in establishing what we now can arguably claim as a program, one with sequenced courses that share outcomes, and in the first-year courses, also share texts, basic syllabi, and assignment sequences; one with an active learning, workshop pedagogy (as opposed to the traditional lecture previously common in the courses); one with growing upper-level and graduate classes, along with a newly approved certificate program in professional and public writing; one with a professional development program, including ongoing workshops and structured mentoring; and one with program and instructor assessment. The first-year writing curriculum and the process we went through to align it with the WPA OS helped define our program as one in writing and rhetoric within the English department, not as the service arm of the department as a whole, one assumed to be staffed by instructors whose real desire was to teach novels, plays, and poetry. In contrast, we worked to present an alternative view of rhetoric and composition as a field and of composition classes as engaging and rewarding courses to teach. As Gunner notes, seemingly small victories can be large ones, depending on context, and another small, though contextually large, victory for our program is represented in its current placement on the department's website, positioned as visual equals to the department's four programs, along with literature, creative writing, and linguistics. (Previously, the program had been hidden under "undergraduate education.") As represented on the website, composition is now at the table in discussions of potential development of new undergraduate and graduate degrees. Such inclusion indicates, as I interpret it, what has been a gradual, local recognition of the field's intellectual history, its qualified faculty, and its contribution to student learning at various curricular levels.

With such an ethos, the program is better positioned to develop new initiatives and to garner resources for them. For example, in the last four years, we have been able to make additional composition hires that include three tenure track, one tenured, and ten non-tenure track, full-time faculty. Our new tenured faculty member directs the newly funded Center for Excellence in Writing. Previously, this center was located in our Learning and Testing Center and directed by a staff member without credentials in writing center administration or rhetoric and composition. Relying upon disciplinary ethos, we could argue successfully for the importance of a writing center directed by senior faculty with an in-field research and administrative record.

Additionally, the program has recently been funded with fourteen interdisciplinary teaching assistant lines that draw graduate students from across our college who are trained to teach writing, serving first in our program and then returning to their home departments as local "writing ambassadors."[3] The program is to help us put well-trained TAs in our first-year classes, but also to better prepare future faculty to work with student writers in their fields. The move from a literature-based program to one based upon the WPA OS positioned the program to participate in this interdisciplinary effort, while the WPA OS, with its attention to the work of faculty outside of first-year writing, helps participating TAs envision how they will use their training in their home departments and future disciplinary teaching.

The narrative I present here of our local program development omits details of occasional but real resistance from both full- and part-time faculty to program change, and it glosses over the discrepancies in some of our classes between what is reflected in program documents, such as syllabi and classroom pedagogy. It omits stagnation in growth of resources within our current economic climate, even as verbal support for our initiatives has increased. Our program remains under-resourced in comparison with our benchmark institutions, with too-high enrollment caps and, despite our recent hires, over-reliance on part-time faculty, challenges Bishop Morris and Bryant describe in Chapter 10 as those faced by non-program programs. This narrative does not seek to sugarcoat our context, but is offered within efforts to understand and chronicle the impact of the WPA OS in various institutional settings and with attention to strategic uses of the WPA OS in efforts for program development and establishment of professional identity.

Rhetorical Uses of the WPA OS

As stated earlier, the WPA OS served for us as a foundational document for program development and cultivation of a professional identity. As such, it was an important rhetorical tool. Below, I outline the most common rhetorical uses to which we put the WPA OS in our early efforts, with the goal that our strategies might be useful for other WPAs, especially new WPAs in departments without a well-defined writing program.

The Ethos of the WPA and Faculty Members

Clyde A. Moneyhun, in his response to the 1999 iteration of the WPA OS, suggests that the document provides the "kind of clout you get from a directive issued by the American Medical Association" (63). When arguing for a rhetorically-based curriculum, with reference to the WPA OS, we could speak as representatives of a larger professional community, supported by research, theory, and disciplinary consensus. For most of its history, the program had been directed by literature faculty, who—while well-intentioned and dedicated—were not versed in the specialized knowledge of the field. In contrast, we used the

WPA OS and other evidence of disciplinary knowledge to enhance our ethos as specialists in the field. In doing so, we drew upon shared values within the academy regarding disciplinary expertise even as we challenged our audience's commonly held assumptions regarding composition.

In addition to enhancing a WPA's ethos for external audiences, the WPA OS enhances ethos for an internal audience of the self. Especially for new or untenured WPAs, or those working at times in relative professional isolation without like-minded colleagues, documents such as the WPA OS can bolster self-confidence and serve almost as an ally. In Chapter 10, Bishop Morris and Bryant also note a similar value of the WPA OS. Along with Moneyhun, they speak of the clout associated with the WPA OS, but they mention the internal clout that it provides them as program administrators by reinforcing and validating their belief that they are doing the right thing for their students. It served for them to build internal ethos, as it did for us in early program development.

A Professional Ethos of the Field

As Jeanne Gunner points out, personal ethos within institutional contexts is often not enough on its own to encourage change. Contrasting an "ethos-based" and "discipline-based authority," Gunner concludes that when relying on an ethos-based authority, the "attacks we experience are indeed personal," and fears that a WPA's arguments based in evidence and expert opinion "give us credibility as speakers, not agents with disciplinary authority" (36). With such concerns in mind WPAs also have to frequently cultivate not only personal ethos, but also the ethos of the field. Professional documents, such as the WPA OS, assist in such efforts. Through representation of professional consensus, research, and expertise, the WPA OS enhances the "character" of the discipline. First, it helps to define rhetoric and composition as a discipline for unfamiliar audiences, and second, the content and the collaborative process by which the statement was developed articulate disciplinary values of collaboration, consensus-building, and professional knowledge. In practice, the WPA OS helped us locally to communicate a professional ethos of the field as we made it visible in various programmatic locations, such as in our student textbook, on our program website, and as a document used in frequent workshops, orientations, and meetings.

WPA OS in Action: Envisioning Program Possibilities

Bishop Morris and Bryant refer to the importance of tangible documents, like charts and graphs, as they made arguments for program development within challenging contexts. For us, the content of such documents included examples of the WPA OS in practice—charts, tables, and graphs that presented details of reputable writing programs, especially those located in our benchmark institutions or in other universities to which our local audiences would identify. These programs served as models, and sharing details of their successes helped us provide a clearer picture for audiences unfamiliar with developments in the field of how our own program might develop. Contrasting the WPA OS and evidence of it in action with our then-current local practice and supporting resources allowed us to illustrate that a significant number of students leaving our first-year classes were not being given the chance to learn what writing faculty and administrators across the nation thought it important for them to learn, and clarified the need for change. Additionally, the WPA OS and examples of other programs also represented consensus among a diverse group of writing instructors and administrators, indicating the possibility of finding some common ground in our own program.

Student Learning within a National Context

The WPA OS facilitated a productive framing of discussions about the curriculum not around individual instructor preference, but around "the common knowledge, skills, and attitudes sought by first-year composition programs in American postsecondary education" (60). For us, the WPA OS was essential in communicating a vision of the program informed by, in the words of the WPA OS authors, "what composition teachers nationwide have learned from practice, research, and theory" (60). With reference to the WPA OS, we facilitated a productive shift from a primary focus on individual instructor interest to what students needed to learn as first-year college writers, especially important within a program in which goals of the first-year courses often were built upon the individual instructor's literary and critical theory expertise. Kathleen Blake Yancey clarifies the significance of this shift in discourse in her 2002 *College English* response to Derek Soles's concerns that the WPA OS does not give enough attention to individual writing instructors' theoretical and pedagogical preference.

The WPA OS was not based upon instructor interests, she explains, but upon "what students need" (379).

Shifting Purposes

Beginning program development in 2001 as a new WPA, I found, as did my colleagues, that the WPA OS served an important role as a persuasive document for both external and internal audiences. We relied upon it to help us establish our own institutional authority, to help represent rhetoric and composition as a field, and to provide evidence to support the need for program development. Currently, with the program relatively more established within the department and larger institutional context, and with the advantages of the ideas, authority, and expertise of new faculty, the role of the WPA OS in the program has changed and is serving us more as a generative than a persuasive document. It and the current discussions surrounding it (located in collections such as this one and on the WPA listserv) help generate local conversations about better meeting our students' needs. For example, our technology committee has used the WPA OS as a starting place for their discussions and recommendations regarding technology outcomes for individual courses. Additionally, within our institutional context, conversation now often centers on those needs of our many second-language writers. While the WPA OS currently does not explicitly address these students' needs, as Paul Kei Matsuda and Ryan Skinnell point out in Chapter 16, it provides us with some common ground upon which to develop outcomes that are responsive to the presence and needs of second-language writers. The WPA OS, a "living document," as the original authors insist, lends itself to revision as it does to local need (68).

Notes

1. My use of plural pronouns throughout the essay recognizes the collaborative nature of much WPA work, and specifically of the collaborative efforts to define a first-year program based on the WPA OS at FIU; it especially recognizes the efforts of program associate directors Cindy Chinelly, who began work with me at Biscayne Bay, and later additionally Robert Saba and Mike Creeden. It refers also to the work of our part-time faculty and TAs who provided, and continue to provide, essential support and ideas for program development.

2. Such use of the WPA OS is a move to which Mark Wiley, for one, would object as he has argued against "pressure to standardize writing curricula based on the Outcomes Statement" (28). In Chapter 20, Isaacs and Knight respond to Wiley's concerns, asserting that the common syllabus and text that Wiley resists is "reasonable and even laudable from a student learning perspective," a statement to which I agree, speaking from my specific institutional context. Perhaps, within Wiley's context, outcomes are achieved without curricular consensus. Yet, in other contexts, as in ours, it would be unlikely.

3. While our interdisciplinary TA program is context-specific, we have benefited from the work of other writing programs, specifically Rutgers, Cornell, George Washington, and Duke where, in various ways, faculty/TAs from other disciplines teach general education writing.

WORKS CITED

Blakesley, David. "Directed Self-Placement in the University." *WPA: Writing Program Administration* 25.3 (2002): 9–39. Print.

Chase, Geoffrey. "Redefining Composition, Managing Change, and the Role of the WPA." *WPA: Writing Program Administration*. 21 (1997): 46–54. Rpt. in *The Allyn and Bacon Sourcebook for Writing Program Administrators*. Ed. Irene Ward and William J. Carpenter. New York: Longman, 2002. 243–51. Print.

Council of Writing Program Administrators [with an introduction by Kathleen Blake Yancey]. "The WPA Outcomes Statement for First-Year Composition." *College English* 63.3 (2001): 321–25. Print.

Council of Writing Program Administrators [with responses by Clyde A. Moneyhun; Keith Rhodes; Mark Wiley; Kathleen Blake Yancey]. "The WPA Outcomes Statement for First-Year Composition." *WPA: Writing Program Administration* 23.1/2 (1999): 59–70. Print.

Ericsson, Patricia Freitag. "Celebrating Through Interrogation: Considering the Outcomes Statement through Theoretical Lenses." Harrington, et al. 104–17. Print.

Gunner, Jeanne. "Cold Pastoral: The Moral Order of an Idealized Form." *Discord and Direction: The Postmodern Writing Program Administrator*. Ed. Sharon James McGee and Carolyn Handa. Logan: Utah State UP, 2005. 28–39. Print.

Harrington, Susanmarie, Keith Rhodes, Ruth Overman Fischer, and Rita Malenczyk, editors. *The Outcomes Book: Debate and Consensus after the WPA Outcomes Statement*. Logan: Utah State UP, 2005. 104–17. Print.

Rose, Shirley K. "Representing the Intellectual Work of Writing Program Administration: Professional Narratives of George Wykoff at Purdue, 1933-1967." *Historical Studies of Writing Program Administration: In-*

dividuals, Communities, and the Formation of a Discipline. Ed. Barbara L'Eplattenier and Lisa Mastrangelo. West Lafayette, IN: Parlor Press, 2004. 221–39. Print.

Soles, Derek. "A Comment on the 'WPA Outcomes Statement for First-Year Composition.'" *College English* 64.3 (2002): 377–78. Print.

Wiley, Mark. "Outcomes are not Mandates for Standardization." Harrington, et al. 24-31. Print.

Yancey, Kathleen Blake. "A Comment on the 'WPA Outcomes Statement for First-Year Composition': Kathleen Blake Yancey Responds." *College English* 64.3 (2002): 378–80. Print.

4 The Perilous Vision of the Outcomes Statement

Teresa Grettano, Rebecca Ingalls, and Tracy Ann Morse

The material conditions of a first-year writing program include the economic pressures that shape issues like space, funding, staffing, even the paper on which syllabi are written. These conditions are so tangible that they almost acquire a personification of their own, becoming characters in the saga of maintaining those programs and influencing the high hopes many of us hold for the future of those programs. We three new faculty were eager to put our knowledge and passion to work in real ways, to represent the WPA Outcomes Statement for First-Year Composition (WPA OS) for all that it hopes to bring to students' academic, personal, and professional lives. We had read about material conditions and underfunded programs that had no knowledge or ability to support student writing in unified, programmatic ways. We had faith in our ability to be innovative and to evoke within our new colleagues fervor for progressive teaching in writing and rhetoric. What we did not know, however, was how deeply the material conditions of an institution could settle into the hearts and minds of a faculty. Institutional memory is long and complex, and our department, nursing old wounds from a near shutdown the decade before, and new wounds from recent university-wide changes, struggled to maintain its own ethos. Wielding the WPA OS like a sword of valor, we entered this financially challenged institution only to learn that the ideals of the WPA OS are not universal.

This chapter spotlights a piece of the WPA OS that deserves more attention: the introduction, a critical reminder for those who seek with conviction to implement these outcomes in local academic environments, but who experience resistance to change. The introduction to the WPA OS states, "Learning to write is a complex process, both individual and social, that takes place over time with continued practice and informed guidance. Therefore, it is important that teachers, administrators, and a concerned public do not imagine that these outcomes can be taught in reduced or simple ways." Indeed, learning to write *is* complex. It is shaped by the material conditions that have shaped our lives: our exposure to literacy, the landscapes of our neurologies, and the tangible and emotional events of our self-exploration. These words of the WPA OS could—and should—just as easily apply to the development of a program itself: "[developing a unified, progressive, first-year writing program] is a complex process, both individual and social, that takes place over time with continued practice and informed guidance." When a program is one, big, struggling student learning to negotiate its history, its language, and its audience, a vision like the WPA OS can seem unrealistic, if not impossible.

Implementing the WPA OS in any program is partly an ideological task. The WPA OS is a construction of knowledge from a larger body of teacher-scholars, and drawing it into the culture of an institution exacerbates the ideological tensions already at work in the culture of that institution. James Berlin draws from the work of Goran Therborn to explain, "Ideology always brings with it strong social and cultural reinforcement, so that what we take to exist, to have value, and to be possible seems necessary, normal, and inevitable—in the nature of things" (*Rhetorics, Poetics, and Cultures* 78). Berlin elsewhere explains, "Because there are no 'natural laws' or 'universal truths' that indicate what exists, what is good, what is possible, and how power is to be distributed, no class or group or individual has privileged access to decisions on these matters. They must be continually decided by all and for all in a way appropriate to our own historical moment" ("Rhetoric and Ideology" 490). Indeed, and certainly in the hierarchy of academic politics, some folks may perceive themselves to have the power to decide these things, which can be especially challenging for junior faculty who seek to create change based on what is possible. What is more, Berlin's suggestion that the "historical moment" should shape how "what exists, what is good, what is possible" are defined becomes fraught when two groups are defining "historical moment" quite differently.

We feel inclined to share with our larger community of scholars as we look back on the past and present of the WPA OS and the range of historical moments our colleagues in this collection discuss how beautifully and precariously the statement sits in the contested spaces between what exists, what is good, and what is possible. In our case, understanding how our colleagues defined these ideas, and how they viewed the historical moment of the institution and their identities in it, would come to play a pivotal role in understanding what was possible for the WPA OS. Beyond the scope of our specific experience, and for all of us who research and teach from the principles outlined in this document, we may see the WPA OS as more than a road map for a writing program. It is a tool for unpacking and reconstructing the ideologies of a community of faculty.

What Exists: Challenges of Defining the Historical Moment

The medium-sized, comprehensive, private university we're writing about is located in the Southeast. It has swelled in the last five years from approximately 4,200 to approximately 6,800 full-time students. The faculty in the Department of English and Writing at the institution specializes in literature, creative writing, journalism, and rhetoric/composition, most of whom are responsible for teaching first-year writing courses. When we arrived on the scene in 2005, there had not been assessment of the program or assessment of the courses. In fact, there had not been any changes to the curriculum for almost three decades. The catalog descriptions for the required first- and second-semester courses simply stated that ENG 101 "teaches the process of writing effective expository essays. ENG 102 includes extensive instruction and practice in research writing" ("Catalog Course Description"). This vague description allowed individual instructors to create thematic classes, but these classes did not share commonly articulated goals. We gathered that the different disciplines represented in our department influenced the spectrum of what students were taught in first-year writing (FYW). The convergence of specialties in the first-year writing program over the years resulted in a curriculum that was vague and not cohesive, marked by course drift and a lack of dialogue among faculty. As new faculty, we wanted to fix these problems—they seemed so *fixable*—and create clear goals and objectives that would lead to assessment of the courses and of the program.

As we were taught in our graduate training, we used the WPA OS to negotiate between the best practices in our field and considerations of our student population, current curriculum, and faculty specialties. We used its language to offer our voices to our colleagues and to offer an authority we did not yet have. However, this document presented philosophical tensions; though many faculty in the department recognized the values in the WPA OS, others felt that they were not a fit for our institution. We didn't understand this reaction. Furthermore, use of the WPA OS was complicated by our junior and marginal status. How could we tell our senior colleagues, many of whom had been teaching at the institution for over twenty years, that what they were teaching in FYW was not serving current students? How could we convince them that our knowledge in a field that did not exist when they completed their degrees could help make positive changes in the FYW curriculum?

We slowly learned that there was more to our senior colleagues' resistance than we were grasping at the time. While recognizing our expertise to teach FYW, many of them dismissed the administrative experiences and scholarly knowledge we had that could positively influence change in the FYW program. We came to realize that we were hired to teach FYW, not necessarily to improve it, and not necessarily to create and deliver new courses in rhetoric and/or composition. Though we began exposing the disorder that was inaccurately labeled a "program," our colleagues held on tight to that disorder, as they worked in other ways to define themselves as a department to a university that was not paying attention. The university community as a whole was dealing with its own disruption—shifting from a two-college to four-college model, hiring a cadre of new administrators, and overhauling the general education and first-year experience curricula. The Department of English and Writing was the largest department with the fewest majors, and many across campus were under the impression (and still are) that if it were not for FYW, the department would not exist at all. For some of our senior colleagues, our attempt to revise the program threatened to expose their only clout on the university level as a fraud. At the same time, they were actively working to reframe the program to accommodate their expertise and disciplines. Though we perceived our colleagues' resistance, we failed to understand that, while we felt they were undermining our disciplinary expertise, their disciplinary expertise was being called into question across campus. Thus, we were doing to our colleagues what the university had been doing to them for years: we weren't hearing them.

To assuage their concerns, we strategically outlined our goals in programmatic documents. With a junior rhet/comp faculty member as WPA (jWPA), we began to write a mission statement for the program, with the goal of adding some cohesiveness without being prescriptive. Like good recent graduate students, we looked to the literature for support. Berlin's work informed most of what we did in our classrooms, and it also inspired our views of what constituted a current, critical FYW program, views that set us apart from a faculty largely dedicated either to no particular rhet/comp pedagogy, or to expressivist pedagogy. Moreover, Berlin's work helped us begin to understand, at least from an intellectual standpoint, the differences between perspectives among the major (tenured, non-rhet/comp faculty) and the minor (untenured rhet/comp faculty) players in the conversation about the status of the program. Berlin explains, for example, that changing definitions of knowledge, reality, and self have influenced the shifts in approaches to teaching writing. He situates his theories of rhetoric in terms of three epistemological categories: objective (reality is in the external world), subjective (reality is within the individual), and transactional (reality is in the interaction of the elements in the traditional rhetorical situation) (*Rhetoric and Reality* 139–65). As a group, the rhet/comp faculty identified with the transactional. The rest of the faculty, however, employed a mixture of objective and subjective, at times citing Peter Elbow and Donald Murray as authorities, at times insisting grammar and sentence structure be the focus of instruction, and at times wanting to use FYW courses to spark an appreciation for literature and recruit majors. Though we found Berlin's work to illuminate for us some of the reasons behind our colleagues' resistance, it was much more of a knowing-one's-enemy kind of illumination at the time than the kind of awareness of history we would come to understand later.

Because of the contrasting ideologies, change moved glacially, taking five years to move from an incoherent program without stated goals to the resemblance of a program with a clearly stated mission statement, outcomes, and guidelines for at least one course in the sequence. Our colleagues had a difficult time understanding that what existed wasn't a semblance of a program, and we had a hard time understanding why they were resistant to changes that would solidify a program influenced by national best practices and, more importantly, that would best serve the needs of our students. What we experienced, and what we feared, was that our FYW program was one of the many "non-program programs" that Karen Bishop Morris and Lizbeth A. Bryant discuss in Chapter 10, a program that possesses little clout, reinforces a perception of FYW as a service course, and lacks training for teachers. What was our purpose if not to lend our expertise to creating a richer, modern program for the students of the university? To model current trends within the discipline, and to bring a new level of rigor and relevance to composition pedagogy, we wanted the department to consider FYW as an opportunity to cultivate citizenship and cultural critique. But, without any motivation to examine its own culture and the impact of that culture on its slowly diminishing power at the university, the department was in no place to teach tenets.

As much as he might have defended our eagerness to envision what is possible—as the WPA OS encourages us to do—Berlin might also have told us to look more deeply into what exists and what is good and, even, what is impossible. The WPA OS states in its introduction, "This document intentionally defines only 'outcomes,' or types of results, and not 'standards,' or precise levels of achievement. The setting of standards should be left to specific institutions or specific groups of institutions" (WPA OS). It cannot be infused into a program—any program—until those who want to use it fully consider what exists and/or what is good. We fancy ourselves visionaries (Why shouldn't we?), but we can get caught up in what is possible. The WPA OS depicts what is possible, and for this very reason, it can be problematic at many institutions, where what exists is not being recognized for its underlying causes, and what is good goes unrecognized because it is hard to let go of what is possible.

Though it often felt like we were hired to fill another spot in the "but-this-is-the-way-we've-always-done-it" structure, we know we're not alone in our experience. Donna Qualley and Elizabeth Chiseri-Strater point out that it is typically in writing programs—the "dynamic rhetorical space within the specific culture of a department and/or university"—where this status quo is disrupted: "These spaces determine what can be said, how it can be said, and who can say it, but change as the circumstances and individuals change. . . . It is only after conflicts arise . . . that we begin to articulate our 'territorial imperatives'" (175–76). Territories had shifted radically at the institution. Faculty were quickly losing much freedom and power to the emerging bureaucracy, and the rhetoric of paranoia was prevalent. The "new guard," as the associate dean lovingly referred to recently hired tenure track professors, was threatening the authority of the senior faculty. It was also threatening to erase their history at the university.

It was Kathleen Blake Yancey who helped us see what exists with even more clarity. With the then-department chair's support, Yancey made a visit to our institution that was intended to be a mini-review of FYW. She spent a day interviewing literature and rhet/comp faculty, the jWPA, the writing center director, and the department chair. Her fourteen-page report offered her observations of the FYW program:

> Faculty who have been at [the university] for 10 years or more . . . are more inclined to see the composition program as an opportunity to foster better writing in students, and an opportunity to foster critical thinking linked to a liberal-arts-based intellectual life of the mind. Faculty who have been at [the university] a relatively short period of time, especially the recent hires in rhetoric and composition, are more likely to see writing itself—in the terms of rhetoric and composition—as the appropriate focus for the first-year writing program . . . the differences in approach are also located in differences in kinds of expertise, with the more senior faculty citing the expertise of college and departmental citizenship and [the university] history, and the more junior faculty citing the expertise of disciplinary knowledge.

Yancey's perspective was important to us—someone outside the institution, someone we deeply respected—was able to help us understand the critical differences between our colleagues and us. Yes, maybe it was disagreement about how writing should be taught, but lying below that was the tumult of institutional history and the grief over barely surviving as an institution. We kept asking our colleagues, "Don't we want to be in sync with national standards?" Our colleagues responded with, "Don't you want to understand what we've been through before you ever got here?"

We were slowly getting to know them. As a discourse community, as John Swales explains, we rhet/comp faculty shared a language, a way of interacting and getting feedback from one another, a series of goals, and a "critical mass" (212–13). Without a doubt, there was security, creativity, and power we perceived inside of our community. For others in the department, in their own discourse communities, there was also power, creativity, and safety. Between discourse communities, there was fear—of losing territory, hurting feelings, inciting conflict. Certainly, and ideally, the differences in discourse—especially in agenda—could have served as points of productive tension in a department-wide FYW collaboration. This kind of tension might honor Kenneth Bruffee's argument about "abnormal discourse [that] occurs between coherent communities or within communities when consensus no longer exists with regard to rules, assumptions, goals, values, or mores" (648). He argues that abnormal discourse—the odd suggestions coming from all sides of what was assumed to be a mutual understanding—can lead to productive learning: "Abnormal discourse sniffs out stale, unproductive knowledge and challenges its authority, that is, the authority of the community which that knowledge constitutes" (648). Likewise, Patricia Bizzell advises that conflict arising as part of "belong[ing] to several discourse communities, each with its own canonical knowledge . . . is positively an advantage. The more conflicts, the more input from discourse communities at cross purposes, the more chance for an interested critique of one discourse community from another to be sparked" (234). Still, much work had to be done to try to heal wounds in the department before "interested critiques" would be honored.

What Is Good: Searching for Stasis

For a long time, we couldn't identify what was good. We recognized that having so many senior colleagues from diverse backgrounds teaching FYW was a benefit to our program for some of the same reasons it caused strife. The differing experiences and perspectives made our FYW classes robust with readings, including a commitment to a common reading for our first-semester course. We shared with our colleagues a desire to improve students' reading, thinking, and writing abilities, though we did not always agree on the way to do this or the language to use to explain how we would do it. In many ways, identifying the differing ideologies in play moved us forward in the process. Recognizing a shared value, we were able to find common ground in conversations and deliberations on articulated revisions of the FYW curriculum. While the common ground was as simple (and important) as serving our students' needs, it was this common ground that would help stabilize very slow progress over the several years it took to revise curriculum and establish a cohesive FYW program.

We would be remiss if we did not say that the biggest part of what is good was the fact that there were so many new rhet/comp faculty members who shared similar ideologies and teaching philosophies. This commonality afforded us a united front to our colleagues in our vision for the program, and language used to express our vision. Our confidence in our knowledge and experience in our discipline that we often held on to bolstered our resolve. It was because of our differing experiences and common ideology that we were able to slowly convince a few members of our department to recognize the value in what we were proposing. Together, we gained a keener awareness of our audience, and we learned that it was vitally important to articulate the language found in the WPA OS, but also to pull back in our tendency to attribute it to the WPA OS. Referring regularly to the WPA OS as extrinsic proof only further alienated our colleagues.

Good also existed outside our community. While we held junior standing within the department, and our ideas or suggestions were often dismissed or ignored, we slowly became recognized across the university for the knowledge and experience we could bring to core curriculum and first-year experience conversations. In these conversations, citing national standards and the WPA OS actually proved effective, even impressive at times. We held positions on university-wide committees, where we engaged in debates and even decision-making that impacted curriculum across the university. Through this university service, we became sought-out resources for debates and conversations regarding the entire first-year program and the core curriculum revision. We acted as consultants to other departments and administrators across campus.

Despite the discord we were experiencing in our department, we came to learn that the WPA OS has a flexibility and adaptability that, at first, we did not understand. While drafting course objectives, we accepted various language choices suggested by our senior colleagues. We were able to appease their concerns rooted in their ideologies and still express goals for the program and curriculum that we held important. Making accommodations for our material conditions and departmental/institutional history, we were able to create goals influenced by the WPA OS, but not solely based on or attributed to them. The good that was accomplished resulted in a clear framework for a cohesive program. With clear language that reflects the different perspectives in our department, we articulated a central program mission statement with measurable goals. We were also able to gain almost unanimous departmental support for revised curriculum and guidelines to the FYW 101 course (previously ENG 101). The department agreed to move away from a departmental syllabus that supplemented individual instructors' syllabi in favor of guidelines for the course. These guidelines laid out specific types of writing through scaffolded assignments. Providing parameters for writing assignments, we appealed to the different teaching perspectives and ideologies in the department by encouraging individual instructors to create their own assignments that met the goals expressed in the guidelines. We especially thought that these changes would appeal to adjunct faculty, who make up over sixty percent of the faculty teaching FYW.

Since agreeing on the guidelines, we have moved further towards assessing our work. Three of the current rhet/comp faculty (including one of us) worked together to create general rubrics that will work with two of the assignments in FYW 101. As part of a university-wide drive for assessment as accreditation review looms, FYW has been used as a positive example to other programs. We have also made strides in assessing our second semester course; however, discussion regarding the curriculum for the course has essentially halted. The department has once again grown weary with discussions focusing on FYW, and would rather devote its time to other departmental business. However, the work we accomplished with the FYW 101 course is effectively in place.

What Is Possible: Understanding Audience in Cultivating Community

In our endeavors to change the FYW program—to create a mission, to reach some consensus on pedagogy, to revise curriculum—it was not enough that each of us understood ourselves or thought we were hired as experts, nor was it enough to lean on the WPA OS as a national set of outcomes composed by scholars with even more knowledge and experience in FYW than we had. What we faced were some of the most basic human—not just academic—reactions to change: fear, uncertainty, and vulnerability. To us, the WPA OS was a wise leader; to our colleagues, who had seen numerous institutional upheavals in the recent past and were in the throes of even more changes, the WPA OS was yet another outsider coming in to change the system that had "worked" for them for so long. To build common ground and to understand our audience of colleagues as collaborators, we had to become part of the discourse community of the department, learning its language and translating our language in terms that the department could understand. The paradox of it all, of course, was that we had to learn to downplay the WPA OS while still holding on to and expressing its vision.

In his article, "Casing the Academy for Community," H. L. Goodall, Jr. acknowledges—as we do now—that this kind of faculty dynamic, this separateness and lack of community, is not uncommon. One of the keys to cultivating community, he argues, is "balancing an appreciation of people as creative, evolving individuals with an understanding of our thoroughly institutionalized (and therefore, constrained) selfhood and subjectivity" (488). Just as those of us in rhet/comp could not imagine not changing a program that seemed vastly outdated, our colleagues held tightly to the way it had always been done. To criticize the program was to criticize those who had been working in it for a very long time. It took us some time to recognize their vulnerability. It has taken even more time for them to recognize ours.

This vulnerability on both sides was somewhat productive for the program and for our learning as new teachers, scholars, and future administrators. As Qually and Chiseri-Strater explain so eloquently in their depiction of "vulnerable" WPAs:

> It may be in these moments of vulnerability, these moments when our understanding seems tenuous, our knowledge and theories suspect, and our intentions questionable that we eventually find or invent a new rhetorical approach that will allow us to continue to do this work ethically and effectively in conjunction with differing others. (172)

If we had backed down, the program would likely have remained as it was without assessment. But our years of education as rhet/comp teacher-scholars have cultivated in us an expectation that ethos will only come with hard, savvy, peaceful work. We still believe that.

What is Possible: Coming to Terms with Conditions

Though we are tempted, we cannot conclude this chapter without being realistic about what has been impossible. As progress was made to bring coherence to the program through what seemed to be concerted efforts of the department as a whole, the department has not been unified. Some colleagues have stated that the discord in the department is greater now than it was five years ago, and they point again to disciplinary divides. It is partially for these reasons that discussions to tackle other FYW curriculum have stopped. For example, for the second-semester FYW course that focuses on research and argumentation, some members of the department wanted to develop and promote a writing in the disciplines model, which would have supported students' writing across the curriculum, and certainly anchored the program in the department as even more critical to the university's goals for learning. Administration supported this idea on paper, but did not provide funding or opportunities to make it happen. Faced with this roadblock, the department just shut down conversation about FYW, specifically about any more revisions. Once again, the material conditions of the institution strongly influenced the department's position on its FYW curriculum.

Most recently, the department has worked to respond to the material conditions of the WPA position itself by revising it to include more writing across the curriculum initiatives to receive more financial and time compensation. While efforts were successful with the administration supporting the changes, the department used the new position to further remove rhet/comp ideology from the program by hiring an individual who does not have a rhet/comp or related degree. The new WPA has a background in literature, much like the majority of the department. An unexpected outcome of this new hire has been the cessation of assessment talk. At this point, there is no plan to assess the courses or the program. Strides that were made in revising the FYW program to become marked by clear objectives that could be assessed appear to be slipping. Thus, what is possible has changed with the changing conditions of the department and with the gradually changing historical moment.

Conclusion

We ultimately came to see the WPA OS less as a form of ammunition and defense, and perhaps even less a set of outcomes for writing. Rather, it became more of a guide, a wise teacher in the treacherous landscape of academic politics and writing program administration. It has helped us to see the spirit of change as tremendously complex: one that can both bring people together and tear them apart. The bottom line for us, and what we've learned through this process, is that while the WPA OS reflects an invaluable, progressive, holistic understanding of student ability and goals, its sheer existence is problematic when contextualized in many writing programs nationally. What happens when you assert a vision like the one reflected in the WPA OS is that you give a community something to strive for while potentially endangering relationships. New faculty walk in with the statement, and both are immediately (and understandably) seen as aliens, especially in institutions and departments so critically wounded and patching themselves up in non-nurturing ways. As future generations of rhet/comp folks enter departments with even more distinct specialties than we have, they may face an even harder time of establishing commonalities with their colleagues to move forward and build upon. If these individuals choose to continue our work, they will begin the cycle again of examining the conditions of the institution and determining what exists, what is good, what is possible, and what is impossible.

Works Cited

Berlin, James A. *Rhetoric and Reality: Writing Instruction in American Colleges, 1900–1985*. Carbondale: Southern Illinois UP, 1987. Print.

—. "Rhetoric and Ideology." *College English* 50.5 (1988): 477–94. Print.

—. *Rhetorics, Poetics, and Cultures: Reconfiguring College English Studies*. Urbana, IL: NCTE, 1996. Print.

Bizzell, Patricia. *Academic Discourse and Critical Consciousness*. Pittsburgh: U of Pittsburgh P, 1992. Print.

Bruffee, Kenneth. "Collaborative Learning and the 'Conversation of Mankind.'" *College English* 46.7 (1984): 635–52. Print.

Council of Writing Program Administrators. "The WPA Outcomes Statement for First-Year Composition." Council of Writing Program Administrators, July 2008. Web. 20 July 2011.

Goodall, Jr., H.L. "Casing the Academy for Community." *Communication Theory* 9.4 (1999): 465–94. Print.

Qualley, Donna, and Elizabeth Chiseri-Strater. "Split at the Root: The Vulnerable Writing Program Administrator." *WPA* 31.1/2 (2007): 171–84. Web. 28 Jan. 2010.

Swales, John. "Discourse Communities, Genres, and English as an International Language." *World Englishes* 7 (1988): 211–20. Print.

Yancey, Kathleen Blake. "University of Tampa: A Report on the First-Year Writing Program." June 2006. Report.

5 The Outcomes Statement as Support for Teacher Creativity: Applying the WPA OS to Develop Assignments

Sherry Rankins-Robertson

Although many of the chapters in this book demonstrate the heuristic value of the WPA Outcomes Statement for First-Year Composition (WPA OS) for writing programs (Maid and D'Angelo; Wilhoit), we should not neglect the WPA OS's creative possibilities for classroom teachers. As teachers of writing, we expect quality writing that responds to desired learning outcomes. To help students meet those expectations, though, we bear a responsibility to produce assignments that are informed by, and that articulate with, the desired learning outcomes of a course, a program, and/or an institution. This chapter illustrates that when the WPA OS is applied to individual writing assignments, students have a roadmap for meeting course learning outcomes. I describe an assignment as it was originally written, and then discuss the revised assignment, which includes the concepts and language of the WPA OS. Using the WPA OS to reconsider my assignment did not require that I modify the tasks I ask students to do, but rather to clarify how and why I asked students to do them. My goal is not to persuade readers to adopt the writing assignment or topic discussed in this chapter; it is merely an example of an assignment that was improved by implementing the WPA OS as scaffolding for a first-year composition assignment. My experience adapting this particular assignment to incorporate the WPA OS in its entirety could apply to any teacher's practice and current writing assignments.

Resisting McPapers

Because the WPA OS is not a template for how to teach writing, but rather a set of learning outcomes for students to demonstrate in first-year composition, the outcomes can be met through many ways (White, "The Origins"). For many courses, the subject or theme, as well as writing topics, used in first-year composition are determined by the instructor. While many writing programs have a set of goals, and perhaps a pre-determined textbook, ultimately it is the teacher's responsibility to develop writing assignments that meet course and programmatic outcomes. With the WPA OS in mind, teachers continue to have the same flexibility and freedom regarding classroom content—which topics to cover and what types of documents students should produce. The flexibility and clarity of the WPA OS can work to sharpen any effective assignment.

Writing assignments are often so loosely written that they lack basic elements, such as learning goals for the project, or how to analyze the situation and audience for writing; however, the assignment cannot be so rigid that it takes away students' flexibility of making decisions that afford students opportunities for independent learning. In *Assigning, Responding, Evaluating: A Writing Teacher's Guide*, Edward White[1] discusses the need for creativity and specificity in assignment development; he says "we must offer the best assignments we can devise in order to stimulate our students' creativity and convince them to learn what we teach" (1). One of the reasons some students produce what White calls the "McPaper," a document that is "a fast-food version of writing that offers little nutritional value to students and is frequently indigestible for readers" (2), is that writing assignments are often constructed without the details needed for students to produce better work. I would argue, based on White's discussion of assignment development, that teachers generate a fast-food version of the writing assignment, the "McAssignment," that yields vacuous projects due to lack of guidelines that would help students generate worthwhile responses. Many assignments I have encountered, some of my own included, lack the articulated goals students are to respond to in that particular assignment; the method and tools to be used for assessment; the scaffolding for rhetorical knowledge; and the critical reading and research strategies that facilitate thinking and writing. Most importantly, weak assignments provide little motivation for students to write beyond the elusive grade.

Not only is it important that students see application of the overall course content to academic environments and beyond, but also students must see what they gain from each assignment, or they quickly lose interest. Nancy Sommers and Laura Saltz indicate that writing matters most for students who compose to meet a larger purpose beyond completing an assignment, and students write more passionately on topics of "what they know and what they learn" (146). To be effective, the assignment must allow students space to develop topics that matter to them. It helps if students have some previous knowledge or interest on the topic. The assignment, then, provides students with a chance to contribute something new to the conversation. Some teachers feel the best way to accomplish this is to give the students free rein to write on whatever they choose. However, openness of assignments too often allows students to rest in their comfort range without much challenge, suggesting that the course has no particular goals aside from the random production of text. In such cases, the WPA OS becomes particularly helpful to teacher and student alike.

Instead of ordering up a McPaper, first-year composition classrooms can offer a starting place for helping students develop a more robust understanding of academic discourse and academic literacy. When writing assignments are designed with this goal in mind, instructors have the opportunity to challenge and socialize students into academic ways of knowing that can transcend the classroom. Many writing assignments still demonstrate the slow change that occurs for many first-year composition assignments, holding true to what James Moffett observed nearly forty-five years ago in *Teaching the Universe of Discourse*:

> In many of our writing assignments, I see us feverishly searching for subjects for students to write about that are *appropriate for English*; so we send them to the libraries to paraphrase encyclopedias, or they re-tell the plots of books, or then write canned themes on moral or literary topics for which no honest student has any motivation. Although asking students to write about real life as they know it is gaining ground, still many teachers feel such assignments are vaguely "permissive" and not as relevant as they ought to be. Once we acknowledge that "English" is not properly about itself, then a lot of phony assignments and much of the teacher's confusion can go out the window. (7–8)

Asking students to write about real life has gained even more popularity in the decades since Moffett drew attention to the ways writing instructors often feel conflicted when students craft writing that seems to transgress the "accepted" borders of academic discourse. Writing assignments that are perceived to transgress the borders of academic discourse are still at issue today, particularly in many first-year composition classrooms, because of pressure to have students demonstrate writing that can fit within traditional norms of academic discourse. The WPA OS provides the theoretical scaffolding for what students should accomplish, while supporting Moffett's encouragement for instructors to find other forms of writing that not only help students to see academic writing in a larger context, but also engage them in writing about topics that are personally meaningful to them.

If teachers plan to resist the distribution of McAssignments, they need to think carefully about topic selection. In "Writing Assignments: Where Writing Begins," David Bartholomae says, "While I believe it is important for teachers to consider carefully the subjects they present to students, and while I believe students write best about subjects that interest them—subjects they believe in, subjects they know something about, subjects they believe there is reason to write about and for which they can imagine an occasion for writing . . . the very notion of motive is misunderstood if a motive is taken to reside in a subject" (183). Finding topics that all students can relate to and know something about is a challenge, as students come with a variety of interests, talents, skills and backgrounds. As Sherry Rankins-Robertson, Lisa Cahill, Duane Roen, and Gregory Glau discuss, "The classroom then must be a space that supports multiple purposes—a space that allows for students' individual and intellectual growth not only in terms of their academic selves but also for their professional, personal, and civic selves" (63–64). Beyond the scope of finding a topic that all students have in common is locating a theme that is interconnected to many other topics so that students still have the freedom to make decision within a subject area. I believe the concept of family can be used in this way. Students could write about topics such as sports, music, or immigration while still responding to the overarching theme of family.

The Assignment

The institution where I teach has used the WPA OS as the desired learning outcomes for first-year composition for quite some time, as individuals involved in framing the WPA OS have also administrated our writing program. In the fall of 2006, I began using the theme of family history writing in my first-year composition courses to respond to the WPA OS. Family history writing contextualizes life stories in specific places at particular times, and examines, defines, and constructs the framework of a family unit's history. When approaching first-year composition with a family history writing emphasis, students are asked to become ethnographers of one of the most common elements to them: family. The composition experience presents the opportunity for students to become photographers of everyday life in their community, capturing people, places, and events through rhetorical lenses. Family history writing assignments lend themselves to the production of texts in all media (print, oral, and electronic), and in a variety of formats, or genres, due to real-world audiences.

Given these many positive characteristics, many writing programs and writing teachers have already incorporated family writing assignments in composition courses. For instance, Florida State University writing faculty have tested the theoretical concept of using family as the theme of first-year composition in a study that explored student reactions to new types of research assignments (Davis and Shadle). They found that students enjoyed writing about the theme of family, and they had something valuable to say. Additionally, Daniel Melzer and Pavel Zemliansky, in an online course titled, "Writing Home and Family," engaged students in the use of primary and secondary research methods so that they could research their families and home communities. Both studies show that students are interested in, and have a common language and background for, writing about subjects related to the theme of family; however, it's important to note that students can write about the idea of family without writing about their own family. Some students' associations with family trigger emotions that do not allow them to develop responsible texts when writing about their own families; since all family history writing is research-driven, students could respond to assignment prompts in my class using another family and still yield the same results.

As I thought about how family history writing assignments ask students to conduct primary research through interviews with members of families, focus on writing about individuals, places, and cultures, and incorporate historical and social secondary research, I realized that family history writing projects inherently have a relationship to the WPA OS. I believe the theme of family to be worthwhile because it not only engages students with topics in which they have a foundational knowledge and language, but also helps students successfully meet all areas of the WPA OS.

One of my first-year composition course projects asked students to develop a biographical sketch, or profile. Much like NPR's *Story Corps*, I asked students to locate an interviewee, aged sixty or older, who belongs to a family. As part of the assignment, students were asked to develop research questions based on the geographical region and historical context of the interviewee's life and conduct an interview with the individual. In the original writing assignment handout I distributed to the students, I provided the following instructions:

> You will write a non-fiction piece based on your interview to showcase this person's life story. Use any pre-interview research you have conducted along with the interview content to develop a rich biographical essay that you would be proud to share with your interviewee. You will submit your essay, no less than four-typed pages, to me by the designated timeline on the course calendar.

From this passage alone, it is not evident that students were asked to conduct peer review and write a reflective self-assessment; however, I verbally added those requirements in class. Additionally, based on the way the assignment was originally written, students did not have any indication of how their work would be evaluated or what materials were expected for final submission. An element that I am now able to see missing from the original assignment is students were not asked to read and discuss various biographies in an effort to critically analyze the rhetorical choices writers make within this genre of writing. When I revised the assignment, I applied all sections of the WPA OS, allowing for a much more intentional learning experience for students.

When developing a writing assignment, teachers may not be cognizant of how often students reference the writing assignment handout provided at the start of the writing cycle. Most students check the handout throughout the duration of the assignment to ensure they are meeting the requirements; therefore, it is critical that the assignment handout provide clear, concise instructions that lay out the expectations, as opposed to adding verbal requirements along the way. As White notes, students need a written assignment that outlines "what the student is asked to accomplish" with "a description of the purpose of the assignment, its format, and the criteria that will be used in evaluating it" (*Assigning* 5–6). Even now, as I review the material I originally presented to my students for this assignment, I notice that its vagueness must have been problematic for many students. Most importantly, no project goals were identified, so it may not have been evident to students what learning occurred in this particular project. This may have inhibited students' abilities to connect how process and projects contributed to the demonstration of learning outcomes in the course portfolio that students were required to develop and submit for assessment.

Elements from the WPA OS existed in what I had hoped students would do, but the WPA OS was not evident in the assignment handout. For example, students were asked to "find, evaluate, analyze, and synthesize appropriate primary and secondary sources," a hallmark of the critical thinking, reading, and writing area of the WPA OS, but how students should identify the types of research that are appropriate was not included. For novice writers, instruction on locating, evaluating, and integrating sources is important. Also implied in the assignment was the idea of students integrating their own ideas, but the assignment did not provide any direction on how to develop their own writing beyond anything more than a dull research paper, one that simply recounts findings. Students were provided with a purpose for writing (informative writing that showcases another's life story), but the audience and rhetorical situation had not been identified or acknowledged.

The genre in the original assignment was an essay, but to even ask students to produce an "essay" is not very precise. After examining the assignment with the WPA OS, I can see that an essay may not have met the needs of the (undetermined) audience, and how this audience could be reached had not been considered; therefore, it would be more effective to allow students to determine the type of document they would like to produce based on the audience and method of delivery. Lastly, elements of language choice (e.g., voice, tone, and level of formality), which are all determined by audience, were not made evident to students from the way this assignment was originally written.

Again, for students to demonstrate evidence of learning on a project and in the course, these elements must be clearly discussed so students understand the decisions that they must make.

The assignment, as it was written five years ago, does not indicate any process work; however, I did require students to submit drafts for peer review, revision work, and pair share, where students "error-hunted" surface features of draft documents. Additionally, nowhere in the written assignment are students asked to be accountable for "knowledge of [the] conventions" of documentation, when clearly the assignment required both primary and secondary research. When I originally developed the assignment, I wanted it to appear open-ended so that students had the freedom to make decisions. I did not comprehend at the time that the way the assignment was written made it difficult for students to produce high-quality work.

Often, we find ourselves blaming students for the ineffective writing they submit, when the reality is that many strong writers struggle to decode a poorly written assignment—as the one I have described—and many students guess wrongly as they puzzle what we really want. The WPA OS can help clear up the notion that many students carry knowledge of "how to please the teacher" or determine "if this is the 'right' way to write," as the WPA OS can ask students to justify the rhetorical choices they make. Reflecting back to the first semester I assigned this project, three particular students' projects come to mind of work that did not meet my expectations. The projects had interesting topics, but looking back, I can see the projects themselves were underdeveloped due to unclear expectations. Several students who had scored below average revised for a higher grade, but the revisions did not show improvement in areas of rhetorical knowledge (developing a document for a directed audience and purpose) or demonstrating critical thinking. It wasn't until I revised the assignment using the WPA OS as a guide that I could see why students were unable to significantly improve their projects in developing a text that was constructed with a particular rhetorical situation in mind, and in a media and genre that met the needs of a specific audience and purpose.

THE WPA OS AND REVISING THE ASSIGNMENT

During the spring of 2007, I came to understand how important it is to use the language of the WPA OS not only in the assignment, but also in assessment rubrics to help students more clearly understand the learning objectives desired for them to demonstrate. Using the WPA OS, I revised the biographical writing assignment, and in the revision, I used the same concept for the assignment—asking students to develop a biographical project by conducting primary and secondary research.[2] The first revision of the assignment took on the need to better articulate clear goals that students should be able to accomplish by the end of the assignment. So, I outlined the following goals for students:

> By the end of this project, you should be able to (1) locate, evaluate, and use primary and secondary sources, specifically electronic sources, to produce a text that accurately integrates and represents the researched content; (2) effectively weave appropriate voice, tone, and style to capture the human element of an interview subject; (3) balance evidence as support for your ideas in developing a biographical project, rather than allowing the research to drive the project; (4) determine (and justify) an appropriate genre and medium based on the needs of an indicated audience, purpose and rhetorical situation; (5) engage in a series of composition tasks and multiple drafts, including peer review and proofreading partners, to develop a refined project; (6) apply appropriate technologies throughout the research and composition process; (7) demonstrate knowledge of conventions for documentation, format, and surface features; (8) explore social, historical, and cultural research to contextualize the telling of a life story.

In addition to project goals, I added several steps to the research process to offer scaffolding, a strategy by which students begin necessary research prior to the composing of a draft. As Debra Frank Dew states in Chapter 1, "we have worked deliberately to provide our students with the extensive *practice* they need as developing writers—we excel at teaching what it is that we want them 'to do.'" In the assignment handout, one critical element for teachers to articulate is how the series of tasks students complete will result in what they will learn.

Because family history research can be located within a variety of repositories, students have a wide range of research avenues, including online sources and databases, to develop a research plan. The revised assignment accounts for the recommended research skills—as discussed under the WPA OS umbrella of "Composing in Electronic

Environments"—of evaluating, organizing, collecting, and using materials from library databases, internet sources, informal electronic networks, and official databases. In Shelley Rodrigo's workshop, "Can You Digg It," based on her textbook *Wadsworth Guide to Research*, she articulates six stages of research scaffolding, which include helping students: (1) identify a topic through identifying a research interest, narrowing research questions, and making a research plan; (2) find and track sources by assisting students to distinguish types of information, locate authority and appropriateness of the source, and track resources; (3) critically read and evaluate sources; (4) synthesize ideas and resources; (5) draft ideas; and (6) present ideas. Rodrigo's steps echo the WPA OS. By incorporating these steps in my writing assignment, students are better able to engage in activities that foster critical thinking through reading and writing and they are better able to integrate their own ideas.

While revising the assignment, I was informed by the WPA OS, but my work was not limited to the WPA OS, as I included other sources, such as Rodrigo's work and NCTE's "Definition of 21st Century Literacies." The assignment now asks students to engage in a research process that allows for an exchange of ideas with sources to support the students' concepts as the central theme, rather than merely stringing together sources. By using the WPA OS to interrogate and then revise the assignment, I have shifted the openness of the original assignment from an essay that requires students to write to an undetermined audience, for an unknown purpose, to inviting students to get involved in making deliberate, rhetorical choices in response to the area of rhetorical knowledge from the WPA OS (e.g., audience, genre, medium, etc.) The revised assignment now asks students to locate a specific audience for this writing that would benefit from reading this piece (e.g., family members of the interviewee, community and/or workplace associates of the interviewee). If students have trouble locating an audience, I provide a default audience to consider: "This person's biography will be placed in a museum gallery that showcases 'Everyday Lives of Ordinary People.'"

Once students have located an audience and begin thinking about the needs of that audience, I ask students to generate a list of various formats that could be used to reach the student-selected audience, and a means by which those formats can be delivered to an audience. Students spend time exploring common formats for different kinds of texts and the technologies that support the various texts. The revised assignment clearly addresses components of rhetorical knowledge and critical thinking, reading, and writing, whereas the previous version of the assignment ignores these essential elements altogether.

The original assignment did not explicitly reveal the process by which the assignment would evolve, even though I included several drafts along with peer review work in class; the revised assignment states that students will work on several drafts, including a rough draft for peer review, a revised draft for teacher conference, and a third draft (prior to the final copy draft) used for partner sharing and proofreading. The revised assignment goes on to state that students will submit all four drafts to show the progression of their work and a meta-cognitive, self-assessment piece, which discusses the changes (or lack of changes) made from draft-to-draft. The new assignment (and syllabus) makes clear that all students will have the opportunity to revise graded work for a higher grade prior to course portfolio submission.

Students learn from the writing assignment handout that they will engage in not only a self-review process (during the peer review process), but also a self-assessment on each project that accounts for how the student has met the assignment goals and has accounted for the rhetorical decisions made throughout the assignment. Although many teachers ask students to assess themselves in a course reflection to accompany a portfolio at the end of the semester, I have found a self-assessment is most effective as students are taking a moment to pause and reflect on each project. As a result, the course reflection becomes a richer task, allowing students to have a reference point for the ways in which each project moved through and toward specific course outcomes.

Conclusion

My goals in revising the assignment were to directly incorporate the WPA OS into my assignment in an effort to allow students to see the application of the learning outcomes throughout the course. Perhaps more importantly, I sought to provide space for students to become independent thinkers and writers. I desire to see in my students what Stephen Wilhoit calls in Chapter 9 "deep change," requiring them to experiment with novel and innovated ways to think critically about their writing. I want my students to break away from the "box checking" to which they are accustomed and have minimal concern for including font size or the number of mandatory sources. My hope is to shift students from "bean-counting" the number of words on a page, or pages within a document, that they have experienced in classes prior to composition.

Providing space for students to negotiate the project details starts when teachers provide a rich architecture for an interesting assignment—one that includes an audience that is broader than the teacher. I have found that students can achieve a strong grasp of writing for an audience outside of our classroom walls and develop projects that are real-life. Instead of producing dull research essays as the original assignment warranted, my students produced family newsletters, glogs, websites, sound files, and blogs with the revised assignment. Students recounted in the self-assessment pieces how their families collectively contributed photos and stories, and as one of my colleagues likes to say, "They produce 'refrigerator-door-worthy stuff.'" I am convinced that using the WPA OS as a heuristic for assignment development has helped me generate an assignment that not only provides the freedom and creativity for my students, but also aids students in meeting the WPA OS as course goals. Additionally, the revised assignment elicits higher-quality work from students. When teachers use the WPA OS to develop assignments, students are provided clarity in what we are seeking on individual assignments, and they see how the connectivity of projects allows them to meet course outcomes. Family history writing has been a topic that has been creative to teach with, but it was the WPA OS that provided a ladder for assignment revision, and consequently, increased student success.

Notes

1. I owe limitless gratitude to Edward White for his continued support. I am most grateful for his engaging discussions about my ideas, and his critical eye to detail.

2. I am happy to share the revised assignment with those readers who are interested. Please email me at mywritingteacher@gmail.com if you would like a copy.

Works Cited

Bartholomae, David. "Writing Assignments: Where Writing Begins." *Writing on the Margins: Essays on Composition and Teaching*. Boston: Bedford/St. Martin's, 2005. 177–91. Print.

Council of Writing Program Administrators. "The WPA Outcomes Statement for First-Year Composition." Council of Writing Program Administrators, July 2008. Web. 27 August 2011.

Davis, Robert, and Mark Shadle. "'Building a Mystery': Alternative Research Writing and the Academic Act of Seeking." *College Composition and Communication* 51.3 (2000): 417–46. Print.

Melzer, Daniel, and Pavel Zemliansky. "Research Writing in First-year Composition and Across Disciplines: Assignments, Attitudes, and Student Performance." *Kairos* 8.1 (2003): n pag. Web. 07 June 2009.

Moffett, James. *Teaching the Universe of Discourse*. Boston: Houghton Mifflin, 1968. Print.

National Council of Teachers of English. "Definition of 21st Century Literacies." National Council of Teachers of English, February 2008. Web. December 2010.

National Public Radio. *StoryCorps*. (2008) Web. 15 Jan 2009.

Rankins-Robertson, Sherry, Lisa Cahill, Duane Roen, and Gregory R. Glau. "Expanding Definitions of Academic Writing: Family History Writing in the Basic Writing Classroom and Beyond." *Journal of Basic Writing* 29.1 (2010): 56–77. Print.

Rodrigo, Shelley. "Can You Digg It?" (2009): n pag. Web. 20 April 2010.

Sommers, Nancy, and Laura Saltz. "The Novice as Expert." *College Composition and Communication* 56.1 (2004): 124–49. Print.

White, Edward. Personal Interview. 16 Feb 2010.

—. *Assigning, Responding, Evaluating: A Writing Teacher's Guide*. Boston: Bedford/St. Martin's, 2007. Print.

—. "The Origins of the Outcomes Statement." *The Outcomes Book: Debate and Consensus after the WPA Outcomes Statement*. Ed. Susanmarie Harrington, Keith Rhodes, Ruth Overman Fischer, and Rita Malenczyk. Logan: Utah State UP, 2005. 3–7. Print.

6 Released from the Ghost of Platonic Idealism: How the Outcomes Statement Affirms Rhetorical Curricula

Doug Sweet

As I was attempting to explain how I saw the "ghost" of Platonic idealism haunting current-traditional writing epistemologies to a group of interdisciplinary faculty, I was interrupted by one of my putative colleagues, screaming at me: "You must be on LSD," he screeched, face violently contorted, spittle spraying. Obviously, I had hit an intellectual sore spot, but I was not prepared for the vehemence and vitriol. I had been trying to quote George Steiner when the yelling started, disrupting my carefully designed Prezi presentation. This is what I was trying to get out: "Learning and memory are conditioned," Steiner tells us,

> at every level, by social and historical agencies. Information is neither in substance nor conceptually value-free. Ideology, economic and class circumstance, the historical moment do much to define the content, the relative hierarchies, the sheer visibility of knowledge as knowledge . . . The cortex and the 'world outside' in which language can be seen as a form of work, of social production, of economic and ideological exchange, cannot be meaningfully separated. (304)

Just after the "sheer visibility of knowledge as knowledge" part, my colleague began his blustering. He was not voicing some honest disagreement *after* I'd spoken. I was not offended by his intellectual position—this particular discussion has gone on since the pre-Socratics—but he seemed unwilling to allow *my* point to be made. He silenced me by shouting me down.

"What is this crap?" he boomed. "Truth either is or isn't; it's not relative to anything but itself—that's the point." From then on, he interrupted me each time I tried to read a quote, or make a statement. "This is just another example of how we've let knee-jerk intellectuals take over," he yelled later, unaware of the irony since he was making sure my argument could not be heard.

I mention this disheartening meeting to try to establish some visceral contact with what we know all too well when it comes to how faculty in other disciplines often regard our work of talking about language. My detractor's response was not just to George Steiner. It was a response to any ideas of contingency, to any concept, in fact, that did not reflect his Platonic view. His reaction in this instance was apoplectic, but I see it as akin to those who, when hearing a delineation of specific social injustices, ask "But what about the other side of the issue?" Obviously, status quo institutions *are* the "other side"; the person asking *is* the other side. I have seen my heckler's attitude in myriad forms over the course of my academic career. His eruptions echoed what I'm afraid too many in the academy already think about the entire field of rhetoric and composition. While one might argue that every academic discipline looks suspiciously at other fields, the following statements are especially familiar to me as ways in which those in other fields (and far too many of our own) view our work: that all this theorizing about epistemologies and politics and symbolicity is much ado about nothing; that everyone else knows the key factor in academic writing is the correct use of APA style; that the goal is to find truth "objectively"; that you cannot use "I" because it reveals bias; that correctness and error directly determine winning and losing; and that they could teach these writing courses if they weren't so busy doing *real* scholarly work.

In this article, I examine these notions, explore their foundational epistemological assumptions, and trace the ways I see the WPA Outcome Statement for First-Year Composition (WPA OS) as delineating a solid rejection of what I call the long Platonic history of teaching the competitive binaries of forensic rhetoric as *the* mode, method, or means of understanding persuasion or argument. It is a Platonic history in that standards for correctness or persuasion depend upon external or transcendent ideals; forensic rhetoric in that questions of all kinds can be reduced to an either/or binary decided by contestation.

Instead, I want to demonstrate that faculty members who teach writing can use the WPA OS to attend to the roles of deliberative rhetoric—negotiating social relationships for future action—by jettisoning the cramping, past-tense, find-the-one-answer binary of forensic rhetoric in favor of a renewed emphasis on creating spaces of plural, contingent agency for our students. The WPA OS has legitimized and authorized—and in a way, institutionalized—an epistemological shift in pedagogy. As writing program administrators, we can use the WPA OS as a response to the inevitable resistance we encounter from faculty, administrators, and students who still cling to notions of language as a neutral transmitter of meaning (knowledge) found elsewhere, whether that elsewhere is identified empirically, rationally, mystically, or divinely.[1]

Of course, as I have noted, just as we faculty members are often discipline-centric, faculty resistance to any "rhetorical turn" in composition studies is often rooted in differing philosophies and conflicting pedagogical assumptions. Ideologies, philosophies, and pedagogies are inextricably linked in any attempt to shape standards or adopt policies. Susan Thomas, in Chapter 12, describes the writing program she saw at Sydney, one she says had "been left theoretically rudderless, subject to blind trial and error at the whims of non-specialists with strong opinions." I would respectfully add that, in most cases, these "whims" reflect an attitude toward language that elides anything social, political, or contingent. One of the more stimulating aspects of the WPA OS is its direct refutation of such current-traditional practices or attitudes. Under "Rhetorical Knowledge" in the document, for instance, we read the first bullet point as "Focus on a purpose." Notice it is not "Focus on a thesis," and the difference is crucial. Focusing on a "thesis" puts emphasis on something produced, an idea or point which can then be the subject of judgment—is it true or false? Is it correct? Focusing on a "purpose," however, plunges students immediately into the active, generative, heuristic process of writing without demanding a formal reduction to the kinds of expository writing one sees in the SAT essay, for example, rooted as it is in an epistemology and form of the five-paragraph theme. The intellectual positioning I continually see students adopting in response to a charge to "find a thesis" is that "there are always two sides to every issue," or "situation," but only one can prevail. The WPA OS works actively against such positioning, as I intend to demonstrate, and re-charts the terrain of writing instruction in productive and necessary ways. The ghost of the dueling binary, after all, is still a very real presence of sorts, a transcendent paradigm that, for centuries, has lurked behind or above much thinking about language.

Legacies of the Competitive Binary and Forensic Rhetoric

To clarify my operational premises, I take a quick turn through the history of both rhetoric and composition, though necessarily in general terms and broad strokes. Most texts on classical rhetoric identify the three basic rhetorical forms: *epideictic, forensic* and *deliberative,* and categorize (epistemologically define) them roughly as follows:

Epideictic	*Forensic*	*Deliberative*
Focused on present	Focused on past	Focused on future
Ceremonial/Occasional	Agonistic/Competitive	Negotiative/ Contingent
(delivered to audience)	(binary struggle)	(temporal alliances)
"to praise or to blame"	"to find the truth"	"to establish agreement"

In antiquity, these three categories encompassed every formalized rhetorical option, covering the only three time frames conceivable: past, present, and future. Although, from a modern stance, these forms can seem a bit constraining or limiting, we should factor in that the audiences, participants, and occasions for any rhetorical display in ancient contexts were limited to civic or legal matters, and reserved for the very few. I use these forms to highlight their differences, to see what kind of thinking each pre-supposes or encourages, and to point out composition's historical institutionalization of binary thinking. Obviously, in their day, none of the three standing alone was meant to apply to every rhetorical possibility—each relied on different epistemological premises and differing assumptions about what rhetorical agency looks like. Epideictic, focused on the present, most often becomes equated with *entertainment,* although Jeffrey Walker, following Aristotle, suggests that the epideictic was a discourse that "asks its audience to form opinions, or even to revise their existing beliefs and attitudes on a given topic" (9). This is certainly a more layered and intellectually nuanced matter than enjoying a ceremonial or occasional speech, as epideictic is characterized above. But, Walker argues that epideictic was never meant as a purely entertaining form, that it aimed at the *suasive* nature of discourse to change thought. Unfortunately, the epideictic seems not to have aged well, and is often dismissed as "to praise or to blame," another handy binary.

The forensic form, focused on judging past action, always takes the shape and epistemology of a *competition*, one in which two opposing positions vie for supremacy, for "truth," or for victory: it is agonistic, with all the battlefield connotations that term conjures—someone must be defeated by the end of the process. The deliberative form, however, focused on the future (what should or can be done), aims at *cooperation*. Instead of obliterating those who disagree, in deliberative rhetoric, the goal is to forge alliances, to cooperate enough to arrive at some sense of agreement that leads directly to decision or action.

When I suggest that the forensic form—debate—has become *the* predominant shape of argument, I am claiming that this is what gets taught most often as what we mean by persuasion. Even in cases where students are asked to hypothesize about future behavior or thought, they often do their hypothesizing in the form and epistemological constraints of the competitive binary choice. Discursive persuasion (argument) in this light is reliant upon and defined by ideas and methods of contest, where success is measured by smashing one's opponent or by thoroughly discrediting the other's argument. For a clear example, note the assumptions about learning implicit in this flyer on a campus kiosk I pass every day: "Top Tutors Teach You to Kick Ass in Class." Attitudes about learning exhibited in this flyer suggest the whole enterprise of teaching is dedicated to producing winners of some specific kind, and forensic (judicial) rhetoric has historically been the default form of that process. Teaching the modes, for example, situates argument as the pinnacle of writing tasks: After students have learned to reminisce, to describe, to evaluate, they are prepared, in this line of thinking, to engage in the supreme task of persuading about ideas, as long as they embrace very definite attitudes about the sacrosanct need for objectivity and adhere to formalized, logical "steps" or "stages" to ensure rectitude.

The epideictic form, after Ramus,[2] in what appears to be a concentrated effort to simplify, came to be as minimized and intellectually marginalized as *belle lettres*, as literature in general, or as "expressionist" because it does not fit well with formalized ideas of argument. These "formalized ideas" look a lot like a forensic rhetoric that relies on a bifurcated Platonic epistemology of truth and doxology, which is the old philosophy/rhetoric split: *Res/verba?* Mind/body? Western metaphysical dualism? My point in all this is that the posited three rhetorical forms, by the time we get to current-traditional formulations, have shrunken to only two. The deliberative form, with its focus on contingent agency and persuasion as negotiated agreement, seems hard to find anywhere—clashing, as it does, with a mindset that sees persuasion as winning—leaving epideictic (expressionist) and forensic (argument) as rhetoric's lasting contribution to composition studies. We might well consider T.S. Eliot's "objective correlative" as the vestigial backbone of expressionist rhetoric—another case of language identifying some truth outside itself and transmitting that truth to another. "In other words," Eliot tells us, the objective correlative is "a set of objects, a situation, a chain of events which shall be the formula of that *particular* emotion; such that when the external facts . . . are given, the emotion is immediately evoked" (100). Eliot's formulation is yet another case of language being seen as inherently neutral, another example of what I mean by Platonic idealism. Isaiah Berlin has summed it up quite clearly, I think, when discussing how he was taught to understand the world by way of his Oxford education in philosophy.

> At some point I realized that what all these views had in common was a Platonic ideal: in the first place, that, as in the sciences, all genuine questions must have one true answer and one only, all the rest being necessarily errors; in the second place, that there must be a dependable path towards the discovery of these truths; in the third place, that the true answers, when found, must necessarily be compatible with one another and form a single whole, for one truth cannot be incompatible with another. (48)

If this is the operative epistemology of much Western intellectual inquiry, as Berlin suggests, we should note that its binary nature (truth/error) is conveniently compatible with all the other binaries just mentioned, as though centuries of writing instruction have done a hatchet job to reduce linguistic persuasion to the esoteric, often solipsistic, but nonetheless "humanizing" efforts of the epideictic to reach for some aesthetic sense—either we persuade that way, or we resort to intellectual combat; the goal is to eliminate the opponent as a credible voice.

I noted above that, "after Ramus," teaching rhetoric became increasingly "simplified." I am not only referring to his severing of *inventio* and *dispositio* from the rhetorical canons that, as James Murphy described, began with "Ramus's 1543 attack on Aristotle" (vii); his way of thinking simplifies what we have already seen to be the differing epistemological processes of the three forms, quite directly. "As I said before concerning the three styles," Ramus tell us, "this difference between forensic and epideictic speech derives more from the subject matter than from the principle and practice of the oratorical art" (36). From this perspective, the three forms *only* differ in their "subject matter"; we can assume they share the same epistemology in Ramus's system. We might remember, at this point, Walter Ong's opinion that, "[I]t is only after the pedagogical build-up of the Middle Ages that the crucial question for philosophy becomes not, Is it true? but is it teachable?" (23). Ramism teaches us that there is a foolproof method for finding every piece of meaning; in fact, it contends that the method itself is far more important than any individual clear idea or bit of new knowledge. My concomitant point is that much of Western culture's pedagogy for persuasion has been shaped by Ramus's thought. Ong puts it like this:

> The order which the mind found in the universe ... was, radically, an order existing not in terms of fully developed, "logically," consistent sciences, but one which was sustained largely by a curriculum. This in turn was stabilized by the existence of unions of teachers (universities) who tended collectively to view and to purvey knowledge as a commodity. (306)

A curriculum of methodical binaries is certainly teachable, and usually comes in forms such as "do and don't," "true and false," and "correctness and error"—all of which predicate a severely truncated notion of argument.

The ghost of Platonic idealism is its reliance on one truth found by either/or argument, its contention that this truth is "not of this world," universal, and absolute. In the context of teaching composition, then, the Platonic ghost lives on in every pro and con assignment, every comparison and contrast essay, every mock debate, every writing task that asks students to see "both sides" of something in order to find a winner, as though every worthwhile intellectual endeavor can be reduced to one of two clear and distinct choices—and that is forensic rhetoric's essential assumption, its epistemological "given."

The next obvious question is, "So what?" What's wrong with shaping all ideas of argument as agonistic struggles where one combatant wins? Off the top, I would suggest that this configuration denies the efficacy and even the mere possibility of pluralistic thinking, leaving *absolutely* no room for a deliberative rhetoric of contingent agency, where one might use language to arrive at agreement *for the moment* or *in this case*. If the goal of persuasive (rhetorical) discourse (and students learning to shape discourse) in forensic terms is to defeat the opponent, to discredit the other side, to destroy the other's credibility or argument, then it is pretty clear we will not be attempting to act in concert with those opponents in any real way. Forensic discourse inevitably leads to the closure of victory, the vanquishing of the defeated. If our dedicated and understood purpose is to overcome opponents, we cannot very well simply turn around after the dust has cleared and include them. They've been erased as active political agents—neutralized by language—silenced by the strength of a discourse that demands a winner, in the same way I was silenced in the incident I described at the outset.

THE PROBLEMS OF SIMPLIFYING COMPLEXITY

We hear the argument all the time: Beginning writers can't handle too many variables all at once. They need to start with simple steps before they can be expected to juggle complexities. A recent listserv post from Peter Adams speaks directly to this attitude; one shared by many dedicated writing instructors.

> Lots of what apprentice writers are told really amounts to "training wheels" designed to reduce the number of demands on the writer as she or he gradually gains proficiency at this very complicated task . . . Too often, perhaps as several have already suggested about the 5PE [five paragraph essay], we run out of time before we have a chance to take off the training wheels. In fact, too often, students leave our classrooms thinking these temporary restrictions designed to make their learning of the complicated task of writing simpler are really iron-clad rules.

Not only do students who are taught this way often concentrate on following "iron-clad rules," as I have already shown, but also they can leave their introductory writing classes believing that the only kind of reasoning validated in the academy is forensic, after-the-fact judging, which derives its authenticity from its dedication to discovering "truth" or discrediting a clearly delineated opposing position, one in which, much like the interlocutors in Plato's *Dialogues*, the opponent seldom gets the good lines or arguments. Students leave such courses firmly convinced that what always matters most in discourse is "getting it right," both conventionally and conceptually. The difficulty I see inherent in this approach should be clear: Students who learn that the pro and con essay, for example, is emblematic of *all* good argument because their courses have focused on "simple" steps, will be unable and unwilling to entertain any other forms of persuasion—especially not a persuasion predicated on negotiating amongst many options to forge tentative agreement in a material world. Luckily, the WPA OS provides us, as writing professionals, a guide to and justification for teaching more than one epistemology, for escaping Platonic idealism, and for entertaining multiple considerations rather than simple binaries in writing pedagogy.

The WPA OS and Deliberative Rhetoric

My use of the term *deliberative* in this discussion is meant to refer to epistemology, to the way we think about what we're doing, and not to resurrecting the *agora* or having students do all their work in collaborative, communal classrooms. I am certainly not attempting to convince anyone that every binary pairing that crosses our mind or experience is invalid or suspect. Think of it this way: Telling students that finding one "correct" answer from between two options in every instance is "logical" severely disfigures the complexities of thought. Teaching that the debate form is applicable and necessary to every argumentative moment is equally illogical and limiting. By advocating a release from the strictures of Platonic idealism, I am not suggesting that Platonic thought has no place in our lexicon or syllabi. I am maintaining, however, that all our composing philosophies and pedagogies should not be reducible to a Platonic epistemology. My experience tells me, unfortunately, that reducing complex reasoning to simplistic competitive binaries (one wins, one loses) insidiously permeates much writing pedagogy.

The second full paragraph of the WPA OS directly addresses the historical pattern of reducing argument to a "one or the other" in the simplistic method of teaching writing I've been dissecting.

> Learning to write is a complex process, both individual and social, that takes place over time with continued practice and informed guidance. Therefore, it is important that teachers, administrators and a concerned public do not imagine that these outcomes can be taught in reduced or simple ways. . . . [T]erms such as 'rhetorical' and 'genre' convey a rich meaning that is not easily simplified.

Acknowledging from the outset that some complexities about learning to write in our various academic worlds cannot be reduced or simplified immediately shifts the grounds of the discussion away from the debate form of forensic rhetoric, the "both sides" type of framing students are so quick to apply. To admit that we are not in the business of providing simple answers suggests, quite accurately, that language is not a neutral carrier of truths found elsewhere; it is an affirmation of the vital part context plays in making meaning, and therefore echoes George Steiner's point quoted earlier that "information is neither in substance nor in content value free" (304).

In other words, the WPA OS stakes out a fundamentally different academic ground from much previous university writing curricula, especially in the modern, managed institution, and marks a definite break from this long tradition of working from Platonic premises. It affirms a "complex process" that is "social" and "takes place over time," hardly a masticate/regurgitate endeavor, and hardly the individualistic coming to knowledge that relies on contemplating the good or the just. What the WPA OS does not say, in fact, speaks volumes. It does not advocate simple skills acquisition; it does not focus on finding answers; it does not assume *one* truth to find; and it undermines the myth of the individualistic writer working in solitude, coming to knowledge through reason or mystical inspiration alone. The WPA OS shows us that we have moved past writing instruction based on competition to instead validate a complex social process of written inquiry that relies on the features and epistemology of deliberative rhetoric.

In the interest of brevity, let me point out the specific language in the outcomes that I see as re-introducing the collaborative, social, contingent, temporal, and future-oriented elements of deliberative rhetoric; elements that, if used, can release student and teachers alike from the ghost of the Platonic ideal. I list these according to category, acknowledging that I am only selecting those points that speak to my argument. We should also be aware that none of the omitted outcomes argue *against* this reading. Under "Rhetorical Knowledge," the WPA OS notes that students should be able to "[r]espond to the needs of *different audiences*"; "[r]espond *appropriately* to *different kinds* of rhetorical situations"; "[a]dopt *appropriate voice, tone, and level of formality*"; "[u]nderstand how *genres shape* reading and writing"; and "[w]rite in *several genres*" (emphasis added). The italicized terms lay epistemological foundations for writing instruction that do not rely on simple binaries or focus on persuasion as an agonistic competition aimed only at winning. In this crucial act of framing, the WPA OS establishes a rhetorical prism through which acts of composing are, *from the outset*, seen as active social undertakings. Instead of facing a one-size-fits-all, "correct" approach, we are immediately immersed in multiplicities—of audience, of purpose, of genre, of style—that describe a much more nuanced terrain for intellectual activity than just "getting it right." As a writing instructor, I see innumerable possibilities for course design, writing opportunities, and research possibilities, if my operating premises for the class echo the assumptions about the rhetorical nature of discourse made explicit here.

Additionally, for "Critical Thinking, Reading, and Writing," the WPA OS outlines the following outcomes: "Use writing and reading *for inquiry, learning, thinking*, and communicating"; and "[u]nderstand the *relationships among language, knowledge, and power*" (emphasis added). Explicitly saying, for instance, that students should be able to "[u]nderstand the relationships among language, knowledge, and power" assumes a plural (relationships), rather than the Platonic notion that all legitimacy comes from knowledge independent of language, rather than a Platonic denial that power could, in any way, affect our understanding of knowledge. Understanding these "relationships" as a condition of composition means that students must actually engage in "critical thinking" *as* they compose; they must learn to juggle variables in a dynamic and dialectical, on-going process of thinking.

Under "Processes," the WPA OS notes that students should be able to "[d]evelop *flexible strategies* for generating, revising, editing, and proof reading" and "[u]nderstand the *collaborative and social aspects of writing*" (emphasis added). "Flexible, collaborative and social"—to describe writing processes in these ways argues directly against privileging the forensic form, and simultaneously affirms the premises of deliberative rhetoric. Notice that the emphasis is on developing flexible "strategies" for the writing process, not just on internalizing different forms, styles, or citation systems. This does not mean, however, that the forensic or debate form is automatically ruled out as *one* of the strategies possible, but in these iterations, it is clearly not the *only* or automatically *most favored* possibility.

Under "Knowledge of Conventions," the WPA OS suggests that students should be able to "[l]earn common formats for *different kinds of texts*" and "[d]evelop knowledge of genre conventions *ranging from structure and paragraphing to tone and mechanics*" (emphasis added). Acknowledging that "different kinds of texts" necessitate different "genre conventions" that influence "structure" or "tone and mechanics" asserts that decades of composition research have not gone unnoticed in our discipline. One of the hardest icons of current-traditional rhetoric to dispense with has been the notion that somewhere "out there" exists the perfect academic essay, one that would work everywhere and always because its logic is inescapable and its structure and mechanics are perfect. Acknowledging this construct to be a self-defeating fantasy is a lot like finally admitting the prancing emperor has no clothes, but is essential to thinking of discourse rhetorically. The WPA OS predicates a writing pedagogy based on the accumulated knowledge of composition scholars, who understand that persuasion with language is most always contingent on contexts—that it is rarely, if ever, done once and for all.

Under "Composing in Electronic Environments," the WPA OS stresses the importance of digital technologies:

> As has become clear over the last twenty years, writing in the 21st-century involves the use of digital technologies for several purposes, from drafting to peer reviewing to editing. Therefore, although *the kinds of composing processes* and texts expected from students *vary across programs* and institutions, there are nonetheless common expectations. (emphasis added)

This section notes that students should be able to "[u]nderstand and exploit the *differences in the rhetorical strategies* and in the affordances available for both print and electronic composing processes and texts" (emphasis added). Each of these points stresses variability, that there is not *one* kind of composition, *one* kind of program, *one* rhetorical strategy to develop successful college writing. In this very material and liberating way, the WPA OS gives program directors, writing instructors, and students alike a useful vocabulary for negotiating the political and social terrain of composition.

Building a Curriculum from the WPA OS

I would now like to turn to what really matters most in this analysis: *praxis*, or how we can actually *do* anything of consequence as a result of our understanding. I am WPA at a small liberal arts university with a first-year enrollment of about a thousand students. Up until the past few years, entering students were required to take a two-course writing sequence that exactly mimicked the English IA and IB of California Community College curricula. The first semester focused on "expository" writing, while the second was called "Writing about Literature." Syllabi stressed correctness and logical development. For many years, coherence among sections was guaranteed by requiring a common handbook, selection of which was often the major decision reached by writing faculty.

Before my hire, the university adopted directed self placement (DSP)[3] for these introductory writing courses, as they were differentiated by theme: "Self and Society," "Transcendence," "California Living," but a few of the possibilities. Predominant faculty attitudes about writing around campus were mostly of the "make them do it right" variety, with a smattering of folks who lauded the value of literature for its humanizing qualities. It was a fairly recognizable atmosphere for anyone who matriculated in the last half century.

Upon assuming the WPA position, I invited all full-time faculty who taught writing to become members of our composition committee, a committee that makes all decisions concerning the writing program. Collaboratively, then, we set about creating a writing program using the WPA OS as a model for our student learning outcomes, for our rhetorically-based curricula, and as a justification for our pedagogical assumptions. As a committee, we agreed that a rhetorically-based course would introduce students to the ways academics and practitioners wrote in their fields. In other words, we took great pains to stress that sociologists, for example, approached writing with different sets of expectations and conventions than economists, that academic sociologists and practicing sociologists didn't necessarily share the same styles or forms across the board. Necessarily, we shifted from thematic course offerings to more genre or context-based alternatives for students to choose from in their DSP. "Writing in Electronic Environments," "Writing in the Social Sciences," and "Writing about Culture" are just a few examples. What we considered most important in this re-thinking of curricular options was that we could show students someone who did this particular kind of writing outside of the academy. We opened up our pedagogy to include a wide variety of "texts." "Writing about Nature and the Environment," for example, might include scientific articles, editorials, travel literature, case studies, websites, film, as well as fiction. In every section, students encounter a broad range of writing rather than seeing everything through the prism of the academic essay alone. We haven't abolished or discarded the academic essay, but we do not teach it as the *only* or necessarily privileged way in which students learn to negotiate social relationships with language. We still teach entire sections of epideictic rhetoric, such as "Composing the Self." We even offer sections focused entirely on forensic rhetoric in a pre-law section. In other words, we have not substituted our own binary as a means of avoiding binaries. Our program stresses what the WPA OS calls the "flexibility" of thinking required to actively engage in persuasive discourse, and this flexibility, in our minds, lives best in atmospheres that do not mandate a winner-take-all way of thinking, a "getting over" as the measure of success. Currently, entering students can choose from a collection of 100- and 200-level offerings to satisfy their general education writing requirement, each of which foregrounds a specific writing focus without pretending it is the only appropriate form, genre or style of writing.

As our committee began the process of defining to each other, to the rest of the university faculty, and to our students, exactly what a rhetorically-based course would emphasize, we came to assume that writing assignments are clearly aimed at purposes that are shared with students (Why are we asking them to write X? Where else might they find such writing? Who does it? Why?). We also came to assume that students write across a range of styles, modes, forms—any that are appropriate to the course classification. An example might be that, in a course titled "Writing about Nature and the Environment," students could conceivably write op-ed pieces, analytical arguments, or data-driven reports. Our primary intention is that students see a range of writing possibilities that aren't necessarily tied to the essay form. Finally, we came to assume that students' texts are an integral part of our curricula. When talking about writing, student work should be one of the voices in the conversations, a voice considered on an equal plane with other sources, other student and faculty work. One of our committee's aims, as we have negotiated amongst ourselves, is to place students in authorial positions from the very first day of class in all writing courses. To accomplish this positioning, or way of thinking about what they're doing as writers, we begin each semester by talking our students through Kenneth Burke's "unending conversation":

> Imagine you enter a parlor. You come late. When you arrive, others have long preceded you, and they are engaged in a heated discussion, a discussion too heated for them to pause and tell you exactly what it is about. In fact, the discussion had already begun long before any of them got there, so that no one present is qualified to retrace for you all the steps that had gone before. . . . The hour grows late, you must depart. And you do depart, with the discussion still vigorously in progress. It is from this 'unending conversation' that the materials of your drama arise. (110)

Initial class discussions, then, focus on interpreting Burke's passage in the context of our writing classes, positioning our students to add their voices to many "unending" conversations. In conjunction with this strategy, most of us post the WPA OS on Blackboard so that students can access it.

Virtually every facet of our developing program finds its *raison d'etre* in the WPA OS. We've never really looked at it as a set of standards we try to meet; instead, we rely on its epistemological premises to envision and create rhetorically centered writing courses that do not pretend to dictate that all academic writing must use an APA citation system or avoid the use of "I." We firmly believe that the WPA OS has reset the frames, "blasted through the continuum of history" to use Terry Eagleton's words from the unnumbered Preface to his text on Walter Benjamin in another context. The WPA OS has revitalized a deliberative rhetoric through which our students become active agents in on-going discussions of consequence. This is a truly revolutionary development for established writing pedagogy, one that actually uses what we have learned through research to reframe academic givens. Students and faculty alike finally have an epistemologically coherent, rhetorically effective way to talk about writing and how we can teach it with some sense of intellectual integrity while relying on an accessible, codified, disciplinary statement.

Notes

1. For a detailed description of such notions, see Lester Faigley, *Fragments of Rationality* and Earl C. Kelley, *Education for What is Real*, especially Chapter II, "Some Common Assumptions of Education."

2. Ramus's theoretical model was, as Ong elaborates, an entire taxonomy built from and always aiming to reduce complexity to a binary pairing. See *Ramus, Method, and the Decay of Dialogue*.

3. For an explanation of directed self placement in writing courses, see Daniel J. Royer and Roger Gilles' "Directed Self-Placement: An Attitude of Orientation" and David Blakesley's "Directed Self-Placement in the University."

Works Cited

Adams, Peter. "Re: The CHE strikes again." *WPA-L*. 23 Feb. 2010. Web. 23 Feb. 2010.

Berlin, Isaiah. "Three Useful Inventions." *The Truth About The Truth*. Ed. Walter T. Anderson. New York: Penguin, 1995. Print.

Blakesley, David. "Directed Self-Placement in the University." *WPA: Writing Program Administration* 25.3 (2002): 9–40. Print.

Burke, Kenneth. *The Philosophy of Literary Form*. 3rd ed. Berkeley: U of California P, 1973. Print.

Council of Writing Program Administrators. "The WPA Outcomes Statement for First-Year Composition." Council of Writing Program Administrators, July 2008. Web. 2 Oct. 2009.

Eagleton, Terry. *Walter Benjamin*. London, England: Verso, 1981. Print.

Eliot, T.S. "Hamlet and His Problems." *The Sacred Wood*. London and New York: Methuen, 1920. Print.

Faigley, Lester. *Fragments of Rationality*. Pittsburgh, PA: U of Pittsburgh P, 1992. Print.

Kelley, Earl C. *Education for What Is Real*. New York and London: Harper & Brothers, 1947. Print.

Murphy, James J. Introduction. *Peter Ramus's Attack on Cicero.* By Peter Ramus. Ed. James J. Murphy. Trans. Carole Newlands. Davis, CA: Hermagoras Press, 1992. vii-ix. Print.

Ong, Walter J. *Ramus, Method, and the Decay of Dialogue.* Cambridge, Mass: Harvard UP, 1983, c1958. Print.

Ramus, Peter. *Peter Ramus's Attack on Cicero.* Ed. James J. Murphy. Trans. Carole Newlands. Davis, CA: Hermagoras Press, 1992. Print.

Royer, Daniel J., and Roger Gilles. "Directed Self-Placement: An Attitude of Orientation." *College Composition and Communication* 50.1 (1998): 54–70. Print.

Steiner, George. *After Babel.* 3rd ed. New York and Oxford: Oxford UP, 1998. Print.

Walker, Jeffrey. *Rhetoric and Poetics in Antiquity.* Oxford: Oxford UP, 2000. Print.

7 Beyond Composition: Developing a National Outcomes Statement for Writing Across the Curriculum

Paul Anderson, Chris M. Anson, Martha Townsend, and Kathleen Blake Yancey

In July of 2007, a packed room of attendees at the conference of the Council of Writing Program Administrators in Tempe, Arizona, considered how the WPA Outcomes Statement for First-Year Composition (WPA OS) might be extended into the increasingly important realm of writing beyond composition, a term that designates writing in all other courses, regardless of whether the courses are part of writing across the curriculum (WAC), writing in the disciplines (WID), or other institutional initiatives (Anderson, Anson, Townsend, and Yancey). At subsequent WPA and WAC conferences, and at the Conference on College Composition and Communication (CCCC), one or more of us continued this conversation with equally eager audiences at special interest group meetings and informal gatherings.

The growing interest in defining outcomes for writing beyond first-year composition courses can be attributed, in part, to writing specialists' desire to research the actual impact of WAC, WID, and similar institutional initiatives. Many leaders of these initiatives are also finding that expanded or even continued funding depends on demonstrating their programs' ability to achieve specific learning outcomes even though they had not previously defined these outcomes. Interest is also spurred by regional and professional accrediting agencies' focus on students' graduation-level abilities, which has extended the assessment of individual writing courses (including composition) to students' writing experiences throughout the entire curriculum (Anderson and Gorman). In addition, writing specialists have begun to think more deeply about writing outcomes as they question popular methods for measuring students' graduation-level knowledge and abilities, including surveys and competency tests (e.g., the Collegiate Learning Assessment), the Association of American Colleges and Universities (AAC&U) VALUE project focused on ePortfolios, and the Voluntary System of Accountability sponsored by American Association of State Colleges and Universities (AASCU) and the National Association of State Universities and Land-Grant Colleges (NASULGC).

In this context of growing demands for evidence-based accountability and for assessment based on explicit outcomes, it is not surprising that writing specialists find it desirable to have a national definition of outcomes for writing beyond composition, one adaptable to their needs. By defining writing outcomes themselves, they could take a significant step toward ensuring that each institution's writing instruction is evaluated according to appropriate criteria, using valid methods. A national definition would also provide writing specialists a starting point for defining outcomes for their own institutions in much the same way that the WPA OS assisted many first-year composition programs in defining their objectives. In addition to saving time, such a starting point could help administrators increase a program's credibility; by contextualizing their local outcomes relative to outcomes developed through a national conversation, they could demonstrate a program's value or persuade their institutions to adopt more ambitious writing goals. A national statement of writing outcomes would also assist the significant number of schools that are instituting or reviving WAC, WID, and other writing-beyond-composition programs. Many are assigning leadership roles to people who lack much specific preparation for this work. The national statement could provide these individuals with a framework within which to understand the nature of their mission.

These benefits were among the considerations that spawned our ambition, five years ago, to create a national statement of writing outcomes beyond composition. As we soon discovered, such an effort faces many challenges, and we were confronted with a number of theoretical and practical issues that complicated our work in interesting ways, but also stalled our progress far beyond the one year we had given ourselves, after our first panel discussion, to produce a document. By chronicling our journey, we hope to shed light on a variety of these issues and suggest ways that our field can continue to use the inspiration of the WPA OS to create a similarly useful set of outcomes for writing beyond composition.

Outcomes vs. Inputs

Over the past twenty years, accrediting agencies have shifted their expectations from evaluating inputs to examining outcomes—that is, from focusing on what academic programs give their students in the form of faculty qualifications, soundness of the curriculum, size and holdings of the library, or extracurricular experiences, to how they define and measure the desired or expected results of their efforts.

Although we embarked on our project intent on defining outcomes, we now realize that we and the colleagues who joined in our forums and informal conversations were actually preoccupied with inputs. Our discussions concentrated on the kinds of actions that institutions, their component units, and their faculty should take in order to initiate, sustain, or expand the writing-beyond-composition programs we value. What we sometimes mistook for an enthusiasm for outcomes was actually enthusiasm for the kinds of support we hoped others would provide for our programs. While our nominal model was the WPA OS, our inspiration also came from other sources, such as the National Council of Teachers of English's (NCTE) 1987 "Statement on Class Size and Teacher Workload: College." That statement declares that the maximum number of students in any writing class should be twenty. Although the majority of schools have classes that exceed this threshold, directors of composition programs or other writing courses have repeatedly used the NCTE statement to argue successfully against making their classes even larger than they already are. In considering issues like these, we found ourselves devising a similar statement that we hoped would guide the creation and sustenance of writing-beyond-composition programs.

Consequently, most of the points we recorded at our open meetings at conferences concerned *features* or *principles* of beyond-composition writing programs rather than their *outcomes*. Similarly, the draft we began in 2008, which we titled a "Statement of Principles and Practices," included a list of actions—such as providing rewards and incentives, multiple faculty-development opportunities, and consistent oversight—that are desired not only by writing specialists, but also by advocates of programs in quantitative reasoning, information literacy, oral communication across the curriculum, lifelong learning, or proponents of other institutional initiatives whose achievement depends on contributions from faculty outside our own department or program. At the level of courses and assignments, our draft also specified desired inputs: a "balance of formal and informal writing," "appropriately scaffolded" assignments, and "measurement criteria that are explicitly tied to the assignment's goals and are included in the assignment." These are not statements about learning outcomes.

Of course, outcomes have little meaning unless they influence inputs. When specialists in WAC, WID, and WIC (Writing-Intensive Courses) mention the outcomes for their programs, they often want to motivate faculty, departments, and institutions to adopt the specific practices—inputs—they believe will be beneficial. Virtually all models of outcomes assessment involve a cycle that moves from the articulation of expectations to assessment of those expectations to the implementation of curricular and pedagogical reforms that bring a program or institution closer to reaching its goals (Anson, "Assessment"). Not coincidentally, the bond between outcomes and inputs forms the very structure of the WPA OS. Each list of outcomes is followed by another list that describes ways "[f]aculty in all programs and departments can build on the preparation" provided in first-year composition. In fact, a gadfly might observe that some of the outcomes could have been included primarily because the authors wanted their colleagues or institutions to provide the inputs. For instance, the statement that by the end of their first-year composition courses students should "understand the relationship among language, knowledge, and power" may seem to bear a date-stamp that identifies it as belonging to a certain era and group of composition specialists, not an instance of the "common knowledge, skills, and attitudes" sought (the statement implies) by the vast majority of "composition programs in American post-secondary education." Similarly, the desire that institutions provide computer classrooms, which were not common a decade ago when the statement was first published, now seems unnecessary in light of the ubiquitous presence of such classrooms at most colleges and universities. (As Micheal Callaway shows in Chapter 19, there is now an equally urgent need to specify new outcomes for the relationship between writing and emerging technologies.)

Descriptions of the best available means—best practices—deserve the attention they are given by writing-beyond-composition specialists. But such practices are not outcomes. In fact, at the point when we abandoned it, our draft didn't mention a single outcome. The result of our outcomes effort had produced only inputs.

Outcomes and Assessment: A Search for Focus

A second major challenge we faced in producing a national set of outcomes was the wide variety of focuses that emerged as we considered the needs of different institutions. All writing-beyond-composition programs have as their goal the attainment of some level of competence by the time students complete their degrees, whether that involves two years or four years of study. Although some schools choose to certify that students have achieved a graduation-level writing ability at the end of the senior year (for instance, through their writing performance in a senior capstone project), others certify earlier, as with a junior portfolio. No matter when the certification occurs, the criteria reflect the institution's *de facto* learning outcomes for writing.

However, the focus of these outcomes varies depending on where in the curriculum the institution wants to place its emphasis. Interest in general education reform will lead to more generic sets of outcomes, while a desire to prepare students to write in specific disciplines will yield more localized and discourse-specific outcomes. The former involves constructing a set of general categories and traits that characterize "good college writing," which often invokes stereotypical academic assignments, such as thesis/support papers, term papers, and summaries. However, during our discussions of a possible national outcomes statement, a number of participants voiced concerns that such general outcomes would not satisfy the expectations of faculty and administrators in programs that focus on highly specific and disciplinarily-oriented kinds of writing: crits in design disciplines (Dannels); phase reports in chemical engineering (Dannels, Anson, Bullard, and Perretti); or object condition reports and museum labels in art history, to name just a few examples (see Anson, Dannels, Flash, and Gaffney). In these disciplines, general writing outcomes that specify generic features of texts, such as demonstrating the ability to "organize ideas" or state a "topic or point of view in a well-incorporated opening and closing" ("Scoring Rubric") are either useless because they have no relevance to particular genres, or must be instantiated with much more specific details to "fit" those genres, a frustrating process compared with creating unique rubrics from the start. As a result, some program leaders have focused their efforts at the level of individual departments and programs. In one version of this approach—well illustrated in North Carolina State University's longstanding departmental outcomes effort (see Carter, "Process")—faculty within the programs are given control of assessing their students' writing abilities and implementing whatever curricular changes will improve those abilities. At the heart of this process is the development of writing outcomes that reflect the disciplinary goals, expectations, and values driving the curriculum of each program. In one version of this process, a small group of interested faculty within the department (often guided by a WAC expert) holds series of thoughtful, exploratory meetings to discuss the attributes of successful graduates, including their communication abilities, with the aim of working slowly toward the articulation of a set of learning outcomes (Anson, "Assessing"; Carter, "Process"). These outcomes are unique to each program or major, shaped from the disciplinary and curricular goals of the unit, and the competitive aspirations to prepare its students as effectively as possible. In turn, the unit develops unique and localized methods to assess its outcomes. Having gathered and analyzed data from those assessments, it then puts into place unique curricular changes that best fit the structural, ideological, and pedagogical features of the department and curriculum. In another version of this process, program-specific outcomes are developed by converting longstanding writing-intensive requirements to a department-based model. This conversion is perhaps best illustrated in the University of Minnesota's WEC ("Writing-Enriched Curriculum") program. And in a hybridized version of these examples, several departments at the University of Missouri have longstanding agreements with the Campus Writing Program that their multi-course configurations of writing-intensive courses meet the single writing-in-the-major course requirement.

These various discipline-focused efforts try to be sensitive to the significant variations in the "ways of knowing, doing, and writing" (Carter, "Ways" 388) that characterize different disciplines and departments. A further extension of the effort involves looking beyond the institution itself and appealing to professionals in the field. With support from a three-year grant from the National Science Foundation,

Miami University of Ohio, and North Carolina State University are engaged in developing national communication outcomes specifically for computer science and software engineering programs. This process reaches beyond faculty by enlisting participation from managers and executives in the types of organizations that hire graduates of these programs. Although the outcomes are specific to these two disciplines, they will still need to be adapted to the particular goals, students, and emphases of the computer science and software engineering programs at each institution. In fact, the project involves representatives from fourteen schools as a way of assuring that the resulting outcomes are sufficiently adaptable (Anderson, et al.).

Some implications of the choice between discipline-specific and general writing outcomes become apparent in the process of trying to assess the effectiveness of a writing-beyond-composition program. In the context of higher education in the United States, outcomes are as closely tied to assessment as they are to inputs proven or imagined to achieve them. At many institutions, writing outcomes are being defined so that departments and programs can assess the extent to which they achieve the results they, their institutions, or some external body (a regional or professional accrediting agency, state mandate, or funding agency) say they should achieve. Indeed, a national writing outcomes statement appeals to many writing specialists precisely because of the potential to use the outcomes in assessment that demonstrates either the efficacy of their writing-beyond-composition programs or how far their institution falls short of these standards in order to justify more support—both financial and rhetorical—for their programs. However, institutions trying to conduct direct assessment of student writing against a general set of writing outcomes find it difficult to make judgments when evaluating student samples from a variety of disciplines. Even what constitutes an effective introduction or a style appropriate to the audience, purpose, and context varies considerably from field to field (Anson, Dannels, Flash, and Gaffney). On the other hand, programs employing discipline-specific outcomes encounter difficulty in drawing general conclusions about overall program effectiveness because no set of criteria seems adequate.

A third possible focus on general education writing goals may take a different but equally useful form, emphasizing the ability of college graduates to participate fully in the social, political, and civic discourse of their communities. The professional or disciplinary genres found in discipline-based outcomes may be replaced by "public genres," such as letters to the editor, or by a statement of the kinds of public issues students should be able to address and the kinds of contexts where they would address them (such as civic forums where scientific knowledge about the environment needs to be translated into more publicly accessible language and concepts).

In addition to these three options (a discipline-specific, general, or general-education focus), there are many others. As engaging as it was to ask ourselves what focus our national set of writing outcomes should take (beyond simply recommending that institutions and programs make this decision for themselves), this question brought us no closer to resolution—or a document.

ABSTRACT OR SPECIFIC?

Regardless of focus, a set of national writing outcomes will have to be abstract in the sense that it can be interpreted and applied to many writing-beyond-composition programs. A third challenge of creating such outcomes is finding an appropriate level of generality while still being specific enough to distinguish program-level outcomes from the WPA OS. One such attempt, AAC&U's VALUE Rubric that defines graduation-level outcomes for written communication, is almost indistinguishable from the WPA OS. The following analysis, which contrasts these two documents, illustrates the complexity of arriving at a useful outcomes statement differentiated for developmental stages in a student's educational career.

At the capstone level, the VALUE rubric states that the students' writing "Demonstrates a thorough understanding of context, audience, and purpose that is responsive to the assigned task and focuses all elements of the work." The WPA OS advocates that by the time they complete first-year composition, students should "Respond appropriately to different kinds of rhetorical situations" (context); "Respond to the needs of different audiences"; "Focus on a purpose"; "Use the conventions of format and structure appropriate to the rhetorical situation"; and "Adopt appropriate voice, tone, and level of formality." Such similarities between the two documents abound. The main distinction between them is the level of diction—there is nothing, we believe, that first-year composition programs would judge to be foreign to their aspirations for their courses. One outcome on the WPA OS is that students will "Develop knowledge of genre conventions ranging from structure and paragraphing to tone and mechanics." The parallel outcome in the VALUE statement says that acceptable work at the capstone level "Demonstrates detailed attention and successful execution of a wide range of conventions particular to a specific discipline and/or writing task(s) including organization, content, presentation, formatting, and stylistic choices." Aside from the specification of a "wide range" of conventions, there is little besides diction to distinguish the two. The WPA OS says that students completing first-year composition should "Control such surface features as syntax, grammar, punctuation, and spelling." The VALUE statement specifies that at the capstone level undergraduates should be able to use "graceful language that . . . is virtually error-free." The AAC&U understands the highly abstract nature of the outcomes in its VALUE rubrics, and emphasizes that they should be "translated into the language of individual campuses, disciplines, and even courses" in order to be useful (Rhodes 21). Could the AAC&U VALUES rubric be revised to establish clearer distinctions between outcomes for first-year composition and graduation-level outcomes? In fact, there was an earlier, *first* draft of the AAC&U outcomes—the one that was revised into the items above—that articulates more closely with college-completion outcomes. The current AAC&U outcomes, as indicated, echo the WPA OS: context and purpose for writing; content development; genre and disciplinary conventions; sources and evidence; control of syntax and mechanics. The original draft of these outcomes, however, is much more ambitious, especially in its attention to intentionality and purposefulness: engagement with the subject/s of writing; intentional use of evidence; understanding of and thoughtful decisions about structure; connections between interests and writing; awareness and use of genre/disciplinary conventions; reflection/metacognitive awareness; and awareness of and sensitivity to audience expectations. Moreover, of particular note for a possible set of WAC outcomes are three of the items—engagement with the subject/s of writing; awareness and use of genre/disciplinary conventions; and reflection/metacognitive awareness.

The first, *engagement with the subjects of writing*, assumes that such engagement will occur over several courses (and possibly in co-curricular contexts like internships); in that sense, it is both developmental and programmatic, with, presumably, program-supporting development. As important, according to the Harvard Study of Writing, it is the ability to *engage*—with both topic and audience—that characterizes student development in writing. Focusing on a student named Luisa as an example, Nancy Sommers outlines what such engagement looks like:

> From her muddled thinking as a first-year student to her senior paper, she learns to hold a thought and to become, in her own words, "a person with things to say." It is through writing—that is, through understanding a larger role for writing than just completing a single assignment—that Luisa claims her education, argues with views and opinions different from her own, and learns to reach beyond herself to engage readers. And it is through writing that Luisa learns to shape her personal interests into public ones, moving into the wider world as a thoughtful and educated citizen. (162)

As formulated here, institutional writing programs foster both the *engag[ing] of readers and the shap[ing] of personal interests into public ones*. Any good list of outcomes for first-year composition could—and, we hope, does—set the stage for this kind of engagement, extending both vertically through the years and spatially outside the academy. As an outcome achieved, however, such engagement would progress (and, we hope, culminate) inside a WAC program.

The second proposed AAC&U writing outcome, *awareness and use of genre/disciplinary conventions*, resonates with the WPA OS. There are two significant differences, however. The first is that the role of genre isn't entirely clear in the WPA OS, given that it appears in two categories: is it rhetorical knowledge, where it appears as "Understand how genres shape reading and writing" and "Write in several genres"? Or is it conventions, where it appears as "Develop knowledge of genre conventions ranging from structure and paragraphing to tone and mechanics"? In the one case, it appears closer to genre as social action, while in the second, it seems more a matter of format. In fact, under conventions, format is mentioned first—"Learn common formats for different kinds of texts"—thus underscoring its relationship to genre. Genre is related to both categories. In one sense, it's a useful redundancy to have genre appear twice, but if that is the logic, why not have it appear in the writing processes category as well, since genre serves as a heuristic for writing tasks? The point, then, is that genre as a concept and practice doesn't seem well theorized in the WPA OS.

Furthermore, the WPA OS's relationship to discourse communities—as we see in works like Anne Beaufort's *College Writing and Beyond* and Anis Bawarshi and MaryJo Reiff's *Genre: An Introduction To History, Theory, Research, And Pedagogy*—isn't included at all. Without the linkage between genre and discourse communities that is so central to WAC, it is difficult to see how genre performs as much more than format. While genre awareness in the proposed AAC&U outcomes is a good thing—not unlike the understanding specified in the WPA OS—neither understanding nor awareness may be sufficient, according to Bawarshi and Reiff. They acknowledge that conclusions on this issue are difficult to draw, but it appears that for genre to function as a salient factor in student writing, some mix of explicit and implicit attention to it is required. Beaufort makes a similar point, arguing that we would need not awareness or understanding of genre but *knowledge of it*.

The third proposed AAC&U outcome is *reflection/metacognitive awareness*, a familiar feature in the context of portfolios of writing, but increasingly understood as the metaphorical tie that binds, as we see in the general research accounts like the National Research Council's *How People Learn*; in local studies like the University of Washington's *Inside the Undergraduate Experience* (Beyer, Gillmore, and Fisher); and in writing studies research like Yancey's *The Things They Carried: Transfer, Composition, and Cultures of Writing*. Again, while it's not clear precisely what is the appropriate mix of reflective questions, activities, and texts to foster writing development, the research is clear. The University of Washington study demonstrates that when students reflect on their experiences, their performance is enhanced. To build this goal into an outcome would lead us to devise a curriculum supporting this development as well.

We might well ask this: Without the kinds of outcomes described in the AAC&U document, will students progressively engage with topics, genres, and audiences; know and practice diverse genres; and use reflection as the connective tissue mapping this writing knowledge and practice? They may, of course, as our own experiences with students suggest, but when they do so, they do so on their own. If this is the development and achievement we hope for our students, then we owe it to them to articulate it. Such articulation engages and constructs us all—writing specialists, disciplinary faculty, and administrators alike—and is also the purpose of designing outcomes.

Another complication we faced in trying to construct a national writing outcomes statement was determining the extent to which the statement should address writing alone versus the extent to which it should include a larger collection of communication outcomes. In the spirit of the communication-across-the-curriculum movement, our abandoned draft mentioned the communication experts' support for the "widespread integration of writing, speaking, and other media." Some of our lists of "guiding principles" described features of "writing and speaking assignments." Like other professional accrediting agencies, ABET includes "an ability to apply written, oral, and graphical communication in both technical and non-technical environments" among its criteria, without specifying the media, genre, audiences, or purposes of the communication. In the aforementioned project, sponsored by the National Science Foundation, that focuses on computer science and software engineering, Anderson, Burge, Carter, Gannod, and Vouk address writing as intertwined with speaking, reading, teaming, and listening. Similarly, Louisiana State University incorporates written, spoken, visual, and technological elements in its Communication Across the Curriculum program. Integration of writing outcomes with other related communication outcomes makes a great deal of sense, but complicates the project of creating a national set of writing outcomes (see also the process of establishing communication outcomes described in Anson, Carter, Dannels, and Rust, and in Carter, "Process"—which describe the difficulty and theoretical inadvisability of divorcing communication outcomes from other learning outcomes within the disciplines).

WRITING SKILLS OR DISCIPLINARY LEARNING?

As we wrestled with questions of generality and specificity, we also recognized the differences between the role of writing in first-year composition and in content-based courses across the disciplines. Explicit instruction often finds varied support in content-area courses: faculty who feel the pressure to sufficiently "cover" a body of material may devote little time to writing in general-education courses (beyond assigning and grading it), while those who teach limited-enrollment capstone or other courses in the upper reaches of their disciplines may feel compelled to help students develop specific discipline-based writing skills. In general, however, the absence of a focus on "writing about writing" that Debra Frank Dew describes (Chapter 1) in connection with the WPA OS (as a reflection of current practice in first-year composition) is even more dramatically absent in courses beyond composition.

We also found ourselves viewing outcomes for writing in the context of the varied roles that writing plays in courses beyond composition. In some WAC orientations, writing serves the purpose of promoting deeper or more critical reading and analysis of course material or more energized and engaged class discussions—that is, writing used primarily to foster richer learning (see Bean). To achieve these goals, faculty may use low-stakes assignments in a variety of unique and creative genres, whose formal characteristics (structure, presence or absence of a thesis, correct grammar) receive little attention in favor of closer attention to students' connection with the material and their insightful or probing reflection on it. In other cases, faculty may require comparatively high-stakes assignments, ranging from short genre-based papers to longer research papers that are designed to "test" students' understanding of the discipline's concepts and conventions. To achieve these goals, faculty attend to (and assess for) a more stringent level of textual performance, and a student's task becomes "learning to write" in adherence to the rhetorical expectations and discursive characteristics of the discipline.

As we discovered, these varied, course-specific goals are challenging to represent in a generalized set of outcomes. Whereas the WPA OS, precisely because it functions within a more coherent discourse community, could be based on reasonable consensus about what a required first-year writing course should do to prepare entering students for their academic careers, the varied purposes of writing in a wide array of disciplinary contexts militate against such consensus. While there is little question that first-year composition represents an almost bewildering variety of approaches, contents, and pedagogical strategies, it's less difficult for WPAs and writing teachers to agree that students need to "Develop flexible strategies for generating, revising, editing, and proof-reading" than it is for teachers of soil science, mechanical engineering, musicology, or biochemistry to see these strategies as central to their own instruction and to the time they devote to supporting students' learning. Our discussions with faculty in these and dozens of other disciplines suggest that they have highly focused learning goals into which writing may be woven with varied emphasis, from central to peripheral.

The Road Ahead

In spite of the challenges we faced trying to create a national set of outcomes for writing beyond the composition course, we don't think such a project is Sisyphean and should be abandoned. In light of our experience, we propose some suggestions for the form the outcomes might take, and the package in which they might be presented to be most useful at individual institutions.

1. As is clear from our own journey, any attempt to create an outcomes statement that will have some national or international utility must begin by taking the writing-beyond-composition perspective, grounding the statement in what we are learning in our work with WAC, WID, WIC, Communication Across the Curriculum (CAC), and their variants. This perspective enables us to add our expertise in writing as we define graduation-level outcomes that overlap with, but are distinct from, outcomes for first-year composition and from the kinds of general education outcomes presented in documents like the VALUE rubric.
2. Leaders of writing-beyond-composition programs must persuade their institutions to include graduation-level writing outcomes in the larger set of comprehensive outcomes their institutions espouse. Many U.S. institutions are in the midst of creating or refining graduation-level outcomes for regional and professional accreditation. Merely expanding a sentence that says graduates "will be able to communicate clearly and correctly" to include genre, audience, and purpose would be an important step because the addition raises awareness—and assessment efforts—about the complexity of the writing-related knowledge and skills the institution needs to provide. Although this step would not provide specific information needed to create and assess discipline-specific outcomes, it would at least call attention to the need for the process and serve some heuristic value in that effort, paving the way for further refinements.

3. The creation of graduation-level outcomes for writing should take lessons from the AAC&U. Although the process that AAC&U used to develop its outcomes was not identical to the one we envisioned for our project (which was modeled partly on how the WPA OS was created), the two processes have obvious similarities. They both begin by soliciting ideas from writing specialists and they involve checking drafts repeatedly with specialists before settling on the final form. For example, we imagined that, after thorough discussion and multiple drafts within communities of writing scholars, we would send the statement to disciplinary groups, who are crucial stakeholders in all beyond-composition efforts, for their input and suggestions for further revision.

4. An outcomes statement for beyond-composition assessment should emphasize the necessity of adapting them to specific institutions, as does the AAC&U. Through much trial and error, we have learned the futility of dropping generic principles, practices, or policies into institutions such as Historically Black Colleges and Universities (HBCUs), community colleges, large research-extensive universities, small private liberal arts colleges, or tribal colleges, and expecting them to be woven effectively into the fabric of those diverse contexts. Nothing about adapting outcomes to local contexts is easy; no statement should promise anything but the rewards of that labor-intensive adaptation.

5. A usable outcomes statement also needs to be understandable to persons outside of writing studies. The WPA OS was written first for those who administer and teach in writing programs, but with an eye to the broader audiences who have a stake in those programs and/or collaborate with them (such as libraries, teaching and learning centers, or tutorial services). Outcomes for writing beyond composition, however, address even broader audiences and must be comprehensible to administrators and colleagues from other disciplines—in terms they understand and can act on in the context of specialized areas of inquiry. Some of the AAC&U's strategies may help make the outcomes understandable to people unfamiliar with the traditions and terminology used in writing studies. The AAC&U model includes not only a framing statement and glossary, but

also careful attention to the language used to describe the outcomes themselves.
6. An outcomes statement is most effective if unencumbered by many provisions, explanations, and implementation strategies. However, alone, such a statement is also insufficient. Perhaps bound or digitally linked to the outcomes statement, a separate document could include detailed advice and examples useful in adapting to specific institutions the abstractions and programs that a national set of outcomes will necessarily offer. Such a document could provide both advice for starting and maintaining an outcomes-based writing process within programs and majors and national exemplars of what that process has yielded at particular institutions.
7. A supplement could provide advice for using the outcomes to advocate for greater institutional support, both monetary and motivational, for writing-beyond-composition programs. Although it would be naïve to claim that English departments or composition programs can implement the provisions of the WPA OS without additional costs for professional development and curricular re-design, the scope of the work is perhaps greater in other disciplines, in part because they are not already steeped in theories and pedagogies of writing. Achieving writing-beyond-composition outcomes could involve additional investments for faculty support and new assessment and continuous improvement programs.
8. The statement will also need to be supplemented with current thinking about best practices for achieving its outcomes, and that will inevitably involve the inclusion of many voices. When the four of us started this conversation, we began such a document, but we don't claim ownership of it. Many others share the needed expertise and have important talent and credentials to bring to bear on the task.

The Promise of Continued Work

In chronicling our journey toward a national outcomes statement for writing beyond composition, and in outlining steps that might follow, we have become even more aware not only of the complexities inherent in the task, but also in the benefits of having such a document. It may be that no single set of individuals within our own field can accomplish the task, as was possible with the still difficult but nonetheless comparatively disciplinarily-contained WPA OS. Given the far wider set of academic and disciplinary professionals that inevitably must be involved in a WAC outcomes document, it could be that this task more logically belongs to a consortium comprised of teacher-scholars from across the disciplines, one that could be supported by a grant from Fund for the Improvement of Postsecondary Education (FIPSE) or some other funding source. Such a proposal is complicated by the lack of a national WAC organization to lobby for it. While WAC scholars and practitioners claim affiliation with CCCC and WPA, neither of those organizations is charged specifically with WAC responsibilities. One advantage, though, of a multi-disciplinary, nationally-based task force, constituted by a high-level professional organization, is that at such time as a draft document were ready for vetting, access to national discipline-based organizations would be more straightforward. Certainly the influence of such a task force would be greater than that of an *ad hoc* group of individuals no matter how influential they may be in our own field.

To that end, we are eager to continue the conversation.

WORKS CITED

ABET. "Criteria for Accrediting Engineering Technology Programs, 2012-2012." ABET, 29 Oct. 2011. Web. 25 July 2012.

Anderson, Paul, and Raymond F. Gorman. "Be Brave in This New World: Maximizing the 'Use Value' of the Higher Learning Commission Program to Evaluate and Advance Educational Quality." *A Collection of Papers on Self-Study and Institutional Improvement, 2005, Volume 4: Commission Processes for Maintaining Affiliation*. Chicago, IL: Higher Learning Commission of the North Central Association, 2005. 1–10. Print.

Anderson, Paul, Janet Burge, Michael Carter, Jerry Gannod, and Mladen Vouk. *Integrating Communication Into the Computer Science and Software Engineering Curriculum: An NSF-Sponsored Project—October 2009 to October 2012*. n.d. Web. 31 July 2011.

Anderson, Paul, Chris M. Anson, Martha Townsend, and Kathleen Blake Yancey. "Outcomes for Writing Across the Curriculum: Starting the Conversation." 2007 WPA Summer Conference, Tempe, AZ. 14 July 2007. Address.

Anson, Chris M. "Assessment in Action: A Mobius Tale." *Assessment in Technical and Professional Communication.* Ed. Margaret Hundleby and Jo Allen. Amityville, NY: Baywood, 2010. 3–15. Print.

—. "Assessing Writing in Cross-Curricular Programs: Determining the Locus of Activity." *Assessing Writing* 11 (2006): 100–112. Print.

Anson, Chris M., Deanna Dannels, Pamela Flash, and Amy L. Housley Gaffney. "Big Rubrics and Weird Genres: The Futility of Using Generic Assessment Tools Across Diverse Instructional Contexts." *Journal of Writing Assessment.* 5.1 (2012): n. pag. Web. 26 May 2012..

Anson, Chris M., Michael Carter, Deanna Dannels, and Jon Rust. "Mutual Support: CAC Programs and Institutional Improvement in Undergraduate Education." *Language and Learning Across the Disciplines* 6.3 (2003): 26–38. Web. 31 July 2011.

Bawarshi, Anis, and Mary Jo Reiff. *Genre: An Introduction To History, Theory, Research, And Pedagogy.* West Lafayette, IN: Parlor Press, 2010. Print.

Beaufort, Anne. *College Writing and Beyond.* Logan, UT: Utah State UP, 2007. Print.

Bean, John C. *Engaging Ideas: The Professor's Guide to Integrating Writing, Critical Thinking, and Active Learning in the Classroom.* San Francisco: Jossey Bass, 1996. Print.

Beyer, Catherine Hoffman, Gerald M. Gillmore, and Andrew T. Fisher. *Inside the Undergraduate Experience: The University of Washington's Study of Undergraduate Learning.* Hoboken, NJ: Jossey Bass, 2007. Print.

Carter, Michael. "A Process for Establishing Outcomes-Based Assessment Plans for Writing and Speaking in the Disciplines." *Language and Learning Across the Disciplines,* 6.1 (2003). Web. 31 July 2011.

—. "Ways of Knowing, Doing, and Writing in the Disciplines." *College Composition and Communication,* 58.3 (2007): 385–418. Print.

Council of Writing Program Administrators [with responses by Clyde A. Moneyhun; Keith Rhodes; Mark Wiley; Kathleen Blake Yancey]. "The WPA Outcomes Statement for First-Year Composition." *WPA: Writing Program Administration* 23.1–2 (1999): 59–70. Print.

Dannels, Deanna P. "Performing Tribal Rituals: A Genre Analysis of 'Crits' in Design Studios." *Communication Education,* 54.2 (2005):136–60. Print.

Dannels, Deanna P., Chris M. Anson, Lisa Bullard, and Steven Peretti. "Challenges in Learning Communication Skills in Chemical Engineering." *Communication Education* 52.1 (2003): 50–56. Print.

National Council of Teachers of English. *Statement on Class Size and Teacher Workload: College.* NCTE, 1987. Web. 31 July 2011.

National Research Council. *How People Learn: Brain, Mind, Experience, and School.* Expanded ed. National Research Council, 2000. Web. 25 July 2012.

"Scoring Rubric: Generic Writing." Greenwood Skills Center. Santa Barbara: Greenwood Publishing Group, 2010. Web. 31 July 2011.

Rhodes, Terrel L., ed. *Assessing Outcomes and Improving Achievement: Tips and Tools for Using Rubrics*. Washington. D.C.: Association of American Colleges and Universities, 2010. Print.

Sommers, Nancy. "Symposium: The Call of Research: A Longitudinal View of Writing Development." *College Composition and Communication*, 60.1 (2008): 152–64. Print.

Written Communication VALUE Rubric. Washington, D.C.: Association of American Colleges and Universities. Web. 31 July 2011.

Yancey, Kathleen Blake. *The Things They Carried: Transfer, Composition, and Cultures of Writing*. Logan, UT: Utah State UP. Forthcoming.

8 The WPA Outcomes Statement and Disciplinary Authority

Craig Jacobsen, Susan Miller-Cochran, and Shelley Rodrigo

The introduction to the WPA Outcomes Statement for First-Year Composition (WPA OS) notes that the document's purpose is "to regularize what can be expected to be taught in first-year composition." Fulfillment of this ambitious goal is contingent upon a host of critical conditions, some disciplinary, some institutional, and some political. For the WPA OS to effect change across a meaningful percentage of the nation's first-year composition programs requires that the document successfully embody the rhetorical principles it valorizes. It must, appropriately enough, do much of what it asks of first-year composition (FYC) students.

As the WPA OS acknowledges, its writers saw the document's primary audience as "well-prepared college writing teachers and college writing program administrators," for whom the WPA OS is written "in their professional language," a language in which, within the WPA OS's imagined discourse community, "terms such as 'rhetorical' and 'genre' convey a rich meaning that is not easily simplified." The WPA OS also identifies an important secondary audience, stating that "we have also aimed at writing a document that the general public can understand." Recognizing the difficulty of writing effectively to a dramatically bifurcated audience, the WPA OS writers indicate that they have privileged "communicating effectively with expert writing teachers and writing program administrators." The explicit statement of intended audiences provides important cues for the interpretation of the WPA OS as a document composed primarily for an audience possessing a high degree of disciplinary knowledge. As the statement itself acknowledges, its primary audience is the exceptional first-year composition teacher, not the average one.

The process of enacting the WPA OS's purpose of regularizing the outcomes of first-year composition is complicated by the document's intended audience, as regularizing outcomes likely involves rewriting curriculum at many institutions. Curriculum revision, like learning to write, is "a complex process, both individual and social, that takes place over time with continued practice and informed guidance" (WPA OS). Curriculum revision is necessarily collaborative, and often engages participants from within the discipline who possess various degrees of disciplinary knowledge and experience, and staff and administration who do not possess any disciplinary background in rhetoric and composition. Further complicating that process is the reality that many, if not most, of the faculty involved in nationwide curricular revision will neither be part of the "general public," nor what the WPA OS calls "expert writing teachers and writing program administrators." The realities of first-year composition instruction mean that faculty implementing the WPA OS will include a small number of experts and a large number of faculty with backgrounds in areas other than rhetoric and composition—along with a significant number of contingent faculty, graduate teaching assistants, and non-experts.

The ability of the WPA OS to accomplish its stated purpose is inextricably tied up in its utility within a real-world process by which institutional curricula are revised. The revision of the two-course, first-year composition sequence in the Maricopa County Community College District tested the WPA OS's usefulness in changing curriculum within a multi-college system. Although every institution's unique circumstances indicate that there is likely no typical scenario for curriculum change based upon the WPA OS, the complexity of the process in Maricopa presented a particularly wide range of challenges to the WPA OS's ability to address the needs of multiple audiences. Critical examination of its effectiveness within various rhetorical situations can help to illuminate the WPA OS's utility in a process of curriculum revision.

Institutional Context

The Maricopa County Community College District (MCCCD) is a ten-college system serving the greater Phoenix metropolitan area.

Together, the colleges enroll more than 250,000 students annually in a wide range of academic and occupational disciplines. Although the colleges are largely autonomous, articulation agreements are made at the district level, and so the basic curriculum must be common across the ten colleges. To help ensure commonality and consistency, the district instituted a "course bank" format in 1988, which remains largely unchanged. Each course offered is defined in the course bank in three parts: a brief course description that appears in scheduling material, a list of course competencies, and an outline of course content.

Faculty members develop new course definitions and revise existing courses, although few faculty members have coursework or formal training in curriculum design or in the use of the district's own system. Historically, the result has been that course bank competencies, abilities that students should be able to demonstrate by the end of the course, have often been articulated instead as activities, as exercises students undertake within a course. Additionally, course competencies must be tied explicitly to the outline of course content, privileging course competencies that look like descriptions of content instead of student learning outcomes. Instead of defining the aims of courses and providing useful tools for course and program assessment, course bank definitions often have been seen as mere templates for a syllabus.

The multi-college nature of curriculum development and revision in the MCCCD means that, although change can be initiated by a single faculty member, all faculty members in the appropriate discipline in all of the ten colleges can ultimately participate in the process. Because the first-year composition sequence (ENG101 and ENG102) is so embedded within the academic transfer and occupational certificate programs of the district, altering the FYC courses comes with a host of institutional complications. Before those complications could become an issue, however, someone—or those within a particular entity within the district—had to initiate change.

In the case of the MCCCD first-year composition revisions, that change began in Mesa Community College's (MCC) English department. MCC is the largest of the district's colleges, enrolling approximately 25,000 students, approximately 9,000 of whom enroll each semester in classes offered by the department. With forty full-time faculty members, the department hires as many as one hundred part-time faculty members per semester. Just five miles from the Tempe campus of Arizona State University (ASU), MCC has a complex relationship with that institution. MCC's relatively smaller size and accessibility, coupled with significantly lower tuition and fees, helps explain why sixty-eight percent of MCC's students begin at MCC and indicates that they intend to transfer to ASU or another university. Historically, the MCC English department faculty has had strong ties to Arizona State as well, with many full-time and part-time instructors having earned degrees and taught at the university. At the start of the twenty-first century, in fact, MCC began hiring graduates of ASU's PhD program in Rhetoric/Composition and Linguistics, or those who had been trained as teaching assistants by ASU's rhetoric and composition faculty. Further, some MCC faculty returned to ASU to earn doctorates in rhetoric and composition, as many held MAs in literature. Although many long-time faculty members at MCC became instrumental to the revisions of ENG101 and ENG102, the initial impulse had come from a small but growing group of relatively new English faculty at MCC. Frustrated by the outdated and overly restrictive course definitions, and lacking a writing program administrator to lead change, these newer faculty members decided to begin a discussion about how the curriculum might be revised.

WPA OS as Impetus for Revision

In 2002, when serious discussion began about revising the FYC sequence, Mesa Community College's English department had no internal apparatus for managing such work. The department had no standing committees, and decisions were made either by the department chair or within the context of monthly department meetings. Faculty course releases—which had been used primarily for facilitating periodic assessment and maintenance of the existing ENG 101 and 102 courses—had been cut by administration the year before. Despite serving nearly ten thousand students every semester, the department lacked a writing program administrator. Scheduling, faculty evaluations, and all other duties for which a WPA might be responsible were in the hands of the department chair. The task of revising course descriptions, which would affect every academic transfer or degree and many occupational certificate programs at ten colleges, was clearly neither a task for one person (the chair) nor forty (the department). Discussions began within a semi-formal group, not yet a true committee, who agreed to meet twice monthly at lunch.

The makeup of this group is important because it is unclear whether its constituents qualified as the WPA OS's primary audience: "expert writing teachers and writing program administrators." Although the informal nature of the group meant that attendees varied, regular contributors covered the full spectrum of experience and formal preparation in rhetoric and composition. Faculty members who had been teaching writing for nearly four decades worked with those with less than half-a-dozen years of experience. Faculty members with newly minted doctorates in rhetoric and composition attended and participated alongside those who had earned MAs in literature decades before. As a result, and as might be expected, familiarity with recent scholarship within the discipline ranged widely. This diversity is significant because it reflects in microcosm the diversity of the MCC English department, the FYC faculty of all ten colleges in the Maricopa County Community College District, and likely is a fair representation, a microcosm, of the nationwide diversity of those who teach first-year composition.

Despite its modest-seeming claims about itself, the WPA OS is a remarkably coherent statement of what the disparate members of any complex, significant academic discipline could agree should be the baseline expectations for students who have earned FYC credit. For faculty members in institutions that seem to have fallen out of touch with the current state of the discipline, and as a way to educate those outside of the field both in and outside of home departments, such a clear articulation, expressing the philosophy of scholar-teachers in the field, bears a particular kind of authority that would supersede a singly-authored, if equally significant, document. Consequently, the WPA OS proved effective at MCC. Although the WPA OS was not the sole motivator for updating the writing curriculum, the desire to be more in-sync with the WPA OS (and thereby with the current state of the discipline) fueled faculty members' efforts at revision.

WPA OS as Focus of Discussion

While characterized by optimism, initial talks about revising the curriculum were somewhat challenging. Faculty at MCC had a long tradition of autonomy, and it quickly became clear that attempts to develop a shared, coherent vision of first-year composition would be difficult. The MCC English department was characterized by faculty holding divergent philosophies about the ways in which writing should be taught. The range of philosophies and pedagogical approaches reflected the diversity of faculty education and experience. The best starting point for the group meeting at MCC was a review of the existing course competencies:

Pre-Revision MCCCD Official Course Competencies for ENG 101

- Generate essay topics from reading, discussion and observation.
- Select a general topic suitable for development in an essay of a specified length and for a specific audience and purpose.
- Compose a thesis statement suitable for development in an essay.
- Use a thesis statement and support to create a well-organized plan for an essay.
- Write an essay introduction which creates interest and states the thesis.
- Write support paragraphs which develop the thesis statement of an essay; contain topic sentences; display unity, coherence, and completeness; and contain specific information and concrete detail.
- Write a conclusion which follows logically from the body of the essay.
- Use diction which sustains a consistent level of formality; demonstrates originality; has appropriate connotations/denotations; and reflects effective, appropriate, and original imagery.
- In a minimum of five essays select and effectively use appropriate rhetorical patterns for a specific purpose and audience employing any combination of the following: exemplification, comparison/contrast, classification, causal analysis, narration, description, process analysis, definition, and essay response.
- Write an essay of argumentation which demonstrates sound logical development.
- Revise the draft of an essay to demonstrate attention to audience, purpose, organization, style, mechanics and sentence structure. ("Maricopa County Community Colleges ENG 101 19956–20055")

Pre-Revision MCCCD Official Course Competencies for ENG 102

- Select and focus a topic appropriate for one research paper of 1,500–2,500 words or two 1,000 word papers.

- Compile a preliminary bibliography of potential research resources.
- Use a variety of print and on-line library resources, including electronic databases, to locate information on the selected topic.
- Use effective strategies for taking and organizing notes.
- Analyze, interpret and evaluate information found in research sources.
- Paraphrase in language that is distinctly the student's and quote source information accurately in order to avoid plagiarism.
- Summarize a passage to reflect the central idea, most significant supporting details, order, and emphasis of the original work.
- Compose an outline with an effective pattern of organization for the paper.
- Compose a focused and clearly stated thesis for the paper.
- Compose a research paper of 1,500–2,500 words (or two papers of 1,000 words each), integrating cited information in summary, paraphrase and quotation to support the thesis.
- Document information from research sources, using Modern Language Association (MLA) or other current standard documentation form.
- Revise the draft of the paper, incorporating feedback received during editing, to produce a finished research paper that observes standard English usage and manuscript form.
- Explain and practice the principles of academic integrity throughout the research, writing and revision process.
- Write a minimum of three additional papers which involve critical reading and writing. One of these will be an essay exam.
- Write at least one argumentation paper which demonstrates sound, logical development. ("Maricopa County Community Colleges ENG 102 19986–20055")

Initial discussion among the attendees focused on the narrow vision of writing that the course competencies represented and their inconsistent status as competencies. Although members of the group were unanimously dissatisfied (though to varying degrees) with the existing course competencies as accurate descriptions of the courses as taught, it was not immediately clear what direction revision might, or even could, take. The WPA OS was introduced at an early meeting of the revision group and contextualized through an explanation of the process of its composition and revision. Within weeks of the start of discussion of FYC curriculum revision, the WPA OS had already occupied a position of disciplinary authority, reflecting the current state of thought in the study of rhetoric and composition.

Given this authority, it was tempting to simply adopt the WPA OS in its entirety. Researching what other institutions had done with the WPA OS revealed that some, including Arizona State University, had done just that, incorporating the full text into program mission statements or linking to the text from department websites. The nature of curriculum within the Maricopa County Community College District, however, meant that a meaningful embodiment of the ideals of the WPA OS within FYC in the district meant revising course bank definitions of ENG 101 and ENG 102. Adapting the WPA OS to fit the MCCCD course bank format meant engaging in a long and complex process of interpretation, translation, and explanation. Even in small-scale discussions among like-minded colleagues, it quickly became apparent that the document is entrenched in disciplinary knowledge, history, and language whose mastery requires a focus on rhetoric and composition studies far from universal among teachers of first-year composition—and that the MCC audience was far more complex than that implied by the WPA OS.

Although the WPA OS's disciplinary authority kept it at or near the center of discussions of curriculum revision, many of the early meetings of the group were dominated by attempts to come to a shared understanding of the document's history, intentions, and vocabulary. At times, these debates seemed only to delay getting to the point of the group's meetings—revising the competencies for first-year composition. As terminology was negotiated and positions were articulated, however, it became increasingly clear that the discussions were the point of the meetings, and that the revised competencies were a reflection of that work, not the sole product of it.

Even a cursory comparison of the language of the pre-revision course competencies for ENG 101 and ENG 102, with the language of the WPA OS, reveals striking differences that fueled extensive conversation. The pre-revision competencies largely treat writing as a decontextualized exercise in the assembly of discrete elements (e.g., thesis statement, topic sentence, support paragraph, introduction), and even the brief references to audience and purpose in the ENG 101 competencies are lost in the competencies for the sequence's second course.

The WPA OS's concerns with context, and its more conceptual focus, generated lengthy conversation about the context of first-year composition itself. Who is FYC's audience? What is its purpose? How can the course definitions, embodied in the lists of competencies, be revised to reflect the kinds of complex thinking about writing that the WPA OS presents?

WPA OS as Template for Revision

When discussion had advanced to the point that group members felt confident that they largely shared definitions of crucial terms, the first rounds of drafting new competencies for the two first-year composition courses began. Rather than focus on reworking the existing course definitions, the group elected to begin with the WPA OS in-hand, fashioning competencies that reflected the language and philosophy of the statement.

As the WPA OS makes clear, effective writing addresses its rhetorical situation, and the process of adapting the WPA OS to the needs of the Maricopa County Community College District course bank was predominantly an exercise in reframing the concepts to fit the needs of the district's ten colleges. Take, for example, the first competency listed in both the new ENG 101 and ENG 102 definitions: "Analyze specific rhetorical contexts, including circumstance, purpose, topic, audience, and writer, as well as the writing's ethical, political, and cultural implications" ("Maricopa County Community Colleges ENG 101 20056–99999"; "Maricopa County Community Colleges ENG 102 20056–99999"). This competency synthesizes three of the WPA OS outcomes listed under "Rhetorical Knowledge." It also articulates MCC's English faculty members' insistence that students understand the ethical, political, and cultural implications of writing. Less obviously, this competency statement reflects concerns that many of the hundreds of faculty members teaching first-year composition in the district would perhaps lack the disciplinary knowledge to be able to quickly define "rhetorical contexts;" therefore, a definition of that term is incorporated into the competency statement.

The audience of the Maricopa district's course bank was an important consideration in the revision of the first-year composition competencies. Every semester, the colleges hire first-time college composition teachers. Although every instructor must hold at least a Master's degree, and have a minimum number of upper-division and graduate credit hours in English, there is no institutional requirement that FYC instructors have formal training in teaching writing. Some of the colleges provide workshops and other kinds of support for contingent faculty; many do not. In revising the course bank definitions, making them self-explanatory for inexperienced, inexpert instructors remained a high priority, as evidenced in the repeated inclusion of brief explanatory lists within the revised competencies:

Post-Revision MCCCD Official Course Competencies for ENG 101

- Analyze specific rhetorical contexts, including circumstance, purpose, topic, audience, and writer, as well as the writing's ethical, political, and cultural implications.
- Organize writing to support a central idea through unity, coherence, and logical development appropriate to a specific writing context.
- Use appropriate conventions in writing, including consistent voice, tone, diction, grammar, and mechanics.
- Summarize, paraphrase and quote from sources to maintain academic integrity and to develop and support one's own ideas.
- Use feedback obtained from peer review, instructor comments and/or other resources to revise writing.
- Assess one's own writing strengths and identify strategies for improvement through instructor conference, portfolio review, written evaluation, and/or other methods.
- Generate, format, and edit writing using appropriate technologies. ("Maricopa County Community Colleges ENG 101 20056–99999")

Post-Revision MCCCD Official Course Competencies for ENG 102

- Write for specific rhetorical contexts, including circumstance, purpose, topic, audience and writer, as well as the writing's ethical, political, and cultural implications.
- Organize writing to support a central idea through unity, coherence and logical development appropriate to a specific writing context.
- Use appropriate conventions in writing, including consistent voice, tone, diction, grammar, and mechanics.

- Find, evaluate, select, and synthesize both online and print sources that examine a topic from multiple perspectives.
- Integrate sources through summarizing, paraphrasing, and quotation from sources to develop and support one's own ideas.
- Identify, select and use an appropriate documentation style to maintain academic integrity.
- Use feedback obtained through peer review, instructor comments, and/or other sources to revise writing.
- Assess one's own writing strengths and identify strategies for improvement through instructor conference, portfolio review, written evaluation, and/or other methods.
- Generate, format, and edit writing using appropriate technologies. ("Maricopa County Community Colleges ENG 102 20056–99999")

WPA OS as Disciplinary Authority

The process of designing and revising curricula in the Maricopa County Community College District is complicated and recursive. Although any faculty member can design a course or submit revisions, the process requires approval of the district's English Instructional Council (EIC), where representatives of each of the ten colleges' departments of English debate proposed changes and solicit input from their faculty members. The college proposing the change, in this case MCC, also takes the proposal through its campus curriculum committee, and eventually the district curriculum committee makes the final determination. It can be a cumbersome and frustrating process that cycles recursively as each body makes revisions that then have to be approved by the others.

Before any of this process could be engaged, though, the revision committee brought the draft before all of the full-time faculty members in the MCC English department to ensure that the committee's work represented the department's view of FYC. The WPA OS was presented to the department as both an impetus for change and an appeal to disciplinary authority. The case was made that the revised FYC competencies would put the college and district in line with current scholarship on the teaching of writing. Whether this appeal was necessary was unclear, because the department unanimously approved the proposed curriculum revisions with little discussion. In a less complex situation, the revisions would have been near completion, but nine other English departments remained to be convinced.

Approval at the district level required lobbying for the support of all of the representatives to the EIC, who did not receive the proposed changes unprepared. Throughout the process at MCC, representatives of the college's revision committee made informal presentations to the council as the work proceeded. Council representatives discussed the need for revisions, examined the WPA OS, and generally agreed that revision was necessary. When the MCC committee presented its polished draft, it was subjected to district-wide scrutiny through a number of institutional mechanisms, primarily through EIC members' soliciting input from the members of the English faculty at the respective colleges, and from a district-wide, half-day meeting of interested members of the English faculty. A number of concerns surfaced.

One of the primary concerns was that each campus was accustomed to putting its own stamp on the ENG 101/102 sequence, and faculty members did not want their hands tied by what they saw as a curriculum leaning too heavily toward teaching rhetorically-based argument (the focus of many of the faculty members at MCC who had been involved in the informal committee discussions). Conversely, a number of faculty worried that the new competencies were too vague, raising the issue of rigor. For example, the loss of the term "thesis," present repeatedly in pre-revision competencies, but absent in the proposed revisions, sparked heated debate. As had been the case at every stage of the process, the WPA OS was presented to help to contextualize the proposed revisions. Unsurprisingly, this appeal had mixed results, convincing many that the existing course definitions were embarrassingly dated while also engaging resentment of outside authority. In conversations about individual elements of the proposed revisions, individual experience was frequently cited to counter disciplinary authority.

Interestingly, some of the objections to the revisions grew out of precisely the awareness of circumstance that helped to guide the writing of the new competencies. Several faculty members expressed concerns that non-expert adjunct faculty members would be unable to construct syllabi that effectively helped students meet the competencies. Although the course bank definitions were not intended to serve as syllabi templates, the old ENG 101 and ENG 102 could function as such, given that they identified numbers of essay assignments, the kinds of acceptable essays, and even word counts. The revised competencies, adhering to the spirit of the WPA OS, eschewed such guidelines in favor of allowing instructors the freedom to construct classes as they saw fit, so long as they met the competencies. The tension between the desire for campus and instructor autonomy and the concern for rigor was resolved in a change that left the revised competencies intact, but added a course note (unusual for the district course bank) that specified a minimum number of written assignments and a minimum total word count. With approval from the EIC, the proposed revisions moved out of the discipline and into the hands of new audiences.

The next step in the process of revising the curriculum was to submit the proposed changes to the college-level, and then district-level, interdisciplinary curriculum committees. This level of approval required negotiating the revision of courses that have an impact on students in every department, since the courses are near-universal requirements for both academic and professional programs. Campus curriculum representatives raised concerns about how the outcomes would be measured, what impact the members of the English faculty felt these changes would have on the quality of learning in the courses, and what evidence the members of the English faculty could provide in support of the revisions. The representatives also discussed issues of transfer, articulation, and the alignment of courses with a trajectory of increasing complexity over the FYC sequence.

Each presentation of the revised curriculum to a new committee was supported by reference to and discussion of the WPA OS, which provided disciplinary authority to defend decision-making and the claim to a disciplinary expertise. In these situations, the WPA OS as disciplinary authority went unchallenged by faculty, staff, and administrators who made no claim to expertise in the teaching of writing. It was in these meetings where the WPA OS came closest to addressing its stated secondary audience, the "general public." In these instances, the clarity and simplicity of the WPA OS clearly influenced the proposed revisions and helped speed a process during which the potential for bureaucratic delay could have been tremendous.

In a context where knowledge-building and research are often seen as the realm of research universities, the WPA OS helped to pragmatically frame an argument for curricular change for faculty who wished to establish their own disciplinary authority. Like many of the "non-program programs" Karen Bishop Morris and Lizbeth A. Bryant invoke in the opening of Chapter 10, many writing programs in community colleges are non-existent, with no writing program administrator. The WPA OS, then, provides those departments with disciplinary-based authority to enact change.

WPA OS as Rhetorical Document

Ultimately, the course descriptions proposed by the MCC faculty members in English, with revisions made throughout the course approval process, were made official and entered the district course bank, and made accessible by faculty, staff, administrators, students and the general public. The WPA OS was an important tool in the development, revision, and approval of these curriculum changes. Their effectiveness is largely a reflection of the document's embodiment of its own core principles.

Focusing on a Purpose

The introduction to the WPA OS admits that its writers "seek to regularize what can be expected to be taught in first-year composition." Such an ambitious goal requires the text to offer a vision of first-year composition that enables consistency. As the process within Maricopa demonstrates, the WPA OS is capable of accomplishing both of these. It is possible to debate and contest elements of the WPA OS, but it is impossible to simply dismiss it as irrelevant to the field, as our experience at MCC delineates. The vision of FYC that the WPA OS presents is broad enough, and adaptable enough, to be re-framed. Whereas the space that the potential vagueness within the WPA OS leaves open to interpretation is potentially problematic, that same space is also critical to achieve the rhetorical purpose of being applicable within different institutional contexts.

Responding to the Needs of Different Audiences

As we have noted earlier, the Council of Writing Program Administrators claims that the WPA OS is meant for both "expert writing teachers and writing program administrators" as well as the "general public." These two extremes, the general public and the expert, elide an important middle, the large numbers of underprepared graduate teaching assistants, contingent faculty members, and non-rhet/comp specialists who staff FYC courses nationwide. At MCC, including these faculty members in conversations about revising the curriculum involved significant amounts of explanation, translation, and interpretation.

The WPA OS effectively addresses the target audience that it admits to privileging: disciplinary experts. Because it less effectively addresses needs of many, if not most, of the faculty members who teach first-year composition, it likely functions most efficiently in an institutional context such as the one it implies, namely one with a writing program administrator whose expertise and position provide a power base to support curriculum revision that would help to bring consistency to FYC nationwide. In the absence of such institutional structures, faculty members who possess disciplinary expertise may lack the political power to successfully implement change.

Responding Appropriately to Different Kinds of Rhetorical Situations

As we have noted, the WPA OS was routinely presented or referred to in a range of situations throughout the process of revising FYC at MCC. The WPA OS was a subject of discussions with as few as two people and as many as a hundred. The discussions were sometimes within a single department, across multiple departments, and across multiple colleges. They involved faculty, staff, and administration with a range of responsibilities and concerns—and the WPA OS, where necessary, was "translated" for each group. Despite the shifting circumstances, however, the WPA OS was consistently employed as an appeal to disciplinary authority. It helped to justify the assertion that change was necessary and to demonstrate that the particular course revisions being proposed were deliberate, useful, appropriate, and in keeping with national standards. Although institutional politics sometimes requires compromise on the precise nature of revisions, the WPA OS proved a very effective tool in guiding and moving proposals through the process.

Using Conventions of Format and Structure Appropriate to the Rhetorical Situation

The WPA OS's spare structure proved very effective in the context of the many meetings in which it was employed. The document distills volumes of scholarly debate into a format that can be read quickly and referred to easily. This format meant that the document itself could be easily distributed, reinforcing its legitimacy as a print artifact. For the purposes of curriculum revision in the Maricopa County Community College District, this format was ideal because it visually resonates with the required course bank format, making it easy to demonstrate how course competencies could be derived from the listed outcomes.

Appropriate Voice, Tone, and Level of Formality

Whereas the formal and authoritative tone of the WPA OS may appear a little didactic when approached as a document by colleagues for colleagues, it is extremely helpful when used as a researched and theorized document from a professional organization. The document's reasoned voice and neutral tone avoids turning the statement into a manifesto, despite its stated desire for consistency of standards. While the introduction adheres to fairly formal conventions, the WPA OS's open-ended sentences through bulleted lists is reminiscent less of the essay format that some audiences might expect from such a document, and more to the brevity of contemporary business writing. This variable level of formality between introduction and recommendations satisfies desires for both academic justification and simple utility, perhaps accounting for the particular success of the WPA OS in discussions with administration and staff about the need to revise and redefine a course.

Conclusions

As the process of revising the first-year curriculum in composition within the Maricopa County Community College District demonstrates, the WPA OS can provide a powerful tool to those who wish to employ it in the service of change. No text can address all contexts with equal effectiveness, and the successful use of the WPA OS almost inevitably includes some degree of clarification, translation, debate, and adaptation, a situation that should not surprise those who would make use of it. The answer to the larger question—whether the WPA OS embodies its own stated premises—seems to be "yes." The WPA OS demonstrates the rhetorical sensitivity, critical thought, and effective processes that it asks of students in first-year composition. In doing so, it forwards its stated purpose of bringing about consistency within and among first-year composition programs.

Works Cited

Council of Writing Program Administrators. "The WPA Outcomes Statement for First-Year Composition." Council of Writing Program Administrators, July 2008. Web. 2 July 2010.

Maricopa County Community College District. "Maricopa Community Colleges ENG 101 19956–20055." *Maricopa County Community College District*, 1994. Web. 15 August 2010.

—. "Maricopa Community Colleges ENG 102 19986–20055." *Maricopa County Community College District*, 1998. Web. 15 August 2010.

—. "Maricopa Community Colleges ENG 101 20056–99999." *Maricopa County Community College District*, 2005. Web. 15 August 2010.

—. "Maricopa Community Colleges ENG 102 20056–99999." *Maricopa County Community College District*, 2005. Web. 15 August 2010.

9 Achieving a Lasting Impact on Faculty Teaching: Using the WPA Outcomes Statement to Develop an Extended WID Seminar

Stephen Wilhoit

In academics, sometimes we are just lucky: Work on one project fortuitously helps us solve a problem we are having with a different project. This was the case for me about ten years ago when I joined a group of colleagues formulating the WPA Outcomes Statement for First-Year Composition (WPA OS). I became involved in the Outcomes Project at the same time that I was redesigning our institution's faculty support program for writing in the disciplines (WID). The timing could not have been better. The Outcomes Statement Working Group was attempting to answer a question central to my efforts at reformulating our support for WID: How can faculty across the curriculum help students apply and develop, in discipline-specific ways, the skills, knowledge, and attitudes they learn in their first-year composition courses? Working through this question helped me develop an innovative and effective faculty seminar in WID that still draws strong, positive reviews every year. In this chapter, I describe the key role the WPA OS played in the genesis of our school's WID seminar and discuss some of the reasons for its lasting impact.

WID at the University of Dayton

In its 1989 revision of general education, the University of Dayton instituted a two-tiered competency program in writing, speaking, math, and information literacy. Under this program, students were expected to learn a set of "general" competencies in each of these areas as they completed their first-year English, communication, and mathematics courses and a set of "graduation" competencies in each as they completed course work in their majors. To achieve this second goal, every department or program was required to identify a set of discipline-specific reading, writing, math, and information literacy competencies its majors were to attain, and was responsible for both delivering and assessing them.

As WPA, I was asked to prepare faculty members who would be teaching writing-related graduation competencies in their departments or programs. Drawing on my prior experience, I initially offered a number of afternoon faculty workshops, focusing on topics such as writing process theory, writing assignment design, and evaluating student writing. I quickly decided, however, that these brief workshops were inadequate for the task at hand. To have a lasting impact on faculty teaching, program development, student learning, and curricular reform—which were the true intentions of the new general education program—I not only needed to help instructors learn how to teach writing more effectively, but also had to fundamentally alter their view of the relationship between student writing and learning in their disciplines. In short, my goal was to effect "deep change" in faculty practice rather than "incremental change," a distinction Robert Quinn characterizes this way:

> Incremental change is usually the result of a rational analysis and planning process. There is a desired goal with a specific set of steps for reaching it. Incremental change is usually limited in scope and is often reversible. If the change does not work out, we can always return to the old way. Incremental change usually does not disrupt our past patterns—it is an extension of the past. Most important, during incremental change, we feel we are in control. Deep change differs from incremental change in that it requires new ways of thinking and behaving. It is change that is major in scope, discontinuous with the past and generally irreversible. The deep change effort distorts existing patterns of action and involves taking risks. (3)

Deep change is fundamental and lasting. For writing teachers, it can involve a reassessment and realignment of beliefs, commitments, and practices; a new understanding of what it means to teach effectively; and a reconceptualization of the relationship between writing instruction and student learning. As a result of their training in WID, I hoped that faculty members would place a greater emphasis on writing in their courses, commit themselves to the study of student writing in their field, value more highly the epistemic potential of writing, experiment with pedagogies aimed at improving student writing and learning, and come to see WID as central to their professional identities and goals. To obtain these deep, lasting changes, however, I had to change both the structure and the content of WID training at my institution. For guidance, I turned to the literature on faculty development; later, I would discover the valuable contributions the WPA OS could make as well.

My survey of best practices in faculty development indicated that programs designed to bring about the desired transformations in faculty practice and values are usually built around four central principles:

Changing Faculty Behavior, Values, and Commitments Takes Time

Effecting deep changes in faculty teaching or beliefs is not easy. There are few quick, long-lasting ways to achieve these results. In effective development programs, faculty members have time to learn about, consider, discuss, and experiment with new ideas and teaching methods in a structured environment that affords them the opportunity to share their insights and experiences with others. For most faculty, one-and-done workshops cannot achieve lasting results.

Faculty Development is Best Achieved in a Collaborative, Supportive Environment

Faculty members usually learn best from and with peers. Exploring and discussing information, ideas, and experiences with peers supports understanding, prompts the imagination, and spurs insight. Workshops and seminars often move faculty out of comfort zones, out of an accustomed role as expert, and into the role of novice learner, a situation that can prompt anxiety and defensiveness when what is needed for growth and deep change is a sense of openness, curiosity, and security. Working with a supportive group of peers can mitigate these negative feelings and support growth.

Faculty Members Learn Best by Applying Information

Active learning is crucial for effective faculty development. Although our colleagues can learn passively—sitting through lectures and Power Point presentations—they will learn more (and learn it more deeply) by being actively engaged: thinking through and solving problems, discussing or debating ideas or theories, applying material to their own classes or students, and critiquing each others' work.

Faculty Must Recognize the Theoretical Validity and Practical Benefits of Proposed Changes

Due to their training and experience, faculty members tend to be skeptics. In Peter Elbow's terms, when confronted with new ideas, they more often play the "doubting" game than the "believing" game. Their first impulse is to cast doubt on the value of any faculty development program by questioning the theoretical validity and/or practical benefit of the workshop's or seminar's goals or material. Ethos plays a crucial role in making faculty development programs successful. Those planning and delivering the program must establish not only their own credibility, but also the validity and utility of the material they cover.

Based on these principles, I completely revised the structure of our WID training program. Moving away from a series of stand-alone workshops, I instituted a semester-long WID seminar in which ten-to-twelve colleagues from across the curriculum met once a week to discuss a range of topics related to the teaching of writing, including: rhetorical and composition theory and practice, classroom management techniques, and student learning theory. Some sessions resembled the one-day workshops I offered in the past—introductions to and discussions of key concepts of composition instruction and rhetorical theory. Other sessions involved critiques of the faculty member's own work—participants developed classroom applications of the material we covered that their peers discussed and critiqued. Members of the workshop then used these assignments and exercises in their classes and reported back to the group on their experiences. The faculty members participating in the seminar formed a supportive, collaborative community of practice for the semester.

DISSATISFACTION AND CHANGE

By the time I joined the group framing the WPA OS, two cohorts of faculty had completed this new seminar. I had developed a syllabus, chosen readings, designed several activities that promoted faculty learning, and received good assessment results—participants felt they were learning how to teach writing more effectively in their disciplines. Though the extended format was paying dividends, I still questioned whether I was achieving the deep change in faculty practice I desired. I worried that the changes faculty members implemented in their courses as a result of participating in the seminar were more cosmetic than substantive, based more on utility than on a deeper commitment to writing and a fuller understanding of their own professional discourse practices and conventions. My dissatisfaction was based more on a felt sense of how the seminar was progressing than it was on issues that I could clearly articulate. I felt I had improved the structure of our WID training program, but I had not sufficiently changed its content, and wasn't sure what was missing.

Joining efforts to craft the WPA OS changed that, however, and in an unexpected way. As it turned out, the most valuable aspect of the WPA OS for me was not the outcomes themselves, but rather the suggestions for how faculty members across the curriculum could build on those outcomes in their own classes. Thinking through the nature and possible implementation of these suggestions helped me understand how to facilitate the deep change in faculty practice I hoped to achieve.

The WPA OS's suggestions for how faculty across the curriculum can build on the skills students develop in first-year composition are not new for those familiar with the field of rhetoric and composition. Indeed, the suggestions flow naturally from the outcomes: To promote students' rhetorical knowledge, teachers should help them better understand both the main features and uses of writing in their field as well as audience expectations; to enhance students' knowledge of conventions, teachers should help them learn specialized vocabulary, format, and documentation in their fields and strategies through which to better control and employ them; to understand the role of process, teachers should facilitate collaborative peer response activities and allow students to produce multiple drafts of writing assignments.

However, the suggestions contained in the WPA OS presuppose that faculty members already possess the knowledge, skills, and self-awareness required to implement them. In my experience, this is simply not the case. Take, for example, the suggestions for helping students develop their rhetorical knowledge. Of course, college teachers know the main features of writing in their fields—their success as writers in the academy testifies to the fact that they have mastered those features. However, when asked to articulate those features clearly in workshops, most are initially stymied. They possess an expert tacit understanding of those features, but until they purposefully and systematically reflect on, identify, and articulate them, colleagues will have little success teaching them to their students. The same observation holds true for the other suggestions as well. Developing effective assignments, activities, and pedagogies to act on these suggestions requires not only a deep, active awareness of the writing and research conventions and practices in one's field, but also a keen understanding of students' literacy practices and a commitment to reflective teaching.

I stood a better chance of fostering fundamental, lasting changes in faculty practice if I helped them identify, reflect on, critique, and develop ways of implementing in their own classes the skills, knowledge, and attitudes required to act on the suggestions included in the WPA OS. Once that occurred, faculty members would be more motivated and better prepared to develop as teachers of writing in their discipline over the course of their careers, inventing and modifying course content and pedagogies as they learned more about their students' literacy practices and adapted to changes in their field. (See Chapter 12 by Susan Thomas and Chapter 14 by Deirdre Pettipiece and Justin Everett for descriptions of how the WPA OS's suggestions for ways faculty members can build on the instruction offered in first-year writing courses supported the expansion of writing on other campuses.)

As I reviewed the content of our WID seminar in light of these reflections, I retained sessions on writing-to-learn theory and practice, assignment design, responding to student writing, and the like, but added an extensive set of heuristics guided by the suggestions in the WPA OS. These heuristics framed the seminar, serving as the basis for much of the discussion and reflective writing. Their intention was to help workshop participants better understand the writing, research, and rhetorical conventions of their discipline as well as their own composing practices. The exact wording of the questions in the heuristics changes year-to-year, depending on the backgrounds and personalities of the faculty enrolled in the seminar, but their basic intention and focus do not. Throughout the seminar, I raise these questions, explaining that faculty members' answers will largely determine how they actually apply the material we cover in the seminar in their classes, use writing to promote student learning, and help students master the writing and research conventions of their discourse communities.

Rhetorical Knowledge Questions

Sometimes I ask faculty to identify prominent textual features and conventions in their discipline, asking questions such as: What are the main features of writing in your discipline that students should learn? What are the conventions of format and structure students need to know? I ask them to consider how the texts they write in their field are supposed to look and sound, and to identify how and when they learned to adhere to those conventions. I ask them to consider which conventions are most important to their field, which conventions are changing, and how those conventions alter by area of specialty or publication venue. One exercise requires them to provide two model texts that illustrate these conventions and to describe how the readings exhibit a range of voice, tone, and formality that are commonly employed when writing in their discipline. The exercise leads them to consider which types of voices and tones and what levels of formality are acceptable in their field, and which are not acceptable and to identify how the standards vary by specialty in their discipline, by purpose, or by publication venue.

Other questions ask them to consider how the elements of the rhetorical situation commonly manifest themselves in their area of study or to identify primary disciplinary genres. First, I ask them to identify the common purposes of writing in their discipline and then to consider the last time they wrote a document that attempted to achieve each of those purposes. How did they draft and revise each text to ensure it achieved its purpose? Based on this exercise, I ask them to consider what is most important for students to know when they compose texts that attempt to achieve the same ends. Likewise, I ask faculty to consider the audiences they typically address in their discipline: How do they compose texts that appeal to different audiences in their field of study, and how can they teach their students to make the same rhetorical moves? Finally, we focus on the primary genres of their field. They list the types of writing they are most commonly called on to produce in their discipline, note the various purposes for each type of writing, and identify the formal conventions and stylistic expectations for each genre, again with an emphasis on how they would communicate these insights with their students.

Still other times, the questions ask them to consider their own rhetorical practices. When they draft and revise formal writing in their discipline, what reader expectations govern their decisions? How do these expectations influence the content, structure, and style of their writing? How did they learn what these expectations are, and how can they share this information with their students? I ask them to select the most effective piece of writing they produced recently, identify what made it effective, and consider how they would explain its effectiveness to someone unfamiliar with writing in their discipline.

Critical Thinking, Research, and Writing Questions

These questions often ask faculty to develop a discipline-specific definition of critical thinking and to consider the relationships that exist among language, knowledge, and power. For example, what does it mean to "think critically" in their discipline? What differentiates critical from uncritical thinking in their field? What textual features indicate that a writer has thought critically about his or her topic? More specifically, what is the relationship among language, knowledge, and power in their area of study; how does language shape knowledge or influence power? I ask them to consider who owns the language of knowledge and power in their discipline: Who sets language standards in their field, and how those standards changed over time? Finally, I ask them to discuss what discipline-specific aspects of critical thinking they feel they need to teach their students.

Because reading plays such a central role in all disciplines, I often ask faculty members to focus on the relationship between source-based writing and critical thinking. I ask them to consider the relationships that exist among reading, writing, and critical thinking in their field: How does reading and writing in their field aid critical thinking, and how do good critical thinking skills help students read and write more effectively? If reading plays a significant role in learning course material in their discipline, how do they teach students to read more effectively in their field of study?

Other times, faculty members must consider what it means to do research in their respective fields and to identify research-related skills their students ought to learn. In these cases, I ask faculty to consider what it means to do research in their discipline. What types of research are most common in their field, and what types of research are most frequently required of students in their department? I ask them to list the essential research skills their students should learn and to identify where in their program students receive instruction and feedback on these skills. In the end, these questions are largely self-reflective. I ask faculty to consider carefully their own experiences as scholars in their field, identifying how they learned to think critically about the material or ideas they study, outlining what critical thinking skills and attitudes help to define their discipline, and think about how can they best develop these skills and attitudes in the students they teach.

Processes Questions

Every time I run the WID workshop, I ask faculty to reflect on their own writing processes, gaining insights they can share with their students. The first set of questions usually focus on their individual composing process: how they generate material for writing in their discipline, how they tend to organize their material, how many drafts they tend to produce, when and how they revise their writing, and what types of response they find most helpful when someone reviews a draft for them. Next, I ask them to consider how their writing process might vary by context. Does their process change depending on the type of writing they are doing, the type of text they are producing, or the type of audience they are addressing? How has their writing process changed over time, from their undergraduate years, through graduate school, and into their professional lives as researchers and teachers? I ask them to consider how they learned to write like a professional in their field—what lessons or experiences were most influential, and which might be most important to share with the students they currently teach?

Other questions ask faculty colleagues to consider writing processes and conventions commonly used by scholars in their respective disciplines, and how they might be influenced by the elements of the rhetorical situation. What conventions influence the way writers in their disciplines organize, draft, and revise the texts they compose? What steps in the writing process are essential for scholars in their field? What invention, drafting, and revising processes are most commonly employed in their area of study? How might the intended purpose or audience influence the processes they employ to write a text? How might the genre of a text influence how they produced it?

Finally, I frequently ask participants to consider the role collaborative writing plays in their discipline. How often do they collaborate with others when composing texts, and what is the nature of that collaboration? When they do collaborate with others on a project, how are the roles negotiated? How do they decide who does what? How is each author credited for the work he or she does on a collaboratively written texts? Finally, how do faculty in their discipline employ collaborative writing in the classes they teach? When are students asked to compose texts collaboratively? How are they taught to do so effectively?

Knowledge of Conventions

Most often, these questions ask faculty members to identify the dominant formal conventions in their fields (including documentation), to consider how these conventions might vary by genre, and to identify model examples of these conventions they could share with students. I ask faculty to consider the dominant formal conventions of texts in their discipline and to speculate on the range of variation that is possible. Who or what creates these conventions, and how do they differ by genre or publication venue? Are the conventions relatively stable or are they changing? Which formal conventions are most important for their students to learn? How can they best teach them? The same line of questioning applies to conventions governing citation and documentation in their discipline: Are these conventions universal in their field? Do they vary by publication venue or genre? How and when did they learn these documentation conventions? How are they teaching their students about documentation and citation? Which texts best model the conventions governing their discipline?

Almost always, discussing the answers to these questions leads to other questions that focus on the relationship between conventions and power: How do conventions determine "insider" and "outsider" status in their field? What conventions are most crucial for scholars in their field to master? Why? How can they communicate this information to their students?

As we discuss answers to these questions over the course of the seminar, faculty participating in these workshops come to a fuller, more critical understanding of writing practices and conventions in their discipline and are in a much better position to act on the suggestions contained in the WPA OS. They come to understand that teaching writing is a highly reflective and creative enterprise, one they can develop and refine every term. Learning how to teach writing in a discipline is a career-long endeavor: each new writing assignment or activity a faculty member includes on his or her syllabus may demand new, creative pedagogies. The results I have obtained after making these changes has convinced me that focusing the WID seminar on the knowledge, skills, and self-awareness required to implement the suggestions included in the WPA OS is central to bringing about the long-term, deep changes in faculty practice and commitments I had hoped to achieve.

Impact of the WID Seminar

Informal conversations with faculty participants who have completed the seminar since I instituted these changes have been encouraging. These colleagues indicate that the experience had a lasting, positive impact on their teaching; they continue to develop as teachers of writing in their disciplines. To better understand the long-term impact of the revised WID seminar, in 2008 I surveyed fifty-eight faculty and staff members still working at the university who participated in the revised seminar. These faculty members were informed that we were attempting to assess the long-term impact of their participation in the program. Twenty-one surveys were completed and returned.

All faculty participants indicated that the seminar effected lasting changes in their teaching. At least ninety percent of the respondents agreed or strongly agreed that the seminar helped them learn how to design more effective writing assignments, employ a process approach to teaching writing, and respond effectively to student texts. More importantly, however, the same percentages agreed or strongly agreed that their participation led them to increase the amount of writing they require in their classes, increased their confidence as teachers of writing, and changed for the better how they still use writing to promote learning in their classes. These results mirror those obtained by Pettipiece and Everett who, in Chapter 14, describe how discussions of the WPA OS at their institution increased the relevance and authority of writing across the curriculum.

The long-lasting effect of the seminar can be attributed, in part, to its structure—weeks of working through material with peers likely has a greater impact on faculty practice than does attendance at a few, one-hour workshops. However, the reflective exercises and discussions arising from the WPA OS, which are now a part of the seminar, also play a crucial role. Continually reflecting on questions concerning one's profession and practice enables "reflection on action," which—as Donald Schön maintains in *The Reflective Practitioner*—is crucial to long-term faculty development (278).

In academics, sometimes we are just lucky. I was fortunate enough to join a group of colleagues drafting the WPA OS at just the right time. Even the small part I played in the process helped me improve support for WID at my institution and foster deep, lasting change in how faculty members across the disciplines teach writing. Shifting the focus of the seminar to an examination of the rhetorical practices and discourse conventions of the participants' disciplines helped colleagues become deeply engaged in determining how language and knowledge operate in and shape respective fields of study; in identifying discipline-specific knowledge, skills, and attitudes their students need to learn to become successful members of their discourse community; and in developing pedagogies to teach that material effectively. Results like these will benefit faculty members and the students they teach at my institution for years to come.

Works Cited

Council of Writing Program Administrators. "The WPA Outcomes Statement for First-Year Composition." Council of Writing Program Administrators, July 2008. Web. 5 May 2010.

Elbow, Peter. "Methodological Doubting and Believing: Contraries in Inquiry." *Embracing Contraries: Explorations in Learning and Teaching.* New York: Oxford UP, 1986. 254-300. Print.

Quinn, Robert E. *Deep Change: Discovering the Leader Within.* San Francisco: Jossey-Bass, 1996. Print.

Schön, Donald. *The Reflective Practitioner: How Professionals Think in Action.* Farnham, UK: Ashgate Publishing, 1995. Print.

10 Building Clout in Non-Program Programs by Using the Outcomes Statement

Karen Bishop Morris and Lizbeth A. Bryant

The title of writing program administrator represents our responsibilities but belies the authority of the role. As WPAs, our authority comes from a number of sources: It is given to us, in part, by the institutions we serve; it is also inherited and inherent in the disciplinary knowledge on which we rely to make decisions that impact student learning. After all, we can trace our lineage to the larger field of rhetoric and composition. As WPAs, we have created a robust and sustainable community of professionals: We have a journal and access to the expertise of our colleagues on the WPA listserv in just a few keystrokes. As WPAs, we also recognize that perhaps the most important dimension of our authority is not bestowed upon us by a title or transferred by virtue of our membership in an organization. The real work of the WPA is finding a way to create our own authority—to claim our clout—by using tools, like the WPA Outcomes Statement for First-Year Composition (WPA OS), to articulate our program's priorities and values in a way that they become significant and visible to institutional stakeholders.

With our title comes the responsibility to provide the vision, planning, and support for thousands of students in first-year composition courses, and yet many of us continue to buckle under a daunting workload with scant resources—a situation that harkens back to the creation of the Portland Resolution (Hult, et al.). We find ourselves perpetually adjusting our programs to respond to a shifting landscape—new admissions standards, or a new program for international students, or deep budget cuts—while trying to maintain learning outcomes. Oftentimes, as WPAs we have not been included at the level of institutional decision-making, and we find ourselves reconciling what we thought we were doing with what must be done. In our experience, we found ourselves rearranging priorities and shifting gears so many times in response to decisions that were handed to us that our visions became blurred. Quickly, and rather spontaneously, we started referring to our program as a "non-program program" on a regular basis. Here we do not intend to offer a universal definition for non-program programs because WPAs will have their own specific set of challenges in their specific institutional contexts. A non-program program is simply such because of the vast number of constraints imposed upon the WPA, constraints that threaten the program's consistency and growth. It is a program that seeks to play a role in key decisions that affect its ability to operate responsibly, yet—due to the lack of resources, to the lack of a like-minded community of scholars, and/or as a result of unique institutional politics—it lacks the institutional clout and authority to actually influence many of those decisions. To move beyond this state, it is essential that WPAs choose not to play victim to hegemonic structures, but rather position themselves so they become central to these conversations.

Unlike more progressive writing programs with faculty who possess PhDs in rhetoric and composition and with curricula that exemplifies contemporary scholarship, non-program programs cannot automatically operate under the assumptions of the WPA OS or within the theories that characterize the last fifty years of our discipline. In fact, most WPAs in non-program programs find themselves situated in instructional contexts with a fledgling rhetoric/composition community. These WPAs have the added responsibility of introducing and defining the outcomes to their respective populations—an uphill journey at best when one considers all of the competing interests and issues that haunt the first-year experience. In doing so, however, WPAs in non-program programs constantly jockey for position, educate administrators, and—ultimately—agitate to establish clout for themselves and their programs.

Research in this collection on the impact of the WPA OS supports the fact that the WPA OS in and of itself is not a solution. Unless the WPA is empowered to move these outcomes into action, progress is slow. In Chapter 20, Emily Isaacs and Melinda Knight report that the WPA OS failed to effect significant change at the institutions they reviewed, a finding that articulates with the research of Clinton Burhans and Richard Larson, whose statistics suggest that writing programs at many institutions continue to lag in their ability to transfer best practices into the classroom. In 1983, Burhans found that between one and five percent of the courses he studied employed "contemporary" pedagogies (646). A decade later, Larson stated that only thirty percent of the programs he studied taught writing as a process. WPAs cannot know definitively what every writing program and teacher is doing in the process of serving 3.21 million first-year students each year; however, the responsibility concomitant with WPA work requires us to move in the direction of the WPA OS (in the United States).

The following vignettes recount the story of two composition directors who learned to deploy the WPA OS in the documentation of their program to ultimately elevate their program's status. While the names and circumstances vary from program to program and institution to institution, our goal is to demonstrate how new and experienced WPAs, regardless of their specific challenges, can apply a certain consciousness to the documentation of their daily work to strengthen their identity and change the status of their non-program programs.

We share our stories to illustrate how WPAs might rethink their own statistics and the struggles, and begin to view their circumstances as a source of empowerment rather than despair. Like Richard Miller, in his essay "Critique's the Easy Part," we decided not to place blame but rather to "choose a course of action, invent solutions, and then fabricate the conditions that generate the life-sustaining sensation of forward movement" (4). These stories may encourage WPAs in non-program programs to take action by documenting their work—administrative, instructional, theoretical—and by making explicit connections to the WPA OS to help them build credibility and clout.

STORY ONE: READY OR NOT, INCREASED CLASS SIZE

Liz came to a regional university in the Midwest that retains sixty-three percent of its students from their first to second year, and graduates twenty-two percent of its students in six years. The campus is located twenty-five miles outside of Chicago, yet the surrounding community has fallen prey to a dying steel industry, poverty, and violence. The working class population is primarily first-generation college students who work full-time. One third of those enrolled in the first semester writing course withdraw or fail; another third in the second-semester writing course earn "Ds," "Fs," or "Ws."

In spite of these poor success rates, the decision was made to increase the class size. The department chair had a message for Liz at the beginning of her first term as WPA: "Liz, the Dean has increased the number of students in 104 from 25 to 27." Like many WPAs who lack clout, Liz was not privy to the discussion of raising the class size; rather, she was informed that the decision was effective immediately. She was left to inform the instructors and manage the fallout. At this point, she realized her position in a non-program program: Liz possessed a title but lacked the authority to direct and protect the welfare of the students and teachers in that program.

We wish we could report that this practice was endemic to our institution; however, WPAs being excluded from broader institutional planning is woven into our collective experiences (Chase 247; Wingate 100). If given sufficient notice and time, Liz could have pulled together research and experience to explain why and how increasing class size results in diminishing returns. All too often, WPAs in non-program programs find themselves embroiled in this vicious cycle, and over time, in the absence of meetings, minutes, and memos, there is a loss of institutional memory. Eventually, WPAs and other administrators fail to recall why class size is what it is; it just is. In all fairness, WPAs are not the only folks who react to complex, external variables. "The administration" we look to for validation similarly struggles within the same hegemonic structure characterized by shifting priorities and resources. Presidents, provosts, and deans, too, must respond to institutional and economic exigencies that are often out of their control.

As Liz acclimated to the institution and its politics, she found encouragement in the writings of other WPAs and realized that her situation was not unique (e.g., Bishop and Crossley). Even a nationally known WPA such as Wendy Bishop lacked the clout needed to protect a writing program. Recognizing that tension between responsible administration and reality exists for all WPAs, Liz decided to move past the announcement of twenty-seven students per class and proceed with a plan to build a program based on the WPA OS and to create documents that would become part of future institutional conversations.

Story Two: Developing Goals and a Curriculum Using the WPA OS

Liz's first order of business as WPA was to select a text for the first-semester course, 104. She selected *The Call to Write*, based on Purdue University Calumet's (PUC) working class population and the book's focus on the WPA OS. She taught 104, getting to know the students and meeting with the instructors. Liz shared the WPA OS with the department chair, laying out her plans to build a curriculum based on the WPA OS. By now, Liz recognized the importance of educating others about the role and work of the WPA; the department chair gave his approval and blessing. Using the WPA OS, she, in conjunction with instructors, developed course goals and a curriculum for 104, planning to do the same for the second semester course, 105.

WPAs know firsthand how exciting and arduous the task of building a curriculum can be, yet, because of the WPA OS, it was manageable for Liz. The WPA OS is a living document: a portable check and balance system for writing instruction. For example, the course coordinators and instructors came from a variety of backgrounds; however, the WPA OS was the common ground. Simply put, the WPA OS gives WPAs the freedom and the power to establish curriculum and evaluate its effectiveness.

Liz's decision to connect the program's goals and standards to the WPA OS also increased her clout because the WPA OS comes from a professional organization outside of her institution. External clout helped her as a WPA gain the respect of others at the university in the midst of an administrative structure that has little use for a writing program and provides that program with little support. The prestige and authority of a national organization, the Council of Writing Program Administrators (CWPA), was more respected than the perspective offered by one lone compositionist on the English faculty. Just as CWPA moved to articulate the objective of teaching writing for a national audience, our job as WPAs is finding methods to document our work in individual programs in a comprehensive fashion that makes our work visible so that wider audiences are able to read and recognize it as valuable (Bishop 45).

External clout served the program well, but what about internal clout? In addition to the WPA OS gold standard, WPAs also need the confidence to design a series of sequenced, cumulative classes, especially in non-program programs. This responsibility is enormous, and so is the need for validation. WPAs minimally coordinate (1) the needs of student populations; (2) the needs of part-timers who teach writing; and (3) the expectations of the faculty in upper-division classes *in conjunction with* various curriculums, teaching tools, and assessment strategies. To argue for and implement a curriculum for 1600 students at PUC, Liz clung to the WPA OS to ground the program in the best ideas from the discipline. In addition to her professional credentials and twenty years of teaching experience, the WPA OS was the barometer of assurance: that last bit of professional clout to affirm she was making "good" decisions.

As a record that incorporates fifty years of research and scholarship, the WPA OS works this way for all WPAs. The WPA OS represents the consensus of our scholarly community, while at the same time giving WPAs the peace of mind that we are doing the "right" thing by students and instructors alike. Particularly in PUC's program, the WPA OS shapes our work with writing instructors and tutors who have little or no background in composition studies and yet are responsible for putting these outcomes into practice. While Liz served as WPA, all of the full-time writing instructors had degrees in literature with a one-semester practicum in the teaching of writing. Some had been teaching writing for ten years, some for ten minutes. Many were accustomed to a reading-based program and putting grades on drafts of student papers.

The WPA OS also builds a bridge between the first-year composition courses and the writing center. Even though the writing center's main goal is to support writing in the first year, the writing center serves a campus-wide audience—a fact that is also reflected in the diverse staff of tutors who represent English and a range of other disciplines. As writing center director, Karen used the WPA OS to ensure consistency with the goals of the first-year program, while Liz used them to shape and shift the instructors' orientation and approaches to teaching writing. The WPA OS was a critical step in building a unified program, as was the conscious choice of *The Call to Write,* which supported the shift.

However, Liz recognized that to build a true program there must be a set of goals and objectives that do not depend on a single textbook and are specific to PUC students. Once again, this documentation must revolve around the WPA OS. She met with 104 and 105 instructors to begin a draft that articulated assignments and goals in relation to the WPA OS. For instance, in order for students to meet the outcomes in the "Process" section, Liz's team decided to build in attention to students' attitudes toward writing and their individual writing practices. As they worked through each section of the WPA OS in this way, more formal, program-wide discussions of the writing curriculum became the norm. English 104 now focuses on developing writing and reading processes, analyzing rhetorical situations, and composing source-based essays. In English 105, students review the work done in 104 and add synthesis, research, and documentation.

These documents, which declared the existence and validity of the writing program, were approved by the English faculty and moved Liz and her colleagues closer to becoming a real program. Creating these documents allowed Liz to establish common ground among PUC's working class, first-generation college students; instructional material; the writing center; and the WPA OS. Teachers began talking about assessing and responding to student writing. The English faculty became engaged in the program by reading and approving documents that outlined course goals. A new course was developed, English 100, creating a stretch program that gave students who needed more writing experiences two semesters to get through the first-semester of composition. Finally, things started to fall into place for Liz as she embraced her role as WPA.

Story Three: Disappearing Writing Instructors

Over the four years that Liz was developing this curriculum, the number of full-time writing instructors decreased from eight to one. When a full-time person left, Liz's pleas for a replacement were ignored. Only eight percent of the writing courses were being taught by full-time instructors.

Being ignored is worse than being rejected. At least when you're rejected, the administrators acknowledge you exist. Being ignored and lacking a voice in conversations about the writing program, WPAs find themselves relegated to non-program programs. This idea of a non-program program is touched on by Katherine Gottschalk, who describes the "precarious lines" that WPAs and writing instructors hold in programs "situated on the fringes of the university" and set up in "marginalized" positions (23). We use the words "iffy" and "adhocky" to describe aspects of our program that remain outside of our control. Maybe there will be release time to administer our non-program program. Maybe not. Maybe there will be a budget to pay our writing center tutors. Maybe not.

In response to the decreasing number of full-time instructors, Liz developed written pleas. Rather than accepting the news, she created charts that showed the steadily increasing reliance on adjuncts. Armed with enrollment projections, staffing plans, and assessment data, she made her case both publicly and privately. When it seemed that her arguments to the English faculty produced no results, she politicked across the university, involving everyone from the director of admissions to the chancellor. Armed with statistics and the WPA OS, Liz connected the challenges she was facing in composition to the university's broader challenges with their first-year students. She seized an opportunity to seek funding from a first-year student initiative and to inform those outside of the department about the writing program. Eventually, bringing along her charts and proposals, she had an audience with the new provost. She was not ignored, but despite all of these efforts, she received no grants or response—at least not immediately.

Whether our pleas garner a response, we have a duty to lead by voicing the needs of student writers. Recorded in documents, this voice creates a measurable record of a real program with a history upon which our successors can build. We create a real program in large part through our diligence in documenting our work.

Story Four: Program Assessment

With goals and curriculum in place, it was time for assessment, but it was not easy to conduct reliable assessment with one full-time writing instructor to assist. Just when things began to look even bleaker, Academic Quality Improvement Program (AQIP) came to our rescue. The general education curriculum committee decided that all general education courses needed goals, outcomes, and measures to assess outcomes. WPAs study assessment. Rather than being ignored, Liz was invited to the dean's office. Let us write that again: She was invited to the dean's office. Administrators call you to their office when they need something. We were asked to lead this process of assessment. As a result, 100, 104, and 105 have been some of the first courses to make it through the approval process because we employed an outcomes-based approach in our work, from course goals, to curriculum design, to textbook selection, through to assessment.

Never let an opportunity like this slip by. Ed White reminds us to use it or lose it, to "assert that you have power (even if you don't) and you can often wield it" (3). Taking advantage of this university requirement, we were finally in a position to assert and wield a modicum of power. After all, the assessment game was easy for us, and suddenly, we were role models as we set about the business of making our work public and showing others how to shape their general education outcomes and documents. This assessment exercise was important for the ways it validated our work with the English department and beyond. Our documents were read and approved by members of the faculty senate. Since our work was seen as connecting to retention and other university priorities, we became experts. Liz asked the dean for funds to pay writing instructors to read portfolios. He said yes. We began planning this assessment and, in the process, moved closer to becoming a real program.

Liz's collection of emails, letters, reports, proposals, charts, and presentations spawned documentation that eventually permeated university conversations. The importance of archiving our positions and voice has been written about as "raw data for archival purposes" and for "future study" (Harris 13–14), and as a source of "intra-institutional historical research" to strengthen the act of knowledge transfer for WPAs (Mirtz 120). Others have extended the conversation of documentation to include best practices for records management from a *rhetorical perspective*, which involves designing a process for records collection that takes into account the myriad of potential audiences that may someday access a document for a range of reasons (Rose; Elliott; Millar). But, what if we take a step back and begin to think more strategically about the records we create? Karen Bishop explores how the issue of documentation "is very similar to that for archivists and becomes one of constructing ourselves discursively as valuable in a format that is recognizable and intelligible to those external to our subfield" (45). To be seen as a real program, WPAs must create an archive that "harness[es] our discursive representations or *documentary reality*" (45).

To think of the normal paperwork in the life of the WPA as shaping the documentary reality of a real program is a powerful intellectual exercise. Focusing on documentary reality means that we approach the processes surrounding records creation with a higher level of consciousness. If our daily activities get captured in memos and meeting minutes, then the sum total of the significance in these records is much greater than their individual parts. For instance, when Liz rallied the instructors to develop a checklist of standards predicated on the WPA OS, it was much more than just a list of course-specific goals. That final checklist embodies several layers of learning, beginning with the instructors' experiences in teaching our student population and the subject-matter knowledge of each course. The final checklist made understanding the first-year composition program's goals accessible for a range of audiences, including: students, writing instructors, department chair, dean, and the faculty senate who ultimately reviewed and approved the documents.

Though it was not stated in the checklist document, the preliminary analysis and conversations that informed the checklist, including drafting the document and its subsequent implementation, demonstrated all of Liz's arguments for the betterment of the program. The checklist document lives on because it accounts for the history of administrative mandates that have affected composition at PUC, and it anticipates mandates that are, as of yet, unforeseen. The social and political aspects of being a WPA in this institutional context gave Liz the ability to predict, act (with authority!), evaluate, and reflect on curricular decisions. This checklist document imbues the program with a measure of authority and slows, if not stops, the cycle of reacting to administrators' demands. In turn, we became proactive. The standards were the foundation needed to build the rest of the program, and because the foundation integrated the values of the institution, it was stronger and stood a better chance of acceptance.

The collaborative task of writing a checklist was more than just a restatement of goals or standards. Ultimately, the checklist represents the social organization in which it was produced, and presents a framework for inquiry by which we can now critique the organization and ideology behind it (Smith 258). To avoid this conscious and methodical preparation, Dorothy Smith warns, means that we run the risk of confining ourselves to the relationships and circumstances constructed by the system we operate within. After all, WPAs do not gain institutional clout or authority by virtue of their title, but savvy WPAs can create authority by making their work visible to larger audiences across the institution. The dual nature of a WPA's job—first to do the work and then to document it for a greater social purpose—allows the WPA to maintain some control where typically there is none.

That said, we must reconceive the way we approach ordinary tasks and accept the fact that while we may not personally see the benefit of going about our work in this way, ultimately, the program will benefit from the extra measure of care given to the rhetorical awareness we give to documentation.

Story Five: "We're sorry to inform you that your account is overdrawn"

Karen's documentation began on the first day of her job as writing center director, when she met with an administrative assistant from the dean's office, the department chair, Liz (WPA), and another faculty member who supervises the computer labs. This time, it was Karen's turn to be informed:

> The writing center is over budget and this has been an historic problem. One of the things we're looking for you to do is carefully manage the budget so that this doesn't happen again. What will likely happen now is that the dean will pull dollars from another area to cover the shortfall–this time–but going forward, you are expected to hold the line with expenses and think very carefully about the amount of staff you have on the payroll.

Karen wasn't panicked; she was prepared. She began composing a memo to the dean in her head. She would open with justification for the writing center, describing its importance in supporting first-year composition (FYC) programs as well as its impact on campus writing. She would invoke Marilyn Cooper's characterization of the challenge of writing centers to support student literacy: Writing centers are, after all, not only a site of struggle within the university, but quite likely the most important site given the role of the university in literacy and society (49). Karen's mental memo was interrupted as she observed her senior colleague's retort: "Where did the money go in the first place?" She surprised herself, and apparently others, by adding: "Yes, and by the way, what is the total writing center budget, and can you share a copy of it with me, please?" There is a first time for everything.

Karen prefers to think of this budget situation as her big break. Here was a chance to educate administrators about the integral role the writing center plays in promoting campus literacy while using language they understand all too well: "outcomes" and the "bottom line." Rita Malenczyk states emphatically that it is the ongoing job of the WPA to represent the work of composition in similar situations. According to Malenczyk, WPAs "continually strive to 'live in peace with the other,' sometimes many different others at once" (82). In our effort to do so, she continues, "we must persuade those others to the see the world as we do, to see our experiences as theirs" (82). If this is true, then we can no longer consider the writing we do in defense of our programs as ordinary but rather as critical argumentation, as life or death persuasive pieces we compose to sustain our programs.

Buoyed by the authority and reason of the WPA OS, Karen set about the work of building an argument to frame the perpetual "overdraft" as a deficit in dollars and sense. In other words, her task was more than just careful addition and subtraction; her responsibility and role as writing center director was to convince the dean to see the writing center as she saw it: the very hub of literacy in the school, one of the last bastions of support for instructors buckling under the pressure of increased class size, a key resource in the retention game and in the support of writing across the disciplines. Of course, she also needed to assure him of the renewed commitment to balancing the budget while pointing out that a group of students were building their résumés and preparing for the professional workplace while serving as tutors. In the end, building a successful case for the writing center budget meant highlighting how the administration's financial goal and the academic value of the writing center were really one and the same. We didn't say that building documentation would be easy.

Two weeks later came the response to Karen's question about the current writing center budget: an invitation to prepare a writing center budget—a dream assignment. She approached it in earnest by reconstructing a five-year history of the writing center and comparing it to her own vision for the place. She created an Excel spreadsheet with the appropriate columns, line items, and assumptions discussed in the notes section. The cover memo was a masterpiece—just shy of two pages that documented historical budget issues and offered explanations. In short, good detective work illustrated that at least $15,000 (roughly half) of the deficit wasn't a deficit attributable to the writing center at all, and was easily explained: supplemental instruction (SI) and tutoring intended to be charged to the new ESL program was inadvertently attributed to the writing center budget, and thus perpetuated the shortfall. Of course, Karen saw little value in detaching the writing center from the work of the SIs and ESL program. Instead, she shared the tutors, time, and space. The results: "pass rates" in the ESL program began to climb; relationships between comp instructors, SIs, and tutors improved, which meant, in the end, better student retention and better students. The writing center had an overage of goodwill and good data.

Story Six: The Fruit of Dropping Outcome Nuggets

There is and always has been a bright side, despite ongoing claims of an "overdrawn" budget. The writing center continues to open year-round, and to date, it has not been forced to reduce staff. The problem is that WPAs don't always see it: the bright side. In fact, we've even grown by adding a few graduate students to the staff, attracting volunteers, and launching a series of interactive workshops designed to reinforce the WPA OS. Face-to-face meetings with the dean have been promising; he finds comfort in our spreadsheets that track increased tutorials and engagement with other departments and campus units. While these meetings have played a powerful role in reminding the administration of the value of the work in the writing center, we prefer to think the long-term strategy is the real genius.

But what of this long-term strategy?

The strategy is determined by those aspects of our jobs as WPAs that we do have control over; namely, the ways we construct and document our work in the confines of our centers, our programs, and within our institutions. As seasoned WPAs, we choose to be hopeful rather than cynical over the absence of a budget, preferring to capitalize on the flexibility and freedom that the loose definition of such necessities affords. When called on to justify an "overage" or hold the line regarding resources, we are emboldened by the small innovations we have made in the writing program and writing center, which are anchored by the weight of the WPA OS. Thus far, these occasions have been tiny blips. We are not naïve. Karen knows the day is coming when she will participate in a conversation concerning the future of the writing center, arguing vigorously to retain the few resources now in her control. We are squirreling away outcomes nuggets for just such an occasion, leaving a trail of documents in the institutional discourse that will ground our case in history, theory, and practice. Spreadsheets and charts are just one example of outcomes nuggets. We are also in the process of developing an annual progress report as well as a three-year strategic plan for the program.

We are not the first to think this way. Peter Carino, in "Reading Our Own Words: Rhetorical Analysis and the Institutional Discourse of Writing Centers," recounts the inherent "marginality and innovation" of writing centers as peculiar rhetorical spaces—automatically marginalized for the ways writing centers differ from traditional classroom spaces; on the other hand, they are free "to innovate, to experiment, to play, to cross disciplinary and organizational borders–in short, to change the way things are usually done" (91). Carino's contribution of a rhetorical analysis of writing center discourse is helpful here. According to Carino, "this communal sense of marginality and innovation in writing center culture shapes the ways centers represent themselves rhetorically in institutional discourse, such as publicity materials and other communications with faculty, administration and students" (92). Recognizing the institution as a significant audience when creating program materials is essential to the WPA and often overlooked when communicating information to tutors and instructional staff.

Carino's lesson concerns the fact that writing centers, like writing programs, are often undefined in relationship to other academic units: budgets are non-existent or unstable; pools of instructional talent are constantly shifting; and support from administrators is ambiguous and often fleeting. Rather than bemoan the disadvantages inherent in situations, as WPAs, we must use our positioning to our advantage; after all, we have a direct responsibility to shape literacy in our departments and on our campuses. With this responsibility comes power—power that we activate through the rhetorical representation of our curriculum and goals. Part of what makes Carino's lesson so powerful is the fact that our success as WPAs depends on our ability to leverage the written word to secure our own place, requiring that we think carefully about the memos and minutes we draft for the ways they represent our programs. Everything we write—from flyers to placement policies—has the potential to substantiate the existence and importance of first-year writing programs and writing centers. That is why we, as WPAs, must approach the documentation of our work deliberately if we are to shift from non-program to bona fide program status.

In the fall of 2009, Karen took over as director of first-year writing. Soon after, she was invited to a meeting by the vice chancellor of academic affairs:

> Dr. Bishop, we have approved eight new Continuing Lecture positions for first-year writing. We imagine that you, Dr. Bryant, and your chair will want to form a search committee immediately and launch a national search. These positions will pay a competitive salary and full benefits, with opportunities for release time in exchange for service in special department, school, and university initiatives.

Just like that. Or so it seemed. In fact, it didn't happen overnight. It was all of the points we've plotted in this article: defending class size; revamping course goals; creating checklists of goals and objectives for each course; justifying budgets or a lack thereof, and so on. It was documenting the work in a conscious fashion, planting and nurturing the seeds of the WPA OS, and then standing back to watch the seeds take root.

As WPAs, we typically find ourselves embroiled in a myriad of situations. We tend to define our success in terms of the success (or lack of success) of the most recent administrative battle. The truth is more complex. On the one hand, the value of WPA work is rarely readily apparent; it can take years before the effects of careful planning are recognized, much less rewarded. Moreover, WPAs must learn to temper criticism of senior administrators who find themselves operating on the same shifting terrain while striving for the same outcomes for student success. PUC's non-program program is no different. The silver lining, however, is the fact that Liz and Karen are both still around to see the fruits of their labor.

Karen now meets three times per year with an administrative assistant from the dean's office to review the writing center budget. These meetings follow a conversation or a document that analyzes "usage": hard data that serves as evidence of work performed and the need for additional resources. It took time, but the writing center has slowly become part of a larger discourse community, and it happened because the writing center was redefined. Through outreach and workshops, by capturing data and integrating itself broadly and deeply into the first-year courses and beyond, the writing center is finally too embedded in the institutional structure to be ignored.

A component of Liz's legacy as WPA is that the charts, tables, and graphs paid off. Was it documentation alone that paved the way for these improvements? No, not entirely. The approval to hire new staff was a constellation of circumstances: a new vice chancellor and various needs of the institution surfacing at the right place and time that made writing a priority. These documents and their involvement in the university's discourse community have been the work of two WPAs: Liz and Karen's willingness to improve the landscape of their students' education and instructors' professional development. With the WPA OS as a foundation, they are building an innovative and sustainable program. At this rate, who knows what the future may bring? They will be ready with the requisite documents, charts, and studies.

WORKS CITED

Bishop, Karen. "On the Road to (Documentary) Reality: Capturing the Intellectual and Political Process of Writing Program Administration." *The Writing Program Administrator as Theorist: Making Knowledge Work*. Ed. Shirley K Rose and Irwin Weiser. Portsmouth, NH: Boynton/Cook, 2002. 42–53. Print.

Bishop, Wendy, and Gay Lynn Crossley. "How to Tell a Story of Stopping: The Complexities of Narrating a WPA's Experience." *WPA: Writing Program Administration* 19.3 (1996): 70–79. Print.

Burhans, Clinton S., Jr. "The Teaching of Writing and the Knowledge Gap." *College English* 45.7 (1983): 639–56. Print.

Carino, Peter. "Reading Our Own Words: Rhetorical Analysis and the Institutional Discourse of Writing Centers." *Writing Center Research: Extending the Conversation*. Ed. Paula Gillespie, Alice Gilliam, Lady Falls Brown, and Byron Stay. Mahwah, NJ: Erlbaum, 2002. 91–110. Print.

Chase, Geoffrey. "Redefining Composition, Managing Change, and the Role of the WPA." *WPA: Writing Program Administration* 21 (1997): 46–54. Rpt. in *The Longman Sourcebook for Writing Program Administrators*. Ed. Irene Ward and William J. Carpenter. New York, NY: Longman, 2008. 243–51. Print.

Cooper, Marilyn. "We Don't Belong Here Do We?" *Writing Center Journal* 12.1 (1991): 48–62. Print.

Council of Writing Program Administrators. "The WPA Outcomes Statement for First-Year Composition." Council of Writing Program Administrators, July 2008. Web. 8 Aug. 2011.

Elliot, Clark. "Communications and Events in History: Toward a Theory for Documenting the Past." *American Archivist* 48 (1985): 357–68. Print.

Gottschalk, Katherine K. "The Writing Program in the University." *ADE Bulletin* 112 (1995): 1–6. Rpt. in *The Longman Sourcebook for Writing Program Administrators*. Ed. Irene Ward and William J. Carpenter. New York, NY: Longman, 2008. 23–33. Print.

Harris, Muriel. "Diverse Research Methodologies at Work for Diverse Audiences: Shaping the Writing Center to the Institution." *Writing Program Administrator as Researcher*. Rose and Weiser. 1–17. Print.

Hult, Christine, David Joliffe, Kathleen Kelly, Dana Mead, and Charles Schuster. "'The Portland Resolution:' Guidelines for Writing Program Administrator Positions." *WPA: Writing Program Administration* 16.1/2 (1992): n. pag. Web. 25 July 2011.

Larson, Richard L. *Curricula in College Writing Programs: Much Diversity, Little Assessment*. Ford Foundation Report. New York: Ford Foundation, 1994. Print.

Malenczyk, Rita. "Administration as Emergence: Toward a Rhetorical Theory of Writing Program Administration." Rose and Weiser. *The Writing Program Administrator as Theorist*. 79–89. Print.

Millar, Laura. "Myths and Realities: Records and Archives Management for Publishers." *Journal of Scholarly Publishing* 27 (1996): 35–54. Print.

Miller, Richard. "Critique's the Easy Part." *Kitchen Cooks, Plate Twirlers & Troubadours: Writing Program Administrators Tell Their Stories*. Ed. Diana George. Portsmouth, NH: Boynton/Cook, 1999. 3–13. Print.

Mirtz, Ruth M. "WPAs as Historians: Discovering a First-Year Writing Program by Researching Its Past." Rose and Weiser. *Writing Program Administrator as Researcher*. 119–30. Print.

Rose, Shirley K. "Preserving Our Histories of Institutional Change: Enabling Research in the Writing Program Archives." Rose and Weiser. *Writing Program Administrator as Researcher*. 107–18. Print.

Rose, Shirley K., and Irwin Weiser. "WPA Inquiry in Action and Reflection." Rose and Weiser. v–xi. *Writing Program Administrator as Researcher*. Print.

—, eds. *The Writing Program Administrator as Researcher: Inquiry in Action and Reflection*. Portsmouth, NH: Boynton/Cook, 1999. Print.

—, eds. *The Writing Program Administrator as Theorist: Making Knowledge Work*. Portsmouth, NH: Boynton/Cook, 2002. Print.

Smith, Dorothy E. "The Sociological Construction of Documentary Reality." *Sociological Inquiry* 44 (1974): 257–68. Print.

United States Department of Education. Digest of Education Statistics. "Total First-time Freshmen Fall Enrollment in Degree-granting Institutions." April 2011. Web. 30 July 2011.

White, Edward M. "Use It or Lose It: Power and the WPA." *WPA: Writing Program Administration* 15.1/2 (1991): 3–12. Print.

Wingate, Molly. "The Politics of Collaboration: Writing Centers within Their Institutions." *Resituating Writing: Constructing and Administering Writing Programs*. Ed. Joseph Janangelo and Kristine Hansen. Portsmouth, NH: Boynton/Cook, 1995. 100–107. Print.

11 Reframing the Conversation: Can the Outcomes Statement Help?

Darsie Bowden

The yearning for *respect* that often accompanies WPA work—together with the assumption that the accrual of respect entails a corresponding uptick in institutional status and resources—takes us very quickly down a slippery slope. I have been a WPA in one form or another (writing center director, first-year writing director, writing across the curriculum director) since 1991, and I have witnessed and experienced the exhaustion and burnout that results from believing that hard work based on sound (research-supported) principles yields certain kinds of returns, and, in a word, respect. But, the term is too fluid, and the forces at sway in institutions of higher education are just too complex to make this very useful as a goal. Rather, I have come to recognize that positive programmatic change involves responding nimbly to opportunities as they develop to reframe the conversations about writing and the teaching of writing. This chapter, then, chronicles the implementation of the WPA Outcomes Statement for First-Year Composition (WPA OS) at my institution, and explores one opportunity nested among many that can potentially contribute to a sea change.

Some Background

In May 2007, a group of nine tenure track faculty at my university, specialists in various areas within rhetoric and composition, broke from our English department and established a new department of writing. The new department, called Writing, Rhetoric and Discourse

(WRD), also included the first-year writing program, adding about sixty contingent faculty and thousands of students to the departmental rolls. In addition to first-year writing (FYW), the new department brought with it a minor in professional writing; we quickly added a Master of Arts (M.A. in WRD) and initiated the development of an undergraduate major, which was approved in May 2010. As director of FYW, and newly freed from some of the constraints (and well-intentioned, but often misguided, input) of a large and fairly traditional literature department, I felt buoyed and energized, and as a result, I began the work of improving the status and stature of first-year writing classes (and FYW faculty) within a writing department.

Since first-year writing programs are not alike, let me first describe the existing program at DePaul. We have two required courses, one focusing on rhetoric and writing (WRD 103), and the other concerned with the researched argument (WRD 104). Students who need additional preparation before starting this sequence are placed into a basic writing class (WRD 102). Note that the placement procedure (previously a combination of a placement exam, test scores, and a student's grade point average) evolved into directed self-placement in 2011, another new step we have been able to take. Because relying on graduate student instructors (in our case, M.A. students) runs contrary to the mission of the university, FYW courses are taught by contingent faculty, six of whom are full-time, and the remaining fifty-four are part-time. Many of these instructors have taught at our university for a number of years, but their employment remains contingent. Furthermore, after six years of full-time employment, contracts for non-tenure-track instructors cannot be renewed; instructors can work part-time forever as long as they are needed, or as long as they want to work for relatively low pay and a lack of job security.

While under the English department, the directorship of FYW rotated among tenure-track faculty. The director received a one-course reduction from the annual seven-course load. As a result, the commitment of directors varied from year-to-year, but generally directors kept things afloat with an overworked assistant director, two annual staff development meetings, and a list of recommended textbooks. Now, after the departmental split, FYW directors serve three-year, renewable terms with a three-course reduction and the support of a writing department. The directors are, as a consequence, more able to engage in program oversight, including curricular revision, regular classroom observations, intensified staff development, and integration of term-end portfolios across all sections.

INTRODUCTION OF THE WPA OS

With our departmental independence, one of our first actions was to revise the FYW learning outcomes to conform more closely to the WPA OS. We took advantage of what was—at that time—the new strategic plan for DePaul, focusing particular attention on two elements: "raising academic rigor and expectations" and "enhancing DePaul's academic reputation" (*VISION twenty12*). What "rigor" and "expectations" actually mean, or how success in these categories is measured, is not specifically defined in the strategic plan. For example, is rigor illustrated through higher test scores (and on what tests)? Or, is it measured by an increase in degrees granted, a proliferation of new graduate programs, national recognition (also a contested term), or all of the above? We determined that implementing writing program assessment based on national guidelines would be a positive (and positively regarded) step, and that such a step certainly had the potential of enhancing reputation. (Of course "reputation" can also be elusive, leaving much speculation as to what might count as reputation-enhancing. While DePaul's reputation was built on a great men's basketball team in the 1970s and 1980s, the women's team has played in the NCAA championships fifteen times since 1990 without significantly enhancing the school's *reputation*). The advantage to ambiguity, of course, is in the opportunity it can provide—in this case, to define rigor, expectations, and reputation on our own terms.

Introducing the WPA OS into our program was, in point of fact, a comparatively small move because our previous learning outcomes were not substantively different from the WPA OS. Adapting the WPA OS to fit our institutional context and navigating the institutional processes of approving the WPA OS were relatively easy at DePaul. The first-year writing committee drafted the changes, which were then approved at the departmental level; we submitted the resulting document to the college's Liberal Studies Council (LAS). Shepherded through by the associate dean of LAS—with whom I had shared earlier drafts for feedback—approval was swift. My impression, stemming from remarks by the associate dean, was that these learning outcomes were viewed with high regard, since many units in the college were struggling to develop similar learning outcomes with less success and without the benefit of national guidelines.

In terms of ramifications, I hoped this step would accomplish a number of things. First, I knew that the WPA OS could help provide continuity and consistency across the approximately 268 FYW sections (5,600 student enrollments, 22,400 credit hours) that we are responsible for each year. Second, I hoped the WPA OS would help pedagogically by giving guidance and direction to the reflective component of the portfolio in which students examine and explain how their writing reflects the achievement of learning goals. Third, I assumed that adhering to national goals and outcomes would be appealing to a university, and would add value to the work that FYW instructors and their students were doing. They could now hold themselves up to (and meet) national criteria. In other words, we took advantage of the university's strategic plan to introduce nationally instead of locally sanctioned learning outcomes.

The Results

In Chapter 9, Stephen Wilhoit argues that WPAs should strive for "deep change" rather than "incremental change." Citing Robert Quinn, Wilhoit maintains that deep change is long lasting and works at fundamentally changing values and approaches, while incremental change can be transitory and reversible. This, of course, makes sense. Launching nationally established learning outcomes for first-year writing at my university was, by any definition, incremental change. In fact, deep change is often difficult to enact in the conservative environment of higher education. Further, much is dependent upon variables of particular academic institutions and contexts. For example, is there an assertively supportive dean or provost? Is there a culture (existing or developing) that values the importance of writing in learning? Has the groundwork been laid for mutually beneficial conversations about writing, the teaching and learning of writing, and its role in knowledge-making?

We managed, I would argue, to orchestrate a shift, although it has not been quick or easy or decisive. We have, indeed, benefited from a change in administration over the past five years—from one that was preoccupied with other, perhaps equally important, concerns to one that has not only enabled but also encouraged the increased prominence of writing. Though writing in the disciplines initiatives over the years have been short-lived, we have connected with faculty and staff in other departments and units at the university through these initiatives, collaborating in the research and development of resources that reflect best practices in writing, learning, and assessment. Finally, the "we" pronoun that I use here includes a number of rhetoric and composition faculty who have worked at DePaul over the past fifteen years, some of whom are now at other institutions. In one way or another, each has contributed to reshaping conversations—whether it was speaking up during a focus group meeting on the issues with student writing at the university, participating in an internal research study six years ago about the amount of writing DePaul students do (at that time, relatively little), or writing a detailed "exit" memo (as part of the process of taking a new job elsewhere) about the lack of writing support at the university.

What were the results of this orchestration? Perhaps the most enduring changes have been local, within the first-year writing program. Through the use of portfolios and accompanying reflective essays, we seem to have facilitated a situation in which first-year writing students are as familiar with the learning goals and learning outcomes as their instructors, helping with consistency across sections while still allowing some independence as to how these goals are achieved and, hence, how the classes are structured. For the past two years, our assessments of student reflective essays have indicated that the students are much more able to speak to these goals than they were in 2006 and before. Students reflect—with varying degrees of skill and success—on their understanding of the learning goals, the degree to which they feel they have achieved the desired outcomes (by pointing to specific materials in their portfolios), and what they feel they have yet to accomplish. Because the portfolio is a component in all FYW courses, the articulation (or lack thereof) between the courses (102, 103, 104) becomes more readily apparent to all constituencies. For example, a 102 (Basic Writing) student who writes about her understanding and ways of employing revision in that course may construe this differently in WRD 103, where rhetorical tasks invite more sophisticated thinking, writing, and self-reflection. The program syllabi and reflective assignments that we have collected and examined suggest that instructors are consistently incorporating the WPA OS into their courses. An informal survey indicates that many instructors find the learning outcomes to be very valuable in helping them with their course planning, textbook selections, and assignment design and sequencing.

However, a quick and equally informal poll of students was less affirming. Because these are required courses, several students said that they felt they had to do whatever the instructors said, and that the learning outcomes presented a set of hoops they had to jump through before they could complete their university writing requirement. They could not remember much about the learning outcomes, even a few weeks after taking the class. While the number of students with whom I spoke was too small to draw any valid conclusions, their comments may suggest a problem of agency, with students feeling that "official" learning outcomes represent yet another set of institutional goals that may or may not intersect with their personal goals. While this is something we hope to remedy in the coming years as we move toward electronic portfolios and different forms of reflection, this issue needs significantly more study. Longitudinal studies in particular would help determine the degree to which the implementation of WPA OS had any impact on students' critical reading and writing abilities.

Beyond the FYW program, changes as a result of the implementation of the WPA OS are more difficult to quantify. The FYW assessments have, in recent years, been held up as models of productive assessment at the university, in part because of the clarity of the goals and the differentiation between goals and outcomes, and also in part because of the structure of the assessments themselves (i.e., focus on students' reflective essays in their portfolios, collaboratively designed scoring guides, reports that relate results to composition theory). Clearly, we have benefited from the rich body of knowledge on assessment in our discipline, which does not exist in other disciplines. More debatable is whether nationally vetted outcomes have conferred more legitimacy on an often-criticized unit (first-year writing) because too many students *still* can't spell or write a complete sentence. In the long run, the WPA OS certainly has the potential for contributing to a sea change; the statement, with its emphasis on rhetoric, critical reading and writing, process *and* conventions is very explicit: learning to read and write is a complex, multi-faceted activity. Despite the visibility of the WPA OS at DePaul (on websites, in assessment reports, in documents on writing in other units, such as first-year programs), there is little evidence that it has won the day over the folk wisdom that good writing is surface-level correctness.

For universities that seem fixated on ranking and stature, perhaps necessarily so, the benefit of a set of goals and outcomes that bears the imprimatur of a national organization remains to be seen. The university's relatively new culture of assessment has provided an opportunity, a kairotic moment, and we positioned ourselves well enough such that the introduction of the WPA OS and assessment literature enabled us to capitalize on that moment. The associate deans who work with us also have come to recognize that there is indeed a national organization (Council of Writing Program Administrators) occupied with teaching writing and with college writing programs, of which writing assessment is just one component.

Clearly, the use of an officially sanctioned set of learning outcomes cannot, on its own, make change happen. I doubt that this was even part of the original intention of the WPA OS. However, together with other incremental changes in the past ten years, including a new department of writing, there have been many more opportunities to explain what we do. The implementation of the WPA OS has contributed momentum and scope to other activities that have been underway during the past year. Recently, we celebrated the six-year anniversary of the first-year program's student-writing showcase, which continues to promote what first-year students can do in writing. Loosely modeled after the Celebration of Student Writing at Eastern Michigan University (see http://www.emich.edu/english/fywp), thirty-five first-year students present their writing to other students, friends, parents, faculty and administrators. Unlike the process at EMU, the process at DePaul is selective. Students compete for the thirty-five slots, and are awarded small cash prizes. We have been fortunate to invite guest speakers who are well-known Chicagoans (not necessarily "creative writers") to speak about the student writing that is presented and writing in the world, as well as nationally known rhetoric and composition experts (such as Andrea Lunsford). As much as celebrating student writing, we use the event to publicize the work of our writing program.

We also worked to capitalize on national attention to writing by participating in NCTE's National Day on Writing (See http://www.ncte.org/dayonwriting), turning it into a university-wide event. Co-sponsored by the Department of Writing, Rhetoric, and Discourse and the writing center, we extended this into a year-long celebration, "DePaul's Year on Writing," which linked the National Day on Writing to the student showcase (above) and to a week-long event on international writing, to which we invited speakers—both international students and academics—to show their work. These events were promoted in campus newspapers and newsletters that went out to faculty, parents, and alumni. Finally, after several years of pressure from many sectors of the university, but primarily from FYW (given our program's reliance on adjunct faculty), an initiative from the deans of various schools at DePaul has been put forward to make substantive changes in hiring and retention practices of contingent faculty. This has provided yet another occasion to share what happens in writing courses and programs and to promote the value and nature of expertise. This remains an issue, one that I'll take up next.

Ongoing Challenges

The material position of writing at our institution contributes to the problem of implementing deep change. As Jeff Rice, Tony Scott, and others have pointed out, the role of WPAs at most institutions is largely managerial. The WPA at my institution is not much different; she manages a relatively large program in which the mandate is to teach students to *write*. As is the case elsewhere, *writing* at my university has a complicated position. Although it is embedded in curricular planning and the university's long-term plan for academic enrichment, it is still largely misunderstood (and, if you will, *disrespected*)—mostly out of ignorance, but sometimes out of indifference. Symptomatic of this is the strong resistance to the plan that gives stable, full-time, and renewable teaching contracts to our mostly contingent FYW writing instructors (and, as a result, access to adequate salaries, benefits, and some kind of tenure). The resistance is especially strong among tenured faculty who argue that any such effort undermines tenure. They maintain that tenure track faculty should teach the writing courses, despite the fact that this would involve hiring at least fifteen new tenure track faculty in our department. These resistant faculty know, of course, that this won't happen. Among other things, the utilization of a large number of part-time (and hence transient) faculty makes no economic or pedagogical sense. The university is thus left just as it is, relying on part-time faculty. Emerging from these discussions seems to be the assumption that almost anyone can teach writing, that the job is little more than getting students to put one correct sentence after another without plagiarizing. Despite the WPA OS, despite the new department, despite the internal efforts, and, despite *some headway* on this, the idea is strongly entrenched that disciplinary knowledge in writing is superfluous in teaching writing; sometimes, it even gets in the way (say, of rote grammar instruction). If this is so, it *would* make sense to frame the WPA as a manager of operations rather than a faculty director, and the better job we do at program development, teacher training, and assessment under these conditions, the more we solidify our role as managers.

Indeed, the managerial model has had an impact on our university's writing center. Three years ago, the faculty director was replaced by a staff professional—hired and supervised by university administrators—who had little disciplinary training and expertise except what was acquired on the fly. To exacerbate the problem, writing within disciplines and across the curriculum is loosely controlled by the writing center. (I say "loosely" only because the directorship serves at the whim and under the direction of upper administration.) Thus, university alliances between those with disciplinary expertise and those without it are not structural, but rather effected only by the efforts of well-meaning individuals. Fortunately, staff directors at our university's writing center *are* smart and well meaning, and have worked hard to acquire disciplinary expertise in writing or to depend upon those who do. Their positions, though, are as contingent as the adjunct faculty who make up the lion's share of our first-year writing teaching ranks.

GARNERING RESPECT OR REFRAMING THE QUESTION?

One of the principles that my naiveté about the value of the WPA OS has reinforced for me is that we need to more effectively impact the larger picture. This is not a new argument. As Peter Mortensen, Susan McLeod, and others have claimed, part of our jobs as writing program administrators is to be "change agents" (McLeod 112) not just within the university, but outside it, and to contribute to the work of re-shaping public perceptions about what writing is and does and how it is best learned. The visibility of the learning outcomes within our institution *may* have contributed to a grudging recognition—at least internally to some people—that important intellectual stuff can and does go on in classrooms that feature writing, and that this "stuff" can and should be substantiated and valued. I have come to believe that I was overly optimistic by believing the respect could be achieved within institutions without changing the public conversation. Internal coalition-building, as Tony Scott and others have argued for, is important, to be sure. And, in fact, while we are not unionized (one of Scott's suggestions), we have gained supporters from outside our unit. But this is not enough.

In her book *The Activist WPA*, Linda Adler-Kassner offers a compelling argument not just about changing minds, but for changing the conversation entirely, reframing the messages we convey to a public in order to make substantive (and deep) change. After offering examples of how the public (including government) configures writing and the teaching of writing, she argues for concrete actions, developed from her interviews with media strategists at community action organizations including MoveOn.org, Strategic Press Information Network (SPIN), and Wellstone Action.

What are some of the things that WPAs, already overworked in the administration of complex programs, can do on our terms? Drawing from Adler-Kassner, and following the examples and suggestions of others from a number of media workshops in which I have participated, I suggest that WPAs establish relationships with local media, including but not limited to campus media. Often, through the university's media office, one can seek to become the "go-to" person to respond to provocative questions to which media may want immediate answers. When a controversial issue emerges (such as news stories that student writing is getting worse, and that lax and misguided teachers are to blame), we can resist the impulse to complain to sympathetic voices (on a listserv, for example) and instead post comments to a public forum. We can use resources that have been established to make this easier: WPA's Network for Media Action website (http://www.wpacouncil.org/nma), CompPile (http://comppile.org/search/comppile_main_search.php), CompFAQs (http://compfaqs.org//CompFAQs/Home), and the NCTE website (http://ncte.org). We can make use of the *Framework for Success in Postsecondary Writing*, its database of research, and the sample assignments and classroom activities that support the Framework (http://wpacouncil.org/framework).

We can also share our narratives: about writers and writing, about interactions between writing teachers and students, about moments that enact what *we* believe and value—a student writer's insight about something he or she has produced, a teaching success, a dramatic learning moment, or an observation of values in action. We can post interesting, thoughtful commentary (for example, postings from Dennis Baron's Web of Language blog: http://illinois.edu/db/view/25 or Mike Rose's blog: http://mikerosebooks.blogspot.com/, or *Scott Jaschik's articles in Inside Higher Ed)* in public places around the university. We can, in Peter Mortensen's words, "Go public" (182). Clearly, any discussion about the WPA OS is also a discussion about the entire spectrum of work in which WPAs are engaged. The development of the WPA OS itself, the expansion of its use, and the contribution it makes in potentially altering the landscape of writing programs both internally and in the public eye, make it extraordinarily valuable in advancing our profession.

WORKS CITED

Adler-Kassner, Linda. *The Activist WPA: Changing Stories about Writing and Writers*. Logan, UT: Utah State Press, 2008. Print.

Council of Writing Program Administrators, National Council of Teachers of English, and National Writing Project. *Framework for Success in Postsecondary Writing*. CWPA, NCTE, and NWP, 2011. PDF file.

Council of Writing Program Administrators. "The WPA Outcomes Statement for First-Year Composition." Council of Writing Program Administrators, July 2008. Web. 12 Dec. 2011.

McLeod, Susan. "The Foreigner: WAC Directors as Agents of Change." *Resituating Writing: Constructing and Administering Writing Programs*. Ed. Joseph Janangelo and Kristine Hansen. Portsmouth, NH: Heinemann-Boynton/Cook, 1995. 108–16. Print.

Miller, Thomas P., and Jillian Skeffington. "The Pragmatics of Professionalism." *The Writing Program Interrupted: Making Space for Critical Discourse*. Ed. Donna Strickland and Jeanne Gunner. Portsmouth, NH: Boynton-Cook/Heinemann, 2009. 126–136. Print.

Mortensen, Peter. "Going Public. *College Composition and Communication* 50.2 (1998): 182–205. Print.

Rice, Jeff. "Conservative Writing Program Administrators (WPAs)." Strickland and Gunner. 1–13. Print.

Scott, Tony. "How We Do What We Do: Facing the Contradictory Political Economics of Writing Programs." Strickland and Gunner. 41–55. Print.

VISION twenty12: The Plan for Academic Enrichment. DePaul University, 2006.

12 The WPA Outcomes Statement: The View from Australia

Susan Thomas

It is assumed that writing program administrators in the United States, as is the case for many administrators in higher education, know how to get things done through a blend of formal scholarly and pedagogical training and expert troubleshooting, complemented by managerial savvy. Given the politics and struggles of wills seemingly inherent in writing program administration, WPAs often answer endless questions, defend writing instruction, negotiate a program's place in the university, make deals, mediate disagreements, and stroke egos—and this on top of designing curriculum, teaching full loads and often overloads, coordinating and mentoring TAs and adjuncts, and grading all those papers—or, simply, getting on with her "day job."

The situation at the University of Sydney is no different from most writing programs, except that, prior to 2004, there was no writing program and no WPA. Not surprisingly, then, there was certainly no national statement of outcomes to assist in the development of writing courses and writing programs. In other words, there was no "statement articulating what composition teachers nationwide have learned from practice, research, and theory," and until very recently, there was no significant research or theory surrounding first-year writing instruction in Australia.

This chapter relates how the WPA Outcomes Statement for First-Year Composition (WPA OS) has enabled this WPA and the program to flourish, assisting the direction of the writing program at Sydney in explicit, subtle, and sometimes (admittedly) sneaky ways. If not for the WPA OS, the writing program at Sydney would have been left theoretically rudderless, subject to blind trial and error at the whims of non-specialists with strong opinions. Additionally, I outline how the Sydney writing program came to be, how I came to it, and how the WPA OS has facilitated its developments—which include a writing center, a virtual exchange program, and the foundations from which to develop a writing across the curriculum (WAC) program. Like the writing program Teresa Grettano, Rebecca Ingalls, and Tracy Ann Morse discuss in Chapter 4, a social-epistemic approach (Berlin) characterizes the program at Sydney and illustrates the importance of a transactional rhetoric both inside and outside the classroom. I relate below how the WPA OS undergirds this approach.

Background

In December 2002, the ink barely dry on my dissertation, I hopped a plane for Australia, along with my new Australian husband, who had persuaded me to try Australia for a year. Since my rhetoric and composition degree would be virtually unrecognizable in Australia, and given that tenure track academic positions are far scarcer in Australia than in the U.S., I was certain that my trip home was as good as booked, so I settled in for a much-needed holiday. However, in the eleventh month, and at the proverbial eleventh hour, I was hired as a lecturer in University English at the University of Sydney, Australia's oldest university. I would soon learn that "lecturer" means assistant professor in this part of the world, and that "coordinator of University English" meant a peculiar hybrid of a WPA and WAC coordinator position. I was unaware, however, of the cultural stigma attached to the very notion of academic writing, the word "rhetoric" in particular, or the politics surrounding University English in an academically conservative university, one modeled on the British system of higher education.

An initiative mandated by the vice-chancellor, University English marked a bold pedagogical shift for the University of Sydney. My interview and subsequent conversations with colleagues had revealed that the course was a variant of freshman composition, or as it is now more commonly known, first-year writing—a program designed to help students write better by teaching them to think better, usually based on rhetorical theory. I was dismayed to learn that there was a remedial stigma attached to the course, and in fact to any academic writing enterprise in Australia. The term *rhetoric* was recognized only in the popular sense (empty language or the antithesis of reality)—

and worse, it was perceived as having no relationship to writing. Even more disturbing was the widely-held belief that drilling students in grammar and coaching them in style would somehow magically make them good writers, an approach that sounded disturbingly akin to what James Berlin calls current-traditional rhetoric.

The next six years would present a significant learning curve, and the tests would be far more difficult than any I had endured in graduate school. A wise professor had told me, "You never really know your discipline until you are required to teach it," and I would soon learn that I had never fully articulated, even for myself, exactly what my discipline meant to me—or the various communities it serves—until I was forced to define and defend it. All of my teaching up to that point had been as a TA or as an adjunct, and I had happily taught the curriculum I was given, designed by people I respected, and delivered to students who had accepted it mostly without question. It never occurred to me, then, that I might one day have to *be* my discipline. While I'd had excellent mentors and extensive training in writing pedagogies, all I had learned now seemed lost in translation, even in an English-speaking country similar in many respects to the United States, but in others a world apart. Fortunately, I turned to the Council of Writing Program Administrators and its many resources, including the WPA OS. I wondered how it could apply in an educational culture so different from that of the United States, a culture not unlike that of Harvard in the early nineteenth century.

The Challenges

Learning to write is a complex process, both individual and social, that takes place over time with continued practice and informed guidance. (WPA OS)

Shortly after my arrival in the Sydney English department, I explained enthusiastically to a colleague that I intended to create a major in writing studies at the university, to which she replied, "What's *that*? What would students with such a major *do*?" It was immediately clear that I would not only be introducing a new program (the first in English department history not based solely on literary texts), but also navigating my way through a clash of cultures and, in some instances, academic elitism. Moreover, I sensed a healthy skepticism of the American educational system as a whole—and of the "core" in particular. While Australians are generally welcoming of American products, services, and entertainment, the area of education seems more sacred. There is a popular saying in Australia, "Only in America" (accompanied by eye-rolling and heavy sighs), which is usually applied to social trends or politics, but occasionally heard in the academy regarding American educational conventions that seem too "low-brow" (e.g., "freshman comp") for institutions of higher learning, particularly top tier research institutions.

The more I learned of my new university and its educational tradition, the more I considered returning to what I knew, to an environment where my discipline was accepted and where I could simply get on with my work without having to defend its scholarly merits and fight for each new development. At this point, I realized that I would have to let the major in writing studies wait while I dealt with more immediate concerns, and that I would first have to articulate clearly the benefits of a rhetorically sound writing course and build the program one step at a time. I was too naïve and inexperienced at the time to realize that American WPAs are plagued with the same problems, a concept that Susan McLeod describes as "The WPA as Foreigner," and that step-by-step and day-by-day is how WPAs get the job done (108). Besides, I had more pressing problems.

University English had grown quickly from forty to six hundred students per year, so I was faced with recruiting and training adjunct staff (mostly graduate students in literature who had no prior experience in writing pedagogy) to teach up to fifteen sections per semester. During the first two years of my appointment, I carried a teaching load of fourteen hours per week (slightly heavier than a "4/4" load in the U.S. system) and taught and/or coordinated intensive versions of University English in both summer and winter school. The WPA OS informed the "aims and outcomes" of each section of the course—as well as the training program and manual I designed for the other teachers, particularly in its emphasis on writing as epistemic and on Andrea Lunsford's definition of rhetoric as a theory of communication rather than mere persuasion (9; see also Eidenmuller).

In some instances, however, the issues and pressures I faced, while not new to WPAs, were exacerbated by cultural difference, which complicated the already arduous task of building a writing program from the foundation up. For instance, I experienced the following "common" challenges: The perception of writing as a second-class discipline; the difficulty of staffing writing classes and educating adjuncts; the challenge of student (and teacher) diversity in the writing classroom; the challenges of managing a heavy teaching load and performing administrative duties while maintaining (or in my case, establishing) a research profile; and the difficulty of negotiating the same promotion criteria as others who do not face the same institutional challenges.

The following suggest problems originated from or were exacerbated by cultural difference: the lack of established Australian writing across the curriculum or first-year writing programs; the absence of a nationally recognized writing/communication discipline, such as rhetoric and composition and associated scholarly journals and organizations; the definition of English studies as close reading of canonical literature; the various currents of anti-Americanism; the differences in Australian and American English and writing conventions; the Australian connotations of rhetoric; the tendency of Australian universities to hire their own PhDs, which can result in academic departments that are sometimes skeptical of new programs and deviations from tradition; and the lack of peer mentoring and peer review programs.

While all of these presented challenges, my insistence on rhetoric as the theoretical foundation of the writing program was what attracted the most criticism. The pilot of University English had been designed by a graduate student in functional grammar (a derivative of Hallidayan Systemic Functional Linguistics), and focused almost exclusively on the mechanics of writing. When promoting rhetoric to an audience with no prior exposure to the discipline, I was faced with the first of many rhetorical decisions: How to make the discipline responsive to the Sydney cultural climate. Again, the WPA OS would prove invaluable, as it helped me realize that before I could convince others of the benefits of my discipline, I would have to articulate for myself how rhetoric translated in my new surroundings, and I would have to make my colleagues understand that "it is important that teachers, administrators, and a concerned public do not imagine that [writing] can be taught in reduced or simple ways. [Teaching writing] requires expert understanding of how students actually learn to write" (WPA OS). The focus of the program would have to shift—and just how, I did not yet know.

The Solutions: Graduate Attributes and the WPA OS

As writers move beyond first-year composition, their writing abilities do not merely improve. Rather, students' abilities not only diversify along disciplinary and professional lines but also move into whole new levels where expected outcomes expand, multiply, and diverge. (WPA OS)

As Stephen Wilhoit notes in Chapter 9, sometimes the best a WPA can hope for is to get lucky, and serendipity was finally on my side. The year 2004 marked two important events that would impact the academic culture at Sydney: the revision of the university's policy on graduate attributes or outcomes, which led to a greater emphasis on teaching and learning, and a campaign to set that portfolio on equal footing with research. The revised statement of graduate outcomes features two levels of graduate attributes: overarching and specific. The three overarching graduate attributes include scholarship, lifelong learning, and global citizenship, while the specific attributes are grouped into five clusters: research and inquiry; communication; information literacy; ethical, social and professional understandings; and personal and intellectual autonomy. All seventeen faculties of the university were asked to devise their own interpretation of the five specific attributes and embed them in their curriculum. The Faculty of Arts' statement of graduate attributes, as featured on its website, now requires the following (See the Appendix for the full descriptions within each category.): research and inquiry; information literacy; personal and intellectual autonomy; ethical, social and professional understanding; and communication.

Common sense told me to use the WPA OS to demonstrate how a writing program would help the university, particularly the faculty of arts, implement the new policy and demonstrate outcomes. This would not be difficult, since there were so many obvious points of consonance, particularly in the areas of communication proficiency, information literacy, technological competence, linguistic diversity, ethical and social responsibility, and intellectual autonomy.

Results

Despite resistance on a few fronts, University English became enormously popular throughout all seventeen faculties of the university, owing mostly to its grounding in rhetoric and its response to student need. Four degree programs adopted it as a required course, but the English department refused initially to allow it to count toward an English major, claiming that its content was unsuitable. (This decision was later overturned.) The resistance in my home department was unsettling, but I was determined to remain focused on the students, who had always been assessed by written assignments, but until now had never been taught how to write. The most significant problem was having only one course that was expected to meet the needs of ESL students and basic writers, as well as more advanced writers—and having to abide by the lecture/tutorial format, comprised of two, six hundred-person lectures per week and a weekly, one-hour tutorial with twenty-five students per group. Despite the fact that University English did not count toward an English major, students still flocked to it and left wanting more.

In December 2005, I argued successfully for the appointment of a second WPA and for University English to be renamed Academic Writing, which underscored its cross-disciplinary scope and its focus on writing. I also felt it important to free the course from associations with any one academic department, since I envisioned a program in writing across the curriculum, and felt that Academic Writing would have a much better chance of success university-wide than would University English.

In 2006, a new Australian WPA was appointed. Though we had received stellar applications from around the world, my instinct was that an Australian writing program needed at least one Australian WPA, since, according to the WPA OS, writing programs should reflect national goals and priorities. This decision marked the turning point in the acceptance of the writing course into the English major. Rebecca Johinke had a BA in classics, so was no stranger to Aristotelian argumentation. Plus, she had worked with Professor Claire Woods at the University of South Australia in one of the country's best communications departments, which pioneered a rhetorical approach to communications studies in Australia. Woods's vision for promoting a "textual culture" within communications programs served as an example for the adoption of a "rhetorical culture" in the Sydney writing program.

By this point, I had already decided to step down as coordinator and give Rebecca a chance to bring fresh ideas and insights into the program. I was exhausted and very near the point of losing my objectivity—never a good thing for a fledgling program, particularly one showing so much promise. Rebecca, using her background in communications and classics, and remaining committed to the WPA OS, employed her knowledge of local attitudes and made strategic additions to the writing curriculum, including a couple of smart examples of rhetorical theory drawn from English literature. The English department voted nearly unanimously to include Academic Writing among its accredited first-year courses, which would remove the remedial or "dead-end course" tag.

With Rebecca at the helm of the academic writing program, I continued to teach several sections and help out in any way she needed me. Together, we mapped a plan for the future of Academic Writing, including the creation of an online interactive component in lieu of the weekly lectures, in keeping with the WPA OS's focus on writing in electronic environments. We were awarded over $150,000 in grant funding to implement the new online features, which also earned Academic Writing the distinction of being named a best practice model of flexible learning.

Writing Goes University-Wide

In mid-2006, I was appointed Associate Dean of Teaching and Learning for the Faculty of Arts, which meant, among other things, that I would be chairing the faculty's teaching and learning committee and representing the faculty on university committees. My colleagues felt that my experience and skills as a WPA would be beneficial to the faculty, which had its own battles to fight over funding, degree structures, and teaching and learning programs.

My role as associate dean gave me a useful vantage point from which to observe the university as a whole—free of departmental or disciplinary biases and conventions. Most significantly, my colleagues and I articulated how strong academic writing and WAC programs solved a number of the faculty's teaching and learning problems. While first-year writing is still a fledgling concept in Australia, the need for such programs is evident, as student bodies are becoming more diverse, with specific needs and expectations. The University of Sydney has sometimes been jokingly referred to as "a finishing school for the elite," as it has traditionally attracted top-ranking students from prestigious private and selective high schools. With more students enrolling from overseas and through alternative admissions pathways (comparable to the GED option in the U.S.), there is a greater need for what Australians call generic skills, those necessary for life in the real world—particularly writing competence.

This shift in the student demographic inspired the dean of arts, with encouragement from the teaching and learning committee, to make the Faculty of Arts the provider of Academic Writing and other "generic skills" programs for the university. This initiative included the development of the Arts Teaching and Learning Network, which I had the privilege of co-designing with colleagues, and a new degree program, the Bachelor of Liberal Arts and Sciences (BLAS), a partnership between the Faculty of Arts and Science that paved the way for a WAC program.

The Arts Teaching and Learning Network focuses on four key priority areas, led by four directors of specific portfolios: e-learning, academic writing, student support and development, and staff support and development. Again, I used the WPA OS and its alignment with the faculty's focus on graduate attributes to argue for academic writing's place in the teaching and learning network.

The BLAS is the first degree program at the university to feature a type of core system, with Academic Writing featuring as one of three required or recommended courses for all students. In making a case for a writing course in the BLAS program, I used the WPA OS to demonstrate that writing instruction isn't only for English or arts degrees, that "faculty in all programs and departments can build on this preparation by helping students learn the main features of writing in their fields, the main uses of writing in their fields, and the expectations of readers in their fields" (WPA OS). The BLAS necessitated yet another redevelopment of the academic writing program to make it suitable for a university-wide audience. Instead of an ENGL prefix, we settled on WRIT to underscore the interdisciplinary nature of writing and to strengthen the case for a WAC program. At this point, the English department removed the accreditation for the original Academic Writing course, so a team comprised of the chair of linguistics, the director of student development, and I developed a new cross-disciplinary writing course especially for the BLAS: WRIT1001.

The adoption of the WRIT prefix gave me the opportunity to do what I had wanted to do for some time: develop the writing program into three distinct courses, rather than having a single course attempting to meet the needs of all students. In 2009, the faculty offered WRIT1001 as the required course for BLAS students, while English continued to offer WRIT1002, and a committee was convened to design a third course, WRIT1000, for ESL students.

The Sydney Writing Hub

With the WRIT courses in place, the next step would be to create an interdisciplinary home for them. I had been working for some time on attracting external funding for a writing center. My search for a donor proved tumultuous and ultimately fruitless, due in part to the recession and to the Australian perception of top universities as successful corporations in their own right. While it is true that most research one institutions are financially secure, this is often not the reality in cash-strapped and under-resourced faculties such as in the arts. I continued to explore funding options, and finally managed to land a large national education grant covering all infrastructure costs. Once again, I turned to the WPA OS to make a case for a writing center, particularly since the center's mission would be "to build rhetorical knowledge and to teach students to use writing and reading for inquiry, learning, thinking, and communicating, and to understand a writing assignment as a series of tasks, including finding, evaluating, analyzing, and synthesizing appropriate primary and secondary sources" (WPA OS). The Writing Hub, as it is now known, opened in July 2010, and offers two first-year courses, WRIT1001 and WRIT1002 (renamed Rhetoric and Writing 1 and 2), as well as writing courses for graduate students. WRIT1000 is under development and scheduled for debut in 2012.

Conclusion

Since my initial appointment at the University of Sydney, I have come to believe more than ever in Ellen Cushman's description of the rhetorician as an agent of social change, as I have witnessed the university's gradual warming to the idea of writing and rhetoric as a discipline, largely due to its adherence to clearly-stated outcomes and its resonance with the university's statement of graduate attributes (7).

As I reflect upon the past six years, the theme that emerges is learning. I had taken up my appointment determined to *change* the educational culture, to *persuade* my colleagues and students to accept writing and rhetoric as a discipline, and to *defend* the scholarly merits of my discipline. My wise colleagues cautioned me not to worry, that everything would fall into place in time. In retrospect, it is obvious that a strong current of imperialism was at work on both sides, with my advocating for a system of teaching writing without articulating (or even knowing) why I believed in it so strongly, and with Sydney colleagues defending the way things had always been done with no evidence to suggest that the old ways were working. Of course, the answer lay in understanding how Sydney students actually learn to write, and then devising programs to facilitate this. The focus had to be placed on the students—not on the WPA or any individual department or faculty member—which is the very approach the WPA OS advocates, backed by the credibility of an internationally recognized organization with proven results.

I chalk up my initial shortsightedness to the naivety of a novice, the palpable fear of failure, the insecurity of a foreigner, and the inexperience that accompanies one's first "real" job. However, once I decided to take a step back and see what I could learn—from the WPA OS, from my own mistakes, or from colleagues—the task suddenly appeared far less onerous, and I began to see opportunities all around me. Each new experience, even the most difficult, had something to teach me, and along the way I developed that wonderful Australian ability to laugh at myself and not take things so seriously, especially at situations beyond my control. The familiar Australian refrains, "no worries" and "she'll be right," would become mantras, and the relaxed attitude of my supportive colleagues and students would somehow soften my defensiveness. I also employed what Stephen Brookfield calls the four lenses of critical reflection: students, self, peers, and scholarly literature (xiii). As a reflective vehicle, the WPA OS has enabled a fresh look through each lens, with all four lending important perspectives to the development and assessment of the Sydney writing program.

After six years of persistence, buoyed by positive student feedback and the support of the Council of Writing Program Administrators (CWPA), I have witnessed changing perceptions of writing and the university's gradual acceptance of it as a discipline. The writing program has evolved from a single controversial "dead-end course" to a high-tech model of pedagogical good practice for the university. It has earned the support of colleagues across the university, and is now enjoying teaching, learning, and research partnerships with the wider Sydney community, area schools, and leading international universities.

The program has attracted national media attention as the only first-year writing curriculum in Australia grounded in rhetorical theory. In partnership with local high schools, it has been awarded two competitive Australian Department of Education grants, enabling collaborations with secondary teachers and students, and initiated a meaningful professional dialogue on the transfer of student writing from high school to the university. I am currently working with colleagues in the Faculty of Arts to establish a cross-disciplinary major in writing, with George Pullman of Georgia State University to develop a "virtual exchange" program, and with colleagues at Stanford University as a partner in their cross-cultural rhetoric program. With the support and encouragement of the Council of Writing Program Administrators, I have established an Australian WPA affiliate, in response to the need for a national body to devise and implement shared outcomes for Australian writing programs, since "the setting of standards should be left to specific institutions or specific groups of institutions" (WPA OS).

As the program at Sydney has grown, I have developed a new appreciation for WPAs, whose plight is different from that of any other professional. Unlike academics from other disciplines, who work with more clearly-defined curricula, and whose fields have long been accepted as legitimate disciplines of tertiary study, the WPA is faced with the added challenge of creating curricula, meaning, and legitimacy seemingly at every turn—on top of the demand to demonstrate excellence in teaching, research, and service. These are classifications that continue to ignore many aspects of WPA work. But, because of these obstacles, the gains and rewards are even more appreciated, particularly when writing programs succeed and make a difference in the lives of students. As the development of the Sydney writing program has demonstrated, the WPA OS offers new programs the benefit of a collective body of wisdom, which takes much of the guesswork out of program development and assessment for new WPAs. Benefiting from the guidance of dedicated colleagues and the WPA OS, the Sydney writing program enters credibly into a new decade—or, as colleagues have called it, a brave new world.

Appendix

Faculty of Arts Statement of Graduate Attributes

Research and Inquiry: Graduates of the Faculty of Arts will be able to create new knowledge and understanding through the process of research and inquiry. They will possess a body of knowledge relevant to their fields of study, and a firm grasp of the principles, practices, and boundaries of their discipline; be able to acquire and evaluate new knowledge through independent research; be able to identify, define, investigate, and solve problems; think independently, analytically and creatively; and exercise critical judgment and critical thinking to create new modes of understanding.

Information Literacy: Graduates of the Faculty of Arts will be able to use information effectively in a range of contexts. They will recognize pertinent information needs; use appropriate media, tools and methodologies to locate, access and use information; critically evaluate the sources, values, validity and currency of information; and use information in critical and creative thinking.

Personal and Intellectual Autonomy: Graduates of the Faculty of Arts will be able to work independently and sustainably, in a way that is informed by openness, curiosity and a desire to meet new challenges. They will be independent learners who take responsibility for their own learning; set appropriate goals for ongoing intellectual and professional development, and evaluate their own performance effectively; be intellectually curious, open to new ideas, methods and ways of thinking, and able to sustain intellectual interest; respond effectively to unfamiliar problems in unfamiliar contexts; and work effectively in teams and other collaborative contexts.

Ethical, Social and Professional Understanding: Graduates of the Faculty of Arts will hold personal values and beliefs consistent with their role as responsible members of local, national, international and professional communities. They will understand and practice the highest standards of ethical behavior associated with their discipline or profession; be informed and open-minded about social, cultural and linguistic diversity in Australia and the world; appreciate their ethical responsibilities towards colleagues, research subjects, the wider community, and the environment; and be aware that knowledge is not value-free.

Communication: Graduates of the Faculty of Arts will recognize and value communication as a tool for negotiating and creating new understanding, interacting with others, and furthering their own learning. They will possess a high standard of oral, visual and written communication skills relevant to their fields of study, including where applicable the possession of these skills in languages other than English; recognize the importance of continuing to develop their oral, visual, and written communication skills; and be able to use appropriate communication technologies.

Works Cited

Berlin, James. *Rhetoric and Reality: Writing Instruction in American Colleges, 1900-1989.* Carbondale: Southern Illinois UP, 1987. Print.

Brookfield, Stephen. *Becoming a Critically Reflective Teacher.* San Francisco: Jossey-Bass, 1995. Print.

Council of Writing Program Administrators. "The WPA Outcomes Statement for First-Year Composition." Council of Writing Program Administrators, July 2008. Web. 11 June 2011.

Cushman, Ellen. "The Rhetorician as an Agent of Social Change." *College Composition and Communication* 47.1 (1996): 7–28. Print.

Eidenmuller, Michael E. *American Rhetoric.* 2001. Web. 6 May 2012.

Lunsford, Andrea A. "Key Questions for a New Rhetoric." *What is the New Rhetoric.* Ed. Susan Thomas. Newcastle-upon-Tyne: Cambridge Scholars Publishing, 2007. 4–15. Print.

McLeod, Susan. "The Foreigner: WAC Directors as Agents of Change." *Resituating Writing: Constructing and Administering Writing Programs.* Ed. Joseph Janangelo and Kristine Hansen. Portsmouth, NH: Boynton/Cook, 2005. 108–16. Print.

University of Sydney Faculty of Arts and Social Sciences. *Statement on Graduate Attributes.* 18 Feb, 2011. Web. 11 June 2011.

Woods, Claire. "Rhetoric and Textual Culture: Constructing a Textual Space in the Curriculum." Thomas. 46–68. Print.

13 Ripple Effect: Adopting and Adapting the WPA Outcomes

Morgan Gresham

> *He spoke of the power of portfolio assessment to "reshape institutional goals," and of its potential to "change the world of assessment."*
>
> —Sharon Hamilton

> *Repurposing as remediation is both what is "unique to digital worlds" and what denies the possibility of that uniqueness.*
>
> — Jay David Bolter and Richard Grusin

Edward White tells us that assessment is both perilous and promising, and that our understanding and interpretation of assessment depends on where we are located: inside or outside the academy, the department, or the discipline (*Teaching* 3). Because of its fluidity, assessment moves with equilibrium, and from even the most non-programmatic attempt at assessment, it pushes us toward systems: of writing, of general education, and of education and teaching in general. The image of an eddy, then, might serve as an apt metaphor for discerning how assessment shapes writing programs.

Reading the other chapters in this collection, I am particularly struck by how similar the many stories are to each other, and to the circular stories that we have been capturing in the WPA literature for more than the ten years the WPA Outcomes Statement for First-Year Composition (WPA OS) has been in place. In "Telling a Writing Program Its Own Story," Louise Wetherbee-Phelps articulates the mission many incoming WPAs face: "In 1986 I went to Syracuse University charged with the task of conceptualizing and founding a new writing program—as it turned out, not from scratch, but by facilitating the self-transformation of a scattered group of teachers and courses into a genuine teaching community" (168). Tim Peeples explains that "budgets, legislatures, students, future employers, the discipline of rhetoric/composition, current program instructors, and so on each can be seen to make legitimate claims on what 'should' be done within a writing program" (164). It is precisely the push-and-pull created by these multiple factors and stakeholders that creates non-program circumstances when there is not strong leadership offered by a WPA. In contrast, as an example of the leadership a strong WPA provides, Phelps describes the positive changes she and others collaboratively created for the Syracuse writing program by piecing together various parts of a non-program. In 1999, Rebecca Moore Howard posted on the WPA-L listserv about the cyclic nature of the WPA and the field's chronic (in)ability to reinvent the WPA wheel with redevelopment of each writing program. She wrote,

> Interestingly, the moment I left Colgate, self-placement ended and they went back to random grouping of students in comp classes—which demonstrates, I believe, not that there's something wrong with self-placement, but that much of a WPA's work doesn't outlive her presence at the site. She departs, and the wheel then gets reinvented by a successor, or the program reverts to default mode. ("Re: Outcomes Assessment")

Howard's "default mode" is the same non-program status that Karen Bishop Morris and Lizbeth A. Bryant describe in Chapter 10. In *WPA as Researcher*, several chapters focus on the need to collect and archive our WPA histories, to create libraries of the memos and other artifacts that document our continuous cycle of powerful and powerless moments (Rose; Mirtz). Without a support network like those created in well-established writing programs, or without the collaborative "Great Groups" Phelps describes, it may be too easy to lose sight, too easy to shift among the powerful versus powerless narratives, in which we WPAs honor in alternating cycles the good and the bad that we encounter; we grow programs and then, as Teresa Grettano, Rebecca Ingalls, and Tracy Ann Morse remind us in Chapter 4, we leave. Upon the WPA's departure—our departure—it becomes someone else's responsibility to reshape and remediate the gone-to-pot non-program

program into a Program. In these instances, WPAs look for and locate moments of power within our not-insignificant powerlessness. Seeking resources, we grasp onto the power of assessment, the WPA OS, and the scholarly cache of the field to show the value of our work both individually and as programs. Further, issues such as assessment and technology create eddies in which programs are forced to change, to remediate themselves in new ways. If or when the WPA remains in place, such eddies have the potential to create positive change (e.g., a new eportfolio system). If the WPA changes, is removed or otherwise disappears, those eddies shift the current away from stability and, at worst, wash the program away when it is not embedded within established departments or anchored by administrative lines. In this chapter, I consider how the swift current of assessment has changed the shape and the scope of the program I direct, and the roles that the WPA OS has served in the changing context of assessment.

I had initially envisioned this chapter as a celebration, noting how my colleagues and I collaborated to create a focus on assessment that engineered power for our small program on campus—a narrative similar to what Bishop Morris and Byrant describe in Chapter 10 as "non-program programs" complete with shared images of squirreling away WPA OS nuggets of power. Instead, what I have discovered is that with great responsibility comes a modicum of power. The moments that we WPAs have to enact significant change are particularly fleeting, and that our programmatic first-year composition (FYC) eportfolio system may in fact serve, as Carl Whithaus warns, as "new tools for enforcing norm-referenced, single-digit or letter scores on wider and wider scales" instead of the innovative tool I had sought as WPA (151). What follows, then, is an exploration of the ways our implementation of the WPA OS has been both programmatically stabilizing and oppressive, and I discuss the ways in which we tenure line faculty who teach in the program have subsequently tried to counter those oppressive tendencies.

Innermost Circle: Place Matters (Not So Much)

My initial thoughts included the idea that place matters, and that it would be important for me to provide a description of the place where I am now. So I do: The University of South Florida St. Petersburg (USFSP) is a small, formerly junior-senior campus that in 2006 received separate accreditation and has shifted from 150 first-year students per year to 500 in the past four years. However, contextualizing my programmatic space was and is important primarily to help recognize the system of the non-program program. My current institution is not special in its uniqueness, but rather in its sameness: From 2004–2008, it existed as a non-program similar to the programs described by Grettano, Ingalls, and Morse and Bishop Morris and Bryant in this volume. Between 2004 and 2008, only seven percent of our composition courses were taught by full-time faculty, and prior to 2008, our small campus did not have a systematic approach to coordinating a program nor to writing assessment. Stepping back from this contextualization allows us to define ourselves institutionally in community with other FYC programs in similar situations, and that community helps us—as mobile WPAs—recognize the larger contextual situation that smaller institutions occasionally arrive late to ongoing national conversations, such as assessment procedures and best practices and the power complexities—both potential powers generated and lost—that will exist in such non-program spaces (Bishop Morris and Bryant; see Chapter 10). Because WPAs may come in with experience from another institutional context and with an ideal of meeting national best practices, even the best laid plans may go awry due to the lack of local institutional knowledge available. Local records, if they existed at all, disappear with the previous WPA, if there was one. It is not with malicious intent that these programs exist in this way, but rather as Shirley Rose suggests, that "failure to retain program records in an accessible location contributes to the view that our work is transient and unworthy of preservation" (116). Although Rose suggests several circumstances in which institutional records may be lost or dismissed, in the case of my current institution, there was neither a true writing program nor a WPA position to catalog. Without the benefit of historical records, my efforts to articulate the national conversation about assessment to the needs of the developing program were inhibited.

Ripple 1: The Story within the Story

In 2008, the then-new provost invited the campus to join the national conversation on student learning outcomes as a part of an accreditation review. As acting WPA, I quickly needed to develop a plan to gather and assess documents and to build a sustainable assessment program for the first-year composition program. Although I was aware of the WPA OS, the day-to-day work of teaching and scheduling in not-quite-a-program type of program quietly pushed the WPA OS out of mind. Yet, the moment it became clear that the program needed a plan, the WPA OS resurfaced as a lifeline to a comprehensive program assessment. Asked by the provost what the writing program was going to do "to close the assessment loop," several members of our faculty quickly developed a systematic and programmatic approach to adopt the WPA OS, choosing a common textbook, constructing common assignments, and developing assessments based on the WPA OS, which included electronic portfolios for FYC and exit-level, general education writing across the institution. From this initial plan, the writing program turned to a number of portfolio assessment models to help shape eportfolio assessment practices (Elbow and Belanoff; Yancey, "Looking Back"; White, "The Scoring").

When we tenure line faculty conducted our first program assessment in spring 2008, only five instructors submitted course artifacts for the assessment, and only three sets of documents from those submitted met the requirements for our WPA OS assessment. Further, in our initial assessment, the mean rating of fifty-four student artifacts was 2.47 on a four-point scale, with a thirty-two percent pass rate. We tenure track faculty charged with developing the assessment practices established a goal for the initial writing assessment at a mean rating of 2.5 or higher, and documents in the assessment fell short of this goal. Given the concerns that our newly instituted FYC program committee had about the materials available and assessment process prior to our joining the faculty, we mandated that, beginning in fall 2008, all first-year composition students would create and develop electronic portfolios that would include three required assignments and two required reflections for midterm and end of term assessment (Conway; Yancey, "Mapping"; White, "The Scoring"). These eportfolios, created and archived in Blackboard, undergo a double-blind holistic scoring for grading and assessment based on a revised scoring guide that reflects our institutional interpretation of the WPA OS. The eportfolios are assessed on students' abilities to demonstrate five areas of the WPA OS: Rhetorical Knowledge; Critical Thinking, Reading, and Writing; Composing Processes; Knowledge of Conventions; and Writing Technologies (officially added in the spring 2010 assessment).

Classroom instructors and two outside readers score student portfolios (0–5) on the WPA OS areas, and the average score counts as part of students' final grades. Average scores of three (3) or higher are considered passing for program assessment purposes. By 2010, after two academic years of WPA OS-based assessment scores, I have a much better sense of how well students are meeting nationally derived expectations for first-year composition: The numbers have remained relatively constant (averaging near 3.5) for both of the FYC courses.

That students' scores have not increased steadily over time is troubling, especially given that scores are highly valued outside of the department. However, the members of our FYC committee recognize the greater improvement to the program created by common assessments built around the WPA OS and the incremental score increases over time. We expect that as our student population levels out, and we continue our programmatic changes based on observations and discussions surrounding student work, we will continue to see positive results.

Of greater concern internally are decreases over time in both students' success rates in completing the eportfolios, and instructors' buy-in for the programmatic changes and requirements. Similar to the conclusions that Liz Hamp-Lyons and William Condon draw in "Questioning Assumptions about Portfolio-based Assessment," our programmatic experiences have clarified that the process of assessment, including our portfolio assessment, affects both the findings and the quality of the assessment. Hamp-Lyons and Condon argue that, over time, portfolio assessment is "a difficult balancing act . . . but one that will become necessary to all portfolio assessment programs as they grow toward maturity" (327). Still far from maturity, our FYC portfolio assessment process is still developing, and how instructors at our institution perceive the assessment process is a large part of that development. Although our committee saw a drop-off in instructor support for our assessment procedures, instructors have been instrumental in refining the portfolio process and expectations.

Ripple 2: Recognizing Our Power Differentials

Unlike the narrative from Grettano, Ingalls and Morse in Chapter 4, and despite our being three, un-tenured junior faculty working together to support the writing program at our small institution, we did have a fairly consistent display of respect and support from our department and our upper-administration. This respect translated to an authority and power (albeit occasionally limited) to enact programmatic changes as we saw fit. Unlike our WPA colleagues elsewhere, the primary location of fear of our programmatic changes was with our contingent faculty.

One of the more difficult pieces has been getting and maintaining instructor buy-in for the programmatic changes. Many of our current adjunct instructors were already teaching at USFSP before my tenure line colleagues and I arrived. WPAs have recognized for some time that institutional change is difficult, especially when assessment is perceived as a form of surveillance (Belanoff; Huot and Williamson). Early in our program discussions, the WPA OS was a rallying point for creating and adopting curricular changes. When the WPA OS was first discussed at professional development meetings, all participants concurred with the goals of the statement, although our instructors each identified different methods for meeting WPA OS-related goals. However, since we have instituted the WPA OS as the basis of our program and its assessment, instructors have become more resistant to the process of assessment, and they have expressed discontent with the WPA OS generally. This discontent seems to stem not from the WPA OS itself, but rather from the programmatic implementation of WPA OS, as embodied by the programmatic assessment.

In our locale, the need for assessment created a strong current that was bolstered by our institution's desire for a positive outcome. Although this strong current initially pushed our non-program toward a positive effect—the consolidation of the non-program into a program—the programmatic approach actually interfered with the effectiveness of the assessment. In this context, where there is significant push-back from instructors toward programmatic initiatives, it is tempting to look at spreadsheets, averages, and standard deviations as the most pressing assessment concerns. Because our FYC committee desired the power and the structure for the writing program that accompanied a systematic assessment approach, we did not pay careful enough attention to the dissent generated by those assessment practices. Further, Whithaus's claim that eportfolio systems may become techno-oppressive is particularly apt here if programmatic or outside expectations cause us to lose track of why we assess student writing. If our purpose is, as Whithaus argues, to measure "how a student is creating new knowledge about composition and about language" (xix), then we must not let the assessment technologies—be they outcomes statements or eportfolios—lose their situated, contextualized experiences. For a period of time, our committee's push toward assessment created this kind of disconnect between what we were doing and why. Yet, our instructors continue, despite some misgivings, to participate in community discussions about assessment and to share the improvements they see in students' demonstrations of rhetorical knowledge, composing processes, and uses of technology. Because they continue to raise concerns about students' abilities to think and write with critical awareness, we are working to share and incorporate instructors' suggested assignments into our writing curriculum. By maintaining and archiving the local conversations we now have, we are better positioned to listen to our instructors' concerns and incorporate our own institutional contexts into our assessments.

A second concern about our programmatic assessment connects with the technologies that house student artifacts for assessment. Although Yancey delivered a persuasive talk to our general faculty in the fall of 2008 about the positive effects of using a common tools approach to course portfolios, in which students create portfolios using a range of website and blogging tools, our committee chose instead to mandate "basic" Blackboard portfolios for our FYC assessment because our students already have access to Blackboard. However, during two years of programmatic assessment, we have encountered an increasing number of technical difficulties that impacted the effectiveness of our assessment. First, because Blackboard portfolios operate in a closed system in which the student has sole control of the portfolio and its contents, we encountered a hole in our assessment practices when we discovered that all students had to share their portfolios with all instructors individually. Although the FYC program created instructions for sharing portfolios with our instructors, some students did not share their portfolios with the intended outside-instructor readers. Therefore, our first sets of assessment numbers had zeros for students who failed to share their portfolios with some or all of the readers assigned to their classes. These zeros negatively affected the overall averages of our student learning outcomes.

Over time, the program added workarounds, both technological and instructive—a Blackboard workgroup, clearer distinctions in our assessment of when a portfolio is "Not Available" for scoring—that have improved the overall averages of submitted and passing portfolios. Similarly, our writing program has made other changes to the portfolio requirements as we encountered un-extractable, downloaded files, incompatible versions of word-processing software, difficulties displaying word-processor to html encoded files, and broken graphics and images. While these technical difficulties initially brought down our students' scores on the portfolios, our program's assessment tools are improving with each iteration of the process. Finally, our campus has opted into Google Applications, providing students easy access to Google Sites, a website building/hosting space that can accommodate files, visuals, and video. As we continue to improve our portfolio assessment practice, we are planning to transition to Google Sites as the primary home for FYC portfolios, eliminating both concerns about sharing portfolios and display errors.

Now that our program has accumulated two years' worth of portfolio assessment data, we on the FYC committee are in a better position to make limited, strategic changes to our program and program assessment. Like a ripple effect, these smaller changes have larger repercussions for our program. One of our changes has been to add the "Composing in Electronic Environments" set of outcomes to our general education outcomes for the university. Because we have been trying for several years to leverage more computer access for our writing classes (our campus currently has only three computer classrooms, and our writing classes are not guaranteed slots in those classrooms), we believe that the WPA OS lends greater credence to our requests for more computer access because we can provide numerical evidence to show that our students are not yet fully meeting expectations for this technological outcome.

Assessment is a moving target, and over the past two years, I have discovered the ways in which that movement works in our favor. A primary concern I had when developing our system was to be aware of and, as Whithaus suggests we should, "honor the impulse behind writing as discovery and communication" (151). Reading and sharing student eportfolios is an important part of our program assessment, and the WPA OS provides the common language to discuss that discovery about communication. Perhaps we did a better job of remaining critically aware of communicative aspects of portfolios in the initial stages of our program assessment when we were in many senses still feeling our way. Whithaus concludes his argument that assessment is a process that necessarily follows the writing process, and that we should not think in terms of having developed a static system but instead a dynamic conversation. My favorite part of teaching writing is "tinkering" with the assignments and the technologies to meet the new needs, goals, and objectives of our writing classes and students (Whithaus 151). I have learned that assessment requires tinkering, too, requiring new technologies, new genres of writing, and new ways to see, hear, and experience young writers' voices. Assessment has many ripple effects; our remediation must extend to our assessment systems so that we may continue to experience these writing conversations.

Stepping Back: Rippling Assessment as Power

Reflecting on this process, I see patterns emerge that foreshadow how eddies will affect the larger system. As WPAs, we often revel in the mysteries of technology and media. In our programs, we push against surges that seek to limit the ways in which we define and compose literacy. We, and our programs, occasionally suffer the consequences—from the light-hearted, "Oh, I won't do that again" remark, to the more severe denial of tenure or removal from WPA positions because of the decisions we make and the battles we choose to fight. Throughout this power negotiation, the WPA OS serves as an "emergent rock" around which powerful currents, such as assessment, can take shape. These currents, then, have the potential to disrupt the traditional flow and provide power opportunities for writing programs—for example, when the provost calls and asks the WPA to lead the assessment parade. Further, the WPA OS eases the field's conscience because it shows that the field, in its participatory and interactive nature, demonstrates an awareness of the chronic and potentially dangerous nature of the non-program-to-Program cycle, and works to provide real tools to WPAs. As a field, we have learned that it is not really possible to create a national archive of writing program documentation: the documents are too context specific and, even when they are not, the working lives of WPAs, especially those of us who exist in the non-program-to-Program world, may prevent us from collecting, distributing, and reading those archives. Yancey is right in her claims that: (1) the WPA OS has succeeded; (2) most teachers are only "vaguely aware of the statement, *if* they are aware at all"; and (3) the reason for the success *is* that the WPA OS has been so proactively pushed in the media in which the non-program-to-Program WPAs can find it: it is web-mediated (Yancey, "Bowling Together" 211, 213, 216). Whereas the scholarly lives of non-program-to-Program WPAs often grind to a halt, with no time to get books from the library or to read them, the WPA OS *can* be Googled, and it only takes five minutes, to read, absorb, and re*media*te for the non-programs in which we find ourselves. Further, because the WPA OS represents best practices for the field, it possesses an ephemeral power that truly is, if we extrapolate from White's illusion of the assertion of power, the best we can hope for.

WORKS CITED

Belanoff, Pat. "Portfolios and Literacy: Why?" *New Directions in Portfolio Assessment: Reflective Practice, Critical Theory, and Large-Scale Scoring.* Ed. Laurel Black, Donald A. Daiker, Jeffrey Sommers, and Gail Stygall. Portsmouth, NH: Boynton/Cook, 1994. 13–24. Print.

Bolter, Jay David, and Richard Grusin. *Remediation: Understanding New Media.* Cambridge, MA: MIT P, 1999. Print.

Conway, Glenda. "Portfolio Cover Letters, Students' Self-Presentation, and Teachers' Ethics." Black, et al. 83–92. Print.

Council of Writing Program Administrators. "The WPA Outcomes Statement for First-Year Composition." Council of Writing Program Administrators, July 2008. Web. 10 Nov. 2011.

Elbow, Peter, and Pat Belanoff. "State University of New York at Stony Brook Portfolio-Based Evaluation Program." *Portfolios: Process and Product.* Ed. Pat Belanoff and Marcia Dickson. Portsmouth, NH: Boynton/Cook, 1991. 3–16. Print.

Hamilton, Sharon. "Portfolio Pedagogy: Is a Theoretical Construct Good Enough?" Black, et al. 157–67. Print.

Hamp-Lyons, Liz, and William Condon. "Questioning Assumptions about Portfolio-based Assessment." *Assessing Writing: A Critical Sourcebook.* Ed. Brian Huot and Peggy O'Neill. Boston, MA: Bedford/St. Martin's, 2009. 315–29. Print.

Howard, Rebecca Moore. "Re: Outcomes Assessment." *WPA-L.* 15 November 1999. Web. 15 August 2010.

Huot, Brian and Michael Williamson. "Rethinking Portfolios for Evaluating Writing: Issues of Assessment and Power." Huot and O'Neill. 330–42. Print.

Mirtz, Ruth M. "WPAs as Historians: Discovering a First-Year Writing Program by Researching Its Past." *The Writing Program Administrator as Researcher: Inquiry in Action & Reflection.* Ed. Shirley K Rose and Irwin Weiser. Westport, CT: Boynton/Cook, 1999. 119–30. Print.

Peeples, Tim. "'Seeing' the WPA With/Through Postmodern Mapping." Rose and Weiser. 153–67. Print.

Phelps, Louise Whetherbee. "Telling a Writing Program Its Own Story: A Tenth Anniversary Speech." Rose and Weiser. 168–84. Print.

Rose, Shirley K. "Preserving Our Histories of Institutional Change: Enabling Research in the Writing Program Archives." Rose and Weiser. 107–18. Print.

White, Edward M. *Teaching and Assessing Writing: Recent Advances in Understanding, Evaluating, and Improving Student Performance.* 2nd ed. San Francisco, CA: Jossey-Bass Publishers, 1994. Print.

—. "The Scoring of Writing Portfolios: Phase 2." *College Composition and Communication* 56. 4 (2005): 581–600. Print.

Whithaus, Carl. *Teaching and Evaluating Writing in the Age of Computers and High-Stakes Testing.* Mahwah, NJ: Erlbaum, 2005. Print.

Yancey, Kathleen Blake. Afterword. "Bowling Together: Developing, Distributing, and Using the WPA Outcomes Statement—and Making Cultural Change." *The Outcomes Book: Debate and Consensus after the WPA Outcomes Statement.* Ed. Susanmarie Harrington, Keith Rhodes, Ruth Overman Fischer, and Rita Malenczyk. Logan, UT: Utah State UP, 2005. 211–21. Print.

—."Looking Back as We Look Forward: Historicizing Writing Assessment." *College Composition and Communication* 50.3 (1999): 483–503. Print.

—. "Mapping ePortfolios: Models, Definitions, Promising Directions." University of South Florida St. Petersburg. Campus Activities Center, St. Petersburg, FL. Aug. 2008. Presentation.

14 Ethos and Topoi: Using The Outcomes Statement Rhetorically To Achieve The Centrality and Autonomy of Writing Programs

Deirdre Pettipiece and Justin Everett

> *American education will never realize its potential as an engine of opportunity and economic growth until a writing revolution puts language and communication in their proper place in the classroom. Writing is how students connect the dots in their knowledge. . . . Of the three 'Rs,' writing is clearly the most neglected.*
>
> —The National Commission on Writing for America's Families, Schools, and Colleges

When the University of the Sciences in Philadelphia hired its first WPA in 2007, writing was physically and ideologically relegated to the margins of the institution. Located in the Humanities Annex, a building at the edge of campus, writing was viewed by students and faculty alike as an essential but distasteful skill inculcated in one basic composition course in the general education curriculum housed under humanities, and marginally addressed in an additional required humanities course, Introduction to Literature. Since this second semester course's content and syllabus identified it as a genres reading course rather than as a composition course, writing *instruction* took place only in the basic composition course. In a private, sciences-based institution whose rigorous disciplinary and professional curricula imposes high expectations and few choices on its students, this isolated writing experience encouraged students to view the single, general education composition course as an irrelevant and burdensome repetition of high school English, and the general faculty to view it as poor preparation for scientific and professional writing tasks related to their upper-division courses. In addition to the "bad taste" the writing course instilled in faculty and students, years of declining performance on the school's writing proficiency examination (WPE) (a rising sophomore assessment) convinced administrators of the need to address the situation.

The step towards appointing a director of writing programs had been hampered for months due to the conflicting ideas of what that director might do and who, precisely, he or she might be. The dean had previously attempted to appoint the director of the writing center to this position. That appointment was rejected by the literature faculty for fear that it would result in a curricular revision that the director had long advocated. While the faculty historically associated with the writing program was eager to hire a candidate who would preserve its autonomy and curricular preferences, administration was determined to have change, and therefore demanded someone from the outside. The dean and the vice president seemed to recognize a point well made by Rebecca Moore Howard, that

> From time to time, those with institutionally sanctioned power recognize and respond to institution-changing power exercised by outer circle individuals or groups. This institution-changing power, which revises established definitions of the university, may also produce institutionally sanctioned power for the group or individual(s) who wield it. (38)

After this contentious and nearly failed search, one of us (Deirdre) was hired as the director of writing programs (WPA), and subsequently was charged by the vice president with a complete program assessment and plan for a more effective and practical writing curriculum in confluence with the university's mission and students. Upper administration in this context seemed to unknowingly echo ideas regarding the need to centralize writing articulated in the epigraph preceding this chapter, essential to implementing the entirety of WPA Outcomes Statement for First-Year Composition (WPA OS).

In essence, our problem was threefold. First, several of our colleagues in the humanities department deeply believed in a liberal arts approach to literacy with the study of literature at its center. Second, the university faculty and administration as a whole perceived a need for curricular revision, particularly with a focus on professional and scientific writing. But, third, the university community as a whole was unaware of rhetoric and composition as a field distinct from literary study in its ideology, body of research, and methods, (For more on the role of ideology in curricular reform, see Grettano, Ingalls, and Morse in Chapter 4.)

Because our attempts at curricular revision met strong ideological resistance from certain quarters, we became aware that we needed to educate the university community about our field. We believed this would allow us to engage in a public conversation about the need for curricular change in our private conversations, public presentations, and eventually, our 130-page, research-based *Strategic Plan for Writing Programs*. This document, with the WPA OS as its core, allowed us to (1) address the ideological concerns of our humanities colleagues; (2) provide reviews of primary research to support the need for curricular revision given the particular mission of the university and its programs; and (3) educate the university community in the field of rhetoric and composition as distinct from literary study.

While our approach—literally taking our argument for curricular revision to the floor of faculty council—may seem bold, it was necessitated by long-standing resistance to significant curricular revision. Though the administrative support for a practical and effective writing curriculum would prove crucial to the revisions and restructuring the program needed, the charge seemed nearly impossible to exercise due to the lack of understanding of and appreciation for theories of teaching and assessing first-year writing within the Department of Humanities in which the existing courses—and the WPA—were housed. With a faculty comprised almost solely of specialists in literatures and cultures, the department felt strongly that while the existing courses might need some revision, literature in and of itself was a solid and valuable focus for undergraduates and their writing; further, the department believed that no student should graduate from the institution without taking a required course in literature and two semesters of Intellectual Heritage, a "great works" sequence that focuses on the "interrelationships among ideas, events, attitudes, values, and artifacts produced within various cultures past and present" ("Intellectual Heritage").

It was within presentations and discussions in department meetings that we first introduced the WPA OS and made arguments for curricular reform. While humanities faculty engaged in numerous discussions of the assessment and revision of writing program courses, and with the writing proficiency exam now the principal responsibility of the director, these discussions never resulted in an understanding that while literature was a vital, rich discipline with its own desirable student-learning outcomes, *reading it* was not necessarily a useful or appropriate mechanism for increasing students' writing ability. We reinforced our presentation of the WPA OS by drawing on Jeanne Rose's ideas on how to "foster a more inclusive view of language" by introducing ideas of *how to use literature effectively* in the writing classroom to achieve WPA OS goals. What ensued was an ongoing and increasingly unproductive battle for disciplinary preference that was less about learning than it was about values.

Our literature colleagues insisted that good writing was more a matter of "talent" than "technique," and was best "absorbed" by studying and imitating the great works. The views of our literature colleagues can best be summed up in Edward White's observation that

> for them, arguments, data, and allies are irrelevant; these are elitists or others living in a fantasy world, and they believe deeply that writing programs are not a proper part of higher education. Often . . . they have an equal contempt for pedagogy and for composition, and their motives are sometimes obscured, even from themselves. Their perceived calling is for higher things, and they have no intention of debasing themselves by learning anything about composition, which they avoid teaching to the equal relief of the students and themselves. ("Use It or Lose It" 7–8)

This was the situation in which we found ourselves. We attempted, as Karen Fitts and William Lalicker suggested, establishing a middle ground based on the assumption "that 'literary' texts and 'everyday' texts make meaning by the same principle", and that these texts could be a part of a multidisciplinary writing program (447). In spite of this, our colleagues continued to insist that the study of literature trumped the need to teach writing and research as a practical skill, going so far as to say that teaching research and documentation was not the responsibility of the humanities department.

Compounding issues related to working on the preliminary planning for program assessment and revision was that it was not these experienced—and very capable—literature faculty members who were teaching the bulk of the general education composition courses; instead, these courses had historically been taught by a small group of adjunct faculty members with no instruction, oversight, or professional development. In this regard, University of the Sciences, in many ways, reflected the "long history of institutions outsourcing first-year writing to barely qualified and/or under-compensated adjuncts" (Moscovitz and Petit 87).

As a result of an adjunct and tenure track faculty little versed in current theories and pedagogies related to first-year and other writing instruction and assessment, the new WPA turned to the director of the writing center (Justin) for assistance, as the only other humanities faculty member with a significant background in rhetoric and composition. This collaboration was crucial to achieving any significant change in the place writing instruction and assessment occupied at the institution; for although writing centers and their direction have a set of disciplinary practices and a body of scholarship of their own, in a small, private, professional institution, collaboration and cooperation between the writing center and the program was imperative.

In addition to the director of the writing center, the WPA solicited assistance in program revision and assessment through the creation of an ad hoc, interdisciplinary writing task force so that faculty in key programs could provide feedback regarding the writing skill sets and expectations their curricula demanded. This task force was the second stop for the WPA OS, and allowed us to continue the process of discussing why the existing belletristic model was inappropriate for the university's mission, how curricular revisions would help the university fulfill its educational mission, and how the field of rhetoric and composition is particularly well-suited to accomplish this task. This group, which reviewed the WPA OS in addition to other literature from our field, invoked some of the vital collaborative, communal engagement practices associated with creating a successful writing across the curriculum program identified by Barbara Walvoord, Elaine Maimon, and Toby Fulwiler.

The interdisciplinary writing task force met bi-weekly to discuss writing needs and expectations; their insight and contributions proved invaluable to our arguments in favor of specific curricular revision for first-year, general education, writing courses. We then used the input from that group in tandem with the WPA OS to inform the design of our research and best-practices-based strategic planning document. This plan opened an institution-wide conversation about the place of writing in the curriculum that resulted in moving writing from its condition of peripheral and departmental irrelevance to a position of centralized and interdisciplinary authority. Moving beyond brief goals, objectives, and assessments associated with a conventional strategic plan, our document was in effect an extended argument introducing our readers to the literature of our field in order to justify our recommendations for curricular revision. We followed the guidance of Chris Anson, who indicated that

> if we continue to rely on *belief* in our pedagogies and administrative decisions, whether theorized or not, whether argued from logic or anecdote, experience, or conviction, we do no better to support a case for those decisions than what most detractors do to support cases against them. (11)

Although we realized that our humanities colleagues would likely not initially be swayed by evidence, we felt strongly that only through the use of *data* could we fairly expect positive outcomes across interdisciplinary faculty, particularly at an institution immersed in scientific study. We knew that it was precisely the interdisciplinary faculty we really had to reach to make the sweeping changes we ultimately proposed. We also knew that by infusing the data into our arguments for change, we could produce "a more robust plan for building on the strong base of existing research into our assumptions about how students best learn to write" (Anson 12). In our *Strategic Plan for Writing Programs*, we specifically linked the five WPA OS goals with literature in the field, followed by a description of the curricular reforms we would make to operationalize these goals.

As a result, the WPA OS provided the backbone of the plan and allowed us to help our colleagues understand the necessity of change along two trajectories:

> *Ethos*: That the field of rhetoric and composition is a discipline independent of the study of literature with a body of empirical research based in social science methods.

Topoi: That the successful implementation of interdisciplinary writing programs that address the broader needs of the university community must exist in intellectual, administrative, and physical independence from colleagues in literature.

In calling for independent authority and structural separation from humanities and literature, while also focusing on the interdisciplinary writing skills valued by programs and faculty all over campus, we were responding differently to the idea of *what students needed* in writing instruction and assessment. Engaging with our interdisciplinary colleagues while still investing in our specific curricular goals posed a serious challenge; we knew that even as we solicited input from those in other disciplines, the construction and execution of curriculum and assessment had to remain with us. We were mindful of White's statements that "we cannot leave these matters to others," because "decisions can determine the future of an entire department" ("Opening" 307).

We were also still engaging in discussions with our humanities colleagues who, operating from current-traditional assumptions, privileged a legitimate and deep-felt belief in the fundamental role literature plays in undergraduate education. When they discussed "good writing," they referred frequently to stylistics, whereas we were more concerned, as Derek Soles noted in his response to the WPA OS in 2001, with designing a writing program that "contributes to academic and career success" (378). We believed, as Barry Maid has suggested, that "writing is not one of the humanities but rather an applied discipline," and therefore we finally sought separation from the humanities department as the only means for removing writing from its marginalized position and infusing it across curricula as an essential professional skill (99). By using the statement—and a wealth of research—as the foundation of our *Strategic Plan for Writing Programs*, we were able to legitimize our plan with a statement that at once was accessible, authoritative, and which validated our approach as representative of the best practices in the field.

Rhetorical Contexts

Though, in 2004, the director of the writing center (Justin) had presented the chair of the writing proficiency committee with data demonstrating that high-stakes examinations like the university's assessment were unreliable and invalid, the examination continued. By 2007, the failure rate on the examination was in danger of exceeding forty percent in spite of the high quality of students admitted to the university and the remediation undertaken in the writing center.

Our initial analysis of the writing proficiency exam, based partly on an extensive review of student exams and on surveys of focus groups of students, faculty, and administrators, conducted by the director of the writing center in 2006, and by both directors in 2007, determined that students were being tested on a specific set of skills—writing an argument in a timed test—that they were *not being taught* in their single composition course. Setting aside the wealth of literature problematizing timed tests in their entirety, having students respond to a challenging argumentative topic in a multi-paragraph essay within a two-hour timeframe must have *seemed* like a fair and useful indicator for second-year assessment to those responsible for implementing it; however, without related coursework or assignments in the writing of academic argument, and given the historically culturally diverse and multi-lingual nature of the student body, students only did well on the exam if such skill sets were present beforehand. It was clear that the writing proficiency exam was not a useful measure of what students had learned in writing courses; therefore, as a graduation requirement, it acted only as an impediment to success. In our conversations with faculty, we utilized the WPA OS descriptions of rhetorical knowledge, critical thinking, writing processes, and knowledge of conventions to point out the exam's fundamental weaknesses.

However, while eliminating the writing proficiency exam was a major goal for the revised writing program, because the interdisciplinary faculty on campus highly valued the ability to construct an academic argument as a vital skill and communicative practice, we determined that our revision of the curriculum would include a strong emphasis on argumentative writing. Since this was also in line with what was being offered by most of our competing four-year institutions in the greater Philadelphia and Delaware areas, we felt certain that the inclusion of and focus on argumentative writing skills ensured that our program was in line with employer and graduate school expectations. While these deliberations about the exam widened the divide between the humanities faculty and the WPAs, they also fostered a very constructive and inclusive review of the course curriculum and of the ways in which writing and its assessment was perceived.

An additional piece of information that came out of the interdisciplinary task force and our surveys of the students and faculty was that what students focused on in the first-year courses was unique to the instructor of the course taken; while shared outcomes were articulated on the model syllabus, these outcomes were often absent from instructors' syllabi. Moreover, perhaps because the adjunct instructors assigned to first-year courses were also teaching at a number of local community colleges, the courses often bore little resemblance to either the model syllabus or each other. Since the general education program at University of the Sciences had clearly identified outcomes and intentions, the wildly divergent nature of the general education courses identified with writing skill competencies was a crucial issue that had to be addressed in the curricular revision. Many of these courses—including those in literature, history, and pharmacy—while requiring writing assignments, contained little or no formal writing instruction. Others, such as those in creative writing, did include significant writing instruction. As a result, student competence in writing was inconsistent at best.

These combined test design problems and curricular issues led us to propose a new two-semester composition sequence based in the WPA OS's hope "to regularize what can be expected to be taught in first-year composition" (60). Although we shared Sheila Carter-Tod's "uneasiness about the standardization process" (76), and had to recognize that our attempt to "regularize" first-year writing at our institution ran afoul of Mark Wiley's warning "that at some institutions these outcomes may be misinterpreted precisely in order to impose a uniform curriculum upon the composition program" (27), we operated from the assumption that our profession's expectations, as articulated by the statement, could legitimize and guide our reform of first-year writing once local conditions were taken into consideration. While the WPA OS explicitly rejects the idea that common syllabi are required to accommodate common outcomes, it does allow for this when it is institutionally appropriate. These kinds of complex, individualized decisions are precisely *why* the WPA OS addresses outcomes rather than standards. The difference is far more than semantic.

Using the WPA OS to guide our reforms, we were able to propose a program that addressed the university's mission that "graduates will have the knowledge, skills, and values to be successful in their professional careers" ("USP Mission Statement"). With this in mind, our new two-semester sequence in writing consisted of a course in research-based, informational writing followed by a course in research-based, argumentative writing. We included virtually all of the explicit outcomes included in the WPA OS into the two syllabi. Though the outcomes were condensed on the syllabus, the full statement was used to engage faculty in the goals of the curriculum during workshops held three times a semester. Additionally, expanded versions of the WPA OS were used to develop shared assignment sheets and common rubrics for all classes.

Ethos: Legitimizing Rhetoric and Composition as Independent of Literature

The first step in formally establishing disciplinary independence in first-year writing involved the establishment of an interdisciplinary writing committee that served as a working group for re-conceiving writing as a central concern across campus. An extension of the initial interdisciplinary task force, this standing committee brought together faculty from all colleges in addition to the director of assessment and the director of the Teaching and Learning Center. This step removed the centralization of authority for writing from the humanities department where, in the language of the much-discussed Boyer Report:

> Unfortunately, today's students too often think of composition as a boring English requirement rather than a life skill ... Faculty too often think of composition as a task the English or composition department does badly, rather than understanding that an essential component of all faculty members' responsibility is making sure that their students have ample practice in both writing and speaking. In evaluating examinations and papers, faculty members are willing to forgive grammatical and stylistic blunders, thinking such matters the responsibility of composition teachers, as long as they believe they can grasp the essence of the student's text; that behavior reinforces the assumption on the part of students that clear communication is not important. (Boyer Commission 24)

While respectfully aware of Rita Malenczyk's legitimate concern that the report endangers the very disciplinary authority that the WPA OS represents (164), we embraced the Boyer Report's analysis of the problem as accurate and perhaps counter-intuitively as the most direct path to gaining independent disciplinary authority outside of the humanities department. Within our home department, writing was unquestionably under the control of English (literature) faculty, but this very appropriation of writing as an exclusive property had the undesirable effect of marginalizing writing as unimportant, irrelevant, and something for students to get through and forget, as our student surveys and focus groups revealed. While we recognized Malenczyk's observation that teaching writing well requires not just writing experience, but a specific set of disciplinary skills, it was by sharing curricular authority with the interdisciplinary writing committee that we were able to trade absolute control of writing for a better positioning of writing across campus as relevant to the university mission and the professionalization of our students. Through a collaborative, "needs based" discussion of interdisciplinary writing, the courses we created met the goals of upper-division assignments—and by extension, instructor expectations—even as they also met the needs of our incoming first-year students and the general education competencies.

Though the interdisciplinary writing committee responded positively to our proposed changes, they were rejected by our home department out-of-hand, beginning with the elimination of "Introduction to Literature" and the revision of the lone composition course into a new two-semester sequence. Since the department, not the committee, held the power to approve or disapprove our courses, this dismissal terminated any possibility of effective program revision. At this point, it was crucial to establish recognition of rhetoric and composition as an authoritative field in its own right. As Linda Bergmann argues, departments housing literature *and* composition faculty "need to initiate and sustain ongoing, productive discussions and collaborations between the fields of literature and composition, rather than merely serving as sites for exerting disciplinary power" (3). However, our own attempts to do this failed. The debate boiled down to the disagreement over replacing the literature course with an argument course; even when the compromise of allowing literature to remain the subject matter of the course was offered, it was rejected by our humanities colleagues. The real issue was privileging the "pure" study of literature over the lower concern of teaching applied writing.

In a last ditch attempt at demonstrating the current goals of writing programs, we presented the WPA OS to the humanities literature faculty hoping to establish disciplinary authority as compositionists and to demonstrate the need to enact curricular change. It was during this presentation that one senior faculty member flew forward, slapped a hand on the table, and bellowed, "What's a compositionist? There's no such *thing* as a compositionist!" The disintegration of the discussion into such a heated situation was evocative of a sentiment Jim Corder articulated a decade before, when he said,

> We are always in a rhetoric. We may see others in a rhetoric not our own; if we do, they are likely to seem whimsical, odd, uninformed, selfish, wrong, mad, even alien. Sometimes, of course, we don't see them at all—they are outside our normality, beyond or beneath notice; they don't occur as humans. (95)

Although we worked hard for many months to establish a dialogue with our colleagues, unfortunately and ultimately, we failed. We finally had to admit, as Timothy Doherty has written, "that change is needed when literacy instruction is constrained because of a prevailing belletristic tradition, which can result from location in an English department" (37). This called for moves to establish an independent *ethos* for the writing program, soon to be followed by new administrative, disciplinary, and physical *topoi*.

Our first move in this direction—our declaration of independence, if you will—was a decision to revise the rejected course proposals with a new prefix. Previously, all writing courses had borne the conventional "EN" prefix. Following this stalemate, we determined that a new prefix—"WR"—would better help us communicate to the university community as a whole the disciplinary and academic distinctiveness of writing programs. (As interim WPA, Justin notes that, as of the fall of 2009, students no longer refer to their writing courses as "English," but as "Writing.") With the refusal of the home department to approve the courses as newly designated, the provost removed writing programs administratively—and physically—from the department.

Topoi: Establishing Independent Intellectual, Administrative, and Physical Spaces

Essential to the success of this move was a reconceptualization of the ideological, academic, and ultimately physical places—*topoi*—eventually occupied by writing programs. In his *Topica* and later in the *Rhetoric*, Aristotle's definition of *topoi* is elusive. It is generally agreed that the term may be viewed in at least two ways: as references to specific "places" in particular texts and as a method for developing particular lines of argument. Using Aristotle's special and common topics (*topoi*) as a starting place, we sought to move first-year writing from its peripheral, relatively irrelevant *topos* in the curriculum to a more relevant, centralized position that infused writing throughout the entire university curriculum. By extending the use of *topoi* beyond Aristotle's meaning to refer to both physical and rhetorical places, and viewing writing programs as places that have physical and rhetorical dimensions, we considered the role "place" plays in defining the relationship of writing programs to their institutions. Our analysis began with the recognition that writing was housed in an isolated building, instructed in an isolated course, taught by marginalized adjunct faculty, all of these "located" in a private, science-based institution in a very urban metropolis populated by a fairly successful, multi-lingual, multicultural student body.

Each of these factors was, of course, loaded with political overtones and institutional history. To begin unpacking the complexity of how writing programs and those involved in them had been so marginalized, we had to identify the power of place in our institution and address the underlying and often subliminal influence marginalization had over perception and value. Our position was one similar to that articulated by John Schilb, and his comments on the problem of defining rhetoric and composition in terms of both disciplinary and physical grounds are worth noting here: "I doubt that I would have had to fight for adequate physical space," he observes, "if my department had given composition adequate conceptual space—that is, seen composition as a central part of 'English'" (165).

Once again citing the WPA OS and our *Strategic Plan for Writing Programs* to establish our legitimacy to campus stakeholders, we made successful arguments for curricular, administrative, and physical relocation. After public argument, administratively, our place was relocated from the Department of Humanities to the Center for Interdisciplinary Studies, a stop-gap program created for several similarly challenged academic areas and administered by a long-time faculty member. From this new administrative location, we were able to propose to the faculty as a whole a model for curricular integration and dispersion of writing across the university that placed a reinvented Center for Interdisciplinary Writing at its core, linking first-year writing, writing in graduate courses, a minor in professional writing, writing across the curriculum, and workshops in grant writing for both students and faculty. Echoing Ann Jurecic in her description of changes undertaken at Princeton, our "faculty did something very surprising: they voted to support a proposal to restructure the teaching of writing . . . a decision that led the university to build a new writing program from the ground up" (69). In particular, this interdisciplinary faculty was most impressed by the outcomes they would be able to focus on from the WPA OS, namely that faculty in all programs and departments could build on this preparation by helping students learn to (1) build final results in stages; (2) review work-in-progress in collaborative peer groups for purposes other than editing; (3) save extensive editing for later parts of the writing process; (4) apply the technologies commonly used to research and communicate within their fields (WPA OS). With the administrative relocation and with faculty buy-in and support of an entirely new curriculum and assessment plan, one that included the phasing out of the well-intended but misguided writing proficiency exam, we felt that our final goal of a geographic relocation of the program to a recognized site on campus would operate as a physical cue to both faculty and students, demonstrating that the place of writing was now much more "central" to the entire curriculum. Our choice was the long-established writing center, a fairly large and well-appointed ground floor building near the dining hall, library, and student health center. With some administrative support, our faculty now shared offices in the writing center along with a visiting professor of writing and the adjunct faculty. Through this centralized physical location, we hoped our curriculum and pedagogy would become what David Gruenewald described as "more relevant to the lived experiences of students and teachers . . . to work against the isolation of schooling's discourses and practices from the living world outside the increasingly placeless institution of schooling" and into "the firsthand experience of local life" (620).

The geographical move to the writing center proved to be an exceptionally rewarding relocation, bringing with it a sense of "home" far greater than expected. The writing program's faculty, as we were now known, including our adjuncts, began to collaborate in a historically new way, supported as we all were now by an administrative budget that accommodated the following: professional development of adjunct faculty through *paid* workshops in the new curriculum and pedagogies; release time for the WPA to observe classes of all writing programs faculty; online software for technology-infused courses; summer pay for *both* WPAs (the director of the writing center had by then become the assistant director of writing programs) to continue curriculum development; increased salaries for all writing programs adjuncts (by the second year of the new program, average adjunct salaries had nearly doubled); and the establishment of new tenure-track lines in writing programs. Through the new physical home and increased budget, the faculty development program we established allowed us to address ways to standardize outcomes for writing in all general education courses and for *all writing faculty*. Sharing the concerns Joseph Eng identifies "that the assessment approaches and grading patterns used by tenure-line and adjunct faculty alike should agree reasonably well," we met together as a body throughout the semester to discuss assignments, rubrics, collaborative learning activities, and outcomes (60). These kinds of shared opportunities had been entirely absent in the lives of the adjunct faculty members, and the increase in ownership and involvement of the curriculum was perhaps the most rewarding element of the new program.

While through the new program we have consistently offered workshops and institutes in key areas across campus, we are still working to achieve many of our loftier goals; however, the establishment of the interdisciplinary writing committee provided us with the first step toward removing writing from its isolation in the humanities department, and infusing it with an authority grounded in providing students with skills relevant to their future professional lives. As of this writing, the new first-year writing sequence is in place along with a minor in professional writing, a course-integrated tutoring program, and the beginnings of a writing across the curriculum program currently under development.

Our independent program is, by all accounts, a success story—if the increasing number of independent programs and writing departments is held in evidence—but the struggle is far from over, as the collection of essays in Bergman and Baker's *Composition and/or Literature: The End(s) of Education* clearly attests. Even though the argument—with the Tate/Lindemann debate frequently invoked as the representative example—is often made on ideological and disciplinary grounds, as Barry Maid suggests, the divide may have less to do "with 'normal' ideas of academic disciplinarity and everything to do with issues of privilege, power, and economics" (93). In other words, Maid continues, "this one really is about class differences and the privileges accorded to some and denied others determined solely on their teaching schedule" (94).

Works Cited

Anson, Chris. "The Intelligent Design of Writing Programs: Reliance on Belief or a Future of Evidence?" *WPA: Writing Program Administration* 32.1 (2008): 11–36. Print.

Aristotle. *Aristotle: Selections*. Trans. Terence Irwin and Gail Fine. Indianapolis: Hackett P, 1995. Print.

Bergmann, Linda, and Edith M. Baker. *Composition and/or Literature: The Ends of Education*. Urbana, IL: NCTE, 2006.

Bergmann, Linda. Introduction. "What Do You Folks Teach Over There, Anyway?" Bergmann and Baker, 1–13. Print.

The Boyer Commission on Educating Undergraduates in the Research University. *Reinventing Undergraduate Education: A Blueprint for America's Research Universities*. 1998. Web. 15 Apr. 2010.

Carter-Tod, Sheila. "Standardizing a First-year Writing Program: Contested Sites of Influence." *WPA: Writing Program Administration* 30.3 (2007): 75–92. Print.

Corder, Jim W. "From Rhetoric into Other Studies." *Defining the New Rhetorics*. Ed. Theresa Enos and Stuart C. Brown. Newbury Park: Sage, 1993. 95–105. Print.

Council of Writing Program Administrators [with responses by Clyde A. Moneyhun; Keith Rhodes; Mark Wiley; Kathleen Blake Yancey]. "The WPA Outcomes Statement for First-Year Composition." *WPA: Writing Program Administration* 23.1–2 (1999): 59–70. Print.

Doherty, Timothy J. "Restructuring in Higher Education and the Relationship between Literature and Composition." Bergmann and Baker, 36–53. Print.

Eng, Joseph. "Beyond Quality Control: Writing Assessment and Adjunct Accountability at a Small Public University." *WPA: Writing Program Administration* 29.1–2 (2005): 59–79. Print.

Fitts, Karen, and William B. Lalicker. "Invisible Hands: A Manifesto to Resolve Institutional and Curricular Hierarchy in English Studies." *College English* 66.4 (2004): 427–51. Print.

Fulweiler, Toby. "Evaluating Writing Across the Curriculum Programs." *Strengthening Programs in Writing Across the Curriculum*. Ed. Susan McLeod. San Francisco: Jossey-Bass, 1988. 61–75. Print.

Gruenewald, David. "Foundations of Place: A Multidisciplinary Framework for Place-Conscious Education." *American Educational Research Journal* 40.3 (2003): 619–54. Print.

Howard, Rebecca Moore. "Power Revisisted; Or, How We Became a Department." *WPA: Writing Program Administration*. 16.3 (1993): 37–49. Print.

"Intellectual Hertitage—General Information and Course Structure." *University of the Sciences in Philadelphia*. University of the Sciences in Philadelphia, n.d. Web. 29 April 2010.

Jurecic, Ann. "Writing Beyond the Headline: Building a Writing Program at Princeton." *WPA: Writing Program Administration* 27.3 (2004): 69–82. Print.

Maid, Barry M. "In This Corner . . ." Bergmann and Baker. 93–108. Print.

Maimon, Elaine P. "It Takes a Campus to Teach a Writer: WAC and the Reform of Undergraduate Education." *Composing a Community: A History of Writing Across the Curriculum*. Ed. Susan McLeod and Margot Soven. West Lafayette, IN: Parlor Press, 2006. 16–31. Print.

Malenczyk, Rita. "What the Outcomes Statement is Not: A Reading of the Boyer Commission Report." *The Outcomes Book: Debate and Consensus after the WPA Outcomes Statement*. Ed. Susanmarie Harrington, Keith Rhodes, Ruth Overman Fischer, and Rita Malenczyk. Logan, UT: Utah State UP, 2005. 162–68. Print.

Moscovitz, Cary, and Michael Petit. "Insiders and Outsiders: Redrawing the Boundaries of the Writing Program." *WPA: Writing Program Administration* 31.1–2 (2007): 86–103. Print.

Pettipiece, Deirdre and Justin Everett. *Strategic Plan for Writing Programs*. Philadelphia: University of the Sciences in Philadelphia, 2009. Print.

Rose, Jeanne Marie. "Standards of English: Literature as Language Standard." *Composition Forum*. 14.2. (2005): n. pag. Web. 15 Feb, 2010.

Schilb, John. "The WPA and the Politics of LitComp." *The Writing Program Administrator's Resource: A Guide to Reflective Institutional Practice*. Ed. Stuart C. Brown and Theresa Enos. Mahwah, NJ: Erlbaum, 2002. 165–79. Print.

Soles, Derek. "A Comment on the 'WPA Outcomes Statement for First-Year Composition.'" *College English* 64.3 (2002): 377–78. Print.

The National Commission on Writing for America's Families, Schools, and Colleges. *Writing and School Reform, Including the Neglected "R": The Need for a Writing Revolution*. College Board, May 2006. Web. 12 May 2012.

"USP Mission Statement." *University of the Sciences in Philadelphia*. University of the Sciences in Philadelphia, n.d. Web. 29 April 2010.

Walvoord, Barbara. "The Future of WAC." *College English* 58 (1996): 58–79. Print.

White, Edward. "Opening of the Modern Era of Writing Assessment: A Narrative." *College English* 63.3 (2001): 306–20. Print.

—. "Use It or Lose It: Power and the WPA." *WPA: Writing Program Administration* 15.1–2 (1991): 3–12. Print.

Wiley, Mark. "Outcomes are Not Mandates for Standardization." Harrington, et al. 24–31. Print.

15 Adoption, Adaptation, Revision: Waves of Collaborative Change at a Large University Writing Program

J.S. Dunn, Jr. Sarah Fabian, Suzanne Gray, Kimberly Coupe Pavlock, Hava Levitt-Phillips, Sarah Soebbing, Heidi Estrem, and Linda Adler-Kassner

In Chapter 9, Stephen Wilhoit describes how his involvement with drafting learning outcomes contributed to the reshaping of the writing in the disciplines seminar at his institution, the University of Dayton. Wilhoit refers to this process as affecting "deep change," a kind of change that requires rethinking one's own position as well as "taking risks." Our chapter, like Wilhoit's, describes how the process of working with learning outcomes served as a catalyst for deep change. Here, though, the focus is on the collective experience we've had with learning outcomes over the past decade in the first-year writing program (FYWP) at Eastern Michigan University (EMU). EMU is an access-oriented public institution enrolling over eighteen thousand undergraduates, including a sizable population of transfers, as well as five thousand graduate students on an urban campus near Detroit, in Southeast Michigan. Among the only courses required of most undergraduate students is first-year composition. As a unit within an English department that hosts six major degree programs, EMU's first-year writing program includes three course offerings, two of which figure in the present discussion: English 120, an elective-credit course introducing knowledge of genre and of the composing process, enrolls about six hundred students per year via guided self placement; and English 121, a general education requirement, focused on college-level research writing, serves approximately 1,650 students yearly. The FYWP staffs these courses with competent, committed, and creative faculty, but about fifty-five percent of them (somewhere between twenty and twenty-five) are part-time adjunct instructors, and eighteen others are graduate teaching assistants, who typically stay for only two years. Overall, just a small number of our instructors are full time, with between three-to-five lecturers, and two-to-four tenure line faculty. (For more background about the history and institutional context of the first-year writing program at EMU, see Irvin.)

Based on this description, much about our circumstances will seem familiar to many readers and similar to other large, public, access-oriented campuses around the country. However, just as we teach our composition students that effective writing needs to address and adapt to specific rhetorical situations, we have sought to attend actively to the particular rhetorical dynamics that situate our writing program. On our campus, these include, among other factors, the needs of various constituencies, such as students and colleagues—both those who teach writing and those with other affiliations across campus—as well as administrators, staff, and the communities that surround us. Being attentive to the situated nature of our work follows from traditions of scholarship in rhetorical theory (Bitzer; Burke) as well as writing assessment (Broad; Huot), and most importantly, guides our approach to the major initiatives we've undertaken over the years, not least our past decade of experience with the WPA Outcomes Statement for First-Year Composition (WPA OS). Throughout this process, we have attempted to adapt rhetorically the discourse of the WPA OS to fit our institutional situation, trying to reinvent these situations through our discourse.

With this perspective in mind, in this chapter, we would like to illustrate what we mean by rhetorically adapting the WPA OS, beginning with a comparison of three sets of student learning outcomes. The original WPA OS outlined the following outcomes: rhetorical knowledge; critical thinking, reading, and writing; processes; and knowledge of conventions. In 2001, EMU's FYWP adapted the WPA OS to fit its institutional context, constructing the following learning outcomes: rhetorical awareness; critical thinking, reading, and writing; writing processes; reflection; use of conventions; and use of technology. In 2009, though, EMU's FYWP revised the learning outcomes to critical reading and analysis; research practices and processes; writing processes and representation; use of evidence; and syntax and mechanics. The particular adaptations of the WPA OS have been in response to the series of constraints and affordances that have operated on our particular campus and in our writing program for a number of years.

We note briefly that several reviewers of this chapter in earlier drafts have reacted with befuddlement to this depiction of our writing program's learning outcomes in relation to the WPA OS, with one slightly exasperated reviewer going so far as to wonder whether we're actually still talking about the WPA OS in this chapter at all. Needless to say, we believe we are, but this plausible reaction reveals a deeper tension manifested in how our profession approaches matters of learning outcomes and assessment that we consider vital. Over forty years ago, composition scholar Donald Murray called for "teaching writing as a process not product," giving rise to a series of passionate debates that continue to animate our field (3). The reactions that Murray and other early advocates of the writing process movement provoked demonstrate what can happen when we shift our expectations about fundamental matters of education. Space limitations prevent us from fully unpacking the aspects of meaning that reside in either set of our outcomes listed above. Instead, our focus with this chapter follows from Murray's lead in exploring learning outcomes and assessment as "a process not product," or more specifically, a series of narratives about how different stakeholders in our writing program adopted, adapted, and revised the WPA OS to support episodes of meaning making. If we're successful, the reaction that some readers may have to our sets of outcomes will perhaps generate a sort of exigency that carries the plot of this chapter forward, ideally until some of this narrative tension resolves itself through a better sense of the interplay between product and process perspectives in outcomes assessment, just as recent genre theorists have argued the decades-long debate between product and process in composition theory should seek (Bawarshi).

Using the metaphor of waves to organize this chapter, we recount our involvement with different aspects of outcomes assessment around the WPA OS at our institution over the past decade. The chapter consists of three overlapping and repeating waves that we have labeled: (1) invention and implementation, (2) inquiry and assessment, and (3) revision and reinvention. Like waves in an ocean, each of these stages has gathered up different participants and brought us together in ways we could not have predicted in the moment, but that now seem to us part of a larger pattern.

First Wave: Invention and Implementation, 2000–2002 (Linda Adler-Kassner and Heidi Estrem)

After we were both hired in 2000 as director and associate director of the first-year writing program (in separate searches, and without knowing one another), we soon discovered that we shared some goals that would eventually help the FYWP to develop as it did. We were simultaneously committed to augmenting the existing best practices pedagogy in the program with ideas from new research, and to working collaboratively with the instructors in the program (some of whom had been there for many years) to consider how we might collectively adapt our courses, English 120 and 121, based on these approaches. We also wanted to enhance the sense of the program *as* a program (rather than two distinct courses taught by a variety of people), and to enhance instructors' senses of participation in the creation and development *of* this program. This was particularly important—and challenging—given the physical spaces in which we work, the differences of status and affiliation among instructors in the program, and the politics of the institution.

When we arrived, the WPA OS, which had recently been published, gave us a place to start the conversations we knew we wanted to have within our program. Equally so, it gave all of us language to wrestle with: to wrap our own heads around, to discuss amongst each other, and to consider in light of our courses. As today, our first-year writing committee (FYWC) was open to anyone who was interested. Discussions of the outcomes were collaborative, productive, and involved markers and large sheets of paper. Now, however, in composing a chapter about this experience that must be linear, these efforts seem somehow much more orderly than they did at the time. While we would have been hard-pressed at the time to lay out these efforts as tactical steps toward a ten-year strategy, as teachers and researchers, we were committed to and immersed in an inquiry stance, and were thus not exactly operating without a net, either. We knew that beginning with the WPA OS was a very good place to start. First, it gave us a *text* to look at. In other words, it wasn't about *us*, at least not initially. Instead, we could begin by discussing and appreciating the WPA OS language. Then—and only then—we thought about how that language might apply (or not) to our courses. These slightly more abstract conversations provided a safe place to think about those ideas, to interact, and to learn from each other. Second, we could use the WPA OS as a national lens on first-year writing. As a group of instructors, it was useful for us to think about how (and whether) the outcomes might be relevant to the specific context of our institution, our colleagues, and our students. Third, it gave us a sort of anchor that we could use for a process of thinking through our own first-year composition courses—both what existed as well as a vision for a future to which we might aspire. In this way, the WPA OS served a kind of dual purpose for the FYWP at EMU: It provided a central focus for conversation about what we were and wanted to be, which likewise provided a way for everyone in the program to get to know one another; it also helped us situate the work we were doing in the classroom—and the language that we were using to describe this work—in a broader, national context.

During these early years, the WPA OS, and the projects that extended from it, pushed us to invent new questions about the nature of our work as well as help create an energy that spread across the program. As an example, we found ourselves coming back repeatedly to certain broader issues related to learning outcomes in our 2001 adaptation of the WPA OS, specifically the category *rhetorical awareness* (What did it mean to understand research writing as a public activity?) and for parts of the category *use of conventions* (How could we help faculty across campus discover new rhetorical frames for imagining student writing beyond typical complaints about mechanics, such as "Why can't my students use a comma correctly?"). One key response to these questions happened in the winter of 2001, when members of the FYWC developed the basis of an activity that now serves as the program-wide final exam in English 121 at EMU, what has since become known as the Celebration of Student Writing (CSW). Asking students to perform a genre transformation on the academic research papers they composed during the semester so that research might appeal to a public audience beyond classmates and instructors in our writing classes represented one attempt to address questions prompted by our revisions of the WPA OS. As the CSW enters its tenth anniversary, the energy it generates at the end of each semester has been transformative, with an average of a one thousand EMU composition students displaying genre transformations of their research in an event that resembles an enormous science fair and attracts hundreds of spectators, including fellow students, faculty from across the curriculum, university administrators and staff, and parents and visitors from off campus. Outreach was on our mind as we considered the CSW, but more importantly, it allowed us to explore questions raised through attending to outcomes assessment via the WPA OS (Adler-Kassner). The energy around the CSW has supported our students in learning to write, and it has drawn into the process a growing number of colleagues who joined our collaboration with different expertise, backgrounds, and affiliations.

SECOND WAVE: INQUIRY AND ASSESSMENT, 2002–2006: CONTINUING THE COLLABORATION (LINDA ADLER-KASSNER AND HEIDI ESTREM)

Following this first wave of implementation and invention, we began to wonder about how the changes we had collectively made in the FYWP were affecting our students. First, we developed an indirect assessment, a survey to use in sections of English 121, asking students to indicate how their confidence with our learning outcomes had changed based on their work in the course. Among its intriguing results was that assessment called attention to the complexity of expectations associated with college-level reading, a finding that led us to rethink our approach to reading pedagogy (see Adler-Kassner and Estrem, "Reading Practices"). A second and more important initiative, however, grew out of a question asked in passing by a then-dean of the university when we presented those results to her: "What did people *other* than students think about students' work in the program and the effects of English 120 and 121 on student writing?" At about the same time the dean's question arose, we had encountered ideas in three books—Brian Huot's *(Re)Articulating Writing Assessment*, Anis Bawarshi's *Genre and the Invention of the Writer*, and Bob Broad's *What We Really Value*—changing our thinking about outcomes. Based on these authors' works, we began to wonder what it would mean to engage in assessment as a collaborative, community-based process. More specifically, two questions about assessment helped focus our efforts going forward: "If qualities of 'good writing' are context-specific, what are the qualities of good writing in our specific context at EMU?" Following from that question, "To what extent are these qualities present in portfolios students produce at the end of our English 121 composition course?" Finding methods through which to address these questions launched us into the second wave of our experience with the outcomes assessment.

The plan we settled on involved extending the notion of context-specific assessment that Huot and Broad advocate, consisting of two major phases. First, working with members of the FYWC, we convened a series of campus-wide focus groups, including students, faculty from both inside and outside of the first-year writing program, as well as EMU administrators and members of the university's non-academic staff, with the goal of discovering the qualities of good writing these constituencies valued in their professional, personal, and public lives. We then analyzed the discussions and created maps representing what we found, sharing these with participants, and recording their feedback. The results of all this work appeared in a new three-part portfolio assessment instrument. (For more details about the process, see Adler-Kassner and Estrem, "The Journey.") The next several sections of this chapter offer the perspectives of participants from this phase of outcomes assessment at EMU and beyond, starting with Kim Pavlock, now a full-time lecturer in the FYWP, who describes her involvement with the portfolio rating process.

Third Wave: Revision and Reinvention, 2006–2010—Widening the Context of Collaboration (Kim Pavlock)

As a new adjunct lecturer, one of the first opportunities I had to meet and work with other instructors involved in the FYWP was at the portfolio assessment meeting that Linda convened in the fall of 2006, a meeting during which professors, graduate students, full-time lecturers, and adjuncts reviewed preliminary assessment work completed the previous year and looked at how the findings related to the writing of our current students. Although I had heard we needed to change our outcomes, I didn't know why. During this initial gathering, we met in small groups, focusing on one piece of student writing at a time, and talked about the findings. It was an opportunity for me to meet my colleagues, learn more about the FYWP, and grow as a teacher by looking at student work and listening to other teachers' perspectives. I felt welcomed and encouraged to share my thoughts with the group.

It didn't seem to matter who was a professor or who was a graduate assistant. We worked collaboratively all morning, and I left the meeting feeling much more a part of the program than I had earlier.

Based on this meeting, subsequent discussions, and my teaching that semester, I better understood the assessment work we were doing as well as the reasons why, and I also felt good about getting to know other first-year writing instructors with whom I could talk and share ideas. As I continued to think about that first experience of reading student work with colleagues, I was reminded of a faculty development activity I had encountered through my work with the National Writing Projects of Michigan and the Collaborative Assessment Conference, both of which sought to help teachers more effectively notice, with a non-judgmental mindset, the qualities and characteristics of student writing. This "noticing" protocol involved, first, looking at a text with other readers and individually noticing—rather than evaluating—what one could observe about its features. Next, group members contributed their individual "noticings" to a collective description of the piece of writing: A participant might say, "I notice that this writing uses concrete details," and in tandem with multiple observations from other group members, a collective picture of the text emerges that is both more complex and generous than any single reader might compose in isolation. When I mentioned the benefits of using the Collaborative Assessment Conference protocol, the FYWC subsequently devoted two meetings in October and November, 2007, to doing just that: noticing various aspects of a student's work instead of immediately judging quality by the most obvious standards. Going around the room, we took turns sharing what we observed in a student's writing, trying to distinguish as much as possible between the expectations we brought as readers and the potential meanings available in the text. We were all informed by what our colleagues identified in a piece of writing that we hadn't noticed. Everyone contributed—from long-time faculty in the program to then-first-year graduate instructors like Hava Levitt-Phillips and Sarah Soebbing, who describe their experiences below.

Joining The Collaboration: Newcomers' Perspectives On The Process (Hava Levitt-Phillips and Sarah Soebbing)

As graduate instructors at the time, we were happily surprised, but also more than a little nervous, at the opportunity to participate in the FYWP's assessment efforts involving the WPA OS. We were eager to learn everything we could about the work of academic professionals, even as we were still very, very conscious of not having yet arrived at that level. Despite our official status, however, we were immediately welcomed as colleagues, and our contributions received the sorts of acknowledgment and validation that we've come to associate with the FYWP's approach to professional development generally.

Participating in the noticing sessions Kim Pavlock describes above was especially rewarding. As first-year instructors, we were right in the middle of trying to figure out how, for the very first time, to enact these outcomes in our own English 120 and 121 classes. Before we even began working with the noticing protocol, we both found it valuable just to look at examples of what members of our program saw as excellent, passing, and failing student portfolios. Then, in the discussions that followed each round of noticing, we were able to see how the group's ideas about writing meshed together and how they diverged. It was instructive for us as graduate students and novice instructors to see that both these similarities and differences were valued. This experience helped us to develop a richer understanding of what people in our program saw as good writing. It also showed us that the FYWP really did walk the talk of its claim that the quality of writing is always context specific.

We also found this experience helpful in dealing with our anxieties about our authority as novice teachers. Listening to our colleagues explain what they saw as excellent and problematic in the portfolios affirmed and clarified the values we were using to read our own students' work. Moreover, looking at these portfolios through vocabulary associated with the WPA OS helped us make concrete those outcomes as grading tools in our courses. For example, after this experience, we found ourselves using language related to the WPA OS as well as the noticing protocol in our written feedback to students. The terminology of the WPA OS, combined with the protocol's emphasis on reserving judgment in the initial rounds of assessment, helped us convey our expectations constructively to students while remaining open to the surprises that we inevitably encountered in their work. We might otherwise have rushed to judgment and searched for error as nervous new teachers; instead, we felt supported in taking the time to more fully engage with our students' writing. The sense of collegiality we experienced during this assessment initiative based on the WPA OS extended not just to our fellow writing instructors, but also to like-minded faculty elsewhere on campus, especially EMU librarians, Sarah Fabian and Suzanne Gray, who brought their own contributions to our evolving understanding of the WPA OS.

More than "Writing" in "Good Writing": The Contribution of University Librarians (Sarah Fabian and Suzanne Gray)

As the narrative of Hava Levitt-Phillips and Sarah Soebbing suggests, the FYWP's assessment efforts depended upon the input of multiple stakeholders, and just as importantly for us, the conscious attempt to incorporate perspectives not typically associated with "writing instruction," such as ours. Like the other co-authors of this chapter, our involvement with the WPA OS benefitted from good timing. Among other developments during this time, the university library at EMU had the opportunity to hire two new faculty librarians to fill two, brand new positions in the library—one of us, Sarah Fabian, was hired as the first-year experience librarian in 2005, and the other, Suzanne Gray, was hired as the information literacy librarian in 2006. Since research is such a large component of the English 121 curriculum, and since English 121 is one of only a small group of general education courses that most EMU undergraduates must complete, it seemed an obvious place for us to start collaborating.

Our efforts took several forms. As mentioned above, during the fall semester, new graduate assistants teaching in the FYWP take a practicum seminar on composition pedagogy, and in fall 2007, Sarah audited this course to gain knowledge of FYWP's philosophy as well as to support the graduate students who would soon teach strategies for research writing in English 121. During this time, the library also developed two online tools to assist FYWP instructors in teaching research. First, we produced a series of videos, now available on youtube.com, that introduce students to the technology-related abilities necessary to find information in the library. Second, we adapted the University of Washington's Research 101 Tutorial package, a modular online tutorial introducing key concepts for college-level research, drawn from a study of information literacy, such as the information lifecycle and research process.

Moreover, we met with Linda and others from the FYWP to share germinal literature in our respective fields and to also begin mapping out the ways in which the FYWP's outcomes and the WPA OS related to the Association of College and Research Libraries' Information Literacy Competency Standards for Higher Education. During these conversations, we considered ways we could embed information literacy concepts and the idea of research as a process into the FYWP curriculum to provide students with multiple opportunities to practice these processes and build upon them throughout their experiences at EMU. One important opportunity came when we participated in the portfolio assessment meetings that featured Kim's noticing protocol. Like Hava and Sarah above, we also felt initially flattered to be included, and subsequently gratified, at the supportive reception our contributions received.

When we think about it now, it all makes sense: If you bring together a group composed mostly of *writing* instructors, show portfolios of student *writing*, and then ask them what they "notice," you're likely to get a lot of talk about, well, *writing*. And so it happened; we, too, found ourselves drawn to instances when the FYWP's student writers used language purposefully, creatively, or persuasively. As *research* librarians reading portfolios of student *research* writing, we discerned another pattern: Rather than words, sentences, or paragraphs, we noticed quotations, citation formats, the content of students' works cited pages, and a host of other cues and strategies through which students incorporated outside sources in the context of their own writing.

Often our comments converged with those of the writing instructors, as when a well-written portfolio featured relevant, credible sources to support the student writer's claims. In other instances, however, we found ourselves noticing the sorts of patterns that Rebecca Moore Howard and her colleagues have recently documented in their important study of the challenges students face with source use and academic writing tasks: the well-written research paper with missing or inaccurate citations, in which the sources included seem less relevant or credible in relation to the student's topic (Howard, Serviss, and Rodrigue). At moments like these in particular, the collegial atmosphere around the FYWP that our co-authors describe stood out to us most tangibly. Instead of ignoring, dismissing, or marginalizing the divergent patterns we noticed, our colleagues simply added them to the accumulating list of noticings and, equally importantly, returned to them in subsequent conversations that transpired during the FYWP's most recent round of outcomes revision.

An important synergy developed through this period of dialogue with members of the FYWP: As we broached the kinds of issues related to evaluating and integrating sources that the information literacy movement has long considered crucial, we benefitted from the insights of our rhetorician colleagues, who helped us reframe matters of citation and the like through larger concerns about use of evidence, which is included in the FYWP's most recent iteration of the learning outcomes. Back then, we knew far less about the WPA OS than we do now, but even then, it impressed us that colleagues from another academic unit and field of study had a process in place that not only drew us into conversations about areas of shared interest, but also incorporated our contributions into something as important as their program's student learning outcomes. Having now studied the history of the WPA OS in relation to the field of rhetoric and composition, we're doubly impressed that our perspectives could be incorporated into elaborations on a project as significant as the WPA OS. Going forward, we hope our respective fields can foster the sorts of collaboration and dialogue we've experienced through FYWP's efforts around outcomes assessment and the WPA OS, and thereby benefit from the intriguing overlaps of knowledge, values, and priorities that scholars in both fields have begun to recognize (D'Angelo and Maid; Elmborg; McClure and Clink).

Assessment As Inquiry: A New Set Of Questions For A New Set Of Outcomes(J.S. Dunn, Jr.)

Throughout this chapter, all of us have mentioned the first-year writing committee (FYWC) and its involvement in our work with student learning outcomes. What's important about the function of EMU's FYWC is the collaborative dynamic it helps maintain within our program. Perhaps best described as an ongoing cycle, the workings of the FYWC, and of our other activities related to the WPA OS, often depend on three major components: (1) an initial idea, problem, and/or task that calls for attention by the program as a whole; (2) a forum or conceptual space that invites input from a variety of stakeholders who bring a range of perspectives to the ensuing conversation over weeks, months, or in the case of our work with the WPA OS, years; and (3) a conscious attempt to articulate, build upon, and circulate across the program the insights that arise from these conversations. The cycle then repeats, often many times. As a result, the idea, problem, and/ or task that begins with one set of meanings surrounding it inevitably takes on new meanings through the input of multiple stakeholders.

From this process orientation toward leadership, then, the work of writing program administration involves a balance between *setting the agenda* that participants follow in conjunction with established precedents, and *documenting the process* that emerges from our collaborative encounters so as to foreground how our multiple contributions lead to new insights that may alter prior assumptions. In this way, a process orientation toward writing program administration tries to push against the fundamental hierarchies that an organizational chart depiction of a writing program always assumes. Here the "process" orientation we describe around the workings of the FYWC begins to explain the evolving "products"—the learning outcomes we discuss above. Rather than dictating ahead of time the products of assessment, we consciously seek to develop the sort of workshop environment among stakeholders in the FYWP that we value in our writing courses, one that supports a particular notion of process out of which, we trust, rhetorically adapted meanings emerge.

To illustrate this dynamic more fully, and to indicate our current directions regarding outcomes assessment and the WPA OS, it's worth considering briefly how we've dealt with some limitations in our earlier approaches. During the 2008 FYWP faculty retreat, Kim Pavlock and other instructors articulated what several rounds of work with the noticing protocol began to suggest—that our existing outcomes weren't able to capture a range of what Kim termed "attitude stuff," which we often associated with students' habits of mind and performance when our courses felt most successful to us. At first, our terminology for describing matters such as our students' engagement with the writing process, and their sense of self-confidence as learners was, as you can see, somewhat vague, but the collaborative process we established allowed us to slowly articulate what we valued in our students' performance, both to our colleagues and, more importantly, to ourselves.

Working empirically from student texts and other artifacts, as well as the observations of instructors during the 2008 academic year, we devised language that attempted to capture some of the habits, dispositions, and qualities of mind we associate with the success of students in the FYWP. After the requisite series of drafts, revisions, and adjustments, we've begun speaking to each other and our students about goals for the learning process in our courses, including the following:

1. *Investment and Engagement* (the writer's sense of connection to her subject matter, texts, and processes of composing);
2. *Autonomy and Authority* (the writer's ability to experience herself and her ideas as credible);
3. *Sense of Perspective* (the writer's ability to acknowledge and take into account ideas and viewpoints that contrast with her own);
4. *Competence and Confidence* (the writer's agency and perseverance in relation to the assignment or task at hand);
5. *Resource Use* (the writer's ability to consciously seek out ideas, people, and other affordances, including technology, appropriate for completing the assignment); and
6. *Reflection* (the writer's awareness of her available choices involving writing, reading, and research, as well as ability to explain her decision making).

Such habits, dispositions, and qualities of mind surely lend themselves to the composing of texts that we associate with "college-level writing" (Sullivan and Tinberg). However, to the extent that students develop such habits while in our classes, they prepare themselves for success with a host of activities in life beyond simply composing effective texts, not least of which those associated with persevering and eventually graduating from college (Powell).

Within the FYWP, instructors and students now speak of Composing Process Outcomes (CPOs), represented by our 2009 iteration of outcomes that play off the WPA OS, as well as Learning Process Outcomes (LPOs), including the six habits of mind above, based upon the original "attitude stuff." Distinguishing these two categories of outcomes also allows us to conceive of our recent assessment activities in a sequence, beginning with attention to the CPOs through our established, program-wide portfolio grading rubric that Linda and Heidi originally developed, and turning now to strategies for documenting students' encounters with the LPOs in our writing courses. In this case, our longstanding commitment to portfolios has led us to explore Edward White's notion of Phase 2 assessment as a means to begin documenting our LPO outcomes. Under White's approach, faculty develop shared and clearly articulated learning outcomes that then guide the planning of assignments and other activities from which student writers can generate material, allowing them to document their development toward those outcomes. Within this framework, portfolios become collections of evidence that allow students to make a case for their learning.

Although still early in this new phase of outcomes assessment in the FYWP, a few observations seem noteworthy. First, based on a small pilot study asking students to document their experiences with the LPOs through a version of Phase 2 portfolio assessment, we've been intrigued by the range of texts, artifacts, and other representations that students have chosen as evidence demonstrating their learning processes (Dunn; Dunn, Guillean, McBain, Pavlock, and Varty). Far from being too difficult or obscure, LPO assessment has proved well within the abilities of students thus far, leading us to new insights about the nature of our writing courses as environments for learning that we wish to investigate further (Dunn, Varty, and Guillean). Moreover, in the spirit of the process approach to writing program administration described above, this recent assessment work has spawned other unexpected but fruitful initiatives. For instance, the range of artifacts, often multimodal and untraditional, that students claim as evidence of their learning processes, has led us toward developing an in-house system of electronic portfolio assessment to better support the collection, display, and archiving of such materials, a project that has already changed aspects of the FYWP's community of practice for the better (Dunn, Karlis, Luke, and Nassar).

Finally, we're excited to see a developing national trend emerge that parallels our local efforts to assess students' learning processes here in the FYWP at EMU. The Council of Writing Program Administrators' recent collaboration with the National Council of Teachers of English and the National Writing Project has led to an important set of learning outcomes, the *Framework for Success in Postsecondary Writing*, which promises to spur a new era of research and scholarship around outcomes assessment, just as the original WPA OS did over a decade ago. Beyond its significance as a policy statement, the *Framework* figures prominently in our own thinking because it follows the same patterns of categorizing expectations for student learning that we've come upon through our own process here in the FYWP. Although our efforts at Eastern Michigan University pre-date it by several years, and adopt a slightly different terminology of descriptors, the *Framework*'s categories of outcomes for "Experiences with Writing, Reading, and Critical Analysis" and "Habits of Mind" mirror our own priorities around Composing Process Outcomes and Learning Process Outcomes in ways we find intriguing (Dunn).

CONCLUSION: RIDING OUR WAVE INTO THE FUTURE

In their recent *Guide to College Writing Assessment*, Peggy O'Neill, Cindy Moore, and Brian Huot touch on a key challenge that underlies the work of all the contributors to this volume: "[M]any programs lack a sense of program-ness; that is, the faculty who teach the courses have not thought about who they are—what distinguishes them as a program and why. The values are there but they remain hidden or, if visible, they remain unarticulated" (62). Among the ideas and experiences described in this chapter, perhaps the underlying theme holding them together has been an attempt to imagine, and more precisely to *invent* rhetorically, our own "program-ness," to articulate in discourse for ourselves and for other audiences on our campus and in the public sphere those values that guide our work around writing, teaching, and learning. Here, more than anything else, the WPA OS represents an opportunity for us to invent ourselves, as we have used it to define, guide, and ultimately revise our theories and practices over the past decade. A number of instances stand out when the WPA OS helped us invent our program-ness. As Linda Adler-Kassner and Heidi Estrem point out, it provides a starting place for discussions. Other contributors to this volume, notably Karen Bishop Morris and Lizbeth Bryant, have documented the challenges and inherent vulnerabilities that new WPAs face when they enter an existing program and attempt to advocate for change. Whether we choose to describe these emergent relationships among faculty of various ranks as the forming of "community," a term that Joseph Harris has rightly sought to complicate, such a process depends on risk-taking for all parties involved. Building an environment where moments of risk-taking seems not just worthwhile but do-able, especially when participants appear initially marked more by their diverse differences than any shared affiliations, calls for all the means of persuasion available to those who would orchestrate such encounters.

If our shared sense of program-ness began in part when we could look past the risky process of forming new relationships with one other and embrace the apparent stability of a text like the WPA OS, we found that this process grew, paradoxically, when we empowered ourselves to remake that text based on the shared visions that soon emerged from our collaborative encounters. Kathleen Blake Yancey and the other developers consciously authorized such a move in their original framing of the WPA OS, and we sought to foreground this move by presenting the various iterations of our program's learning outcomes. As we mentioned at the outset, some readers have questioned the extent to which this chapter can even be said to deal with the topic of the WPA Outcomes Statement for First-Year Composition itself, rather than merely "what Eastern Michigan University's First-Year Writing Program has been up to during the past decade." While obviously a false dichotomy, this contrast deserves attention because it highlights a key principle we try to enact at all levels of our WPA work: the idea that the program develops and becomes stronger with and through continual work with outcomes (and curriculum and assessment linked to those outcomes). Such a principle offers a rationale for the related but distinct sets of outcomes we discuss in the beginning of the chapter and, more importantly, for our claim that today, in 2012, with the third version of student learning outcomes and its extensions, our first-year writing program continues to enact the WPA OS more than a decade later. Likewise, our willingness to view the WPA OS as an emerging draft, calling for re-vision as well as re-writing, carries over to the attitudes we hope to instill among our colleagues as they work with the WPA OS in everyday practice. That is, as Linda and Heidi discuss above, rather than standardizing our curriculum through the WPA OS, we've consciously sought to prompt, nudge, and support faculty across our program in finding creative pedagogical means to accomplish the shared curricular ends that our outcomes help articulate.

Perhaps the greatest danger in developing an outcomes statement like the WPA OS comes from the possibility that, once articulated, such outcomes function less as a heuristic for inventing and articulating shared practices than as a mechanism of surveillance that limits the agency of faculty. Mark Wiley attempts to forestall these concerns when he argues that "outcomes are not arguments for standardization" (24). Acknowledging the potential risks, however, he points out, "one of the prevalent charges is that setting standards means standardization—that is, standardizing the curriculum in a given subject area so that teachers have no choice in what they will teach" (25). Indeed, the same decade that witnessed the development of the WPA OS has seen the rise across all levels in American education of another assessment tool closely related to the learning outcome: the grading rubric. Here, in the case of rubrics, as scholars such as David Martins, and Erin Turley, and Chris Gallagher document, choices about implementing assessments have actual, and sometimes dire, consequences for teachers and students that unfortunately parallel the potential risks Wiley alludes to for learning outcomes. In light of these trends, perhaps our best option as a profession entails attending consciously to the necessary interplay of the sorts of "product" and "process" perspectives on assessment work that we raise at the start of this chapter, and that our narratives foreground.

The work of writing program administration is fraught with challenges that often seem closer to flux than stasis. As we complete this chapter documenting the past ten years of collective action in our program, we embark on a new era of transition, with Linda Adler-Kassner and Heidi Estrem having left for new positions on other campuses, and John Dunn taking over as director of the first-year writing program at EMU. During moments like these, we all experience, perhaps most powerfully, the impact that the communities we invent around our work as literacy educators have upon the nature of that work. Attempting to identify patterns of development in the early writing across the curriculum movement (WAC), Jeff Jablonski distinguishes broadly between *first-stage* and *second-stage* WAC programs, according, among other things, to the kinds of issues each faces and the resources each has available for addressing those challenges (181–190). During first-stage WAC initiatives, the major exigencies involve establishing and building—often from scratch—a new program. Here the main priorities concern bringing people together around new ideas and ways of doing things. In first-stage WAC programs, charismatic leaders frequently provide the necessary vision through which to make sense of otherwise unfamiliar, often intimidating, proposals for change. The personal qualities of such leaders, the *ethos* they invent in each moment through words and actions, draw together and motivate participants, becoming a catalyst that prompts others to join the new initiative and a resource that supports them in the face of complexity and the unexpected. Successful writing across the curriculum programs in their first stage depend on a powerful sense of ethos, most often conveyed personally by leaders gifted with such. However, for this reason, the viability of a first-stage WAC program often depends primarily upon the duration of its leader's tenure at the particular institution (Jablonski; Young and Fulwiler 288). By way of contrast, Jablonski identifies second-stage WAC programs through a change in emphasis they make over time. Rather than depending on specific leaders or charismatic personalities, second-stage programs transition toward greater emphasis on documenting the priorities and practices they value, generating texts—mission statements, policies, and in our case, the various incarnations of the WPA OS we have adapted to our specific rhetorical situation over the past decade—that embody the shared commitments of stakeholders across the program. By doing so, they gain both greater stability over time as well as the capacity to adopt, adapt, and revise more flexibly to waves of change, as our chapter title alludes. In this sense, they rhetorically invent a collective or communal ethos that goes beyond any one participant's vision. Or, put another way, during the past ten years, we have found that the WPA OS has provided us in the first-year writing program at Eastern Michigan University with the ability to plan for, effect, and navigate constructively the sorts of deep change all writing programs face.

Works Cited

Adler-Kassner, Linda. *The Activist WPA: Changing Stories about Writing and Writers*. Logan: Utah State UP, 2008. Print.

Adler-Kassner, Linda, and Heidi Estrem. "Critical Thinking, Reading, and Writing: A View from the Field." *The Outcomes Book: Debate and Consensus after the WPA Outcomes Statement*. Ed. Susanmarie Harrington, Keith Rhodes, Ruth Overman Fischer, and Rita Malenczyk. Logan: Utah State UP, 2005. 60–71. Print.

—. "Reading Practices in the Writing Classroom." *WPA: Writing Program Administration* 31 (2007): 35–47. Print.

—. "The Journey is the Destination: The Place of Assessment in an Activist Writing Program—Eastern Michigan University." *Organic Writing As-*

sessment. Ed. Bob Broad, Linda Adler-Kassner, Barry Alford, and Jane Detweiler. Logan: Utah State UP, 2010. 14–35. Print.

Association of College and Research Libraries. *Information Literacy Competency Standards for Higher Education*. Association of College and Research Libraries, 2000. Web. 8 March 2010.

Bawarshi, Anis. *Genre and the Invention of the Writer*. Logan: Utah State UP, 2003. Print.

Bitzer, Lloyd. "The Rhetorical Situation." *Philosophy & Rhetoric* 1 (1968): 1–14. Print.

Broad, Bob. *What We Really Value: Beyond Rubrics in Teaching and Assessing Writing*. Logan: Utah State UP, 2003. Print.

Burke, Kenneth. *A Grammar of Motives and A Rhetoric of Motives*. Cleveland: World Company, 1962. Print.

Council of Writing Program Administrators, National Council of Teachers of English, and the National Writing Project. *Framework for Success in Postsecondary Writing*, Jan, 2011. Web. 6 May 2012.

Council of Writing Program Administrators. "The WPA Outcomes Statement for First-Year Composition." Council of Writing Program Administrators, July 2008. Web. 11 Oct. 2010.

D'Angelo, Barbara. J., and Barry. M. Maid. "Moving Beyond Definitions: Implementing Information Literacy Across the Curriculum." *Journal of Academic Librarianship* 30 (2004): 212–17. Print.

Dunn, J.S., Jr. "Exploring Possibilities for Assessment in the *Framework*'s 'Habits of Mind': A Large University Writing Program's Recent Experiences Leveraging the Washback Effect." The 2011 Conference of the Council of Writing Program Administrators. Louisiana State University, Baton Rouge. 2011. Presentation.

Dunn, J.S., Jr., Cindy Guillean, Amy McBain, Kim Pavlock, and Nicole Varty. "Assessing (and Advocating for) What We Value: Documenting Our Contributions to Students' Learning Processes in College Writing Programs and Writing Centers." East Central Writing Centers Association Annual Conference. Western Michigan University, Kalamazoo. 2011. Presentation.

Dunn, J.S., Jr., Sarah Karlis, Carrie Luke, and Dave Nassar. "Assessing Technology Needs in a Large University Program: A Pilot Study to Identify Options for Implementing E-Portfolios." Computers & Writing 2011 Conference. University of Michigan, Ann Arbor. 2011. Presentation.

Dunn, J.S., Jr., Nicole Varty, and Cindy Guillean. "Documenting What We Value: Making the Case for Student Learning in One Basic Writing Class." Eastern Michigan University. 2011. Manuscript.

Elmborg, James. "Locating the Center: Libraries, Writing Centers, and Information Literacy." *Writing Lab Newsletter* 30.6 (2006): 7–11. Print.

Harris, Joseph. *A Teaching Subject: Composition Since 1966*. Upper Saddle River: Prentice Hall, 1996. Print.

Howard, Rebecca Moore, Tricia Serviss, and Tanya K. Rodrigue. "Writing from Sources, Writing from Sentences." *Writing & Pedagogy* 2 (2010): 177–92. Print.

Huot, Brian. *(Re)articulating Writing Assessment for Teaching and Learning.* Logan: Utah State UP, 2002. Print.

Irvin, Lennie. "The Activist WPA in Action: A Profile of the First-Year Writing Program at Eastern Michigan University." *Composition Forum* 20 (2009): n. pag. Web. 1 July 2009.

Jablonski, Jeffrey. *Academic Writing Consulting and WAC: Methods and Models for Guiding Cross-curricular Literacy Work.* Cresskill: Hampton, 2006. Print.

McClure, Randall, and Kellian Clink. "How Do You Know That? An Investigation of Student Research Practices in the Digital Age." *portal: Libraries and the Academy* 9 (2009): 115–32. Print.

Martins, David. "Scoring Rubrics and the Material Conditions of Our Relations with Students." *TETYC: Teaching English in the Two-Year College* 36 (2008): 123–37. Print.

Murray, Donald. "Teach Writing as a Process Not Product." *Cross-Talk in Comp Theory: A Reader.* Ed. Victor Villanueva. Urbana: National Council of Teachers of English, 1997. 3-6. Print.

O'Neill, Peggy, Cindy Moore, and Brian A. Huot. *A Guide to College Writing Assessment.* Logan: Utah State UP, 2009. Print.

Powell, Pegeen Reichert. "Retention and Writing Instruction: Implications for Access and Pedagogy." *College Composition and Communication* 60.4 (2009): 664–82. Print.

Sullivan, Patrick, and Howard B. Tinberg. *What Is "College-Level" Writing?* Urbana: National Council of Teachers of English, 2006. Print.

Turley, Eric D., and Chris W. Gallagher. "On the Uses of Rubrics: Reframing the Great Rubric Debate." *English Journal* 97 (2008): 87–92. Print.

White, Edward M. "The Scoring of Writing Portfolios: Phase 2." *College Composition and Communication* 56.4 (2005): 581–600. Print.

Wiley, Mark. "Outcomes Are Not Mandates for Standardization." *The Outcomes Book: Debate and Consensus after the WPA Outcomes Statement.* Ed. Susanmarie Harrington, Keith Rhodes, Ruth Overman Fischer, and Rita Malenczyk. Logan: Utah State UP, 2005. 24–31. Print.

Yancey, Kathleen Blake. Afterword. "Bowling Together: Developing, Distributing, and Using the WPA Outcomes Statement—and Making Cultural Change." Harrington, et al. 211–21. Print.

Young, Art, and Toby Fulwiler. "The Enemies of Writing Across the Curriculum." *Programs That Work: Models and Methods for Writing across the Curriculum.* Ed. Toby Fulwiler and Art Young. Portsmouth, NH: Boynton/Cook, 1990. 287–94. Print.

16 Considering the Impact of the WPA Outcomes Statement on Second Language Writers

Paul Kei Matsuda and Ryan Skinnell

The adoption of the WPA Outcomes Statement for First-Year Composition (WPA OS) by the Council of Writing Program Administrators (CWPA) in April of 2000 represents a watershed moment for mainstream rhetoric and composition specialists. It was the first attempt by a national organization to define a set of common outcomes for first-year composition that was supported by research in rhetoric and composition. In the ensuing years, according to Edward White in his 2006 review of *The Outcomes Book: Debate and Consensus after the WPA Outcomes Statement,* the document "seems to have struck a chord that resonates throughout the profession" (111). White's sentiment is commonly shared among people writing about the WPA OS (Ericsson; Harrington xv; Rhodes, et al. 9–10), and it is not exactly inaccurate depending on how one defines "the profession"—and the kind of students with which the profession is concerned.

The resonances of the WPA OS "throughout the profession," however, have not extended to second language writing teachers or students. Although the development of the document "engaged quite literally over a hundred teachers," (Yancey, "Kathleen Blake Yancey Responds" 379), and "managed to attain remarkable agreement among a very disparate but important group of leaders in the field" (Elbow 178), second language writing specialists were not involved in the conversations out of which the document was formed. In addition, a survey of second language writing research demonstrates that, during the decade since the WPA OS was adopted by CWPA, it has scarcely been cited in the literature concerned with second language writers, suggesting that it has had minimal impact in discussions of first-year writing instruction among second language writing specialists. In fact, almost nothing has been written by anyone, including second language researchers or rhetoric and composition specialists, about the implications of the WPA OS for second language writers in spite of the presence of a growing number of second language writers in institutions of higher education in North America (for a notable exception, see Preto-Bay and Hansen 49–50). The minimal work that has tried to consider the implications for second language writers often does little more than note that outcomes in general can be problematic for any group of writers, usually second language and basic writers, who are less proficient than others (Sternglass 207–09).

The lack of systematic and sustained conversation about the implications of the WPA OS for second language writers is problematic, especially at a time when their presence is increasingly felt. In 2008-2009 academic year, there was an all-time high of 671,616 international students enrolled in U.S. colleges and universities, most of whom came from countries where English is not the dominant language (Institute of International Education). In addition, many colleges and universities, in order to secure additional funding, are rigorously recruiting international students, resulting in a surge of second language writers even at institutions where there have traditionally been very few. Also increasing is the number of resident students—long-term residents of the United States, including permanent residents and citizens—who grew up speaking languages other than privileged varieties of English. By one estimation, there already were over 1.3 million "foreign-born" U.S. citizens enrolled in higher education in 1990, and this population seems to be growing steadily (Otuya). Since many of these students go through the first-year writing requirements, spending at least as much time as native-English-speaking students, it is important to consider how their presence and needs are reflected in any attempts to articulate the goals and outcomes of the first-year writing curriculum. To this end, this chapter examines the extent to which the WPA OS reflects (or does not reflect) the presence and needs of second language writers.

SECOND LANGUAGE CONSIDERATIONS IN THE WPA OS

A quick glance at the WPA OS reveals that there is no explicit reference to second language writers (or anyone who comes with various degrees of language differences) or specific issues they may face in the classroom in the statement. This is not to say that language issues are non-existent in the WPA OS—there are two outcomes in the statement that are related to language. One of them appears under the heading, "Critical Thinking, Reading and Writing." It suggests that, at the end of the first-year composition curriculum, students should "[u]nderstand the relationships among language, knowledge, and power." While an understanding of those relationships is a noteworthy outcome for any writer, the term *language* as it is used here seems to refer to a socio-political notion of language rather than many of the language issues that challenge second language writers who are in the process of developing their English proficiency—namely, sentence structures, vocabulary, and idiomatic expressions, as well as sociolinguistic and pragmatic concerns ("pragmatic" not in the sense of "practical" but in the sense of issues related to pragmatics). Notions of how language is related to power and knowledge are directly tied to the expectation that students are both aware of and sensitive to the prevailing linguistic and cultural norms of the socio-rhetorical context in which they write. Making students aware that language is tied to power alone does not enable students to assert or negotiate power through language if they have not developed proficiency in the target language.

Another language-related outcome appears in the section, "Knowledge of Conventions": "Control such surface features as syntax, grammar, punctuation, and spelling." This item seems more closely related to the needs of most second language writers with regard to language issues than the other outcomes. However, the faulty parallelism in the phrase "syntax, grammar, punctuation, and spelling" seems indicative of a lack of attention to language issues—syntax is a subset of grammar along with morphology, phonology, and vocabulary. The goal of "control" seems to suggest that the students are expected to have an implicit knowledge of the English language and its structure; that is, it is supposed to be a matter of controlling *performance errors* that arise in translating the implicit knowledge of linguistic structures into language production. That the WPA OS does not also mention the development of implicit linguistic knowledge seems to suggest that students are expected to have such knowledge before even enrolling in the first-year composition course. In other words, the document seems to take for granted the native English speaker norm, suggesting the influence of the myth of linguistic homogeneity—the assumption that students in U.S. higher education are always already native users of a privileged variety of English (Matsuda, "Myth" 638).

Even the outcomes that address language-related issues seem not to be attuned to issues related to second language acquisition or the negotiation of language differences. Rather, the WPA OS seems to focus largely on rhetorical issues. As Barry M. Maid and Barbara J. D'Angelo note in Chapter 18, although four categories are explicated in the WPA OS, rhetorical knowledge seems to supersede the others. For instance, the WPA OS states that, by the end of the first-year composition sequence, students should: "Use writing and reading for inquiry, learning, thinking, and communicating [Critical Thinking, Reading, and Writing]"; "Develop knowledge of genre conventions ranging from structure and paragraphing to tone and mechanics [Knowledge of Conventions]"; and "Understand and exploit the differences in the rhetorical strategies and in the affordances available for both print and electronic composing processes and texts [Composing in Electronic Environments]."

These desired outcomes represent well the majority of the document in that they assume a level of linguistic knowledge that supports a focus on higher-order concerns in first-year composition courses. As Ana Preto-Bay and Kristine Hansen question, "how will L2 students who are still developing their linguistic ability perform in these areas if they do not receive further *and* explicit instruction in how to use academic English language as well as support in the large cultural transition they must make?" (49). The lack of language issues may reflect the assumption that students enrolled in first-year composition courses already have a native-like proficiency in a dominant variety of English so they can focus on other aspects of writing—an issue that pertains not only to second language writers, but to users of non-dominant varieties of English. That is, even when teachers and administrators are aware of the presence of second language writers in their classes and programs, they may choose not to address some of the common issues faced by second language writers because the WPA OS does not include those issues. The focus on rhetorical awareness in itself is not a problem. In fact, all writers, regardless of their linguistic or cultural background, can benefit from attention to rhetorical issues. What is problematic, however, is that the rhetorical focus in the WPA OS seems to come at the expense of language issues that a growing number of students in first-year composition courses face.

The Impact of the WPA OS on Second Language Writers

To examine the extent to which second language writers are affected by the WPA OS, it is important to consider the statement's domains of influence. The impact of the WPA OS is probably most prevalent in the mainstream sections of first-year composition courses (see Isaacs and Knight in Chapter 20). In many parts of North America—especially at urban, open-admissions institutions—it is no longer unusual to find mainstream first-year composition courses that are dominated by students who come from diverse linguistic backgrounds. In recent years, large, research-intensive institutions are also seeing an increase of both resident and international second language writers in mainstream sections. Although many of those institutions have traditionally had separate sections of first-year writing courses for international students, the growing student enrollment seems to have surpassed, in many cases, the capacity of those sections. Even when separate second-language sections are available, recent research on placement practices of second language writers have shown that students, for complex, identity-related considerations, choose to enroll in mainstream sections (Braine; Costino and Hyon; Ortmeier-Hooper). Other institutions simply do not have separate sections; students have no choice but to enroll in the mainstream first-year composition courses. This is often the case at many rural and small liberal arts institutions. Although these smaller institutions have not traditionally had large international student enrollments, many of them are beginning to see a surge of international students from countries that are trying to globalize by sending out their citizens to earn degrees in English-speaking countries.

Yet, mainstream composition courses and pedagogical materials that are commonly used in those courses are likely to be designed with the monolingual norm in mind (Matsuda, "Myth"). While some second language writers are able to perform well in mainstream composition courses, others struggle as they try to keep up with fast-paced reading and discussions filled with tacit conventions as well as cultural and historical references with which they are not familiar. The struggle of those students may not become apparent to teachers who are not used to considering issues of linguistic and cultural differences. Students, on their part, may not feel entitled to ask teachers to provide additional linguistic or cultural information for a variety of reasons, including having internalized the monolingual assumptions. When those issues become apparent to the teacher, students may still be expected to fill in the gap themselves by going to the writing center, where they will meet with peer tutors who are, in many cases, even less prepared to address those issues than are the classroom teachers (Trimbur, "Peer Tutoring" 27–28). Other students may simply drop out of the class, requiring them to spend additional time and money in completing the requirement. For example, in a study comparing mainstream and multilingual sections of the first-year composition course at a university in the South, George Braine found that 24.4 percent of second language writers in the mainstream section withdrew from the course, in contrast to the withdrawal rate of 4.8% for the second language section (96).

The impact of the WPA OS on second language writers is probably most prevalent in the mainstream sections of writing courses, where the monolingual ideology embodied in the statement resonates with the dominant assumptions in the classroom. The use of the WPA OS, therefore, reinforces monolingual assumptions, especially when the WPA OS is used as a guiding principle for designing or redesigning these courses. Even when second language writers are placed in separate sections, however, they may still be affected by the WPA OS. By default, second language sections at many institutions are considered equivalent to the mainstream sections, and students are expected to meet the same set of outcomes regardless of differing backgrounds and needs. In fact, some teachers who have taught both mainstream and second language sections claim that they do not change their teaching materials or practices, regardless of which type of classes they are teaching (Saenkhum, Matsuda, and Accardi). Yet, the question of whether and to what extent the expected outcomes should or should not vary across placement options has not been explicitly addressed in the professional literature. The common expectation is that multilingual sections will help students to reach the same goals as do students in mainstream courses, only with more attention to the language learning needs of those enrolled. Still, to this point, there has not been a serious and sustained conversation among WPAs about whether or not it is reasonable to expect that second language composition sections should accomplish the same goals as mainstream composition sections. Put another way, second language students, especially international students, come from much different backgrounds than their mainstream counterparts, and often enroll in U.S. institutions of higher education with much different goals. Any guidelines and policies applied across mainstream and second language sections must account for those alternative backgrounds, needs, and goals.

Another related issue is that of the standards—or the level of outcomes—that students are expected to meet. Given the limited time and the range of issues that teachers and students are expected to address in second language sections (and the long-term nature of second language acquisition), it would be unreasonable and unrealistic to expect that the proficiency level of students at the end of the semester will be the same as native-English-speaking students who already come with a high level of English language proficiency. The WPA OS, as it currently stands, has a built-in mechanism that accounts for this difference: The document does not specify the level of the outcomes (Wiley; Yancey, "Standards"). Rather, it only stipulates what aspects of writing proficiency need to be addressed in the first-year writing program. The benefit of not specifying the level of outcomes is that it accounts for the varied levels of language and writing proficiencies students bring to the first-year writing program. Yet, faculty across the disciplines who are not aware of the distinction between outcomes and standards may expect students to come out of all writing program courses with the same level of linguistic and rhetorical achievements. What the WPA OS does, in effect, is to let WPAs and writing instructors off the hook—because WPAs do not have to guarantee a specific level of achievement—while students are still being held accountable to unreasonable expectations based on the myth of linguistic (and cultural) homogeneity prevalent in U.S. higher education in general.

The Global Implications of the WPA OS

As we have mentioned, the WPA OS does not specify the level of outcome students are expected to reach at the end of the first-year composition sequence. By the same token, and in a positive light, the WPA

OS also does not specify how the outcomes are to be achieved; instead, it provides parameters within which writing teachers can develop their pedagogical practices. This is the beauty of the document—it makes the statement acceptable to WPAs and writing teachers from a wide variety of instructional contexts and philosophical orientations. The outcomes are also intended to help students become flexible writers who can function in a wide variety of rhetorical contexts. For example, under the first category, "Rhetorical Knowledge," students are expected to learn how to: "Focus on a purpose"; "Respond to the needs of different audiences"; "Respond appropriately to different kinds of rhetorical situations"; "Use conventions of format and structure appropriate to the rhetorical situation"; "Adopt appropriate voice, tone, and level of formality"; "Understand how genres shape reading and writing"; and "Write in several genres."

In theory, these outcomes help all students—regardless of their linguistic or cultural background—adapt to a wide range of rhetorical situations. In practice, however, the examples of "different audiences" and "different kinds of rhetorical situations" found in composition textbooks are often limited to those that are found in North American (especially U.S.) contexts. For instance, writing pedagogy that focuses on civic engagement—to prepare students to understand and engage in the public sphere—usually implies participation in U.S. public discourse. Another popular pedagogical approach that focuses on the critique of pop culture often means critiquing dominant U.S. pop culture. Examples presented in textbooks and in class often come from U.S. contexts—contexts that are familiar to the teacher and to a perceived majority of U.S. students, but not to those who come from less-dominant cultural backgrounds both in the States and elsewhere.

In some cases, students from other countries may choose to write on topics that are situated in other linguistic or cultural contexts, and teachers may even encourage students to do so. Yet, teachers who are unfamiliar with those linguistic and cultural contexts may not be able to respond in ways that would help those students develop their critical awareness. Furthermore, the supposed audience for student writing is likely to be prototypically educated readers who come from the dominant U.S. context. Even when the teacher is from another linguistic or cultural context, it is difficult to resist the institutional and cultural tendencies to focus on the dominant image of the audience. (In fact, one of the co-authors of this chapter who is familiar with non-U.S.

linguistic and cultural situations also continues to struggle with this dilemma in his teaching.)

As a result, students who will be going back to non-U.S. rhetorical contexts may not be adequately prepared to understand and engage those rhetorical contexts; even worse, they may end up perpetuating the dominant U.S. cultural assumptions in those contexts, serving as agents of cultural imperialism. There are consequences for students—both first and second language writers—who remain in the U.S. context as well. With the globalization of economy and the prevalence of the Internet, the rhetorical contexts in the U.S. are also becoming increasingly global. Many employers these days, for example, are multinational, and employees and managers often come from different linguistic and cultural backgrounds. Preparing students for different audiences and different kinds of rhetorical situations can no longer mean preparing them for monolingual audiences and rhetorical situations that are dominant in the U.S. context; it also needs to include a broader range of audiences and situations that are found around the globe.

Where Do We Go From Here?

What do we need to do to make the WPA OS reflect the global reality both within and outside first-year composition classrooms? The first and most obvious step would be to integrate language issues more explicitly. It entails the recognition of language acquisition as an important instructional goal of first-year composition courses—rather than something that is expected to happen naturally and without effort. It would also entail that teachers, regardless of the sections they teach, be prepared to address those language issues at the point of need. Just as writing teachers are expected to be able to help students who struggle with rhetorical concepts (such as the rhetorical situation, audience, persuasive appeals, and genre) by providing explanations, examples, and feedback, so too should they be expected and trained to provide instruction in issues related to language. If the WPA OS were to articulate the need to address a wide range of language issues, it would be able to promote the necessary shift toward linguistically inclusive first-year writing courses.

Some may argue that the issues of language acquisition and cultural differences should not be included in the WPA OS because they are not within the purview of first-year composition, and therefore should be handled in "remedial" courses or intensive English courses. This position, however, seems to ignore the reality of today's first-year composition classrooms, which already enrolls a growing number of students who are in the life-long process of acquiring the English language as they also develop a high level of writing proficiency. As the CCCC Statement on Second Language Writing and Writers points out, "second language writers have become an integral part of writing courses and programs." Another possible argument against the inclusion of language issues is that they are not relevant to all students—that is, native English users who grew up as part of the mainstream U.S. communities may not need those components. However, because the WPA OS delineates what all students should be able to do by the end of the first-year composition curriculum, it needs to encompass all aspects of writing rather than limit itself to what the perceived majority of students need to develop. Some students may already be proficient in some of the areas that are articulated in the WPA OS; in that case, those students can focus on meeting the remaining expectations. The same principle should apply to language issues.

It is also important to point out that the burden of developing language proficiency does not belong only to students learning the dominant variety of English. As the English language continues to spread throughout the world and diversifies itself, it is becoming increasingly important for users of the dominant variety of English to learn to interact and negotiate with users of various Englishes. As we have pointed out, the current WPA OS allows for such global applications of rhetorical principles, but because it does not explicitly include an understanding of linguistic and cultural differences that enable students to imagine the global rhetorical situations, it also allows teachers and students to neglect those possibilities. What this means is that there needs to be more explicit discussion of the ways in which the WPA OS can be implemented to meet the needs of students—both U.S. and international—who will inevitably be writing in global contexts.

Another important consideration is how language issues are articulated and communicated to faculty across the disciplines and to the wider public. If language issues are simply enumerated, it could create or reinforce the perception that students coming out of first-year writing courses should have "mastered" the dominant variety of English language by the end of the first-year writing sequence. To avoid perpetuating this problematic assumption, the WPA OS—and WPAs who will use it—need to continue the concerted effort to emphasize that the document does not guarantee a certain level of achievement, and that faculty across the disciplines also need to contribute to students' rhetorical and linguistic development by building on what students have developed in the first-year writing courses.

Finally, to further develop the WPA OS in ways sensitive to language differences and different placement options, it would be important to involve in the revision process writing teachers and researchers who have intimate knowledge of those issues. Developing the next generation of writing teachers and program administrators who are knowledgeable about evolving student needs requires a sustained collaboration between rhetoric and composition scholars and second language writing specialists. Only through such collaborations can the WPA OS become more versatile and inclusive, reflecting the diversity of the profession and of the student populations with whom our profession is concerned.

Works Cited

Braine, George. "ESL Students in First-Year Writing Courses: ESL versus Mainstream Classes." *Journal of Second Language Writing* 5.2 (1996): 91–107. Print.

Conference on College Composition and Communication. *Statement on Second-Language Writing and Writers*. CCCC Committee on Second Language Writing, 2001. Web. 02 Oct. 2009.

Costino, Kimberly A., and Sunny Hyon. "'A Class for Students Like Me': Reconsidering Relationships among Identity Labels, Residency Status, and Students' Preferences for Mainstream or Multilingual Composition." *Journal of Second Language Writing* 16.2 (2007): 63–81. Print.

Council of Writing Program Administrators. "The WPA Outcomes Statement for First-Year Composition." Council of Writing Program Administrators, July 2008. Web. 02 Oct. 2009.

Elbow, Peter. "A Friendly Challenge to Push the *Outcomes Statement* Further." Harrington, et al. 177–90. Print.

Ericsson, Patricia Freitag. "Outcomes Use Table: Current Uses of the WPA Outcomes for First-Year Composition." Washington State University. May 2006. Web. 4 Dec. 2009..

Harrington, Susanmarie. Introduction. Harrington, et al. xv-xix. Print.

Harrington, Susanmarie, Keith Rhodes, Ruth Overman Fischer, and Rita Malenczyk, eds. *The Outcomes Book: Debate and Consensus after the WPA Outcomes Statement.* Logan, UT: Utah State University, 2005. Print.

Institute of International Education. *Open Doors 2009: International Students in the United States.* Institute of International Education. 16 Nov. 2009. Web. 20 Nov. 2009.

Matsuda, Paul Kei. "The Myth of Linguistic Homogeneity in U.S. College Composition." *College English* 68.6 (2006): 637–51. Print.

Ortmeier-Hooper, Christina. "'English May Be My Second Language, But I'm Not 'ESL.'" *College Composition and Communication* 59.3 (2008): 389–419. Print.

Otuya, Ebo. "The Foreign-Born Population of the 1990s: A Summary Profile." *Research Briefs* 5.6 (1994): 1–10. Print.

Preto-Bay, Ana, and Kristine Hansen. "Preparing for the Tipping Point: Designing Writing Programs to Meet the Needs of the Changing Population." *Writing Program Administration* 30.1/2 (2007): 37–57. Print.

Rhodes, Keith, Irvin Peckham, Linda S. Bergmann, and William Condon. "The Outcomes Project: The Insiders' History." Harrington, et al. 8–17. Print.

Saenkhum, Tanita, Paul Kei Matsuda, and Steven Accardi. "From Awareness to Action: Making a First-Year Writing Program ESL Friendly." Conference on College Composition and Communication. Louisville Marriott Downtown, Louisville, KY. 18 Mar. 2010. Presentation.

Sternglass, Marilyn S. "Practice: The Road to the Outcomes over Time." Harrington, et al. 201–10. Print.

Trimbur, John. "Peer Tutoring: A Contradiction in Terms?" *Writing Center Journal* 7.2 (1987): 21–28. Print.

White, Edward M. "The Origins of the Outcomes Statement." Harrington, et al. 3–7.

—. "Review of Susanmarie Harrington, Keith Rhodes, Ruth Overman Fischer, and Rita Malenczyk's *The Outcomes Book: Debate and Consensus after the WPA Outcomes Statement.*" *WPA: Writing Program Administration* 29.3 (2006): 111–13. Print.

Wiley, Mark. "Outcomes are not Mandates for Standardization." Harrington, et al. 24–31.

Yancey, Kathleen Blake. "Kathleen Blake Yancey Responds." *College English* 64.3 (2002): 378–80. Print

—. "Standards, Outcomes, and All That Jazz." Harrington, et al. 18–23. Print.

17 Competing Discourses within the WPA Outcomes Statement

Judy Holiday

> *In short, the study of writing is a major subset of the study of the history of human consciousness, institutions, practice, and development over the last five millennia; and composition—the learning and teaching of writing—is in the middle of all that. It appears, then, that composition is a serious intellectual endeavor.*
>
> ----Charles Bazerman

> *[C]omposition has nothing whatever to do with rhetoric. I can now insert the adjective "modern" in front of "composition" to indicate that when I refer to composition from here on out I mean the course is required of all first-year college students. As far as I can see, there is no necessary reason that rhetoric could not be taught in this course.*
>
> —Sharon Crowley

In addition to varying applications such as assessment and teaching assistant training, the WPA Outcomes Statement for First-Year Composition (WPA OS) continues to serve its original goal of providing some curricular consistency across first-year composition (FYC) courses in the United States. Because some readers may balk at the use of "curricular" in conjunction with the WPA OS, I should explain that I am not using "curricular" in its usual sense of referring to the design of individual courses. Rather, I am using the term in the sense that because outcomes (i.e., what we expect students to be able to know and to do by the end of a course) are inextricably tied to course content, the

WPA OS does take up the subject of curricula, but does so in the sense of conceptual knowledge and practice applicable to *any* writing course (see Johnson). The WPA OS organizes this curricular knowledge into sections: "Rhetorical Knowledge"; "Critical Thinking, Reading and Writing"; "Processes"; "Knowledge of Conventions"; and "Composing in Electronic Environments." Used in this way, "curricula" denotes neither topical course context (e.g., writing in the life sciences or business writing), nor standards (specific levels of achievement), as the introduction to the WPA OS illustrates: "This statement describes the common knowledge, skills, and attitudes sought by first-year composition programs in American postsecondary education." Such knowledge, skills, and attitudes should, the introduction suggests, "[t]o some extent . . . regularize *what* can be expected to be taught in first-year composition" (emphasis added). This *what*, the subject matter of first-year composition, the introduction continues, does not reflect a mere "compilation or summary of what currently takes place" but rather represents what has been learned from "practice, research, and theory."

With these words, the WPA OS makes a claim to reflect rhetoric and composition's current disciplinary knowledge with respect to writing instruction. Following this emphasis upon disciplinary knowledge, the framers understandably highlight the need for educators who are members of the profession, "expert writing teachers and writing program administrators" who can provide "informed guidance" and "the expert understanding of how students actually learn to write" (WPA OS). Here, the framers of the document adeptly speak to multiple audiences. While invoking composition's vexed history of tenuous disciplinary control for those familiar with that history, the framers simultaneously claim disciplinary expertise in the teaching of writing to wrestle control from external forces that might maintain that anyone can effectively teach writing. The introduction thus makes clear that the framers well-understood the need to claim disciplinarity—the production of disciplinary knowledge—as a means to prevent the teaching of outcomes "in reduced or simple ways."

In the leading epigraph to this chapter, Charles Bazerman alludes to teaching composition in ways that are not reduced or simple, squarely locating the teaching of composition in a social context. According to such an approach, the social nature of language and meaning, discourse, and the social bases of literacy are intrinsic to the teaching of composition. In Chapter 11, Darsie Bowden represents a large, although not-formalized, group of compositionists who advocate that writing instruction should situate the subject of writing within a much larger context of all of human relations as an integral part of a very rich intellectual history (e.g., Berthoff; Bizzell; Boland; Hardin; Olson; Rose; and Shaughnessy). As an intellectual endeavor, the teaching of writing eschews a merely procedural view of writing instruction in favor of attention to the socially constitutive nature of discourse.

The framers of the WPA OS prevail upon readers of the document to understand that the document's target audience is comprised of "expert writing teachers and writing program administrators" so that writing instruction remains in the hands of the experts, those immersed in the rich epistemic knowledge conferred by the study of the discipline. Acknowledging that the majority of writing instructors are not necessarily experts in the field of composition, however, this section of WPA OS might also be seen as a caveat reminding WPAs that varying ranks of writing instructors may need expert guidance in interpreting and executing the outcomes in ways that attend to the social nature of language.

This chapter examines the efficacy of the document to instantiate the curricular consistency and disciplinary currency espoused by the WPA OS, and conceivably may be used in graduate/professional training with respect to the use of the WPA OS. As frames of analysis, I use "big rhetoric" and "little rhetoric" (terms adopted from David Fleming) as key components of what may be considered representational of our disciplinary knowledge. It is my hope that, after discussing the use of these terms as analytic frames in the next section, readers will agree that reading the WPA OS, through these frames, reveals tensions in the document, particularly between one-way and multi-directional acculturative approaches to the teaching of writing.

As I will show, both "big rhetoric" and "little rhetoric" operate in the WPA OS. Because the WPA OS alludes to both "big" and "little" rhetoric, I believe that the framers generally understood the need to organize and fuse both components to construct a coherent and theoretically rich foundation for writing instruction. However, the design of the statement unfortunately obscures its coherence by presenting the outcomes as co-valent, rather than as embedded. This weakness in design allows the two explicitly "big rhetoric" outcomes to be underemphasized, or even jettisoned,[1] and thus establishes the potential for an emphasis of "little rhetoric" over "big rhetoric" or, far worse, the teaching of the former divorced from the latter. Consequently, TAs in training programs could read the document to legitimate a more procedural approach to writing (little rhetoric), even while their WPA in charge of the program might be trying to encourage a more socially attentive rhetoric.

Recognizing a *potential* pitfall of the document may reduce the risk of writing instruction that is assimilatory or one-way acculturative (normative)—the very pedagogies of exclusion the field of rhetoric and composition has so ardently sought to overcome. In considering the widespread use of the WPA OS, and as someone who (like this audience) would like to ensure that our classrooms are as inclusive of and responsive to the interests of our students as is possible, I offer the following analysis and recommendation for re-designing the document, both to contribute to ongoing discussions surrounding the WPA OS (e.g., in teaching assistant training) and to support the framers' articulated purpose to regularize writing instruction without simplifying it.

Rhetoric: The Big and Small of It

"Big rhetoric" contextualizes writing as the production and reception of texts situated within larger cultural and historical contexts. In *Authoring a Discipline*, Maureen Daly Goggin describes "big rhetoric" by distinguishing between compositionists who "tend to conceive of our discipline as a subfield of English studies with composition (i.e., writing instruction, usually in first-year composition) as its focus," and rhetoricians who tend to perceive writing instruction as a pedagogical component of the field of rhetoric (198). Goggin writes,

> In short, whereas compositionists tend to equate their enterprise with the teaching of writing only, rhetoricians situate their enterprise within a much larger, and richer, framework of theories and practices that have been concerned with the reciprocal relationship between discourse and social, political, and cultural contexts. (198)

Although the actuality of this taxonomy might not be as clear cut as the taxonomy itself, the point that composition is seen as part of the discipline of rhetoric by many within the field highlights the curricular aspect of an approach to writing instruction that situates writing within a larger social context (e.g., Bazerman; Bizzell; Boland; Brodkey;

Crowley; Hardin; Goggin; Olson; Rose; Selfe and Selfe; Shaugnessy; and Smitherman).

In "Composition Is Not Rhetoric," Sharon Crowley proffers a useful definition of rhetoric that illustrates the difference between "big" and "little" rhetoric. While Crowley never uses either term, her definition connotes the two, and is thus useful for distinguishing "little rhetoric" (defined in her first sentence) from "big rhetoric" (defined as a combination of both sentences):

> Any theoretical discourse that is entitled to be called "rhetoric" must at minimum conceive of rhetoric as an art of invention, that is, it must give a central place to the systematic discovery and investigation of the available arguments in a given situation. Furthermore, it must conceive of the arguments generated by rhetorical invention as both produced and circulated within a network of social and civic discourse, images, and events.

Here, "little rhetoric" refers to available arguments in a given situation, such as in a specific discourse community. While "knowing one's audience" and being familiar with the conversations that take place among that audience are necessary features of rhetorical study, the second part of Crowley's definition of rhetoric (as indicated by "furthermore") sounds very much like Goggin's discussion of writing instruction from a rhetorician's perspective. Both Goggin and Crowley highlight the point that "little rhetoric" is necessary to but not sufficient for rhetorically rich writing instruction, the disciplinarity the WPA OS invokes in its introduction. (The second epigraph to this chapter indicates that Crowley stands in the camp of compositionists who advocate "big rhetoric" and the possibility of teaching FYC as a rich, intellectual endeavor.)

Big rhetoric pedagogies explicitly present a metacognitive view of writing that examines the production and circulation of discourse. Big rhetoric is most clearly indicated in the following bullet from the WPA OS: "Understand the relationships among language, knowledge, and power." Big rhetoric fosters students' awareness that they themselves are *produced by* and *producers of* cultural narratives and texts that are in constant play with each other "within a network of social and civic discourse, images and events." David Fleming describes big rhetoric as "a globalized metadiscourse oriented to the interpretation and criticism of symbolic inducement in all its forms and settings" (171).

Such metacognitive study of the cultural arbitrariness and historical formation of texts serves to denaturalize the immutability of texts and the discreteness of discourse communities, encouraging students to see themselves as communicative participants who are already inside many fields at play—not outside them. Learning to play in new fields and learning explicitly about new fields become, then, simply natural aspects of human development—accomplishments students have already achieved. Nevertheless, denaturalization of students' positionalities—their backgrounds, beliefs, and abilities—does not erase those subject positions, particularly the epistemic knowledge and cultural capital students acquired while in those positions. Rather, denaturalization facilitates students' abilities to reflect upon their own and others' subject positions, and to understand themselves as both socially constructed and socially constructive (see Holiday for fuller discussion of benefits of this approach).

In contrast, "little rhetoric" situates full agency in the rhetor to understand whatever arguments are available in a given situation, and to wield those same arguments successfully. Fleming describes little rhetoric as "a supplemental art directed to performance" (171). Little rhetoric often works well for students eager to enter a new discourse community, yet when little rhetoric is taught as divorced from big rhetoric, it runs the risk of presenting discourse communities as somewhat discrete and unified. When decontextualized from the playing field of multiple discourse communities, issues of power and language do not surface. Little rhetoric divorced from big rhetoric, then, can potentially reinforce the ideology of a meritocratic playing field that rhetoric and composition has so roundly criticized, and through which so many students have been neglected or alienated (see Matsuda and Skinnell in Chapter 16). Little rhetoric divorced from big rhetoric will not necessarily meet the needs of resistant and marginalized students who, for whatever reasons, might not see themselves acculturating to the new discourse community they are expected to join (Bizzell). Little rhetoric alone will not serve, even fairly, homogenous and privileged student populations who subsequently miss out on learning the self-reflective praxis embedded within big rhetorical theory. Teaching within a big rhetoric social paradigm benefits *all* students, encouraging them to self-reflectively examine their cultural predispositions and socializations, thereby augmenting their understandings of public and private discourses.[2]

Nevertheless, we must not forget that little rhetoric (i.e., argument) is integral to big rhetoric and essential to communicative skill; therefore, it is important not to pitch it against meta-rhetorical discussion. Teaching big rhetoric does not neglect the teaching of argument and persuasion, since writing instruction underwritten by big rhetoric necessarily contains discussion of little rhetoric—as Crowley's two-part definition of rhetoric aptly demonstrates. Little rhetoric is clearly indicated in the following outcomes in the WPA OS: "focus on purpose," "respond to the needs of different audiences," and "understand the conventions appropriate to the rhetorical situation." On the other hand, big rhetoric (the combination of both little and big) can be clearly seen in the outcomes: "understand how genres shape reading and writing," and "understand the relationships among language, knowledge, and power."

"Service" as a Subset of "Little Rhetoric"

"Service" writing instruction—the expectation that students will learn Standard English and how to write for the academy in first-year composition courses—has seen many changes since its inception at Harvard, particularly in its move away from a deficiency model of schooling. In addition, the discreteness of such concepts as Standard English and academic discourse have been challenged within our field, their homogeneity having been interrogated in the understanding that language tasks are always rhetorical and, subsequently, situational. Although the tasks of acculturating students to Standard English and academic prose have remained somewhat uncontested goals in first-year composition (given that most writing instructors want to facilitate their students' entries into the academy and other public and professional domains—places where facile use of Standard English is esteemed), first-year writing pedagogies have made some significant positive changes. For one, an acculturative rather than deficiency model of student capability has been theoretically embraced by the field (e.g., Bizzell; Rose; and Shaughnessy). As a result, first-year composition courses generally present the academy as a new discourse community that students are expected to learn about, struggle with, and join—an unfamiliar place that students are not expected to enter knowledgeably and well-informed. Thus, academic discourse is often taught as a form of "little rhetoric," subject to a rhetorical situation, and produced within one or more discourse communities. Ideally, once students become familiar with the various conversations taking place, they should, to varying degrees, be able to understand their audiences and wield arguments accordingly.

Patricia Bizzell tells us in "Opinion: Composition Studies Saves the World!" that composition research has greatly improved acculturative service pedagogies, and she reminds us that acculturative narratives are incomplete when told as narratives of initiation and transition, a one-way process that ignores the actual multi-directional process of incorporating people who bring "their own rich discursive resources to the academy" (178). "Teachers and students alike," Bizzell observes, "found that what was needed was not a one-way acculturation process, but a two-way, indeed a multidirectional, process of collaboration and change whereby new forms of discourse were incorporated into academic ways of doing things, and new types of intellectual work were thereby enabled," and she provides Black English as an example of a dialect that "enables types of academic work that could be done in no other way" (178). The field of rhetoric and composition has theoretically recognized the value of multidirectional acculturation, setting it against both assimilatory ideals and one-way acculturation (e.g., Delpit; Powell; Shaughnessy; and Smitherman).

Mention of diverse student populations and multidirectional acculturation, however, is absent in the WPA OS introduction. Socially attentive implementation of the outcomes is therefore contingent upon the pedagogical orientation of writing instructors to enact multi-directional, rather than assimilatory, classroom pedagogies. In a less-than-optimal scenario, for example, inexperienced practitioners of the WPA OS could conceivably shut down interaction in a classroom by "correcting" students for their dialectical non-standard use of English, a move that might occur during instructors' sincere attempts to remind students of the outcome that stipulates "control such surface features as syntax, grammar, punctuation, and spelling." In "The Road to the Outcomes over Time," Marilyn S. Sternglass questions the expectation that students be able to "control surface features." Non-standard speakers and ESL writers should not be expected to have complete control of such features, and she reminds composition professionals of their supposed postmodern orientation to language that prohibits such students from having "their work evaluated on the correctness of the forms rather than the sophistication of their ideas" (208). She suggests that the statement be revised to read that "students should have been *practicing* the conventions of syntax, grammar, punctuation, and spelling," and should, most importantly, be made "familiar with the patterns they are having difficulty in controlling" (209).

Similarly, Christiane Donahue writes, in "'Internationalization and Composition Studies," that one-way acculturative models (discourses of initiation and transition) can replicate much of the social and academic stratification already extant in the classroom, leaving many students disenfranchised. Referencing the heterogeneous sociolinguistic backgrounds of students within U.S. writing classrooms, she writes that "the fundamental problem of imagining internationalizing composition as export is that this is precisely its source as colonialist activity" (215). Donahue thanks second language scholar Ann Johns "for moving us beyond the simple integrative model" (217), which, Johns says, "'[m]any linguistically-diverse students object to, or are intimidated by,' for its 'subjugation of their lives and habits to academic languages and discourses" (qtd. in Donahue 217). John's observations of such common student experiences demonstrate that under the guise of empowering students to communicate "equally" and within global contexts, one-way acculturative service composition classes often alienate and marginalize those students who don't enter college already literate or interested in academic discourses. Although the verbs "develop" and "practice" in the outcomes, "develop knowledge of genre conventions," and "practice appropriate means of documenting their work," implicitly acknowledge students as evolving learners who acquire strategies, the *ways* that these conventions are presented to marginalized students are not discussed anywhere in the WPA OS. There is nothing that explicitly situates these outcomes in a socio-historical context that might reduce the intimidation to which Johns refers.

In a related body of scholarship, Steven Aragon and Brad Kose offer an outstanding literature review of a growing body of research devoted to cultural capital, a concept associated with the sociologist Pierre Bourdieu, who is largely known for explicating academe's complicity in the reproduction of social inequity and stratification. Aragon and Kose note, for example, that many students of color feel a discomfiting incongruency between their personal identities and "the culture and practices of school" (110), and subsequently resist the socialization process as an exercise of their agency and pride in their minority identities. Multiple studies underscore this minority perspective, and Aragon and Kose explain these studies' implications: "the need to avoid secondary and postsecondary practices that attempt to assimilate African American students or American Indian students into schooling without affirming their background identities" (110). Similar critiques of one-way acculturative pedagogies can be made with respect to class, sexuality, and other aspects of identity, suggesting that multidimensional acculturative practices that affirm and incorporate students' already existing knowledges, literacies, and capacities within first-year writing instruction are of crucial importance. Viewed otherwise, writing instruction might perpetuate normative teaching.

A Brief Analysis of the WPA OS

We can see that writing instruction that incorporates big rhetoric automatically provides students with a meta-discourse that situates little rhetoric within it. Yet, the WPA OS mentions only two explicitly metacognitive outcomes that encourage big rhetoric: "Understand how genres shape reading and writing"; and "Understand the relationships among language, knowledge, and power." Since there is no specific acknowledgement in the WPA OS that these two outcomes need to be retained when teaching first-year composition, it is possible that they may be under-emphasized or even dropped from a curriculum. Since this possibility exists, it is important to point out that if writing instruction maroons the only two explicitly big rhetoric outcomes, the remaining outcomes run the risk of being taught from normative, one-way acculturative approaches.

Although we might expect the rhetorical knowledge section to be the most attentive to the social constitutive nature of language, its overall tone suggests a more *pre*scriptive than *de*scriptive approach to the cultivation of rhetorical awareness: By the end of first-year composition, students should "Focus on purpose," "Respond to the needs of different audiences," "Respond appropriately to different kinds of rhetorical situations," "Use conventions of format and structure appropriate to the rhetorical situation," and "Adopt appropriate voice, tone, and level of formality." The verbs "focus," "respond" (appropriately), "use," and "adopt" emphasize performance, which may be achieved in the absence of a larger socio-historical context. Such a focus on performance might legitimate a procedural view of writing instruction, as advocated by Richard Fulkerson. For example, learning "what is appropriate" with respect to audience, structure, voice, and tone constructs writing as prescriptive and lockstep, unless it is taught within a big rhetoric context that frames "appropriateness" as a rhetorical choice that is culturally and historically influenced. Without such a perspective, students may be forced to focus on purposes of no interest or consequence to themselves, adopt insincere voices, and respond to audiences that they don't wish to engage. Thus constricted, demonstration of their ability to use an appropriate format or convention in their work does not accurately indicate the quality of their engagement. Indeed, many students have capitulated to the immediate demands of merely "showing off" their ability to fulfill an assignment while being disenfranchised by the process, with some students dropping out of school as a direct or indirect result of writing pedagogies that, as discussed earlier, Donahue disparages as "colonialist activity" (215) and Johns deems "'intimidating'" (qtd. in Donahue 217). In Chapter 16, Matsuda and Skinnell use the term "monolingual ideology" to refer to this form of colonialism, and they elucidate the struggles that students suffer as a result of its negative effects.

If taught decontextualized from the disciplinary purview of big rhetoric, the "Knowledge of Conventions" section can likewise be taught from a colonizing or one-way acculturative perspective: Students should "Learn common formats for different kinds of texts"; "Develop knowledge of genre conventions ranging from structure and paragraphing to tone and mechanics"; "Practice appropriate means of documenting their work"; and "Control such surface features as syntax, grammar, punctuation, and spelling." Here again, we see that students are, first and foremost, expected to learn formats, practice documentation, and control sentence-level mechanics and paragraphing. These outcomes might come across to students as prescriptive and unnecessary if not taught within larger contexts that explain why appropriate documentation is important, or elucidate the rhetorical persuasion operating in paragraphing and mechanics. Understanding how language *works* provides students with reasons to choose appropriate forms and helps liberate them from compulsory compliance that is potentially stifling or intimidating, as is often the case for users of non-dominant varieties of English. Big rhetoric explains to students why such seemingly minor details as genre or punctuation are rhetorically important while simultaneously fostering metacognitive transference of such persuasive knowledge to other domains.

From a pedagogical standpoint, even "write in several genres" (one of the two primary big rhetoric outcomes) runs the risk of being taught from a little rhetoric, or one-way acculturative, perspective. As Barbara Little Liu astutely explains in her critique of the WPA OS in *The Outcomes Book: Debate and Consensus after the WPA Outcomes Statement*, the framers of the WPA OS were aware of the potential complications of using "loaded" terms such as "rhetoric" and "genre." At issue, Liu explains, is that many instructors unfamiliar with contemporary genre theory misunderstand genre as being synonymous with form (73). Thus, the outcome stating that students should be able to "write in several genres" or "understand how genres shape reading and writing" could be diversely interpreted, and ultimately morph into modes-based instruction that does not accurately reflect the richness of genre as a complex historically and culturally situated, dialogical interaction between writer, reader, and discourse community.

Conclusion

I hope to have conveyed the importance of a big rhetoric or multi-directional, acculturative approach to writing instruction: What gets taught with respect to writing is clearly determined by the theoretical context in which writing instruction takes place. Since the outcomes in the WPA OS are weighted equally, the two "big rhetoric" outcomes can be too easily divorced from an instructor's implementation of the WPA OS, and I see that as problematic.

In "What's Theorizing Got to Do with It?" Michael Stancliff and Maureen Daly Goggin demonstrate the viability and value of teaching from a big rhetorical standpoint, specifically the ways such pedagogy avails itself to addressing the many needs of students as they arise. Working within the context of preparing graduate teaching assistants, Stancliff and Goggin draw upon four categorical approaches to teaching: functional, organic, conversion, and multiphilosophical. They demonstrate that a metacognitive approach accommodates each of these four approaches, teaching the nuts-and-bolts (functional), responding to the experiences and needs of any given student population (organic), acculturating students into a discourse community (conversion), and bridging students' intellectual paradigms via reflective engagement (multiphilosophical). Since all of these needs come into play in a writing classroom, the need to teach nuts-and-bolts, engage students where they are, and motivate students to acculturate to whatever discourse communities to which they aspire, a multiphilosophical approach makes sense and serves as an umbrella for all approaches, leaving none uncovered. This multiphilosophical approach is closely related to "big rhetoric" in that both require metacognitive rhetorical instruction that deals with much larger social, political, and cultural contexts in which discourses, beliefs, and students circulate. What differentiates a literacy education from the mere accumulation of literacies is acquiring and incorporating a meta-perspective of human epistemology, of humans as interpretive beings who always make meaning, whether consciously or not.

Big rhetoric more accurately describes our disciplinary knowledge than its diminutive. The WPA OS implicitly iterates this disciplinary knowledge, yet the WPA OS runs the risk of being used in reduced ways if little rhetoric is taught as anything other than a subset of its big sister. As a training and curricular tool, then, we should be careful to responsibly ensure that the WPA OS is used to encourage multidirectional, acculturative pedagogies. One way to better ensure such praxis is to change the design of the statement so that the outcomes are "nested," with little rhetoric outcomes embedded within big rhetoric ones.

Notes

1. For example, some programs that have adapted the WPA OS for their own purposes have dropped the outcome "understand the relationships among language, knowledge, and power," one of only two outcomes that can be seen as encapsulating the rich intellectual history of which I speak. Touting their use of the WPA OS as a template for devising a first-year composition curriculum concerning critical thinking at Eastern Michigan University, Linda Adler-Kassner and Heidi Estrem, in "Critical Thinking, Reading, and Writing: A View from the Field," incorporate every outcome in the "Critical Thinking, Reading, and Writing" *except* the one referring to the relationships among language, knowledge, and power. Their choice to relegate such content to courses *outside* of first-year composition may suggest that the subject of composition is not a disciplinary subject (see Boland).

2. A "big rhetoric" approach, however, should not be conflated with cultural studies pedagogy. As mentioned earlier, any choice of course topic, including business, technical, and writing for a particular profession, can be taught from a perspective of "big rhetoric."

Works Cited

Adler-Kassner, Linda, and Heidi Estrem. "Critical Thinking, Reading, and Writing: A View from the Field." *The Outcomes Book: Debate and Consensus after the WPA Outcomes Statement*. Ed. Susanmarie Harrington, Keith Rhodes, Ruth Overman Fischer, and Rita Malenczyk. Logan: Utah State UP, 2005. 60–71. Print.

Aragon, Steven R., and Brad W. Kose. "Conceptual Framework of Cultural Capital Development: A New Perspective for the Success of Diverse College Students." *Diversity and the Postsecondary Experience*. Ed. Jeanne L. Higbee, Dana B. Lundell, and Irene M. Duranczyk. University of Minnesota, 2007. 103-28. Web. 6 May 2012.

Bazerman, Charles. "The Case for Writing Studies as a Major Discipline." *Rhetoric and Composition as Intellectual Work*. Ed. Gary A. Olson. Carbondale: Southern Illinois UP, 2002. 32–38. Print.

Berthoff, Ann E. "Is Teaching Still Possible? Writing, Meaning, and Higher Order Reasoning." *Cross-Talk in Comp Theory: A Reader*. 2nd ed. Ed. Victor Villanueva. Urbana, IL: NCTE, 2003. 329–43. Print.

Bizzell, Patricia. "Opinion: Composition Studies Saves the World!" *College English* 72.2 (2009): 174–87. Print.

Boland, Mary. "The Stakes of Not Staking Our Claim: Academic Freedom and the Subject of Composition." *College English* 70.1 (2007): 32–51. Print.

Brodkey, Linda. *Writing Permitted in Designated Areas Only*. Minneapolis: U Minnesota P, 1996. Print.

Council of Writing Program Administrators. "The WPA Outcomes Statement for First-Year Composition." Council of Writing Program Administrators, July 2008. Web. 7 March 2011.

Crowley, Sharon. "Composition Is Not Rhetoric." *Enculturation* 5.1 (2003): n. pag. Web. 6 May 2012.

Delpit, Lisa. "The Silenced Dialogue: Power and Pedagogy in Educating Other People's Children." *Harvard Educational Review* 58.3 (1988): 280–98. Print.

Donahue, Christiane. "'Internationalization' and Composition Studies: Reorienting the Discourse." *College Composition and Communication* 61.2 (2009): 212–43. Print.

Fleming, David. "Rhetoric as a Course of Study." *College English* 61.2 (1998): 169–91. Print.

Fulkerson, Richard. "Composition at the Turn of the Twenty-First Century." *College Composition and Communication* 56.4 (2005): 654–87. Print.

Goggin, Maureen Daly. *Authoring a Discipline*. Mahwah, New Jersey: Erlbaum, 2000. Print.

Hardin, Joseph Marshall. *Opening Spaces: Critical Pedagogy and Resistance Theory in Composition.* Albany: SUNY P, 2001. Print.

Holiday, Judy. " In[ter]vention: Locating Rhetoric's *Ethos.*" *Rhetoric Review* 28.4 (2009): 388–405. Print.

Johnson, Robert R. "Craft Knowledge: Of Disciplinarity in Writing Studies." *College Composition and Communication* 61.4 (2010): 673–90. Print.

Liu, Barbara Little. "More than the Latest PC Buzzword for Modes: What Genre Theory Means to Composition." Harrington, et al. 72–84. Print.

Olson, Gary A. "The Death of Composition as an Intellectual Discipline." Olson. 23–31. Print.

Powell, Malea. "Dreaming Charles Eastman: Cultural Memory, Autobiography, and Geography in Indigenous Rhetorical Histories." *Beyond the Archives: Research as Lived Process.* Ed. Gesa E. Kirsch and Liz Rohan. Carbondale: Southern Illinois UP, 2008.115–27. Print.

Rose, Mike. "The Language of Exclusion: Writing Instruction at the University." Villanueva. 547–69. Print.

Selfe, Cynthia L., and Richard J. Selfe. "The Intellectual Work of Computers and Composition Studies." Olson. 203–20. Print.

Shaughnessy, Mina. "Diving In: An Introduction to Basic Writing." Villanueva. 311–18. Print.

Smitherman, Geneva. *Talkin' and Testifyin': The Language of Black America.* Boston: Houghton Mifflin, 1977. Print.

Stancliff, Michael, and Maureen Daly Goggin. "What's Theorizing Got to Do With It? Teaching Theory as Resourceful Conflict and Reflection in TA Preparation." *WPA: Writing Program Administration* 30.3 (2007): 11–28. Print.

Sternglass, Marilyn S. "The Road to the Outcomes over Time." Harrington, et al. 201–10. Print.

18 Is Rhetorical Knowledge the Über-Outcome?

Barry M. Maid and Barbara J. D'Angelo

The introduction to the original WPA Outcomes Statement for First-Year Composition (WPA OS) clearly indicates that, although the WPA OS is intended for first-year composition (FYC), it is expected that as students progress in their academic careers, their writing abilities will not only "diversify along disciplinary and professional lines but also move into whole new levels where expected outcomes expand, multiply, and diverge." Clearly, the intent of the original outcomes group was that the WPA OS be flexible and adaptable to other curricular contexts and types of writing programs. As a result, we, in the technical communication (TC) program at Arizona State University (ASU), felt comfortable first adapting the original WPA OS to fit the context of a technical communication program incorporating technology (Maid, "Using the Outcomes"), and then modifying those program outcomes by including information literacy (D'Angelo and Maid, "Moving Beyond"). We presently apply our revised version of the WPA OS for both curriculum development and to assess students prior to graduation, using electronic portfolios and Phase 2 scoring with a scoring guide that incorporates language of the WPA OS (D'Angelo and Maid, "Assessing Outcomes").

As originally adopted by the Council of Writing Program Administrators (CWPA), the WPA OS is divided into four categories: rhetorical knowledge; critical thinking, reading, and writing; processes; and knowledge of conventions. However, our assessment results and an examination of three semesters of portfolios from graduating seniors indicate that one category is possibly emerging as a particularly significant, *über*-outcome: rhetorical knowledge. Although the small sample of portfolios precludes definitive conclusions, we have identified patterns in the claims that students make about their success at reaching these outcomes. Students believe they have achieved the outcome of rhetorical knowledge, particularly those related to audience and purpose, more often than outcomes related to the other three categories. In addition, students' discussion of other outcomes, particularly those related to research and technology, are infused with an exceptional awareness of the rhetorical aspects of their work.

In this chapter, therefore, we explore the claim that having successfully completed FYC, students do, indeed, "expand, multiply, and diverge" in their writing abilities. Our graduating students do, through their coursework, appear to have mastered outcomes in critical thinking, reading, and writing; understand and use appropriate writing processes; and demonstrate knowledge of conventions. However, our assessment results and an examination of student portfolios indicate that rhetorical knowledge has possibly emerged as a kind of über-outcome for our students. Now, it is possible that since courses in our major are all taught by writing instructors, our own bias toward the importance of rhetoric is mirrored by our students. However, it may also be that our students have come to understand that rhetoric is crucial to producing effective writing in the workplace. The possibility may also exist in that, as writers gain experience and confidence, rhetorical issues simply emerge as the most pressing. We intend to explore all of these and other possibilities as potential reasons that rhetoric emerges as an über-outcome for these students. As a point of clarification, when we create the term "über-outcome," we do so to refer to an outcome that reveals itself to be not only most important among the others, but also one that works on a higher level; it is an outcome that also has a tendency to influence other outcomes.

Program History and Evolution

The undergraduate technical communication program at Arizona State University adopted the WPA OS as a foundation on which to build outcomes, and we did so for several reasons. Barry Maid, who was hired to build the program, had just been active as a member of the original outcomes group. He knew that it was important to have clearly delineated outcomes in place, and he understood that it would be much easier to start building a program with a clear set of outcomes rather than try to impose outcomes after the fact. He also saw that using the WPA OS as a basis for outcomes for an undergraduate technical communication degree was a wonderful opportunity to prove the versatility of the WPA OS, because it was intended to be modified to meet different institutional needs and curricular contexts. That versatility, in fact, was key to our adoption of the WPA OS, as it allowed us to integrate two components: technology and information literacy, which is the ability to find, organize, analyze, and report on information. The Association of College and Research Libraries has established standards for higher education regarding information literacy, a set of standards that hold the same relationship to the teaching of information literacy as the WPA OS holds for the teaching of writing. Initially, the technical communication program integrated technology, and later, information literacy, with the original WPA OS to modify it to fit the local context of an applied, professional, and technical writing program. Moreover, from the program's inception, a senior capstone course was required. Originally, the capstone was conceived as a way for students to demonstrate their mastery of the program outcomes. The method for this demonstration was, from the beginning, the construction of an electronic portfolio of the student's work in the program and then a public presentation of the portfolio. From the beginning of the program, we felt our students would best understand the significance of the artifacts they chose to include in their portfolios if they needed to explain the choices to an audience of their peers. Over time, our presentations have moved from face-to-face to virtual environments.

After a short while, we began to realize that just having program outcomes and then working with students in the capstone course to show how they had achieved those outcomes wasn't enough. Faculty and students both knew about the outcomes. They were posted on the unit's website. They were attached to syllabi. Still, some kind of connection was missing. Unlike the situation described in Chapter 15, where faculty members in other disciplines used a process similar to that of the Outcomes Group to develop mutually agreed upon outcomes, our faculty members inherited outcomes we developed from the WPA OS. In addition, our faculty lacked the approach to implement these outcomes into every course they taught. We needed to make sure that faculty and students understood that the program outcomes were the essential fabric of our entire curriculum. The first step we took to facilitate the complete integration of our program outcomes with our curriculum was to map these outcomes onto each course. We accomplished this by compiling a list of which program outcomes were covered in every course in the program. We (Maid as program head, and D'Angelo as director of assessment and curriculum) then used that information to create a curriculum map for our program. To ensure both curricular consistency and to help students understand the role of the program's outcomes, we then required that each syllabus list the outcomes for the specific course. In the past, the custom had been simply to list all program outcomes or give a link where the program outcomes could be found online.

The second change as a result of the curriculum mapping was the method we chose with which to assess the capstone portfolios. As the program grew, the number of graduates each semester also grew so that a more formal process to evaluate portfolios was necessary. As the number of portfolios grew, in order to keep the scoring process from slowing down in the details of each artifact in every portfolio, we decided to implement Phase 2 Scoring (White) as a rigorous method to assess portfolios. The construction of the portfolios is a large part of the content of our capstone course. In their final semester, students enroll in the capstone course, where they analyze their artifacts (assignments from courses and other work) in the context of technical communication program outcomes, which they then use to compose the portfolio. Portfolios are evaluated by two faculty members using a six-point scoring guide and Phase 2 scoring procedures (see D'Angelo and Maid, "Assessing Outcomes" for more details). After scoring is complete, students present their portfolios to invited faculty and students. Originally, presentations were held on campus; however, we quickly realized that requiring students in an online program to travel to campus wasn't working well. Most of our students work full-time, and many live far from campus; some are out-of-state. Further, many of our faculty members live out-of-state and are working practitioners, precluding their attendance at presentations. We first attempted using Internet conferencing software so that those who couldn't attend in-person could view presentations. However, using Internet conferencing didn't solve problems with scheduling for working professionals who would either have to take time off (students) or not be able to attend (faculty).

As a result, we moved the capstone course from Blackboard to Ning, a social media environment. As a platform, Ning provided several advantages over Blackboard for a course that is run as a workshop. It is password protected so that students' work remains private, and it includes tools, such as forums, chat, notifications, and blogs, that allow students to engage with each other and with each others' work. However, the main advantage in using Ning is that it provides an environment in which we can securely host student presentations asynchronously. As a result, we are able to maintain the requirement that students "present" their portfolio without requiring students or faculty to travel to campus. Using Ning allowed us to move the public presentation of student portfolios online in video format so that faculty and students can view and comment on portfolios at their convenience. Another advantage is Ning's better capacity than Blackboard's for larger file uploads. Since narrated portfolios composed in PowerPoint (or videos) tend to be large, file size limitations in Blackboard on the ASU system proved problematic. Next, unlike Blackboard, in which access is restricted to course enrollment, we can easily invite technical communication faculty members, students, and guests to join the site during a period of time so that they may view and comment on student presentations. In the two semesters we used Ning, we saw a significant increase in the number of faculty, students, and guests of students (family, friends) viewing presentations and commenting on them.

    Clearly, the logistics of using Ning proved advantageous in overcoming problems with capstone requirements for an online program. More importantly, since appropriate use of technology as a medium for organizing and presenting information is an outcome for our students, the use of Ning and video presentations is a demonstration of students' proficiency. On-site presentations tended to be delivered using PowerPoint in a fairly traditional oral presentation format. The move to Ning required students to focus more closely on how to adapt the use of the medium, whether using narrated PowerPoint or video, to address audience needs. The portfolio is the final artifact that students compose in the program. We suspect that on-site presentations were seen by many students as insignificant, since their portfolio had already been submitted and scored. With the transition to Ning, the portfolio and presentation are combined into one artifact, which results in the need for students to pay more attention to the rhetorical context and use of media in shaping their argument to demonstrate outcomes and to deliver it effectively.

Researching Portfolio Results

Following a grounded theory approach (see Charmaz), D'Angelo coded and analyzed the persuasive statements in ten portfolios from fall 2006, spring 2007, and fall 2007 semesters to code outcomes as they were manifested in student compositions. She coded and analyzed artifacts (work from courses, internships, and workplaces that students chose to incorporate in their portfolio) to determine what students included as evidence to support their argument that they achieved specified outcomes. In addition, she coded and analyzed rater comments that accompanied portfolio scores to determine patterns related to student claims about outcomes and faculty assessment of them.

The results of the study indicate that students made the most claims about outcomes related to rhetorical knowledge (see Table 1). Further, and among the latter, students most often supported their claim to have met the purpose of the assignment or task by pointing to evidence in an artifact. The second most frequently supported outcome in the rhetorical knowledge category was student claims related to meeting audience needs. As such, student work was rhetorically driven.

In discussing the concept of rhetorically driven prose, we focus particularly on audience and purpose as embedded or contextualized within a rhetorical situation. In this view, discourse is situated in recognizing that rhetoric is concerned with both content and presentation of information, and that it is influenced by the rhetor, audience, and context in which it takes place. As Elizabeth Turpin points out in "New Lamps for Old: A Reevaluating of Technical Communication in the Context of Classical Rhetoric," classical rhetoric lends a theoretical basis to technical communication, just as it does to the broader field of rhetoric and composition. Turpin points to Aristotle's and Plato's articulation of audience relationships as factors in determining context and presentation of a product so that content and form are inseparable from achieving a given purpose.

Table 1 Coding Results for Persuasive Statements and Artifacts.

Outcome Category	No. in Persuasive Statements*	No. in Artifacts*
Rhetorical Knowledge	23	17
Critical Thinking, Reading, and Writing	18	13
Processes	12	7
Knowledge of Convention	8	9

Rater comments acknowledged students' support of claims to have met both audience and purpose as rhetorical outcomes. Here is a sampling of raters' comments: one rater notes that a portfolio "demonstrates a clear understanding of rhetorical knowledge"; another rater comments that a portfolio exhibits "solid analysis of purpose, audience, situation." Other raters' comments express positive aspects of sample portfolios, noting that a writer is "aware of audience needs and purpose," "presents her evidence," and are "sensitive to different audience needs and purposes."

As mentioned above, the technical communication program integrated technology with the WPA OS. Analysis of portfolios and rater comments reflect students' claims of an awareness of the rhetorical nature of technology choices. Students made claims related to selecting and using technology or software. In addition, they demonstrated recognition of the rhetorical selection and use of software and media based on audience and purpose. Clearly, then, their decisions about technology and the application of technology were rhetorically driven. Again, the focus here is on audience and purpose as over-riding rhetorical concepts, or, as we have termed it, the über-outcome. This is clearly consistent with our intent in integrating technology with the original WPA OS in that we wanted students to go beyond thinking and learning about technology as mere tools whose mechanics they simply need to master.

The incorporation of technology as an outcome for writing and composition programs—both choosing and using technology—is problematic, as is evident in the debate about its inclusion in the WPA OS. For technical communication, how to articulate technology outcomes is even more contentious due to the discipline's applied nature and close association with industry practices. (See Maid's "You Don't Always Need a Hammer"). Students often enter technical communication programs expecting or desiring to learn the latest applications used in industry and listed in job ads as the skills or proficiencies required for employment. Such beliefs make rhetorical concepts and "learning how to learn" abstract concepts to students who are driven by the need to meet the qualifications required (or perceived to be required) by employers. As scholars and instructors, technical communication faculty members want students to understand broader rhetorical and social contexts of technology use as evident by the inclusion of outcomes related to understanding social, economic, legal, and ethical impacts of technology selection and use in the technical communication program outcomes statement.

As a group, students in D'Angelo's case study were aware of the rhetorical nature of technology selection and use in the context of audience and purpose for the assignment or task in which they were engaged. However, the tension between learning technologies (or software) and learning how to select and use applications or media within rhetorical contexts is evident in the analysis of the portfolios. Several students included evaluative statements about the technical communication program in addition to persuasive statements in the portfolio. One of the most frequent and negative comments students made in these evaluative statements was that the technical communication program does not offer courses in technology training. These comments were related to students' beliefs that they should learn the software necessary to meet employer expectations in job ads. Ironically, the analysis of student portfolios uncovered that they not only had learned software and technology use, but they had done so in a way that was rhetorically driven. As such, students went beyond learning the mechanics of how to use software to an understanding of how their selection of media and software had an impact on content and design decisions.

Another way of looking at the issue of technology and the WPA OS is the difference between short-term and long-term goals. Students and employers often focus on the short-term goal of learning a specific version of a specific software program, commonly to learn a structured, task-specific function. As educators, however, we are more concerned with long-term goals, wanting our students to understand that rhetorical choices of audience, purpose, and task should drive software selection—not the other way around. Certainly, ten portfolios is too small a number to state categorically that the way we integrated technology into our outcomes is successful. However, the prevalence of student choices of technology in the context of audience and purpose indicates that rhetorical knowledge may have emerged as an über-outcome, although we cannot be sure whether students do this consciously.

In addition, portfolio analysis revealed that students engaged in research that was appropriate for the rhetorical situation (audience, purpose). Student research, as represented in the ten student portfolios analyzed during the case study, was rhetorically driven; that is, research practices were influenced by the audience for results and by the purpose for which results would be used. While, in all cases, student research was completed as part of an assignment for a course or an internship, the claims made in persuasive statements as well as in the application of concepts in artifacts demonstrated that an awareness of audience and purpose was at work beyond the classroom when students made choices to do research and how to conduct, complete, and present it (D'Angelo, "Student Learning").

Critical thinking, reading, and writing (CTRW) outcomes were the next most frequently claimed by students. The majority of the claims about the CTRW outcomes related to research and to the use of information from research to produce documents. Students also discussed in their persuasive statements various issues related to technology, including the impact of technology on audiences, the presentation of information, the legal and ethical issues involved in using technology, and the use of technology for online work and collaboration. In student persuasive statements, claims about process outcomes focused on editing, on drafts and revisions, and on collaborative or group work. Claims related to knowledge of conventions focused on intellectual property, on understanding and application of standards or regulations, and on documentation of sources in academic research. The processes and knowledge of outcomes were difficult for the raters to evaluate. Both categories included the most rater comments, proclaiming that students did not support claims with evidence.

So, What Have We Learned, and What Do We Need to Learn?

Our initial assumption was that students majoring in an undergraduate technical communication program would lean more heavily toward the outcomes related to processes and knowledge of conventions when framing their arguments in their capstone persuasive statements. It was a natural assumption based on the demographics of the students with whom we work. Our students are typically older than traditional students; they come to us with workplace or military experience, and they are extremely career focused. Just as they look at our program because it is an applied program, they expect us to give them skills that they understand will be directly applicable in the workplace. Our assumption proved to be wrong. Rhetorical knowledge clearly emerged as the outcome that seemed to outweigh the others. Why?

Our initial thoughts are that there are likely to be several related issues at work. First of all, our instructors are all rhetorically biased. Both by training and world-view, they tend to value rhetorical skills above all others. Understanding audience, purpose, and context, encompasses everything they do and teach. As a result, it is most likely their pedagogy, even when the mapping says otherwise, that may be described as having the tendency to over-emphasize rhetorical knowledge. Our curriculum map, for example, indicates that rhetorical knowledge should be emphasized in the three "introductory" level courses: TWC 301 General Principles of Multimedia Writing, TWC 400 Technical Communication, and TWC 401 Principles of Technical Communication. Our initial thoughts when creating the curriculum map were that once students were grounded in these initial, required courses, the remaining courses would primarily focus on other outcomes while building on that foundation. However, looking at the list of courses (Table 2) from which students chose to include assignments as artifacts in their portfolio, TWC 411, Principles of Visual Communication, and TWC 446, Computer Documentation are most heavily represented. Is there something about the pedagogy of these courses, or the approach of the instructors, that lends itself to a stronger emphasis on rhetorical knowledge than is indicated in the curriculum map? Or, have students received such a foundational understanding of rhetorical knowledge by the time they compose their portfolios that they look back on their assignments from these courses through that lens? We can't answer those questions at this point; however, what is clear is that in their portfolios, rhetorical knowledge is emphasized more frequently than the other outcomes.

Another possible interpretation of the information is that since rhetorical knowledge is clearly emphasized in the "more basic" courses in the program, such as TWC 301, Principles of Multimedia Writing, and TWC 401, Principles of Technical Communication, our instructors present students with a strong base in rhetorical knowledge, and that base is transferred to other courses and finally to the persuasive essay in the senior capstone portfolio. That interpretation may provide the "best possible spin" on what we're seeing. It just seems unlikely to us that we would consistently see that level of transference across sections and instructors, unless the importance of rhetorical knowledge weren't also being taught in the other courses in the curriculum, despite what our curriculum map says.

Table 2 Courses Represented by Artifacts in Ten Portfolios.

Course	No. of artifacts
TWC 301 General Principles of Multimedia Writing	4
TWC 401 Principles of Technical Communication	5
TWC 411 Principles of Visual Communication	9
TWC 421 Principles of Writing with Technology	1
TWC 431 Principles of Technical Editing	4
TWC 443 Proposal Writing	3
TWC 444 Manual and Instructional Writing	1
TWC 446 Computer Documentation	7
TWC 451 Copyright & Intellectual Property in the Digital Age	1
TWC 452 Information in the Digital Age	1
TWC 453 History of Information and Technology	1
TWC 494 Writing for Non-Profits	3
TWC 494 Medical Rhetoric	2
TWC 447 Business Reports	1
TWC 484 Internship	3

Of course, other possibilities exist as to why rhetorical knowledge is so frequently emphasized. The rhetorical bias may influence our choices in textbooks, so that the tendency towards rhetoric is emphasized and reinforced by the texts used in our courses. Second, our students are smart. If our instructors are emphasizing rhetoric, and our students are sensitive enough to pick up the instructional emphasis, even unconsciously, then one might argue that when the students write their persuasive essays for the capstone portfolio, they naturally highlight rhetorical knowledge since they know instructors in the program are the audience for the essays. Of course, this further demonstrates the über-outcome nature of rhetorical knowledge: students are composing the portfolio to meet the expectations of their audience of faculty raters.

Is it possible to overemphasize rhetorical knowledge? We expect that the question could be debated for a long time. However, looking at our curriculum map, it becomes clear that for many of our courses, rhetorical knowledge is not the primary outcome that should be included in the curriculum. Has our assessment of senior capstone portfolios shown us that we might not be teaching what we claim we're teaching? Should we change, and if so, in what way?

The Feedback Loop and Where We Go From Here

It is a given in all good assessment strategies that information learned from the assessment should influence curricular revision in the program being assessed so that the program can be improved. Our assessment of senior capstone portfolios based on our program outcomes reveals that our rhetorical knowledge outcome seems to dominate everything our students do. This is clearly seen in the rhetorical nature of students' claims of their use of technology and research practices. In particular, given that we expect students to emphasize learning and use of tools, the fact that their portfolios demonstrate rhetorical context shows that rhetorical knowledge may be an "über-outcome"—at least in this case study. However, our study is not the only assessment results to show this is the case. An unpublished study done by Edward M. White and Norbert Elliot for McGraw-Hill indicates similar findings. For a program more concerned with long-term than short-term outcomes, perhaps this is a good thing.

However, the implications of rhetorical knowledge as an über-outcome are less clear. As we take what we have learned and use it to revisit our curriculum, we are left with many questions, such as the following: Do rhetoric and rhetorical knowledge always trump other strategies and influences in our curriculum? Is our current curriculum somehow overvaluing rhetorical knowledge? Do our instructors over privilege rhetorical knowledge? Do our students, aware of our instructors' propensity to privilege rhetorical knowledge, overstate the rhetorically personal perspective when they write in their persuasive statements?

We are aware there may be a theoretical advantage to teaching, say, knowledge of conventions as a subset of rhetorical knowledge. Doing so gets students to understand that it is imperative not only to know the conventions, but also to know that conventions may shift given a different context or a different audience. Can we say the same unequivocally about processes or critical thinking, reading, and writing? Would we really want to?

We think we have a solid, sensible curriculum. However, to this point, only one course (TWC 447, now TWC 347) has been seriously revised (D'Angelo and White; D'Angelo, "Using Portfolio Assessment"). We expect, as we use the information obtained through our program assessment to revisit our curriculum, that the answers will appear on a course-by-course basis. We still assume our original curriculum map makes sense. However, as we look at individual courses, we may decide that some of the outcomes mapped to those courses may need to be revised or—and this may be even more likely—that some of the curriculum and assignments in those courses need to be rethought to make sure our students are achieving all of the program outcomes, not merely some of them—and not just one possible uber-outcome.

WORKS CITED

Association of College and Research Libraries. *Information Literacy Competency Standards for Higher Education*. Association of College and Research Libraries, 2000. Web. 6 May 2012.

Charmaz, Kathleen. *Constructing Grounded Theory: A Practical Guide Through Qualitative Analysis*. Thousand Oaks, CA: Sage Publications, 2006. Print.

Council of Writing Program Administrators. "The WPA Outcomes Statement for First-Year Composition." Council of Writing Program Administrators, July 2008. Web. 9 Sept. 2011.

D'Angelo, Barbara J. "Student Learning and Workplace IL: A Case Study." *Library Trends* 60.3 (2012): 637-650. Print.

—. "Using Portfolio Assessment to Discover Student Learning." *Proceedings of the 74th Annual Convention of the Association for Business Communication*. The Association for Business Communication. Nov. 2009. n. pag. Web. 6 May 2012.

D'Angelo, Barbara. J., and Barry M. Maid. "Assessing Outcomes in a Technical Communication Capstone." *Handbook of Research on Assessment Technologies, Methods, and Applications in Higher Education*. Ed. Christopher Schreiner. Hershey, PA: IGI Global, 2009. 152–66. Print.

—. "Moving Beyond Definitions: Implementing Information Literacy Across the Curriculum." *Journal of Academic Librarianship*, 30.3 (2004): 212–17. Print.

D'Angelo, Barbara J., and Otis White. "Learning from Our Stakeholders: Using Research to Redesign a Business Writing Course" *Association of Business Communication Annual Conference*, Lake Tahoe, NV. 1 November 2008. Address.

Maid, Barry M. "Using the Outcomes Statement for Technical Communication." *The Outcomes Book. Debate and Consensus after the WPA Outcomes Statement*. Ed. Susanmarie Harrington, Keith Rhodes, Ruth Overman Fischer, and Rita Malenczyk. Logan, UT: Utah State UP, 2005. 139–49. Print.

—. "You Don't Always Need a Hammer." *Kairos: A Journal for Teaching Writing in Webbed Environments* at "CW 2001 Townhalls." 6.2 (2001): n. pag. Web. 4 June 2010.

Turpin, Elizabeth R. "New Lamps for Old: A Reevaluating of Technical Communication in the Context of Classical Rhetoric." *Writing on the Edge* 1.1 (1989): 87–96. Print.

White, Edward M. "The Scoring of Writing Portfolios: Phase 2." *College Composition and Communication* 56.4 (2005): 581–600. Print.

White, Edward M., and Norbert Eliot, et. al. "McGraw-Hill Assessment Research in Composition: Portfolio and Survey Analysis." Conference on College Composition and Communication. Louisville, KY. 18 March 2010. Address.

19 The WPA Learning Outcomes: What Role Should Technology Play?

Micheal Callaway

When the original WPA Outcomes Statement for First-Year Composition (WPA OS) was adopted by the Council of Writing Program Administrators (CWPA) in 2000, it was groundbreaking, codifying the central tenets of first-year composition and playing a significant role in legitimating writing classes and the place of writing program administrators in English departments. The document, as numerous contributors to this collection note, continues to resonate throughout the field and shape the way people teach first-year writing and train first-year writing instructors. In Chapter 8, Craig Jacobsen, Susan Miller-Cochran and Shelley Rodrigo articulate a similar point when they state that the WPA OS "occup[ies] a position of disciplinary authority." As a result, even though the initial WPA OS and subsequent revisions have been the result of contentious negotiations between a wide variety of scholars, the document allows the field to articulate *a* worldview about writing. Nevertheless, any time that one document is used to shape a field, some concerns will not be addressed, and those omissions resonate as thoroughly as the included content.

My concern in this chapter is how technology is currently discussed in the WPA OS, specifically as it relates to delimiting the scope of what is considered writing. Writing appears to mean words, only and words in a row, and there are few references to how writing technologies shape writerly decisions. As Kathleen Blake Yancey puts it, the original WPA OS reflects the history of the field: "historically, writing for print has played a central role in the development of students intellectually and socially . . . . This document speaks to that history and to that role"; however, she also notes that "on the street and in the classroom, we have already migrated to the screen and to multimedia" (221). Rhetoric and composition is beginning to move in new directions, so the WPA OS should move in those directions as well. Cynthia Selfe and Patricia F. Ericsson sound a similar alarm. They believe the WPA OS "focuses largely on traditional writing outcomes, with only the briefest nod to emerging technologies and their impact on literacies" (32). Yancey, and Selfe and Ericsson understand that the focus of writing instruction is expanding, and they reach that conclusion not through an appreciation for technology in and of itself; rather, they were led to that conclusion after careful consideration of the online literate practices of their students. Future revisions of the WPA OS must take into account and articulate a more thorough consideration of students' online writing practices.

This chapter examines the WPA OS's orientation towards technology, and posits that the reason for the lack of substantive change between the two versions is due to the overemphasis on the technology and the lack of explicit references to how technologies shape writerly decisions. Focusing exclusively on the technological applications used to write in electronic environments overlooks the symbiotic relationship created when a writer reflects on previous training, experiences, and expectations, and chooses to write to a specific audience, using a specific writing technology. Taking the emphasis off the technology and placing it on values and practices allows for a reading of literacy that is not solely skill based. Literate practices are not just applied skills; they are engaged practices. Students do not only need instruction on how to *use* or apply technology, but also they need instruction on how to *critically engage* technology. Students should also receive instruction in how they shape and are shaped by digital mediums, and how their identities and literate practices are constructed and promulgated by digital mediums and within digital environments. Currently, only traditional, print writing seems to be identified as writing in the WPA OS. As further revisions are made to the WPA OS, less focus should be placed on how technological applications relate to skills, such as research and revision, and more focus should be placed on the writerly decisions, such as genre, purpose, audience, that occur in electronic environments.

The Outcomes Statements: The Past and Current View of Technology

The following section outlines the way that technology is framed in the 1999 and 2008 versions of the WPA OS, and problematizes the instrumentalist bifurcation of writing technology from writer. In the 1999 version of the WPA OS, technology is only mentioned under the categorical heading of "Process." The document reads, "Use a variety of technologies to address a range of audiences," and the statement suggests that faculty facilitate student growth in this area by "[applying] the technologies commonly used to research and communicate within their fields" (62). Even though the word "technology" appears in the statement, the relationship between writing technology and writer is not sufficiently delineated. Based on the suggestion for how to facilitate growth in this area, it seems as if technology in the original WPA OS is simply a reference to tools, such as pencils, word processors, and computers that are *used* to write. Moreover, placing technology under the heading of "Process" further implies that selecting the writing technology is just one more step in a systematic, linear series of actions that writers go through when writing.

Although the reference to technology signals that the 1999 version of the WPA OS addresses the potential effects of technology on writing, the outcome doesn't speak to the dynamic relationship between the writer and the writing technology. Rather, it seems to distance writer from writing technology. Using specific technologies to research and communicate is important. However, the statement lacks a corresponding call to question the added value of using one technology over another, to acknowledge that technologies might alter communication, or to consider how technologies impact literacy and literate practices. Without the call to question added value, this outcome appears to stress application without critical theorizing. Students should recognize that specific technologies might modify their writing and research practices in addition to being able to use the technologies. Application may be stressed over theory because the writing technology is the instrument through which writing tasks are completed. However, the instrument doesn't seem to have any bearing on the invention possibilities or the modes of construction of the text.

Omitting a call to critically theorize technology in the WPA OS might be explained by positing that rhetorical knowledge trumps all. As Barry M. Maid and and Barbara J. D'Angelo note in Chapter 18, rhetorical knowledge can be seen as an "über-outcome," one that seems to supersede the others in importance. The lack of language in a national outcomes statement that specifically addresses the elasticity of the concept of rhetorical knowledge may reflect the assumption that rhetorical knowledge is an über-outcome that renders explicit recognition of technology moot. However, Maid and D'Angelo find the need to add a supplemental technology outcome for local purposes. This requirement acknowledges that instruments never stand alone; writing technologies are always paired with "the learning, training, discipline, and practice that always guides use" (Porter 385). Rhetorical knowledge may be an über-outcome, but the rhetorical knowledge needed to write in electronic environments sometimes differs from the rhetorical knowledge needed to write in print. The WPA OS's "Rhetorical Knowledge" section is excellent and can be applied to any context. All students can benefit from explicit discussions of rhetorical awareness. Nevertheless, some emerging technologies are different enough from traditional, print writing to necessitate an in-context outcome that draws attention to the ways that writing technologies impact writerly decisions.

On the Web, writing can move far beyond the capabilities of pen and paper or word processing programs. People can write documents that include collages of pictures, movies, remixes of songs and revise their work based on comments left by readers. My emphasis on networked computer technology is important because the Internet can shrink the distance between writer and audience, authorize more people to speak, reduce the lag time between production and distribution, and allow for quick feedback for reshaping messages. Networked computer technology also enables people to create new genres of writing, such as blogs and wikis. In *The Language of New Media*, Lev Manovich maintains that, "All existing media are translated into numerical data accessible for the computer. The result: graphics, moving images, sounds, shapes, spaces, and texts become computable, that is, simply sets of computer data. In short, media become new media" (25). The last sentence is particularly important. The media are not necessarily "new," but the possibilities for remixing, remediation, and reproduction are, influencing how people view these writing genres.

Over time, the new media genres of writing call upon different conventions (i.e., page construction, transitions, or subheadings) and the ability to input links, create non-sequential texts, and use graphics and sound clips. These technology-specific concerns could make documents created for the Web different from their traditional print counterparts. Because of the different considerations that writers of new media documents might have, writing teachers cannot rely solely on what has worked in the past; rather, they need to get students to broaden their horizons and think beyond the linear, print page.

Although the 2008 revision of the WPA OS addresses some of these concerns, it does not move much beyond the 1999 version in terms of its focus on technology as a tool. The technological instrumentalism in the 1999 version can be attributed to the times. In the late 1990s, some people wrote weblogs and other new media texts, but these forms of writing were not pervasive. Likewise, access to computer technology, especially networked computer technology, was inconsistent. These two factors lessened the need to prioritize technology in the WPA OS. However, by 2008, millions of people were writing and reading new media texts, and access had greatly expanded. Surely, the digital divide still exists and should be taken seriously, but access shouldn't be an impediment to including technology more fully into the WPA OS, especially if the emphasis is on critically engaging with technology. Adam Banks discusses the need to move beyond a mere instrumentalist notion of the digital divide to understand that "technological literacies, and critical understandings of technology are needed to gain meaningful access to any technology" (30). Currently, discussions about the digital divide often equate access with having a computer with network capabilities at home, but there is more to being a sophisticated user of technology than having a computer. Excluding students who lack Web access at home from critical discussions about technologies further disenfranchises them.

The addition of a "technology plank," a component previously seen as controversial, signals that the field of rhetoric and composition is adapting, but the outcomes presented in that section do little more than reiterate the points from the 1999 iteration of the WPA OS. The first outcome, under the "Composing in Electronic Environments" heading, states the following: "Use electronic environments for drafting, reviewing, revising, editing, and sharing texts." The key term is "electronic environments." There are wide ranges of electronic environments: this outcome could be interpreted broadly to include using programs that enable digital interactivity or narrowly to emphasize using a reviewing feature in a word processing program. This is not to suggest a good or bad binary, but simply to note possible interpretations. Clearly, the language in the 2008 document was extensively negotiated and considerate of the weight that a national outcomes statement carries. A major problem still remains—students are asked to "use" as opposed to "be aware" or "learn to" engage with electronic environments. They aren't asked to critically reflect on how the environment impacts drafting, revising, or sharing texts.

Moreover, this outcome seems to emphasize peer review. Using technology for peer review is appropriate, of course, but if peer review is the primary way of including technology, the emphasis remains on the tools. As further evidence to support my reading that technology is positioned as a tool, the introduction to the section explicitly singles out drafting, peer reviewing, and editing as reasons for why an electronic environments outcome is necessary. Neither how the "electronic environments" might impact what the writer writes, nor how the writing technology limits what is possible receives adequate attention. So, the environment is described as an element for manipulation instead of an element one considers and factors into the writing process.

The second outcome, "Locate, evaluate, organize, and use research material collected from electronic sources, including scholarly library databases; other official databases (e.g., federal government databases); and informal electronic networks and internet sources," is equally limiting in its present state. Just as the first outcome seems to emphasize peer review, the second outcome seems to privilege traditional research. Again, there is nothing wrong with encouraging students to "locate," "organize," and "research," and it is especially important to urge them to "evaluate" their sources. However, this outcome could be stronger when paired with a call to think about how work published in electronic environments alters conventional notions of credibility and reliability.

Students do use their computers for research, but many of them also write online. Without explicit discussions in class, students are often left to negotiate the space between the print and online spaces on their own. To avoid reifying the technological instrumentalist binary, the WPA OS's technology section could be updated to focus on how writing technologies necessitate specific kinds of rhetorical decisions. Technologies impact emerging literacies, so theories of technology need to move beyond skills to consider the values and practices of technology users. Jeff Rice's contribution to scholarship on digital rhetoric furthers our understanding of potential divergences between new media writing and traditional print writing. In "The 1963 Composition Revolution Will Not Be Televised, Computed, or Demonstrated by Any Other Means of Technology," Rice argues that new media writing is audience-centric. It is highly participatory and the writing is "not necessarily preempted by feelings of purpose or direction" (65). On the other hand, limited to linear, print text and guided by assessment criterion, traditional print writing is often divorced from audiences (59–62). Although his work doesn't specifically reference the WPA OS, Rice presents a cogent argument for why the document needs to be reconsidered. Andrea Lunsford's "Writing, Technologies, and the Fifth Canon" also seeks to show technology as something more than a neutral tool. Like Rice, Lunsford argues that the methods of invention and construction in electronic environments differ from traditional print writing, and implores readers to view "writing as epistemic, performative, multivocal, multimodal, and multimediated" (171).

Opening space for discussions about writing technologies is important because first-year composition students might not understand rhetorical situations or think about how environments affect writing. Barbara Duffelmeyer's "Critical Computer Literacy: Computers in First-Year Composition as Topic and Environment" underscores the importance of discussing technology and writing together. When she made computer technology a topic of conversation in class, and not just a tool to complete tasks, she found that students grappled with how their personal usages of technologies were shaped by cultural messages. She also found that students became more aware of their rhetorical decision-making process as a result of the conversations (304). Definitive evidence to confirm that networked computer technology affects writing may not exist. However, there is compelling evidence that traditional print writing and reading and their new media counterparts rely upon different theories of invention and that those theories are not necessarily transferable.

Writers and Writing Technologies

The "Composing in Electronic Environments" section contains three outcomes, but only one provides a deeper consideration of technology. Future revisions should move away from the first two outcomes and toward expanding the third, which urges students to "Understand and exploit the differences in the rhetorical strategies and in the affordances available for both print and electronic composing processes and texts." This is the only outcome in the electronic environment section that suggests that writing technology can impact how a writer writes, or that there are differences between writing situations and writing technologies. Rhetorical knowledge is emphasized here *in the context of the* electronic environment, as is the possibility that print and electronic composing practices can be different. The 1999 version of the WPA OS and the first two outcomes in the 2008 statement seem to assume that writing is writing, and all people need to do is "figure out" the technology that they are using. One interpretation of "figure out" the technology is that writers are separated from the technology when they write. I don't believe contemporary Americans can be pre-technology. As long as people are members of technologically dependent societies, the technological devices impact what they do and what seems possible. People cannot be technologically neutral subjects, and technologies cannot be neutral, either.

Even this configuration doesn't quite disentangle the issues. Michelle Kendrick's "Cyberspace and the Technological Real" offers a way of questioning the ideological assumptions about subjectivity at the heart of the technology-writer binary. The "technological real" posits that "subjectivity is always in the process of being reconstructed by the technologies—material and semiotic—which it purports merely to manipulate" (144). So, there can be no pre-technological self because technologies are constantly intervening in our lives and altering our sense of self (144). Underlying Kendrick's theory is the assumption that people repress the recognition that technology intervenes in their lives, and that repression drives them to imagine a self that is free from the taint of technology (149). To assume that writers are writers regardless of the writing technology used is to assume that the repeated exposure to technology has no impact on our processes and ways of being. Technology may not make us physically different, but it does influence our orientation towards and our ways of being in the world. Identities and literate practices are construed and proclaimed by and through digital mediums and within digital environments.

Because writing is a means of communicating, there may be occasions where words alone are not enough. Discussions of audience awareness may cover this terrain, but viewing writers as symbiotically connected with writing technologies goes much deeper than understanding the audience to whom one is writing. In linguistics, the concept of code-switching is used to describe how people can simultaneously move back and forth between different dialects. Code switchers are often moving between a prestige dialect, such as Standard American English and a disparaged dialect, such as African American Vernacular English. For the code-switcher, the switch is not just about audience. It's also about identity maintenance. Experiences with technology can shape actions in much the same way that experiences with language can. I'm not suggesting that code-switching and orientations towards technology are equivalent, but both are issues that move beyond mere audience awareness and into identity maintenance; both necessitate considerations that run deeper than knowing one's audience.

If a student views herself as a "techy," she may shy away from multimodal writing, even if she believes that extra-verbal cues or a non-sequential structure might be more appropriate because she believes that formal writing is linear writing. Sherry Turkle sums it up well when she writes, "In the story of constructing identity in the culture of simulation, experiences on the Internet figure prominently but these experiences can only be understood as part of a larger cultural context" (10). Cultural context is the ever-evolving exchange between emerging, new media literacies and existing, print literacies (10). As Turkle suggests, experiences with technology help people fashion ideological orientations towards technologies. For example, people don't join social networking sites because they only want to post stuff in cyberspace. They do it because they want to be connected, to share who they are, and to make themselves anew, writing themselves into being and subconsciously or consciously making rhetorical decisions along the way. Technology cannot be removed from the process. Mastery of computer technology won't necessarily make students better writers. Discussions about writing technologies, though, might help them better understand their relationship to the technology and make better choices when matching writing technologies to writing situations. Discussing technology in this way is not teaching the tools; it is discussing technological interactions as value driven, writerly decisions. The degree to which writers consciously see a symbiotic relationship between themselves and their writing technologies will depend on how they have learned, through formal and informal means, to orient themselves to those technologies.

Considering the Technological Orientations of Our Students

The inclusion of a technology section in the 2008 iteration of the WPA OS is an advance; however, I hope to push the boundary a little more to consider what is still missing from the WPA OS. If orientations towards technology are shaped in formal and informal ways, writing instructors need to be considerate of the formal message they communicate in class. Writing instructors also need to consider the literate practices of their students and the informal messages that their students receive about writing. In a 2008 Pew Research Study, titled "Writing, Technology," Pew found that eighty-five percent of teens age 12–17 use instant messaging, phone text messaging, email, and social networking sites to communicate (ii). Although this isn't surprising, the enlightening part of the study is the revelation that sixty percent of respondents do not view those communicative acts as "writing" (Lenhart, et al. ii). So, writing may be writing for some college-writing teachers, but for students, only certain kinds of writing are actually writing. This is a problem because a large number of students are using technologies and writing without necessarily considering the rhetorical choices that they make when writing. To complicate the matter, sixty-four percent of students reported incorporating practices from their out-of-school, text-based communications into their school writing (ii). The Pew study focuses on lack of capitalization and use of emoticons, but the bigger issue is that students see an important distinction between the writing that they do at home and the writing that they do at school, possibly erecting boundaries between their school and out-of-school selves.

When asked what might facilitate their growth as writers, the overwhelming response was "teachers having them spend more time writing in class, and teachers using more computer-based tools (such as games, writing help programs or websites, or multimedia) to teach writing" (Lenhart, et al. iv). Although some may think that these findings of do not merit the concern of the Council of Writing Program Administrators (CWPA), I suggest that the WPA OS should be revised to expand the scope of writing to include digital and multimodal production of texts. Omission of these forms of writing from even casual consideration in classrooms implies to students that such forms are not "writing." The current version of the statement uses the word "electronic," but the references don't speak to the possibility that certain writing technologies call upon different writing conventions. The statement doesn't have to list specific kinds of technologies to be useful, but it should be broad enough so that new media technologies can be read between the lines. As a way to remove specific technological applications from the statement, a revised WPA OS could ask students to consider their own use of technology: "Be aware that personal usage of technology shapes usage of technology in educational settings and vice versa." An outcome that connects home and school could start discussions of technology where students are and would stand the test of time, because students' experiences with technology would drive conversations.

Also, if students utilize technology as they write, they need to consider the rhetorical and ideological forces affecting their interpretations of writing. An outcome could be added to emphasize reading online, such as "Understand that reading in online environments may call for adapted reading strategies and influence the interpretation of texts." An outcome that emphasizes reading is important so that students gain a better understanding of how print and new media texts play off of each other to create context and meaning. If students engage with these issues in class, they will be better positioned to deal with the diversity of rhetorical situations they encounter outside of class. Many teachers already have these kinds of conversations. Anytime writing teachers tell their students not to blindly rely on sentence structure suggestions from MS Word's reviewing feature, they are discussing the effects of writing technologies on writing practices. Or, when students complain about the perpetual changes to social networking sites' interfaces, they are speaking about the ideologies that support technologies. Moreover, an outcome could be added to draw attention to the role of ideology in shaping writerly decisions, such as "Understand that constructed ideologies support writing technologies, and those ideologies shape the ways that people write." The next step is to consciously address writing technologies more so in class. For instance, whenever a celebrity or political figure gets into trouble for an online post, the door is opened to discuss invention and construction of texts in online writing environments. A revised WPA OS could encourage students to think about this aspect by including the following outcome: "Understand that digital writing and traditional print writing sometimes call for different forms of invention and construction."

A revised WPA OS that includes these sample outcomes would facilitate conversations about technology and users of technology—not one or the other. These sample outcomes also subtly encourage students to think about how the available means of persuasion are influenced by writing technologies. Now and in the future, students will have to account for the constraints and possibilities that writing technologies offer, and they will need to prepare themselves to read and write in traditional print and new media formats because they have been acculturated in a time when multiple literacies are emerging at a rapid pace (Selfe and Selfe). Given these realities, a revised, more technologically friendly WPA OS should present outcomes that emphasize the interconnectedness of writers to writing technologies, encouraging students to critically consider their writerly decisions and online writing practices, especially in regards to how these online writing decisions and practices influence the interrelation of self-formation and the public sphere. Currently, students may not think about the writing that they do in their English 101 class in this way, but they might think about their online writing in such terms. A set of outcomes that emphasizes the interrelation of rhetorical awareness, writing, and writing technology could challenge the false binary between students' online writing and school writing practices. For example, when people use social networking sites, it is possible for them to construct selves and identities through multimodal texts, strategically advancing and revising those identities as they receive feedback from others. They must make tough rhetorical decisions about language, genres of texts and how these genres mesh to produce multimodal texts, purpose, audience, etc. A revised WPA OS needs to acknowledge and encourage this rhetorically complex process, and it needs to help students make this process conscious. As new iterations of the WPA OS are considered, I hope that stakeholders seriously consider the sample outcomes above. Since new literacies and new technologies are rapidly emerging and meshing, the discipline bears the responsibility of developing outcomes that broaden and enrich the discipline's understanding of writing, one that acknowledges the interrelation of writer, writing technology, and self-formation, and that recognizes and encourages the multiple literacies that students bring with them when they enroll in composition courses.

Works Cited

Banks, Adam. *Race, Rhetoric, and Technology: Searching for Higher Ground.* Mahwah, NJ: Lawrence Erlbaum, 2005. Print.

Council of Writing Program Administrators [with responses by Clyde A. Moneyhun; Keith Rhodes; Mark Wiley; Kathleen Blake Yancey]. "The WPA Outcomes Statement for First-Year Composition." *WPA: Writing Program Administration* 23.1/2 (1999): 59–70. Print.

Council of Writing Program Administrators. "The WPA Outcomes Statement for First-Year Composition." Council of Writing Program Administrators, July 2008. Web. 6 May 2012.

Duffelmeyer, Barbara. "Critical Computer Literacy: Computers in First-Year Composition as Topic and Environment." *Computers and Composition* 17.3 (2000): 289–307. Print.

Kendrick, Michelle. "Cyberspace and the Technological Real." *Virtual Realities and Their Discontents*. Ed. Robert Markley. Baltimore: Johns Hopkins UP, 1996: 143–60. Print.

Lenhart, Amanda, Sousan Arafeh, Aaron Smith, and Alexandra Rankin Macgill. "Writing, Technology and Teens." *Pew Internet & American Life Project*. Pew Research Center, 24 April 2008. Web. 13 Feb. 2010.

Lunsford, Andrea. "Writing, Technologies, and the Fifth Canon." *Computers and Composition* 23.2 (2006): 169–77. Print.

Manovich, Lev. *The Language of New Media*. Cambridge, MA: MIT Press, 2001. Print.

Porter, James. "Why Technology Matters to Writing: A Cyberwriter's Tale." *Computers and Composition* 20 (2002): 375–94. Print.

Rice, Jeff. "The 1963 Composition Revolution Will Not Be Televised, Computed, or Demonstrated by Any Other Means of Technology." *Composition Studies* 33.1 (2005): 55–73. Print.

Selfe, Cynthia L. *Technology and Literacy in the Twenty-First Century: The Importance of Paying Attention*. Carbondale: Southern Illinois UP, 1996. Print.

Selfe, Cynthia L., and Patricia F. Ericsson. "Expanding Our Understanding of Composing Outcomes." *The Outcomes Book: Debate and Consensus after the WPA Outcomes Statement*. Ed. Susanmarie Harrington, Keith Rhodes, Ruth Overman Fischer, and Rita Malenczyk. Logan, UT: Utah State University, 2005. 32–35. Print.

Selfe, Cynthia L., and Richard Selfe. "'Convince me!' Valuing Multimodal Literacies and Composing Public Service Announcements." *Theory Into Practice* 47.2 (2008): 83–92. Print.

Turkle, Sherry. *Life on the Screen: Identity in the Age of the Internet.* New York, NY: Simon and Schuster, 1997. Print.

Yancey, Kathleen Blake. "Bowling Together: Developing, Distributing, and Using the WPA Outcomes Statement—and Making Cultural Change." Harrington, et al. 211–21. Print.

20 Assessing the Impact of the Outcomes Statement

Emily Isaacs and Melinda Knight

The aim of the Outcomes Statement project with which we are in particular agreement is the originating one: that writing programs should articulate what they seek to have students learn, and that these learning outcomes should be tied to research-based findings on best practices for teaching first-year college writing. As Harrington, et al., members of the Outcomes Statement collective, argue in 2001 (when they published the WPA OS in *College English*), "it's useful to see some common assumptions undergirding all our programs" (322). That there are legitimate conflicts within the scholarly community as to which particular practices are best—for example, focusing on the argumentative genre versus focusing on practicing several genres—is ultimately of less importance than the principle of tying one's program values to the scholarship-defined values of the discipline of rhetoric and composition. We choose the term "values" here because outcomes statements, as much as mission statements or course descriptions, reveal the teaching, learning, and writing values that the institutions that adopt them hold.

An explicit purpose of the WPA Outcomes Statement for First-Year Composition (WPA OS) was to promote consensus on outcomes for first-year writing. We also believe that a focus on outcomes implicitly suggests directions for teaching methodology and curriculum. Despite the existence of the WPA OS, however, first-year writing and writing programs (and the teachers who work in them) are too often developed without sufficient reference to these agreed-upon values of the field, and that, in turn, has led to an overly large spectrum of approaches to teaching writing nationwide. This is a strong assertion, to which we imagine many may nod, while others may question both the evidence and whether it is important to even address issues of disciplinary coherence. One might wonder, for example, if any of us in the field can reasonably estimate what percentage of the nation's BA-granting institutions teach writing as a process. Fifty percent? More? Fewer? We just don't know. As a field, we appear unaware of the extent to which most colleges and universities do—or do not—teach first-year writing in ways that reflect the discipline's dominant values as embedded in the WPA OS.

As Richard Fulkerson notes as recently as 2005, "There is no available and current synthetic account of what goes on in college writing classrooms in the United States: the syllabi, writing assignments, readings, classroom procedures" (682). There are, of course, a number of historical or localized accounts, the most useful of which are those written by Albert Kitzhaber and Edward M. White and Linda Polin. Kitzhaber analyzes the "present state of composition studies" in 1963 by collecting syllabi from ninety-five, four-year colleges and universities, visiting eighteen of those schools (8–9). While his data are out of date, he makes a useful set of recommendations regarding administration (class size and teaching load), exemption, faculty status, assignment design, commenting, and standards for evaluation—categories that have become part of our larger study. In a 1986 report funded by the National Institute of Education, White and Polin examine the effectiveness of college writing programs in California, with a focus on administrative structure, composition faculty and the composition program, and students. In their five-year study of all nineteen campuses, they used questionnaires, interviews, outcome measures, and other data points, producing a "California Construct" of six instructional approaches to teaching composition (38–54). The most recent systematic and large-scale study of college writing programs appears to be Richard Larson's 1994 report to the Ford Foundation, which we discuss in more detail later in this chapter.

Increasingly, efforts towards gaining greater knowledge of what it is that is "done" in the field have been demonstrated through publications on particular issues (Lunsford and Lunsford's "Mistakes Are A Fact of Life," most notably) and ongoing research projects (e.g., CCCCs Professional Database, analyzed by Gere, which focuses on survey data from CCCs members, and Thaiss's WAC/WID mapping project). Nonetheless, there is an enormous amount of work to be done if we are to be able to provide the kind of report called for by Fulkerson, echoing Richard Haswell.

In partial response to this dearth of knowledge, this chapter investigates to what extent there is a "widespread understanding of these outcomes," as WPA OS initiator Edward M. White ("Origins" 7) hopes, by those programs that are judged "best in class" in various institutional types (classes are diversely defined, as detailed below) by the *U.S. News and World Report,* and by our own professional organization, the Conference on College Composition and Communication. It is the purpose of our research project, "Top College Writing Programs" (from which this chapter is drawn), to offer scholarship that empirically explores how first-year writing is taught in the United States. In this chapter, we specifically address the question of how and to what extent the WPA OS, other outcomes, or the values embedded in the WPA OS, have been adopted (or adapted) in 101 four-year colleges and universities, selected as type-representatives from the approximately 2,500, that currently grant BAs in the United States today (Carnegie Foundation). In determining our categories of analysis and the particular data points we have collected, we used earlier research as an initial guide (Kitzhaber; Larson; and White and Polin in particular).

Whether we like it or not, ranking schemes play a major role in public discourse about the value of post-secondary education, both in the United States and throughout the world. The Institute for Higher Education Policy, for example, in a report funded by the Lumina Foundation, discusses how rankings might, in fact, play a positive role in institutional decision-making in the four countries studied (2). Despite the scorn often heaped upon the surveys reported by *U.S. News and World Report* and *Business Week,* among others, consumers and policy makers do indeed pay attention to them, and almost all universities and colleges cooperate in the data collection process. Schools proudly announce how they are ranked, and there is great anticipation about each new release of rankings. *U.S. News and World Report* even has a countdown clock in days, hours, and minutes on its main website to alert visitors when the next year's rankings will be released.

To develop a sample for our study, we chose as a starting point the annual rankings published by *U.S. News,* not because we endorse their selections and methodology, but because of the stature and power of these lists for prospective students, administrators, and decision-makers. *U.S. News* purports to measure reputation for academic quality, via a set of indicators from seven categories (assessment by administrators at peer institutions, retention, faculty resources, student selectivity, financial resources, alumni giving, and the publication's determination of graduation rate).[1] Significantly, we have chosen not to find out what is happening at the "average" institution, but rather at various types of "bests"; our belief is that this sample allows us to see what trends are occurring in highly regarded national and regional institutions of various types. More specifically, to develop a representative sample for our study, we made our selection of schools based on several different *U.S. News* 2009 rankings categories. While the *U.S. News* survey may be best known for the overall college rankings, the annual report breaks down the lists by many categories, allowing us to select among the lists to create a broad view across four regions of public and private spheres and of different types of institutions: BA-focused, Master's (term used by Carnegie, formerly known as comprehensive), and doctoral-granting. The specific 2009 *U.S. News* lists we drew upon are as follows: top national—ten schools; top public—twenty; top liberal arts—ten; top Master's—five in each region (North, South, Midwest, and West); and top BA—three in each region ("America's Best Colleges").

We also selected schools from two other lists: "Top Historically Black" (the top five schools in the list), and all the "writing in the disciplines schools" (WID) mentioned in the list of "academic programs to look for." While we focus on first-year writing in this study, we believe the WID list captures schools that otherwise might not have made it into our sample. Further, we believe it is important also to include programs rated highly by our own discipline. To that end, we included schools within the United States whose writing programs have been awarded the CCCC Writing Program Certificate of Excellence from 2004—when the award was established—through 2009. Our exclusion of schools in other countries in this group relates to the focus of this study, which is to look at first-year writing programs located within the United States. Clearly, much exciting work in rhetoric and composition is being done outside the United States (see Susan Thomas's chapter in this collection), although the concept of first-year writing is by no means a universal curricular paradigm throughout the world. All these selection criteria (and some schools fit into more than one category) resulted in a sample size of 101, which we believe offers a rich trove of data for discussion and analyses. We began our data collection in the fall of 2008, and continued for the next year. The findings we report in this chapter are current as of summer 2009.

Once we selected our sample, we then began to investigate schools by examining what is publicly available on websites, replicating and expanding an approach first used to examine professional schools (Knight). We wanted a methodology that would be comparable across schools, and we believe that how an institution presents itself, how it demonstrates what it values, gives us the best indication of the extent to which the WPA OS has had an impact. For this chapter, therefore, we focus on the first-year writing requirement itself, course descriptions, mission statements, policies, catalogs or bulletins, program reports posted on websites, and any other documents posted or linked. We essentially reviewed all information available to the public. Although retrieval was often challenging and occasionally difficult, we were careful to crosscheck for accuracy within a website wherever possible. This methodology is very different from traditional surveys sent to WPAs, where the response rate can have an impact on results, and where it can be difficult to compare and crosscheck data.

Our method is a critical part of our research design, as we wanted to see how schools presented themselves to the public, including the ways in which an institution represents itself to important stakeholders. A public affirmation of first-year writing outcomes can be a powerful indicator of consensus building in the discipline. With higher education under increasing duress because of demands for accountability and transparency, we would argue that it is important to consider how information is presented and to whom. Because of the dominance of the various rating schemes, some schools have taken it upon themselves to provide verifiable data as a counterpoint. Consider, for example, the Voluntary System of Accountability (VSA), which provides "basic, comparable information on the undergraduate student experience to important constituencies through a common web report—the College Portrait" ("Home"). One goal of the VSA is to measure "educational outcomes and facilitate the identification and implementation of effective practices as part of institutional improvement efforts" ("About VSA"). Our own findings for first-year writing programs, we believe, will also provide important information to stakeholders, including the ways in which research in rhetoric and composition has, or has not, had an impact on how programs represent themselves, including, we would hope, an indication of actual teaching and curricular practices.

Perhaps the greater concern that those of us active in the field have is the extent to which, in practice (not in theory), the field is dominated by what is most frequently called current-traditional or traditional approaches to teaching writing. The available evidence suggests that the current-traditional model of teaching writing continues to dominate first-year writing instruction (Burhans; Connors; Larson). It's useful to recall that in 1983, Clinton Burhans' review of 263 college and university catalog descriptions of first-year writing courses led him to conclude that between eighty-three percent and eighty-nine percent of courses were taught in a "traditional" model, with only one-to-five percent employing "contemporary" pedagogies (645). A decade later, Larson's research finds that thirty percent of programs teach "the writing process," but that, at most schools, the focus is on attention to formal aspects of writing and that approaches are widely divergent, and reflect little current scholarship in the field (24). With the proliferation of graduate programs in composition/rhetoric, and with writing programs' increased influence on graduate students' pedagogical practices, it is reasonable to assume that the field has progressed in translating knowledge from scholarship to pedagogy, though significant barriers to broad adoption of best practices undoubtedly remain present (Bartholomae; Isaacs).

Part of the reason we have an apparent disconnect between theory and practice is that we have had a relatively short timeframe to establish ourselves as a discipline, and with the majority of programs in first-year writing still within other established departments, which may have other concerns and priorities, changing curricula and pedagogies is extremely difficult. Additionally, providing training for the faculty that must teach millions of students is, to say the least, challenging, particularly when we consider that most first-year writing faculty are contingent and turn over with great frequency. As David Bartholomae notes, the impact of the discipline is primarily trickle-down, as allocations for tenure lines has decreased, so that writing specialists are primarily running programs, conducting research, and teaching pedagogy courses, not actually teaching first-year writing sections in significant numbers (1953).[2] Of course, a commonplace view is that the translation of theory into practice would seem to require a half- century. Beyond these practical challenges that have impeded the widespread adoption of agreed-upon values in the classroom, however, are some genuine disagreements among those who are conversant with rhetoric and composition research and theory as to how first-year writing should be taught and whether or not we should, in fact, even have a broadly unified position on teaching first-year writing. Significantly, we have largely originated within a discipline (English) that eschews regulation, standardization, and anything that might compromise what is often characterized as "academic freedom." Sometimes, it seems to us that academic freedom is raised overly broadly, inhibiting institutional efforts to provide students with a common set of expectations, experiences, and learning outcomes. Note that even within the WPA OS community there is considerable anxiety about standardization. In Chapter 17, Judy Holiday is concerned about the WPA OS leading to a "one-way acculturation process" and "little rhetoric" at the expense of "big rhetoric"—largely because of what she perceives as an implicit call for standardization from the WPA OS. Similarly, Mark Wiley is greatly concerned about what he sees as potential misuse of the WPA OS, writing, "It is possible that at some institutions these outcomes will be misinterpreted precisely in order to impose a uniform curriculum upon the composition program. Individual teachers might be forced to use a common syllabus, text, and a reductive form of assessment to evaluate student writing at the end of the term" (27). To this, we respond that with the exception of the "reductive form of assessment," all of these uses Wiley suggests are reasonable and even laudable from a student learning perspective. In any event, we hope it is clear from this example that the entire issue of establishing shared content and pedagogy is vexing for many of us, and in particular, we would assert, to those of us who originate from the humanities and carry with us that distaste for standards—a term the framers of the WPA OS explicitly rejected—of any sort.

James Williams notes that the discipline's valuing of individual perspectives has led to the "deprofessionalization of the field," a strong statement for which we have considerable sympathy (223). Notably, even among the WPA Outcomes Collective—a relatively homogenous group compared to a randomly selected pool of academics (WPA or otherwise) responsible for "running" (we use the term loosely) writing programs—there are significant problems with agreement. Keith Rhodes, Irvin Peckham, Linda Bergmann, and William Condon, in their history of the development of the WPA OS, note, "we confronted an unpleasant fact: the term *first-year composition* varied widely in meaning" (12). In 2005, Fulkerson, based on his review of several popular "how-to-teach expository writing" books by major figures in the field, advances an even stronger assertion of his point of view that the discipline had become increasingly fractious, haphazard, and disjointed in its approach to teaching writing: "We differ about what our courses are supposed to achieve, about how effective writing is best produced, about what an effective classroom looks like, and about what it means to make knowledge" (680–81).

Fulkerson's dismal conclusion comes from a non-empirical review of the field: a review of several general texts on teaching writing. We characterize Fulkerson's conclusion as dismal because we are in assent, though this is not to say that we are not aware that many in higher education value diverse approaches to teaching as a strength. Our concern is with the broad degree of disparity in approach, and in particular, with approaches that are contrary to cumulative research and which indicate that important developments in the field are virtually unknown or ignored at many institutions. Fulkerson's conclusion is supported by empirical data for a similar conclusion by Larson in his 1994 report, *Curricula in College Writing Programs: Much Diversity, Little Assessment*. Under commission from the Ford Foundation, Larson sought to "describe [the nation's college] writing programs, locate their underlying assumptions, identify the theories on which they were based, and understand main features of the context within which they operated" (3). Using a voluntary survey methodology in which 575 data requests (randomly selected from 3,000, with the addition of a dozen or so specially selected schools) yielded 240 usable surveys. Larson analyzed documents that program administrators sent him: sample syllabi, internal memos, and other documents describing programs and policies (5). Larson found great diversity in approaches to teaching writing, declaring that the Ford Foundation's contention that there was no "center of gravity" was well-supported by his study (18). To the extent that he did find consistency, it was in an emphasis on "formalism" and, in particular, a "predominant emphasis on teaching forms of writing, patterns of arrangement, compliance with formal requirements (in paragraphs and sentences)" (18). In this 1994 report, there is no mention of outcomes or standards per se, although Larson examines program documents for evidence of concern for the development of students' skills in rhetoric; critical thinking, reading, and writing; and processes. Larson ends by asserting that it would be a waste of the Ford Foundation's money to invest in the "improvement of college writing programs" on the grounds that there is overly "wide disagreement on what a college writing program should be or should teach" (40). Finally, as precursor to the assessment movement that we have seen develop in recent years, and of which the WPA OS is a part, Larson calls for accountability and program review, declaring that "one of the most troubling findings from the study was the almost complete *absence* in most institutions of any effort to determine *whether the first-year writing program is achieving its purpose*" (46–47).

Central to the WPA OS project is, of course, accountability through assessment, as well as the broader goal of developing a set of expected outcomes that individual institutions and the broader public can consult as a reference and comparative appraisal. Beyond local value, the WPA OS's success at creating unity in the ways that Fulkerson, Larson, Williams would admire is contingent upon whether widespread adoption of the WPA OS occurs. Patricia Freitag Ericsson documents the impact of the WPA OS in a chapter for *The Outcomes Book* collection. Ericsson's methodology for assessing the extent of the adoption of the WPA OS was to review the WPA Listserv archives (where the WPA OS originated and has been frequently discussed since then) to identify individuals who described or mentioned using the WPA OS at their schools and to additionally query the WPA Listserv. From these methods, Ericsson developed a list of individuals to contact, resulting in a list of fifty-nine institutions whose responses to surveys led Ericsson to state that the "Outcomes Statement technology has been broadly adapted and successfully implemented in a wide variety of venues" (105). At the outset of our research, we wondered if this was an overly optimistic conclusion, even considering that Ericsson's methodology was not comprehensive and was conducted not long after the Council of Writing Program Administrators adopted the WPA OS and took steps toward promoting it. With our research and analysis now complete, however, we have found that the WPA OS has had little influence on the 101 institutions we reviewed. That being said, we do see some influence of the larger outcomes movement that has reverberated through higher education, and finally, we notice significant dispersal of the WPA OS's "values," a finding we believe Fulkerson, Larson, and Williams would find uplifting.

Before sharing our data, we must briefly share our challenges with terminology. Kathleen Blake Yancey makes an important distinction between standards—which define levels of achievement—as opposed to outcomes—which define what we would like students to know or do. She further notes a significant difference between objectives, which "tend to be very specific statements of achievement," whereas outcomes "do not specify *how well* students should know or understand or do what the curriculum intends" (21). This distinction seems simple enough, until one starts looking at 101 first-year writing programs that do not always use these terms precisely. The slipperiness of the terminology made it a challenge to determine exactly what schools in our sample were doing and the extent to which the WPA OS has had an impact. We address this challenge by developing the following six categories that best represent how first-year writing programs have been engaging in the issues raised by the WPA outcomes movement. We assign schools to each of the categories.

1. No first-year writing requirement: 8 schools
2. First-year writing requirement
   a. No outcomes; no goals or objectives: 29 schools
   b. No outcomes; no goals or objectives, but WPA skill areas in course description: 19 schools
3. First-year writing requirement—standards, as opposed to outcomes (note that a standard could be an outcome achieved at a particular level): 6 schools
4. First-year writing requirement—concept of outcomes or equivalent absent, but goals and/or objectives present
   a. No connection to WPA: 0 schools
   b. 1-to-3 WPA OS outcomes embedded: 20 schools
   c. 4-to-5 WPA OS outcomes embedded: 8 schools
5. First-year writing requirement—outcomes or equivalent
   a. No connection with WPA OS: 1 school
   b. 1-to-3 WPA OS outcomes embedded: 3 schools
   c. 4-to-5 WPA OS outcomes embedded: 6 schools
6. Adopted WPA OS: 1 school

The first category was, for obvious reasons, very easy to determine. Some of these schools have first-year seminars, although we make distinctions between those that focus on teaching writing and those that are merely topical or thematic. For subsequent categories, it is important to note that first-year writing requirements are not always met by courses, as many schools offer exemption through a variety of measures (Advanced Placement and International Baccalaureate, among others, which have their own outcome statements or something resembling them).

The second category indicates whether or not these schools' first-year writing requirements had any language related to outcomes or goals or objectives present at all in course descriptions and other publicly available materials. In the schools categorized as 2a, we find no language relating to outcomes, but in 2b, one or more of the WPA OS's areas (rhetorical knowledge; critical thinking, reading, and writing; processes; knowledge of conventions; or composing in electronic environments) may appear in descriptions of course content or activities. (Thus, in this category, institutions may describe what will be covered in a first-year writing course, but do not articulate outcomes, goals, or objectives.) For example, a course description may indicate that the course is about critical thinking, but does not indicate what students will learn; or, the course approaches writing as a process, but doesn't specify what students will be able to do or learn as a result. The third category includes institutions that indicate standards, levels of achievement to be measured, in addition to or in place of outcomes or goals or objectives.

The fourth and fifth categories make a distinction between schools that use the term "outcome" specifically and those that do not; the latter group most often uses the term goals or objectives or both, and from here on we use the phrase "goals/objectives" for simplification. In both of these categories, we further distinguish among schools that do not use any of the language or concepts of the WPA OS and those that do. The sixth and final category indicates the wholesale (word-for-word) adoption of the WPA OS. With all these categories, we are making assumptions about what first-year writing programs value.

We were not surprised that most of the eight schools in category 1 (no first-year writing requirement) represented elite liberal arts colleges (Amherst, Sarah Lawrence, Kenyon, Oberlin, among others). Most of these, nevertheless, did stress the value of writing in courses throughout the curriculum, although there appeared to be no active instruction in writing. Additionally, a total of six schools fell into the third category, stressing standards as opposed to outcomes. Notably, of the schools with a first-year writing requirement, fifty-four—more than half—did not give any indication of specifying outcomes. Within that group, nineteen used some of the concepts in the WPA OS in a description of course content, but not in terms of outcomes or goals/objectives. In our sample of 101, thirty-nine schools listed goals/objectives or outcomes. However, only eleven schools specifically referred to outcomes. One school clearly indicated that it adopted the WPA OS (the statement appeared word-for-word on the website), and three others made reference to its existence by simply directing readers to it for more information or indicating that it had been used in crafting program outcomes.

Our study reveals a wide range of approaches to what students should learn or do in first-year writing programs. With only eleven schools using the term "outcome," it would appear that the WPA OS has not (yet) had the intended impact. On the other hand, twenty-eight schools consider goals/objectives important, and given the imprecision of these terms, that means thirty-nine out of ninety-three schools with required first-year writing courses are emphasizing more than course content or a description of activities in their public discourse. To give a fuller picture of our findings, we offer some snapshots of schools in each of our categories.

As mentioned earlier, most of the schools without first-year writing programs are what could be considered elite liberal arts colleges. Students at Amherst, for example, are required to take a first-year seminar that introduces students to liberal studies. Amherst has a writing center, as do most other schools in this category, but the notion of a required first-year writing course is absent. In these schools, while writing may occur in the seminars, it may be only one of the capabilities emphasized. Oberlin, also in this group, has a graduation proficiency requirement, which can be met in several ways, including writing certificate or intensive courses, but the instructor's judgment is the basis for fulfilling the requirement. Yet, Oberlin also has a writing center, a writing associate's program, and a separate department of rhetoric and composition. Thus, these schools, while typically articulating value for student writing, do not define academic writing very closely, much less define outcomes.

Our second category proved challenging. Here we find schools with a first-year writing requirement, but hardly any discussion of this requirement. Bowdoin (2a), another selective liberal arts college, requires a first-year seminar with a focus on writing about a particular topic, a practice that is clearly intended to provide an introduction to a discipline. More typical of the 2a category are schools that describe their courses as intended to help "students express themselves effectively in writing," as is the case at Gonzaga University ("2007–09 Undergraduate" 70). Harvard, a school that has been part of an influential movement of theme-based first-year writing courses, has little to say about goals. In the 2b category, we do not find outcomes or goals/objectives, but we do find significant discussion of the requirement, and in this discussion we observe embedded WPA OS skill areas. Several schools in the UC system bear mentioning. Berkeley describes the first of its two-semester sequence as "designed to offer students structured, sustained, and highly articulated practice in the recursive processes entailed in reading, critical analysis, and composing" ("CWR4A"). Further, "students will write a minimum of thirty-two pages of expository prose during this semester" ("CWR4A"). This description tells a reader exactly what will happen and what are the expectations for measurable course work, but it does not specify what students are expected to learn, or do—which is the essence of defining outcomes. Key areas such as critical thinking, reading, and writing processes, and knowledge of conventions may be mentioned as part of a description, but not as intended outcomes. A critical marker for this category is what a course or program offers.

Category 3 includes schools with first-year writing requirements that have *standards* as opposed to *outcomes*, a focus on measuring achievement via exit exams, review of portfolios, or common grading schemes. A surprise for us was Carleton College, recognized for its superb portfolio initiative. Here, faculty members have agreed upon criteria for good writing, which reflect the values of the WPA OS. For example, students' writing at Carleton are expected to demonstrate an appropriate rhetorical strategy, with a thesis developed with coherence, logic, and evidence and a clear, concise, and interesting purpose, and the writing is to be edited to address surface errors. These criteria, however, do not emphasize what the writer should be able to do, but rather how the paper should look. This distinction is important. The program mandates three papers, revision, and instructor feedback, but processes themselves are not considered in the evaluative criteria. It might be possible to argue that Carleton more properly belongs in category 4b, but its focus on achievement assigns Carleton to category 3. One could also argue that Carleton doesn't have a first-year writing requirement, since the writing requirement for graduation, which must be completed between the third and sixth terms, is a combination of a grade in a writing course and review of the portfolio; there is a first-year course, but it is not required. Clemson presents a similar challenge for categorization. ENGL 103 (for first-year students) provides "training in composing correct and effective expository and argumentative essays, including writing documented essays," and a portfolio is required for graduation, though the purpose of that is much broader, focusing on general education ("Undergraduate Catalogs: 2008–09"). We believe that the decision of the Outcomes Statement Collective to value outcomes over standards is important, as it speaks to our field's long commitment to teaching writers how to be writers, not just to help students produce the best written products.

Categories 4 and 5 are distinguished by whether the term "outcomes" is actually employed and of specifying the extent to which these institutions share WPA OS's values. The University of Massachusetts, Amherst, classified as a 4c school, focuses on first-year writing course aims, and this school's website pays particular attention to the philosophy underlying these aims, as well as to a well-articulated mission statement. Duke, which has a thematic approach to first-year writing and relies on post-doctoral fellows, also fits into 4c for emphasizing that students learn how to engage with the work of others, articulate a position, and situate their writing within specific contexts, while practicing research, participating in workshops, revising, and editing. Absent in all of the schools in this category is attention to the fifth (and most recent) area, composing in electronic environments; as a result, category 4c indicates attention to the first four areas in the WPA OS. Finally, we did not find any schools that would fit into category 4a—programs that indicated goals/objectives, but without any WPA OS values embedded within them. In this data, we find reason for optimism. Schools that have first-year writing requirements with courses that have established goals and objectives also have significant shared values with those articulated in the WPA OS. The WPA OS was not devised to "impose unsuitable restriction" (WPA OS)—and so, the fact that several institutions have developed outcomes and courses that have only partial similarity to the WPA OS would, we believe, be seen by the Outcomes Collective as appropriate and positive, rather than as lamentable.

Category 5, with eleven schools, includes first-year writing courses and programs that specifically employ the term "outcomes," and all but one of these schools includes areas from the WPA OS. The one school in category 5a, the U.S. Coast Guard Academy, specifies institutional outcomes to the effect that "Graduates shall be able to write clearly, concisely, persuasively, and grammatically," along with some outcomes related to reading, speaking, and listening ("Catalog of Courses 2008–09"). Category 5 represents quite a diverse group of institutions (Elon, Georgia Tech, Princeton, among others). As one example, we find the University of Denver, a CCCC award winner, which, while not making explicit reference to the WPA OS, provides a very detailed set of outcomes for the sequence of two courses. This is a program that has given a lot of thought to what students are expected to learn and how. The University of Denver Writing Program also lists eleven features common to both courses, and includes a very specific mission statement: The program aims "to create a robust culture of writing on campus, developing strong student skills through multiple writing experiences guided by the best research and pedagogy" ("Mission"). Four of the five WPA areas are emphasized, and the website includes much information about the program, its goals, course outcomes, and overall mission; yet, we note without criticism, there is no reference to the WPA OS.

Eastern Michigan University is another university that provides very detailed information about outcomes, and these have recently been revised, as discussed elsewhere in the collection (Chapter 15), with the aim of focusing on six key areas: investment and engagement, autonomy and authority, sense of perspective, reflection, competence and confidence, and resource use. The previous version more directly paralleled the WPA OS, reflecting close familiarity with that text; this new version indicates how the statement can be adapted to fit local needs and concerns—thus fulfilling the intentions of the WPA OS framers. The revision also details what students' writing should be able to demonstrate in critical reading and analysis, research practices and processes, writing processes and representation, use of evidence, and syntax and mechanics. We wonder, of course, what led the school to move from using the language of the WPA OS to this new version, especially in the use of evidence and syntax and mechanics; all four of these areas of demonstration focus on proficiency, which suggests standards of achievement, as opposed to outcomes. As with the University of Denver, reference to the WPA OS is absent.

As mentioned earlier, only three schools explicitly refer to the WPA OS (Princeton, the University of California, Irvine, and the University of Florida). The only school that has adopted the WPA OS and posted it publicly on its website is the University of California, Irvine. This composition program is housed in an English department, and its courses are primarily taught by graduate teaching assistants and lecturers. We are not making any judgments regarding what it means for only one institution to adopt the language of the WPA OS, or for only eleven schools in our sample of 101 to use the term "outcome." We do suggest, however, that the very concept of outcomes in first-year writing program is not universally accepted.

We believe our research—limited as it is by sample size and choice, temporality, and dependent on individual schools' abilities to disclose their programs via the Web—enables us to make several tentative conclusions. First, the WPA OS has not been broadly adopted or even adapted by our nation's colleges and universities. That said, we also have found that despite laudable efforts to distinguish standards from outcomes—that is, between institutions that define first-year writing as a kind of minimum competency exam and those that define first-year writing as a place where university students are trained in the intellectual and practical processes and habits of academic writers—these distinctions are extremely slippery and also contestable. In the extremes, it's easy. Of course, we do not support focusing on defining courses for their gate-keeping function, as is the case at many of the institutions we studied, and that is exemplified by course descriptions that emphasize the grammatical and mechanical conventions of Standard American English. However, beyond these extremes are many programs that have not adopted the language and philosophy of outcomes, and we suspect these are conscious, thoughtful decisions, as is the decision to choose more closely defined objectives (or goals) over outcomes. Our second conclusion is that outcomes have not entered into the discourse of how writing programs represent and define their mission. We understand the political choice to use the term "outcomes" by the WPA OS collective, but we are concerned that a kind of "outcomes" language bandwagon is gathering more momentum, when the more specific, student-focused language of objectives and goals, perhaps with some standards as well, is often very appropriate, holding faculty, administrators, *and* students accountable.

Third, it concerns us that so many of our top 101 schools fall in categories 1 (no first-writing requirement), 2a (requirement, but no outcomes, goals, or objectives that even share WPA OS's values), or 5a (requirement and outcomes, but no connection to WPA OS's values)—for a total of thirty-eight, more than one-third of our population. In these schools, it appears that little of our discipline's values are shared. Put another way, only fifteen schools (categories 4c, 5c, and 6), about fifteen percent, have courses or programs that are aligned with the WPA OS.

A fourth conclusion is that the fifth area of the WPA OS, "composing in electronic environments," has had virtually no impact at all. We find this unfortunate given all the public pronouncements and NCTE policy statements regarding the importance of taking into account Web 2.0; these results suggest that even Web 1.0 has not had much effect on actual practice. More optimistically, it may be that technology should be a shared responsibility across the curriculum, and not one specifically connected to first-year writing.

Finally, more optimistically, despite these findings, we nevertheless note that the values of writing and writing pedagogy—presumably propagated via the publication of the WPA OS as well as more broadly through the professionalization and proliferation of rhetoric and composition—have been adopted much more so than Burhans, Fulkerson, Larson, or Williams feared. As we searched the Web pages of schools with which we were quite unfamiliar as well as those of our nation's elite schools, we found evidence of the deep reach of such core ideas as drafting, peer and instructor feedback, and writing as process not product.

Notes

1. For more information on the *U.S. News and World Report* selection process, see Morse. The results are posted online first, followed by a cover story in the print edition. For the 2009 rankings, see also the September 1, 2008 print edition of *U.S. News and World Report*, as the story is no longer accessible on the Internet.

2. See Townsend's 1999 Survey for the Coalition for the Academic Workforce for specific data on percentage of tenure line faculty teaching first-year writing.

Works Cited

"About VSA." *Voluntary System of Accountability, Undergraduate Education Reports.* Association of Public and Land-Grant Universities and American Association of State College and Universities, n.d. Web. 21 July 2010.

"America's Best Colleges 2009." *U.S. News & World Report.* 20 August 2008. Web. 15 July 2009. Print. 1 Sept. 2008.

Bartholomae, David. "Composition, 1900–2000." *PMLA* 115.7 (2000): 1950–54. Print.

Burhans, Clinton S., Jr. "The Teaching of Writing and the Knowledge Gap." *College English* 45.7 (1983): 639–56. Print.

The Carnegie Foundation for the Advancement of Teaching. *The Carnegie Classification of Institutions of Higher Education,* 2000 edition. 2001. Web. 25 July 2009.

"Catalog of Courses 2008–2009." *United States Coast Guard Academy.* USCGA, 2009. Web 10 Aug. 2009.

"CWR4A—Reading and Composition." *College Writing Programs.* UC Berkeley, 2009. Web. 10 Aug. 2009.

Connors, Robert. *Composition-Rhetoric:Backgrounds, Theory, and Pedagogy.* Pittsburgh, PA: U of Pittsburgh P, 1997. Print.

Council of Writing Program Administrators. "The WPA Outcomes Statement for First-Year Composition." Council of Writing Program Administrators, July 2008. Web. 7 Jan. 2011.

Council of Writing Program Administrators [with an introduction by Kathleen Blake Yancey]. "The WPA Outcomes Statement for First-Year Composition." *College English* 63.3 (2001): 321–25. Print.

Ericsson, Patricia Freitag. "Celebrating Through Interrogation: Considering the Outcomes Statement Through Theoretical Lenses." Harrington, et al. 104–17. Print.

Fulkerson, Richard. "Composition at the Turn of the Twenty-First Century." *College Composition and Communication* 56.4 (2005): 654–87. Print.

Gere, Anne Ruggles. *Initial Report on Survey of CCCC Members.* NCTE Report. January 12, 2009. Urbana, IL: NCTE, 2009. Web. 4 Aug. 2010.

Harrington, Susanmarie, Keith Rhodes, Rita Malenczyk, and Ruth Overman Fischer, eds. *The Outcomes Book: Debate and Consensus after the WPA Outcomes Statement.* Logan, UT: Utah State UP, 2005. Print.

Haswell, Richard, H. "NCTE/CCCC's Recent War on Scholarship." *Written Communication* 22.2 (2005): 198–223. Print.

"Home." *Voluntary System of Accountability, Undergraduate Education Reports.* Association of Public and Land-Grant Universities and American Association of State College and Universities, n.d. Web. 21 July 2010.

"Impact of College Rankings on Institutional Decision Making: Four Country Case Studies. Institute for Higher Education Policy." Institute for Higher Education Policy, May 2009. Web. 21 May 2009.

Isaacs, Emily. "Teaching General Education Writing: Is There a Place for Literature?" *Pedagogy* 9.1 (2009): 97–120. Print.

Kitzhaber, Albert R. *Themes, Theories and Therapy: The Teaching of Writing in College*. New York: McGraw Hill, 1963. Print.

Knight, Melinda. "Writing and Other Communication Standards in Undergraduate Business Education: A Study of Current Program Requirements, Trends, and Practices." *Business Communication Quarterly* 62.1 (1999): 10–28. Print.

Larson, Richard L. *Curricula in College Writing Programs: Much Diversity, Little Assessment*. Ford Foundation Report. New York: Ford Foundation, 1994. Print.

Lunsford, Andrea A., and Karen J. Lunsford. "Mistakes Are A Fact of Life: A National Comparative Study." *College Composition and Communication* 59.4 (2008): 781–806. Print.

"Mission." *University Writing Program*. University of Denver, 2006. Web. 10 Aug. 2009.

Morse, Robert J. "How We Calculate the Rankings." *U.S. News and World Report*. 1 Sept 2008: 74.Web. 2 Aug. 2010.

Rhodes, Keith, Irvin Peckham, Linda S. Bergmann, and William Condon. "The Outcomes Project: The Insiders' History." Harrington, et al. 8–17. Print.

Thaiss, Chris. "International WAC/WID Mapping Project." *MappingProjectUCDavis.edu*. University of California, Davis, 14 August 2009. Web. 20 July 2010.

Townsend, Robert P. "Who Is Teaching In U.S. College Classrooms? A CAW Study of Undergraduate Faculty." *Coalition on the Academic Workforce*, 1999. Web. 2 Aug. 2010.

"Undergraduate Catalogs: 2008–2009." *Clemson University Office of the Registrar*. Clemson University, 2009. Web. 10 Aug. 2009.

White, Edward M. "The Origins of the Outcomes Statement." Harrington, et al. 3–7. Print.

White, Edward M., and Linda Polin. *Research in Effective Teaching of Writing, Volumes 1 and 2, Final Project Report*. ERIC Document Reproduction Service. 1986. ED275007. *ERIC EBSCO*. Web. 6 June 2010.

Williams, James D. "Counterstatement: Autobiography in Composition Scholarship." *College English* 68.2 (2005): 209–25. Print.

Wiley, Mark. "Outcomes Are Not Mandates for Standardization." Harrington, et al. 24–31. Print.

Yancey, Kathleen Blake. "Standards, Outcomes, and All that Jazz." Harrington, et al.18–23. Print.

"2007–09 Undergraduate." *Gonzaga's Catalogues*. Gonzaga University, 2009. Web. 10 Aug. 2009.

Appendix: WPA Outcomes Statement for First-Year Composition

Adopted by the Council of Writing Program Administrators (WPA), April 2000; amended July 2008.

For further information about the development of the Outcomes Statement, please see http://comppile.org/archives/WPAoutcomes/continue.html

For further information about the Council of Writing Program Administrators, please see http://www.wpacouncil.org

Introduction

This statement describes the common knowledge, skills, and attitudes sought by first-year composition programs in American postsecondary education. To some extent, we seek to regularize what can be expected to be taught in first-year composition; to this end the document is not merely a compilation or summary of what currently takes place. Rather, the following statement articulates what composition teachers nationwide have learned from practice, research, and theory. This document intentionally defines only "outcomes," or types of results, and not "standards," or precise levels of achievement. The setting of standards should be left to specific institutions or specific groups of institutions.

Learning to write is a complex process, both individual and social, that takes place over time with continued practice and informed guidance. Therefore, it is important that teachers, administrators, and a concerned public do not imagine that these outcomes can be taught in reduced or simple ways. Helping students demonstrate these outcomes requires expert understanding of how students actually learn to write. For this reason we expect the primary audience for this document to be well-prepared college writing teachers and college writing program administrators. In some places, we have chosen to write in their professional language. Among such readers, terms such as "rhetorical" and "genre" convey a rich meaning that is not easily simplified. While we have also aimed at writing a document that the general public can understand, in limited cases we have aimed first at communicating effectively with expert writing teachers and writing program administrators.

These statements describe only what we expect to find at the end of first-year composition, at most schools a required general education course or sequence of courses. As writers move beyond first-year composition, their writing abilities do not merely improve. Rather, students' abilities not only diversify along disciplinary and professional lines but also move into whole new levels where expected outcomes expand, multiply, and diverge. For this reason, each statement of outcomes for first-year composition is followed by suggestions for further work that builds on these outcomes.

Rhetorical Knowledge

By the end of first year composition, students should

- Focus on a purpose
- Respond to the needs of different audiences
- Respond appropriately to different kinds of rhetorical situations
- Use conventions of format and structure appropriate to the rhetorical situation
- Adopt appropriate voice, tone, and level of formality
- Understand how genres shape reading and writing
- Write in several genres

Faculty in all programs and departments can build on this preparation by helping students learn

- The main features of writing in their fields
- The main uses of writing in their fields

- The expectations of readers in their fields

CRITICAL THINKING, READING, AND WRITING

By the end of first year composition, students should

- Use writing and reading for inquiry, learning, thinking, and communicating
- Understand a writing assignment as a series of tasks, including finding, evaluating, analyzing, and synthesizing appropriate primary and secondary sources
- Integrate their own ideas with those of others
- Understand the relationships among language, knowledge, and power

Faculty in all programs and departments can build on this preparation by helping students learn

- The uses of writing as a critical thinking method
- The interactions among critical thinking, critical reading, and writing
- The relationships among language, knowledge, and power in their fields

PROCESSES

By the end of first year composition, students should

- Be aware that it usually takes multiple drafts to create and complete a successful text
- Develop flexible strategies for generating, revising, editing, and proof-reading
- Understand writing as an open process that permits writers to use later invention and re-thinking to revise their work
- Understand the collaborative and social aspects of writing processes
- Learn to critique their own and others' works
- Learn to balance the advantages of relying on others with the responsibility of doing their part

- Use a variety of technologies to address a range of audiences

Faculty in all programs and departments can build on this preparation by helping students learn

- To build final results in stages
- To review work-in-progress in collaborative peer groups for purposes other than editing
- To save extensive editing for later parts of the writing process
- To apply the technologies commonly used to research and communicate within their fields

Knowledge of Conventions

By the end of first year composition, students should

- Learn common formats for different kinds of texts
- Develop knowledge of genre conventions ranging from structure and paragraphing to tone and mechanics
- Practice appropriate means of documenting their work
- Control such surface features as syntax, grammar, punctuation, and spelling

Faculty in all programs and departments can build on this preparation by helping students learn

- The conventions of usage, specialized vocabulary, format, and documentation in their fields
- Strategies through which better control of conventions can be achieved

Composing in Electronic Environments

As has become clear over the last twenty years, writing in the 21st-century involves the use of digital technologies for several purposes, from drafting to peer reviewing to editing. Therefore, although the *kinds* of composing processes and texts expected from students vary across programs and institutions, there are nonetheless common expectations.

By the end of first-year composition, students should:

- Use electronic environments for drafting, reviewing, revising, editing, and sharing texts
- Locate, evaluate, organize, and use research material collected from electronic sources, including scholarly library databases; other official databases (e.g., federal government databases); and informal electronic networks and internet sources
- Understand and exploit the differences in the rhetorical strategies and in the affordances available for both print and electronic composing processes and texts

Faculty in all programs and departments can build on this preparation by helping students learn

- How to engage in the electronic research and composing processes common in their fields
- • How to disseminate texts in both print and electronic forms in their fields

Index

AAC&U (Association of American Colleges and Universities), 89, 95–98, 102
AAC&U's VALUE Rubric, 95
ABET (Accrediting Board for Engineering and Technology, 99
academic discourse, 10, 25, 26, 60–61, 248, 250; universal academic discourse (UAD) 4–6
academic freedom, 34, 291
accountability, x, 89, 289, 293
active learning, 37
Adams, Peter, 78
adjunct, xiii, 36, 54, 118, 143, 161–162, 165, 167–169, 185, 195, 199, 203–205, 210, 215
Adler-Kassner, Linda, 19, 26, 30, 163–164, 209, 212, 214–215, 224, 226–229, 254–255
administration, 24, 56, 108, 110, 121–122, 139, 147–149, 157, 162–163, 185, 192–193, 221, 286
Advanced Placement, 4, 14, 295
African American Vernacular English, 279
Amherst College, 295–296, 298
Anderson, Paul, xiv, 88–89, 94, 99
Anson, Chris M., xiv, 88, 91–92, 94, 99, 196
AQIP (Academic Quality Improvement Program), 143
Aragon, Steven, 250–251

Aristotle, 74, 203, 262
Arizona State University, 26, 109, 114, 257, 258
assessment, xvi, 13, 34, 47, 55, 56, 88, 89, 91, 94, 102, 143, 144, 158, 159, 160, 179, 181, 182–188, 195, 197, 214, 217, 218, 220, 223, 224, 226, 268, 293; outcomes, 91, 211, 214, 215, 220, 221, 223, 224; Phase 2, 223, 257, 260; portfolio, xiv, 24, 27, 183, 184, 187, 215, 219, 223; writing, 18, 160, 182, 183, 198, 210
assessment, self, 63, 68–69
assessment, writing program, 156
Association of American Colleges and Universities (AAC&U), 89
Association of College and Research Libraries, 219, 259
audience, 20, 40, 54, 64, 65, 66, 67, 94, 95, 96, 97, 101, 112, 114, 115, 116, 120–121, 237, 238, 244, 246, 252, 258, 262, 263, 264, 265, 266, 268, 274, 277, 282; awareness of, 53, 55, 265, 278–279; needs of, 261, 262, 263
Australia, 165–166, 168–169, 171–172, 174–176, 178
autonomy, 111, 119, 170, 192, 299

311

312 Index

Banks, Adam, 275
Bartholomae, David, 10, 21, 28, 61, 290
basic writing, xiii, 18–29, 30, 155
basic writing curriculum, 18, 25
Bawarshi, Anis, 3, 11, 98, 211, 214
Bawarshi, Anis, and Mary Jo Reiff: *Genre; An Introduction To History, Theory, Research, And Pedagogy*, 98
Bazerman, Charles, 242–245
Beaufort, Anne, 8, 98; *College Writing and Beyond*, 8, 98
Benjamin, Walter, 85
Bergman, Linda, x, 201, 205, 291
Berlin, Isaiah, 76
Berlin, James A, 46, 49, 50, 76, 166, 167; *Rhetoric and Reality: Writing Instruction in American Colleges, 1900–1985*, 49; *Rhetorics, Poetics, and Cultures; Reconfiguring College English Studies*, 46
Berthoff, Ann, 244
best practices, xiii, 18, 21, 24, 47, 49, 92, 103, 126, 138, 144, 158, 182, 189, 196, 197, 212, 285, 290
Bishop, Wendy, 139
Bizzell, Patricia, 20, 52, 244–245, 247–249
Blakesley, David, 35, 86
Boland, Mary, 244–245, 254
Bolter, Jay David, 179
Bowden, Darsie, xv, 154, 243
Bowdoin College, 296
Boyer Report, 200
Brodkey, Linda, 245
Brookfield, Stephen, 175
Bruffee, Kenneth, 52
Bullard, Lisa, 92
Burhans, Clinton, 137–138, 290, 301
Burke, Kenneth, 85

Cahill, Lisa, 61
Callaway, Micheal, xvi, 91, 271
Carino, Peter, 149
Carleton College, 297
Carter, Michael, 93, 99
CCCC Writing Program Certificate of Excellence, 288
Celebration of Student Writing (CSW), 160, 213
Charmaz, Kathleen, 262
Chase, Geoffrey, 34
Chiseri-Strater, Elizabeth, 50, 55
choice: rhetorical, 11, 63, 65, 67, 252, 265, 280
Clemson University, 298
cognitivism, 20
collaboration, xiii, 36, 40, 52, 195, 201, 214, 220, 223, 240, 249, 265
Collaborative Assessment Conference, 216
College Board, 14
College English, xi, 34, 41, 285
communication across the curriculum (CAC), 99, 101
Composing Process Outcomes (CPOs), 222
composition training, 36
Condon, William:, x, 184, 291
Conference on College Composition and Communication (CCCC), 88, 104
Connors, Robert, 6, 290
conventions, 21, 25, 26, 82, 84, 97, 100, 116, 121, 122, 128, 130, 131, 132, 134, 135, 159, 210, 213, 248, 250, 251, 252, 269, 274,
conventions, knowledge of, 25, 27, 29, 37, 65, 66, 128, 133, 198, 210, 252, 257, 258, 265, 266, 269, 295, 297, 308
conventions, research, 129, 130

Index 313

conventions, writing, 20, 21, 27, 169, 281
Cooper, Marilyn, 146
Council of Writing Program Administrators, xi, 19, 88, 120, 140, 160, 167, 175, 176, 223, 230, 257, 271, 280, 293, 305

creative writing, 36, 38, 47, 199
critical thinking, 25, 27, 29, 37, 51, 64, 65, 67, 68, 81, 131, 132, 177, 198, 210, 254, 257, 258, 265, 269, 292, 295, 297, 307
Crowley, Sharon, 242, 246, 248
Cushman, Ellen, 174

Dannels, Deanna P., 92, 94, 99
Davis, Robert, 62
Delpit, Lisa, 249
development, program, 32, 33, 37, 39, 40, 41, 42, 125, 162, 176
Dew, Debra Frank, xiii, 3, 7, 66, 100
digital environments, 272, 278
digital media, 272, 278
digital mediums, 272, 278
directed self placement (DSP), 35, 83, 86
disciplinarity, xv, 206, 243, 246
disciplinary expertise, 40, 48, 119, 121, 162, 243
Donahue, Christiane, 250, 252
Downs, Douglas, 3–6, 11
Duke University, 43, 298

Eagleton, Terry, 85
education, general, 22, 24, 25, 26, 48, 94, 143, 144, 199, 209, 298
Educational Testing Service (ETS), 14
Elbow, Peter, 49, 127, 183, 230
electronic environments, 29, 172, 272, 274–277, 295, 298, 301, 308

electronic portfolio (eportfolio), 89, 159, 181, 183–187, 223, 257, 259
Eliot, T. S., 76
Elliot, Norbert, 268
Elliott, Clark, 144
Elon University, 299
emerging technologies, 91, 272, 274
EMU, Eastern Michigan University, 160, 209, 213–215, 218–220, 223, 226, 299
English as a Second Language (ESL), 148, 171, 174, 249
epistemology, 6, 27, 49, 72, 73, 74, 75, 76, 77, 79, 80, 81, 85
Ericsson, Patricia Freitag, xii, 33, 230, 272, 293
error, 20, 26, 28, 72, 76, 77, 187, 218, 297
ethos, xiv, 23, 32, 38, 39, 40, 45, 55, 127, 191, 196, 200, 202, 227
Everett, Justin, xv, 129, 134, 191

Fensterwald, John, 27
field, composition/rhetoric, 290
FIPSE (Fund for the Improvement of Postsecondary Education), 104
first-year composition (FYC), xiii, 5, 6, 7, 8, 10, 11, 13, 14, 18, 19, 25, 27, 29, 35, 59, 91, 95, 100, 107, 115, 117, 120, 128, 141, 184, 209, 239, 245, 248, 257, 271, 291; assignments, 25, 58, 60; classrooms, 60, 61, 238, 239; courses, 23, 25, 27, 62, 91, 115, 136, 213, 233, 234, 238, 242, 248; program, 24, 41, 89, 95, 107, 122, 145, 146, 183, 243; sequence, 108, 109, 110, 115, 119, 236

314 Index

first-year writing (FYW), 11, 33, 48, 51, 52, 54, 56, 155, 157, 158, 159, 172, 193, 195, 199, 200, 203, 204, 213, 251, 271, 285, 286, 287, 288, 289, 290, 298, 300, 301; course, xi, 33, 47, 48, 56, 100, 129, 238, 239, 240, 290, 295–298; curriculum, 3, 21, 22, 23, 34, 37, 56, 176, 231, 232, 239, 254; instruction, 25, 231, 251, 290; instructors, 216, 271; requirements, 22, 231, 289, 294–298; sequence, 205, 239

first-year writing program, 45, 46, 47, 50, 51, 53, 54, 149, 155, 158, 166, 169, 209, 210, 212, 215, 225, 226, 227, 236, 288, 289, 293, 294, 295, 296, 300; funding, 45, 56, 88, 94, 104, 143, 172, 174, 231; space, 4, 5, 7, 15, 22, 26, 28, 45, 50, 60, 61, 68, 69, 120, 148, 182, 187, 203, 221, 276, 277; staffing, 22, 45, 143, 169

Flash, Pamela, 92, 94

Fleming, David, 10, 11, 244, 246, 247

Florida International University, 32

Flower, Linda, 13

Ford Foundation, 286, 292

formality, level of, 64, 81, 95, 112, 122, 237, 251

format, 62, 64, 66, 67, 95, 97, 98, 114, 116, 117, 121, 122, 128, 130, 144, 237, 251, 252, 261

Fulkerson, Richard, 252, 286, 287, 291, 292, 293, 301

Gaffney, Amy L. Housley, 92, 94

genre, 3, 4, 8, 11, 14, 27, 92, 102, 107, 133, 173, 188, 209, 213, 238,

genre theory, 8, 9, 11, 15, 253

Georgia Tech University, 299

Gere, Anne Ruggles, 286

Glau, Gregory R., 61

Goggin, Maureen Daly, 245, 246, 253

Gonzaga University, 297

Gorman, Raymond P., 89

Gottschalk, Katherine, 142

grammar, 27, 49, 96, 100, 116, 162, 167, 232, 249, 250, 252

Greene, Nicole Pepinster, 20

Grusin, Richard, 179

Gunner, Jeanne, 3, 5, 37, 38, 40

Hallidayan Systemic Functional Linguistics, 169

Hamilton, Sharon, 179

Hamp-Lyons, Liz, 184

Hardin, Joseph Marshall, 244, 246

Harrington, Susanmarie, xi, 230, 285

Harris, Joseph, 224

Harris, Muriel, 144

Harvard University, 4, 13, 97, 167, 248, 297

Haswell, Richard, 23, 287

heuristic, xiii, 4, 6, 8, 14, 58, 69, 73, 101, 129, 130, 225

Holiday, Judy, xvi, 5–7, 15, 242, 247, 291

Horner, Bruce, 20, 29

Howard, Rebecca Moore, 180, 192, 219

Hult, Christine, 136

Huot, Brian, 13, 185, 210, 214, 215, 224

idealism: Platonic, 71, 76, 77, 79

information literacy, 91, 125, 170, 177, 218, 219, 220, 257, 259

Ingalls, Rebecca, xiv, 45, 166, 180, 182, 184, 193

Institute for Higher Education Policy, The, 287
international students, 136, 161, 231, 234, 236
invention, 11, 133, 211, 214, 246, 273, 277, 281
Isaacs, Emily, xvi, 34, 43, 137, 234, 285, 290

Jacobsen, Craig, xiv, 107, 271
Johns, Ann, 250, 252
Johnson, Robert R., 243

Kaufer, David, 8, 10
Kendrick, Michelle, 278
Kitzhaber, Albert R., 286, 287
Klausman, Jeffrey, 22
Knight, Melinda, xvi, 34, 43, 137, 234, 285, 289
knowledge, rhetorical, xvi, 8, 9, 11, 14, 25, 29, 37, 59, 65, 67, 68, 97, 128, 129, 130, 174, 186, 198, 210, 233, 251, 257, 258, 262, 263, 265–269, 273, 274, 278, 295
Kose, Brad, 250, 251

language choice, 53, 64
Larson, Richard, 138, 286, 287, 290, 292, 293, 301
liberal arts, 10, 192
linguistics, 38, 173, 279
literacy, 22, 146, 147, 149, 188, 192, 243, 259, 272, 273
literary study, 193
literate practices, 272, 273, 278, 280
literature, 27, 34, 35, 36, 37, 38, 75, 83, 84, 192, 193, 194, 195, 196, 197, 198, 199, 201
Liu, Barb Little, 12, 253
Lu, Min-Zhan, 20, 21, 28, 29
Lumina Foundation, 287
Lunsford, Andrea, 160, 168, 277, 286

Maid, Barry, xvi, 25, 58, 197, 206, 220, 233, 257, 258, 260, 264
Malenczyk, Rita, 147, 200, 201, 270
Manovich, Lev, 274
Matsuda, Paul Kei, xv, 42, 230, 233, 234, 235, 247, 252
McAlexander, Patricia, 20
McLeod, Susan, 162, 168
mechanics, 82, 96, 97, 112, 116, 169, 211, 213, 233, 252, 299
Melzer, Daniel, 62
metacognitive, metacognition, 13, 96, 98, 246, 251, 253
Millar, Laura, 144
Miller-Cochran, Susan, 107, 271
Mirtz, Ruth, 144, 180
Moffett, James, 60, 61
Moneyhun, Clyde A., 39, 40
monolingual, 234, 235, 238, 252
Morse, Tracy Ann, xiv, 45, 166, 180, 182, 184, 193, 301
Mortensen, Peter, 162, 164
Murray, Donald, 49, 211

National Council of Teachers of English (NCTE), 67, 90, 160, 163, 206, 223, 301
National Day on Writing, 160
National Institute of Education, 286
National Research Council, 98; *How People Learn*, 98
National Science Foundation, 93, 99
National Writing Project, 216, 223
non-program programs, 33, 39, 50, 119, 137, 138, 139, 141, 142, 180–181
noticing, 216, 217, 219, 220, 221

Oberlin College, 295, 296
objectives, ix, x, 47, 89, 141, 150, 188, 196, 294–298, 300, 301

Olson, Gary A., 244, 246
Olson, Wendy, xiii, 18
Ong, Walter, 77
online writing environments, 281
online writing practices, 272, 282
outcomes, ix, x, xiii, xiv, xvi, 11, 19, 21, 24, 37, 81, 88–104, 128, 143, 196, 199, 200, 204, 205, 225, 248, 254, 257–269, 285–301; assessment, 91, 211, 214, 215, 220, 221, 223, 224; big rhetoric, 244, 251, 253; course, 68, 69, 299; general education, 101, 144, 187; learning, xiv, 34, 35, 36, 58, 59, 62, 64, 68, 88, 91, 92, 93, 99, 109, 136, 156–160, 182, 209–211, 220–223, 225, 226, 285, 291; learning process outcomes (LPOs), 222–224; little rhetoric, 254; program, 59, 257–260, 264, 268, 269, 296; writing, 89, 92, 93, 94, 95, 99, 289

Outcomes Book, The: Debate and Consensus after the WPA Outcomes Statement, xi, xii, 7, 12, 18, 230, 253, 293

Outcomes Collective, ix, xi, xii, 291, 298,
Outcomes Project, 124

Paraskevas, Cornelia, 3
Peckham, Irvin, x, 291
pedagogy, xvi, 9, 27, 29, 54, 84, 204, 212, 218, 253, 266, 290, 291; basic writing, 20, 21, 27, 28; composition, xiv, 28, 50, 218; writing, 13, 20, 79, 80, 82, 86, 168, 237, 301
peer review, 13, 63, 65, 66, 68, 82, 169, 276
persuasion, 72, 75, 76, 77, 79, 81, 82, 168, 225, 248, 252, 282

Pettipiece, Deirdre, xv, 129, 134, 191
Pew Research Center, 280
Phelps, Louise Wetherbee, 179, 180
placement, 23, 38, 155, 180, 209, 234, 235, 240; advanced, 295; self-placement, 35, 83, 86, 155, 180, 209
Plato, 79, 262
Polin, Linda, 286, 287
Porter, James, 274
portfolios, xvi, 98, 158, 159, 173, 186, 187, 217, 219, 223, 258, 259–261, 262, 263, 264, 265, 266, 268
Powell, Malea, 249
praxis, 83, 247, 254
Princeton University, 204, 299, 300
process theory, 4, 9, 12, 13, 125

Qualley, Donna, 50
Quinn, Robert, 125, 157

Ramus, Peter, 75, 77, 86
reform, curricular, 35, 125, 193, 194, 196
Reiff, Mary Jo, 98
remediation, 27, 179, 188, 198, 274
research: primary, xv, 62, 193
research, secondary, 62, 63, 65, 66
retention, 144, 147, 148, 161, 288
revision, curriculum, xiv, 53, 108, 114, 117, 121, 122
rhetoric, xv, 10, 11, 14, 38, 74–79, 159, 166, 168, 169, 171, 200, 202, 242, 245–249, 262, 292, 296, 301; deliberative, 73, 74, 75, 76, 78, 79, 80, 81, 82, 86; epideictic, 74, 84; forensic, 72, 73, 74, 76, 78, 80, 84; transactional, 166

rhetoric, and composition, xv, 32, 40, 47, 72, 108, 111, 114, 128, 136, 154, 169, 193, 195, 200, 201, 203, 220, 230, 243, 245, 249, 262, 275, 285
rhetorical awareness, 146, 210, 213, 233, 251, 274, 282
rhetorical decisions, 68, 169, 276, 279, 282
rhetorical practice, 10, 11, 131, 135
rhetorical theory, 7, 9, 11, 127, 166, 172, 210, 247
Rhodes, Keith, x, xvi, 230, 291
Rhodes, Terrel L., 96
Rice, Jeff, 161, 277
Rodrigo, Shelley, xiv, 67, 107, 271
Roen, Duane, 61
Rose, Mike, 20, 164, 244, 246, 248
Rose, Shirley, 32, 144, 180, 182
Russell, David, 3, 5, 10
Rust, Jon, 99

Saltz, Laura, 60
Sargent, Elizabeth, 3
Schön, Donald, 135
second language (L2), 230–240
second, language writers, xv, 230–240
Selfe, Cynthia L., 246, 272, 282
Selfe, Richard, 246, 282
Shadle, Mark, 62
Shaughnessy, Mina, 19, 20, 28, 244, 248, 249
situation: rhetorical, 7, 49, 64, 95, 108, 115, 121, 130, 132, 142, 237, 238, 239, 249, 262, 265, 277, 281
Skinnell, Ryan, xv, 42, 230, 247, 252
Smitherman, Geneva, 246, 249
Soles, Derek, 41, 197
Soliday, Mary, 28
Sommers, Nancy, 13, 14, 60, 97

Stancliff, Michael, 253
standardization, 34, 226, 291
standards, ix, x, xiv, 19, 50, 53, 73, 85, 94, 122, 130, 140, 145, 199, 226, 236, 243, 292–295, 297, 299, 300; national, 53, 121
Steiner, George, 71, 72, 80
Sternglass, Marilyn, 18, 231, 249
Stretch Program, 26
syntax, 96, 211, 232, 249, 250, 252, 299

technology plank, xi, xvi, 25, 275
technology, writing, 272, 273, 276, 278, 282
Thaiss, Chris, 286
The Carnegie Foundation for the Advancement of Teaching, 287
Therborn, Goran, 46
Thomas, Susan, xv, 73, 129, 165, 288
tone, 64, 66, 81, 82, 95, 96, 97, 116, 122, 130, 233, 237, 251, 252
Townsend, Martha, xiv, 88
Townsend, Robert P., 301
Turkle, Sherry, 279
Turpin, Elizabeth R., 262

U.S. News and World Report, 287, 301
United States Coast Guard Academy, 299
universal academic discourse (UAD), 4, 5, 6, 7
University of California Berkeley, 297
University of Dayton, 124, 209
University of Denver, 299
University of Florida, 300
University of South Florida St. Petersburg, 181

University of Sydney, 165, 166, 172, 174
University of Washington, *Inside the Undergraduate Experience*, 98

voice, 64, 66, 95, 103, 116, 122, 130, 237, 251, 252
Voluntary System of Accountability (VSA), 89, 289

Wardle, Elizabeth, 3, 4, 5, 6, 11
White, Edward M., ix, x, xi, 59, 64, 69, 144, 179, 183, 189, 194, 197, 223, 230, 260, 268, 269, 286, 287; *Assigning, Responding, Evaluating: A Writing Teacher's Guide*, 59, 64
Whithaus, Carl, 181, 185, 187, 188
WID (writing-in-the disciplines), 56, 88, 89, 91, 101, 124, 126, 127, 128, 129, 132, 134, 135, 209, 286, 288
Wiley, Mark, 19, 43, 199, 226, 236, 291
Wilhoit, Stephen, xiv, 58, 68, 124, 157, 170, 209
Williams, James, 291, 293, 301
Wilson, David McKay, 29
Wingate, Molly, 139
Woods, Claire, 171
writing: expository, 73, 83, 292; family history, 62, 63

writing about writing (WAW), xiii, 3, 4, 5, 6, 7, 8, 9, 10, 14, 15
writing across the curriculum (WAC), xiii, xiv, xv, 56, 88, 89, 91, 93, 96, 97, 98, 100, 101, 104, 135, 166, 172, 173, 195, 226, 227, 286
writing assessment, 18, 160, 182, 183, 210
writing centers, 146, 149, 195
writing process, 8, 12, 13, 14, 20, 25, 26, 27, 29, 82, 97, 103, 132, 133, 188, 198, 204, 221, 258, 276, 295, 297, 299; movement, 211; theory, 9, 12, 13, 125
writing program administration, xii, 18, 32, 37, 56, 165, 221, 223, 226
Writing Program Administrator: junior WPAs, 49, 51
Writing Studies, 4, 36, 98, 102, 167, 168

Yancey, Kathleen Blake, x, xiv, 4, 6, 7, 8, 9, 11, 13, 15, 34, 41, 51, 88, 98, 183, 186, 188, 189, 225, 230, 236, 271, 293
Young, Art, 227
Young, Richard, 8, 10

Zebroski, James, 13
Zemliansky, Pavel, 62

Contributors

Linda Adler-Kassner is Professor and Director of the Writing Program at University of California, Santa Barbara. She is author, co-author, or co-editor of seven books and many articles and book chapters. Her book *The Activist WPA: Changing Stories about Writers and Writing* was awarded the Council of Writing Program Administrators Best Book Award in 2010. Her work has appeared in *College Composition and Communication, College English, WPA: Writing Program Administration, Composition Studies*, and other publications.

Paul Anderson is the Roger and Joyce L. Howe Director of the Howe Center for Writing Excellence at Miami University, Ohio. He is a Fellow of the Society for Technical Communication, Association of Teachers of Technical Writing, and Miami's Institute of Environmental Sciences. His publications have won awards from the National Council of Teachers of English and the Society for Technical Communication. Current interests include ethics, assessment, and cloud and intercultural collaboration.

Chris M. Anson is University Distinguished Professor and Director of the Campus Writing and Speaking Program at North Carolina State University. A scholar of writing, language, and literacy, he has published fifteen books and over one hundred articles and book chapters, and has spoken or run faculty-development workshops across the U.S. and in twenty-five other countries. He is currently Associate Chair of the Conference on College Composition and Communication.

Nicholas N. Behm is an Assistant Professor of English at Elmhurst College in Illinois, where he teaches courses in composition and rhetoric and studies composition pedagogy and theory, whiteness studies, and critical race theory. His research examines how first-year composition textbooks may reinforce white privilege and maintain white hegemony.

Karen Bishop Morris currently serves as the Director of First-Year Writing and Director of the Writing Center at Purdue University, Calumet. Previously, she directed the writing program at the University of Southern Indiana. Her current teaching includes graduate seminars in writing program administration, writing assessment, and the theory and practice of teaching composition. Her scholarly interests include civic engagement, integrating social media into the freshman year, and public rhetoric and practice around disease disparities. Her work has appeared in *English Education*, *WPA: Writing Program Administration*, and Rose and Weiser's *The Writing Program Administrator as Theorist*.

Darsie Bowden is a Professor in the Department of Writing, Rhetoric, and Discourse at DePaul University, where she is director of first-year writing and teaches courses at both undergraduate and graduate levels. She has published books on voice (*The Mythology of Voice*) and screenwriting (*Writing for Film*). and her essays have appeared in a number of journals, including *College Composition and Communication*, *Composition Studies*, *WPA: Writing Program Administration*, and *Writing on the Edge*.

Lizbeth A. Bryant is an Associate Professor of English at Purdue University, Calumet. The former director of the writing program at Purdue Calumet and of the Mid-Ohio Writing Project at Ohio State Mansfield, Bryant has published books on grading, *Grading in the Post-Process Classroom*, and on voice, *Voice as Process*. Her most recent work is a collection of pieces on writing for students, *Essays on Writing*.

Micheal Callaway is Residential Faculty at Mesa Community College in Mesa, Arizona, where he focuses on teaching and developing curriculum for developmental writing courses. He is the co-author of *Argument in Composition* with John Ramage, Jennifer Clary-Lemon, and Zachary Waggoner (Parlor Press, 2009).

Barbara J. D'Angelo is Assistant Clinical Professor of Technical Communication at Arizona State University on the Polytechnic Campus. She teaches courses in technical communication, business communication, and intellectual property. She has presented and published articles on writing assessment, business communication, and information literacy.

Debra Frank Dew is Associate Professor of English at the University of Colorado at Colorado Springs, where she directs the UCCS Rhetoric and Writing Program. Her work on WPA advocacy appeared in *CCC* (2009). With Alice Horning, she co-edited *Untenured Faculty as WPAs: Institutional Politics and Practices* (2007). She is currently assessing the impact of writing conferences on writing performance and students' affective response to FYC.

J.S. Dunn, Jr. is an Assistant Professor of English at Eastern Michigan University, where he serves as Director of the First-Year Writing Program and teaches courses in the graduate and undergraduate programs in Written Communication. His scholarship focuses on writing assessment, writing program administration, and the discourse of public policy debates around higher education reform.

Heidi Estrem is the Director of the First-Year Writing Program and an Associate Professor of English at Boise State University. She teaches a range of writing courses, from first-year writing to the graduate pedagogy seminar for new teaching assistants. Her ongoing research interests in writing assessment and writing instructor development are reflected in recent publications, which include the co-authored book *Organic Writing Assessment: Dynamic Criteria Mapping in Action* (Utah State UP), as well as articles in *WPA: Writing Program Administration*, *Composition Studies*, and edited collections.

Justin Everett is an Assistant Professor of Rhetoric and Composition at the University of the Sciences, where he serves as Interim Director of Writing Programs and Chair of Health Communication faculty. He is co-author of *Dynamic Argument: A Rhetoric and Reader* (2007) and *Introduction to Professional Writing* (forthcoming). His research interests include writing program administration and rhetoric of science.

Sarah Fabian is an Assistant Professor at the Halle Library of Eastern Michigan University, where she serves as the Subject Specialist for the First-Year Writing Program. In addition to other responsibilities, she regularly participates in the English Department's graduate pedagogy seminar for new writing instructors.

Gregory R. Glau is Associate Professor and Director of the University Writing Program at Northern Arizona University. With Duane Roen and Barry Maid, he is the co-author of *The McGraw-Hill Guide: Writing for College, Writing for Life* and has published numerous academic essays, especially focused on basic writing. His latest book, co-authored with Chitra Duttagupta of Utah Valley University, is *Everyday Writing* (Pearson, 2012).

Suzanne Gray is an Associate Professor at the Halle Library of Eastern Michigan University, where she is the founding director of the Academic Projects Center, an initiative to provide integrated tutoring support for writing, library research, and technology. She also serves as the library liaison to the Women's and Gender Studies Program and the Writing Across the Curriculum Program. Her research interests include Information Literacy.

Morgan Gresham is an Associate Professor at the University of South Florida St. Petersburg, where she serves as the writing programs coordinator. Her works span feminism, computers and composition, and writing program administration.

Teresa Grettano is an Assistant Professor of English at The University of Scranton, where she teaches classes in writing. Her work has been published in *WPA: Writing Program Administration*, *Composition Studies*, and the collection *Activism and Rhetoric*. She currently serves on the steering committee of Rhetoricians for Peace.

Kimberly Harrison is an Associate Professor of English and Director of the Writing and Rhetoric program at Florida International University in Miami. Her research has focused most recently on nineteenth-century women's rhetorical history. She has edited *A Maryland Bride in the Deep South: The Civil War Diary of Priscilla Bond*, co-edited *Victorian Sensations: Essays on a Scandalous Genre*, and co-authored *Contemporary Composition Studies: A Guide to Theorists and Terms*. She is currently completing a study of southern women's rhetoric during the American Civil War.

Deborah H. Holdstein is Dean of the School of Liberal Arts and Sciences and Professor of English at Columbia College Chicago. Holdstein recently completed a five-year term as editor of *College Composition and Communication*. She has published widely in composition and rhetoric, film, technology, and literature and has also directed the Consultant-Evaluator Service of the Council of Writing Program Administrators. She has served on the MLA Publications Committee, the Executive Board of the CWPA, the Executive Committee of CCCC, and as an Officer of the CCCC. Her most recent book, co-edited with Andrea Greenbaum, is *Judaic Perspectives in Composition and Rhetoric* (Hampton Press, 2008), and her work has appeared in such journals as *CCC, College English, WPA: Writing Program Administration,* and *Pedagogy.*

Judy Holiday is an Assistant Professor in the Writing Program at the University of La Verne. Her current research contributes to recent recovery of Lillian Smith (1897–1966) as a rhetorician and public sphere theorist. She has published "In[ter]vention: Locating Rhetoric's *Ethos*" in *Rhetoric Review* and "Still Sophistic [after All These Years]: An Interview with Susan Jarratt" in *Composition Forum.*

Rebecca Ingalls, Ph.D., is an Assistant Professor and Director of the Freshman Writing Program at Drexel University. Her work in composition and cultural rhetoric may be found in *inventio,Academe, The Review of Education, Pedagogy, and Cultural Studies, POROI, Harlot,* the *Journal of Teaching Writing,* and the *Journal of Popular Culture* (forthcoming). She is currently working with colleagues on an edited collection about plagiarism.

Emily Isaacs is an Associate Professor of English at Montclair State University, where she teaches and administers the first-year writing program and a graduate certificate program in teaching writing. Recent articles have appeared in *College English, WPA,* and *Writing Center Journal,* and in several book collections. She is co-editor of *Public Works: Student Writing as Public Text.*

Craig Jacobsen is Residential Faculty at Mesa Community College, where he teaches composition, literature, and film. He is the co-author of *Scenarios for Writing* and co-editor of *Practicing Science Fiction: Critical Essays on Writing, Reading and Teaching the Genre.*

Melinda Knight is Professor of English and Director of the Center for Writing Excellence at Montclair State University, where she teaches undergraduate and graduate courses in writing center theory and practice, teaching writing through technology, and American cultural studies. Her research focuses on program evaluation and assessment and writing in the workplace, and she is the editor of *Business Communication Quarterly*.

Hava A. Levitt-Phillips teaches composition and literature at Washtenaw Community College in Ann Arbor, Michigan. Her teaching and research interests include self-disclosure and representation in student writing and textual interpretation, praxis pedagogy in literary studies, and the literary and theoretical work of Muriel Rukeyser.

Barry Maid is a Professor, and for ten years was program head of Technical Communication at Arizona State University. Along with numerous articles and chapters focusing on technology, independent writing programs, and program administration, he is a co-author, with Duane Roen and Greg Glau, of *The McGraw-Hill Guide: Writing for College, Writing for Life*.

Paul Kei Matsuda is Professor of English and Director of Second Language Writing at Arizona State University, where he mentors doctoral and master's students in applied linguistics, rhetoric and composition, and TESOL. Former director of writing programs at Arizona State University and the University of New Hampshire, Paul has published widely on second language writers in writing programs in such journals as *College English, College Composition and Communication, WPA: Writing Program Administration,* and *Written Communication*.

Susan Miller-Cochran is Associate Professor of English and Director of First-Year Writing at North Carolina State University. Her research focuses on the intersections of technology, second-language writing, and writing program administration. She co-edited *Rhetorically Rethinking Usability* (2009) and *Strategies for Teaching First-Year Composition* (2002), and co-authored *The Wadsworth Guide to Research* (2009).

Tracy Ann Morse is an Assistant Professor in the Department of English at East Carolina University. Her work has appeared in *Rhetoric Review, Disability Studies, inventio,* and *The Journal of Teaching Writing*.

Wendy Olson is Assistant Professor of English at Washington State University Vancouver, where she directs the undergraduate composition program. She has published on feminist rhetoric and basic writing, and is currently co-editing a collection titled *On Language and Value: Political Economies of Rhetoric and Composition.*

Kimberly Coupe Pavlock is a full-time lecturer at Eastern Michigan University, where she serves as Assistant Director of First-Year Writing and Co-Director of the Eastern Michigan Writing Project. Her interests include teacher education, writing centers, and family literacy.

Deirdre Pettipiece is Associate Dean of Arts and Sciences at West Chester University of Pennsylvania. A former editor of *WPA: Writing Program Administration*, she has published chapters on writing and assessment. Her co-authored textbook, *Introduction to Professional Writing*, is forthcoming from Pearson.

Sherry Rankins-Robertson is an Assistant Professor of Rhetoric and Writing and Director of First-Year Composition at the University of Arkansas at Little Rock, where she teaches the graduate seminar in teaching writing. She has designed curriculum and taught courses in family history writing, non-fiction, and business writing. Her publications have focused on uses of multimodal composition in first-year composition, strategies for successful online teaching, and prison education.

Rochelle (Shelley) Rodrigo is an Assistant Professor of Rhetoric & New Media at Old Dominion University. She was as a full time faculty member for nine years in English and film studies at Mesa Community College in Arizona. Shelley researches how "newer" technologies better facilitate communicative interactions, more specifically teaching and learning. As well as co-authoring *The Wadsworth Guide to Research*, Shelley was also co-editor of *Rhetorically Rethinking Usability* (Hampton Press). Her work has also appeared in *Computers and Composition, Teaching English in the Two-Year College, EDUCAUSE Quarterly, Journal of Advancing Technology, Flow,* as well as various edited collections.

Duane Roen is Professor of English at Arizona State University, where he also serves as Assistant Vice Provost for University Academic Success Programs, Head of Interdisciplinary and Liberal Studies, and Head of Technical Communication. In addition to more than 250 articles, chapters, and conference presentations, he has published eight books. He has served as secretary of the Conference on College Composition and Communication (2007–2011). He currently serves as president of the Council of Writing Program Administrators (2011–2013).

Ryan Skinnell is an Assistant Professor of Rhetoric and Composition at the University of North Texas. His research is focused on the history of rhetoric, composition, and writing programs. He has published articles in *JAC*, *Rhetoric Review*, and *Enculturation*.

Sarah Soebbing teaches composition at Eastern Michigan University and Jackson Community College, and received her MA in Written Communication, with a specialization in the Teaching of Writing, from Eastern Michigan University. She is the media editor for the Eastern Michigan Writing Project and a writing project teacher consultant.

Doug Sweet is Director of Undergraduate Writing at Chapman University, and teaches courses on rhetorical history and theory. He is co-author, with Jeanne Gunner, of *Grounds for Writers* (Pearson, 2008) and author of the forthcoming *Contexts & Choices: A Guide to Practical Writing* (Kendall-Hunt, 2012). He publishes primarily on rhetorical theories of argument and epistemology.

Susan Thomas is a Senior Lecturer (associate professor) at the University of Sydney, Australia, where she serves as the founding director of the writing center and university writing program. She is the editor of *What is the New Rhetoric?* And is the recipient of the 2007 Sydney University award for Teaching Excellence.

Martha Townsend is an Associate Professor of English at the University of Missouri, where she teaches graduate and undergraduate courses in rhetoric and composition, writing across the curriculum, and writing in the disciplines. Formerly the director of MU's Campus Writing Program, her current book project is a literacy study of high profile football players who earned undergraduate degrees while playing at a Division I university.

Stephen Wilhoit is a Professor of English and Assistant Director of the Ryan C. Harris Learning Teaching Center at the University of Dayton. He has published *A Brief Guide to Writing from Readings*, *A Brief Guide to Writing Academic Arguments*, and *The Longman Teaching Assistant's Handbook*.

Edward M. White, a Visiting Scholar at the University of Arizona, has written or edited fourteen books and about one hundred articles or book chapters on writing, writing instruction, and writing assessment. His best-known books are *Teaching and Assessing Writing*, which won a Shaughnessy award from the Modern Language Association in 1994, and *Assessment of Writing*, an MLA research volume, published in 1996. He received the 2011 Exemplar Award from CCCC, and is featured in *Writing Assessment in the 21st Century: Essays in Honor of Edward M. White* (Hampton, 2012).

Kathleen Blake Yancey, the Kellogg W. Hunt Professor of English at Florida State University and Director of the Graduate Program in Rhetoric and Composition Studies, is the author or editor of ten scholarly books and over seventy articles and book chapters. Her leadership experience includes the presidency of the Council of Writing Program Administrators; the chairship of CCCC; and the president of NCTE. Currently, she co-directs the International Coalition on Electronic Portfolio Research <ncepr.org> and edits *College Composition and Communication*, the leading journal in the field.

www.ingramcontent.com/pod-product-compliance
Lightning Source LLC
Chambersburg PA
CBHW020330240426
43665CB00043B/201